HARDPRESS.NET
HOME OF HARD-TO-FIND BOOKS

The Farmer's Assistant
by John Nicholson

Address:
HardPress
8345 NW 66TH ST #2561
MIAMI FL 33166-2626
USA
Email: info@hardpress.net

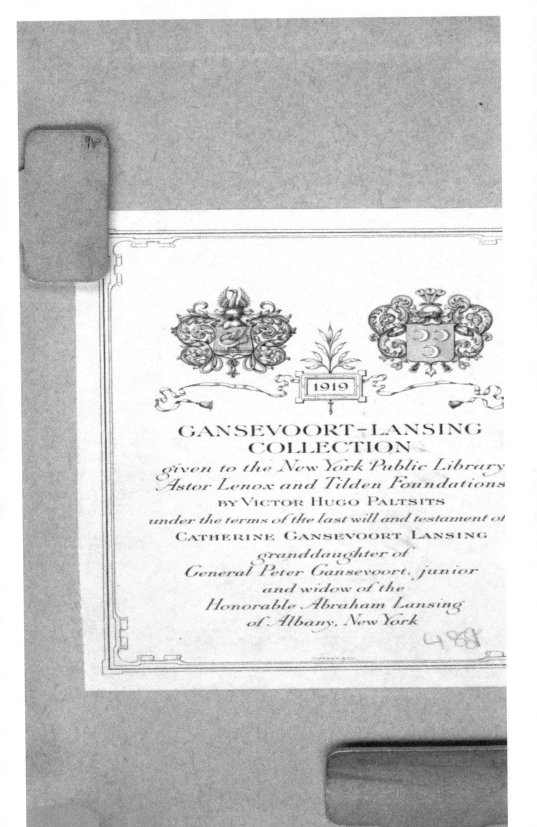

THE

FARMER'S ASSISTANT.

By JOHN NICHOLSON, Esq.
OF HERKIMER COUNTY, STATE OF NEW-YORK.

THE SUBJECTS ON WHICH THIS WORK TREATS, ARE NUMEROUS,
EMBRACING EVERY ARTICLE RELATING TO AGRICULTURE,
ARRANGED IN ALPHABETICAL ORDER.

ALBANY:

PRINTED BY H. C. SOUTHWICK,
No. 94, State-Street.

1814.

BLG

District of New-York, ss.

BE it remembered, that on the second day of July, in the thirty-eighth year of the Independence of the United States of America, H. C. SOUTHWICK, of the said District, has deposited in this office the title of a Book, the right whereof he claims as proprietor, in the words following, to wit:

" The FARMER'S ASSISTANT, by John Nicholson, Esq. of Herkimer County, State of New-York.—The subjects on which this work treats, are numerous....embracing every article relating to Agriculture, arranged in alphabetical order."

IN conformity to the act of the Congress of the United States, entitled " An act for the encouragement of Learning, by securing the copies of Maps, Charts and Books to the authors and proprietors of such copies, during the time therein mentioned." And also to an act, entitled " An act supplementary to an act, entitled " An act for the encouragement of Learning, by securing the copies of Maps, Charts and Books to the authors and proprietors of such copies, during the times therein mentioned, and extending the benefits thereof to the arts of designing, engraving and etching, historical and other prints."

THERON RUDD, Clerk
of the Southern District of New-York.

INTRODUCTION.

THE following Work is offered for the patronage of the farmers and planters of our country. It is particularly calculated for the northern and middle states; but as husbandry has general features of similarity in all countries, it is nearly equally well adapted to those states which lie farther to the south. It is believed to contain a summary of the best means known in this country for the farmer to conduct his business to advantage. The various articles comprising the Work, are arranged in alphabetical order, with proper references to each other, where they have a necessary connexion. The Work is, in part, an abridgment of the essays of others —and, in part, it is original. Acknowledgments are due to the gentlemen whose essays have been published by " the society for the promotion of agriculture," &c. and that " for the promotion of useful arts," in this state ; and, in most instances, the authority of their names has been made use of; particularly that of the learned and worthy President of those institutions, whose exertions in improving the state of farming amongst us, entitle him to the first agricultural honors of the state.

Although, in some parts of Europe, Practical Farming may be considered as nearly reduced to a science....yet, in this country, from inattention to this important subject, (owing, perhaps, to the ease with which a subsistence is acquired, where lands are plenty) the means of making the most of the labors of the field is, in general, but imperfectly understood. On this subject, the existing knowledge in other countries, even if brought home, would not, in all respects, be knowledge for us. A difference in soils, climates, and the productions to be raised, must ever be productive of differences in the best modes of culture. To the agricultural geniuses of our own country, we must, therefore, look for aid in maturing the best system of farming here ; and, no doubt, in a country possessing such varieties of climate and soil, many variations will be found necessary.

Some Chemists of Great-Britain, and elsewhere, have gone into the analyzation of earths, in order to ascertain the constituent parts of those which are fertile, and of those which are sterile ; and thus, by ascertaining the substances which form the rich, to be able to point out the ingredients which are necessary as permanent additions to the poor. It is to be hoped, that the Chemists of our own country, stimulated by the example, will turn their attention to similar enquiries, and to others which are calculated to throw light on the œconomy of the vegetable world, and the means of increasing its products. The Chemical operations of vegetation are, indeed, slow, and apparently hid from our view; but patient investigation will, no doubt, lead to discoveries highly important to the science of agriculture.

The farmers of this country enjoy the peculiar blessing of being lords of the soil which they cultivate. Long may they enjoy this proud pre-eminence over the husbandmen of Europe! This circumstance, while it is pregnant with the blessings of ease, content, independence and freedom, to the cultivator, is calculated, eventually, to draw forth his best talents in the practical improvement of the country; for, to this, the farmer has every inducement, when the result of his labors and skill in improving his lands, becomes a permanent benefit to himself, or his posterity, and not to an avaricious landlord, or a lordly master. It is to be hoped, that improvements in husbandry, and in the face of the country, will become visibly more rapid, as the obstacles to improvement, the general roughness of the land, shall have become removed....as the capitals of our farmers shall be gradually increased, and as the knowledge of the best husbandry shall be more generally diffused. Great as our country is, almost every part, from the ease with which access to markets can be had, is calculated to become highly agricultural —and, if proper encouragement be given to its commerce, may become, as it were, the granary of the world. For the wealth attendant on commerce, overflowing the land, as the Nile does its banks, is calculated to facilitate the means of improvement; and additional improvement is again productive of additional means to meliorate the condition of all, by an additional increase of the products of the earth.

The cultivation of the earth, has been the favorite employment of many of the wisest and best men in all ages; and it is worthy of note, that wherever the lovers of rural life have been called forth as the defenders of their country, or to assist in its councils, they have never been known as the subverters of its liberties. Such is the sterling virtue with which men are usually endued, who have a particular veneration for the plough and the hoe. An ambition for lawless power, and a love of rural life, are, perhaps, incompatible.

It is to be hoped, that from amongst our farmers, many a CINCINNA-TUS may arise in succeeding times—who, after having " ruled the storm of mighty war," or shone in the councils of his country, shall again " seize the plough," and " greatly independent live !"

To him who has a relish for the culture of the earth, it is unnecessary to dilate on its pleasures; and to him who possesses not a taste of this kind, the task would be useless. A taste, however, for particular pursuits, is susceptible of being strengthened and improved ; and to this, nothing is more conducive than to clear the subject of its difficulties, and to render the path plain and easy. We travel with delight on the road which lies plainly before us.... but with perplexity and pain on that which is intricate or unknown. If, therefore, the farmer would derive the greatest pleasure, as well as the greatest profit from his employment, let him be firstly diligent in making his way plain: let him become as fully enlightened as possible in all that tends to render his labors productive, and this will greatly strengthen his relish for his employment, and render its pleasures more obvious and striking. " The FARMER'S ASSISTANT" is intended to simplify and methodise the existing knowledge of Farming in our country ; and as far as the author shall be found to have succeeded in his first attempt, so far shall his most predominant ambition be gratified.

THE AUTHOR.

September 1, 1814.

RECOMMENDATIONS.

Copy of a letter from Simeon De Witt, Esq. Surveyor-General of the state of New-York, to the Publisher.

Sir,

Since you put into my hands, Mr. Nicholson's manuscript on husbandry, entitled " *The Farmer's Assistant,*" I have not had leisure to examine it critically, and to compare its contents with what is to be found in the various authors who have treated on the same or similar subjects. However, after the perusal I have given it, I have no hesitation in recommending it as a book that will be found very useful to the practical farmer. The merit of such works depends principally on a judicious selection from what has been said by the standard writers on such subjects....from what is to be found in periodical and occasional publications—together with the unwritten information collected by the writers themselves, and the results of their own observations, arranged so as best to accommodate readers. In all these respects, I believe the present work will be found to evince considerable research and observation, as well as judgment in the plan of conducting it. It certainly contains a good deal of useful matter, which is not to be found embodied in any one book on husbandry. His gleanings from various publications, are considerable....and these, together with his own observations, are brought together in such a manner as is well calculated to condense the information intended to be communicated. The arrangement of his topics in alphabetical order, will facilitate that recourse to them, for which the farmer will have frequent occasion, and is, therefore, judiciously adopted. Considering this work as a valuable collection of materials, relating to rural economy, adapted to our country, I think it deserving of that patronage which American productions of merit ought to receive from us, and hope it will meet with that encouragement which will enable you to give it to the public.

I am, sir, respectfully yours,

S. DE WITT.

Copy of a letter from T. Romeyn Beck, M. D. to the Publisher.

SIR, ALBANY, MARCH 23, 1814.

I have examined, at your request, the manuscript copy of a work, entitled "*The Farmer's Assistant,*" written by John Nicholson, Esq. The very slight acquaintance that I possess, on the practical part of the subjects treated of in this volume, prevents me from giving a determined opinion on its merits. I can, however, add, with perfect conviction of its truth, that many articles are written with correctness, and convey information which must prove useful. A laudable degree of industry appears to have been exercised in compiling from the writings of foreigners, as well as Americans, whatever may be important to the practical farmer. The plan adopted by the author, appears better calculated for the class of citizens to whom it is addressed, than any other that could have been chosen. A consise, yet comprehensive detail on each of the subjects which, in succession, call for the attention of the husbandman, is one that best comports with his situation and his leisure. From being arranged in alphabetical order, the facility of investigation is increased, as is also the ease of reference from one subject to another. The necessity of a work similar to the "Farmer's Assistant," is acknowledged by most practical men, and, in fact, is absolutely indispensable, in order to keep pace with the improvements made in this highly important branch of industry. The agriculturalist fills an interesting situation in every community, and particularly so in the United States. Patriotism, as well as every social feeling, suggests the encouragement of this most useful, and, in most cases, virtuous section of our population. To render the labors of the farmer more productive, and to increase the comforts of society, in general, appear to be among the motives of this work—and it is sincerely hoped that such exertions may meet with a liberal reward.

T. ROMEYN BECK, M. D.

Mr. H. C. Southwick.

———

I HAVE perused a part of the manuscript above mentioned, and am of opinion that the work will be highly important and useful to Farmers, and therefore concur in recommending it to their patronage.

DANIEL D. TOMPKINS,

Governor of the State of New-York.]

Albany, June 19, 1814.

FARMER'S ASSISTANT.

A.

AIR. Seeds which are buried so deep as to be secluded from their requisite proportion of air will not vegetate; for this reason weeds are constantly springing up in new ploughed grounds; those seeds which before lay too deep for vegetation being turned up nigher the surface.

Let seeds be sown in the glass receiver of an air-pump, exhausted of air, and they will not vegetate; but admit the air and they will grow directly.

The lodging, or falling of some kinds of grain and of grass, is owing to standing too thick to admit a free circulation of air, by means of which they can only preserve a healthy state. Plant one grain of wheat, for instance, in the richest soil, and the stalks when grown, will not fall; but plant a great number of grains in the same soil, so closely together as to preclude a free circulation of air amongst the stalks, and they become unable to sustain their own weight.

Air consists of different *gases*, as they are termed; the *oxygene* gas, or *vital* air, which is essential to the existence of all animals; the *hydrogene* gas, or inflammable air; the *nitrogene* gas, or common atmospheric air, deprived of its oxygen, by having served the purposes of respiration or combustion, and which is also called *azote*; and the *carbonic acid*, formerly called *fixed air*, so often found fatal in the bottoms of wells and elsewhere. These are the principal; but by the application of a sufficient degree of *caloric*, (heat,) all liquid substances can be changed into the gaseous state.

The common atmosphere is principally composed of the oxygene and nitrogene gases, being about twenty-one parts of the former and seventy-nine of the latter.

As the oxygene or respirable air is essential to the existence of animals, so the hydrogene and the azote is absorbed in plants, and is essential to their growth. Plants also, while exposed to the light, emit oxygene. Thus, by the economy of Nature, the vegetable world is

2

continually absorbing that air which is hurtful to man, and is almost constantly reproducing that which is healthful.

See further articles, FOOD OF PLANTS, GERMINATION OF PLANTS, SEEDS, SOWING, &c.

APPLES. The seeds of an apple seldom produce trees which bear the same kind of apples, and hence the necessity of grafting or inoculating, when we would raise the same kind.

A judicious selection of trees which bear the best apples for different uses, is a matter worthy of particular attention.

See articles CIDER, ORCHARD, &c.

For gathering apples for winter use, they should be *picked* from the tree, laid carefully in a heap, under cover, without being bruised; after they have *sweated,* let them be exposed to the air and well dried, by wiping them with dry cloths; then lay them away in a *dry* place where they will not freeze. The time requisite for sweating will be six, ten, or fifteen days, according to the warmth of the weather.

Mr. Forsyth says, that " the most complete method of saving them, so as to preserve them the greatest length of time, is to wrap them in paper and pack them away in stone jars between layers of bran; having the mouths of the jars covered so close as to preclude the admission of air, and then to keep them in a dry place where they will not be frozen.

The fruit should not be gathered till fully ripe, which is known by the stem parting easily from the twig: It should also be gathered in dry weather and when the dew is off.

APPLE-TREE; *(Pyrus Malus.)* This tree flourishes most in a fertile sandy loam, sandy, or rich, warm, gravelly soil. A stiff clay is not good, even though it be rich. It thrives better in a poor sandy soil than in any other poor earth.

Some apple-trees bear alternately and some yearly. The cause of the former is owing to the young tree bearing too large a crop at first; this so exhausts it as to render it unfit for bearing the next year; in the mean time it becomes sufficiently recruited for a heavy crop the third year; and thus it becomes confirmed in the *habit* of alternate bearing, in which it ever after continues. In order, therefore, to prevent young trees from getting into this habit, let the young fruit be stripped off where it appears too plentiful, but gradually, less and less each year, until such time as the tree can bear a full yearly crop, and thus become confirmed in the habit of a yearly bearer. Perhaps a tree that has become confirmed in the habit of alternate bearing might have its habit changed by once or twice divesting it of its young fruit during the bearing year, and manuring it well during that season.

Take a scion from a yearly, and graft it on the limb of an alternate bearer, and it will become alternate, and vice versa.   But if the true reason has been given for alternate bearing, it does not follow that a scion from a yearly bearer, when grafted on a stock that has never borne, will become alternate.   In the first case, the habit of the alternate bearer being already confirmed, regulates the scion; but where the habit of the scion has become confirmed and that of the young stock has not, it would seem that the habit of the scion must prevail. It is said, that about the summer solstice, the bark of the body of an apple-tree may be taken off and a new bark will presently form, which will regenerate the tree, and render such as were before barren, productive; but, perhaps, to ensure an experiment of this kind it would be well to give the part of the tree deprived of its bark, a coat of Forsyth's composition, or something similar.

See further articles; FRUIT-TREES, ORCHARD, NURSERY, &c.

APRICOT.   The same culture that is proper for a peach-tree is also good for an apricot, with this difference, that apricots require a lighter and warmer soil than a peach-tree.   See article PEACH-TREE.

ASH; *(Fraxinus.)*   There are three kinds of ash in this country; the white, the yellow, and the black.   The upland white-ash is the best timber, but is liable to a white rot when kept too much in contact with the ground.   Winter is the best time for felling it to preserve the white part from worms.   The black-ash is the most durable wood for rails, &c.

ASHES.   *See* article MANURES.

ASPARAGUS.   To make a bed of this excellent spring green, open a trench four or five feet wide and one foot deep, in the warmest part of your garden—the warmer the better.   Fill the trench half full of good barn dung; level it, and scatter some good earth over it; then lay on your roots, eight or nine inches apart, in their natural position; or, if seeds be used, about half that distance apart: Fill up the trench with good soil and your bed is made.

If roots be planted, they may be cut the second year; but if seeds, not till the third.   After the bed is fit for use, all the shoots which come up before the middle of June may be cut off; but all after that should run to seed to strengthen the plants.

As this plant is one of the first green vegetables which the opening season presents, and as no substitute equally productive can be had till the season for green peas and beans, which usually is not until some time in summer, it becomes a matter of economy to have two asparagus beds; the first to be brought forward as early as possible, the other late. For this purpose the latter ought to have a northern exposure, and it should be spaded in order to retard its growth; by which means the plants will be equally large and yet very tender. The roots should be laid so deep as to admit of spading the ground over them. The beds should be kept clear of weeds throughout the season. In the fall they should have a layer of rotten dung spread over them, an inch in depth, which may in part be taken off the next spring; and, when the bed becomes too high by the constant addition of dung, part of the earth may be pared off in the spring, before the plants shoot, and the bed covered again with a thin compost of rotten dung.

ASS. This is a valuable animal for carrying burdens, and for being used in small carts. Mr. Livingston observes, that for these purposes they are much used in the country between Nantz and Paris; and, that even loads of wood and hay are there carried on their backs. Their use for many purposes in this country, particularly in villages, would be found an article of economy; they will subsist on the coarsest fare; may be kept at constant service; are subject to few or no diseases; and they live to a great age.

It is also mentioned in " *The Complete Grazier*," that asses have been successfully used in Great-Britain for ploughing light lands, four of them being equal to two horses.

B.

BARLEY; *(Hordeum.)* This is a hardy grain, subject to few diseases; bears the drought well and is profitable for cultivation. When hulled, it may be ground into flour, which makes a bread whiter than wheat and but little inferior in taste. Soups made of it, when hulled, are as good as those made of rice, and are accounted cooling and detersive in fevers. The longer this grain is kept the better tasted it becomes; the cause of its bad taste is owing to its hull. The usual allowance of seed for an acre is two bushels; but this is hardly sufficient; in general, two and a half is better. Barley has frequently been known to yield sixty bushels an acre. It requires a soil in good condition, and like many other crops, turns to poor account when sown on such as are poor. The best for raising it are the loamy, sandy-loamy, or gravelly soil but it will do very well even on a strong stiff clay, provided it be well mellowed with frequent and effectual ploughings and harrowings, and these can be done to the best effect in the fall preceding.

As barley is a dry husky grain and requires considerable moisture to cause it to vegetate, it should be sown when the ground is sufficiently moist : It should also be sown as soon as the ground can be well prepared in the Spring.   This grain receives essential benefit from being soaked in lye, brine, or some other fertilizing liquor.   An English writer mentions an experiment made some years since which may be worth inserting. " The last Spring," says he, " being remarkably dry, I soaked my seed-barley in the black water taken from a reservoir which constantly receives the draining of my dung-heap and stables.   As the light corn floated on the top I skimmed it off and let the rest stand twenty-four hours.   On taking it from the water I mixed the grain with a sufficient quantity of wood ashes, to make it spread regularly, and sowed three fields with it.   The produce was sixty bushels to the acre.   I sowed some other fields with the same seed, dry, but the crop, like those of my neighbors, was very poor, not more than twenty bushels an acre, and much mixed with weeds.   I also sowed some of my seed dry, on one ridge, in each of my former fields, but the produce was very poor in comparison to the other parts of the field."   Adding some saltpetre to the liquor in which the barley is soaked, will probably be found of great service.

See article SOWING.

It is injurious to harvest this grain before it is thoroughly ripened ; and, after it is cut, it should lie a night or two in the dew, in order to make the beards come off more easily in threshing.

This grain, like many others, will degenerate so much in a few years as not to be worth cultivating, if the seed be not frequently changed. The farmer ought, therefore, to procure new recruits of seed brought from some considerable distance.   It may be advisable also, to change the *kind* of barley in order to ascertain which is most suitable to the soil.   These are various : There is the two-rowed, the four-rowed and the six-rowed barley ; and, there is also a species of barley which has no husk upon it, which is commonly called spelt. (*See* article SPELT.)   The six-rowed barley is sowed in England and Ireland, as a winter grain, and is there called bear, bere, or barley-big. It shells very much if suffered to stand until it is sufficiently ripe. The four-rowed barley has generally been cultivated in this and the neighbouring states; probably because, in them, it has generally been found the best for cultivation.

As in some parts farmers have attempted to cultivate this grain without success, it may be well to observe, that perhaps the cause of this failure was owing to their lands not having been made sufficiently *rich*—to not having been *ploughed* and *harrowed* sufficiently—to not having sowed on them a sufficiency of seed; for if this be not done, this grain will often be choaked with weeds—to seed, which had become *degenerated* by having been too long used in one part of the country—or, perhaps, to the *kind* of barley not having been suitable to the soil. If the farmer has satisfied himself as to all these particulars, and still finds himself unsuccessful in the culture of this grain, he may conclude that either his soil, of whatever kind it may be, or the climate in which his farm is situated, is not suitable to the culture of barley.

Wherever a country is found suitable to the culture of barley, and not so suitable for raising wheat or rye, there, particularly, it becomes highly expedient to erect mills for hulling barley; for this grain, when hulled, can be converted into a very good substitute for wheat or rye-bread. Peas can also be hulled at such mills, which renders them excellent for soups, &c.

BARN. The size of the barn ought to be proportionate to the produce of the farm, for in this country, where building is not expensive, all the hay and grain ought to be stored in buildings sufficient to cover them. Many farmers content themselves with a small barn, perhaps not sufficient to hold half their produce, while most of their hay is left in their meadows, in stacks, to be there foddered out to the cattle in the course of the winter. In this way the manure is almost totally lost, as a stack containing five tons of hay, fed out in this way, would not manure an eighth of an acre to any essential purpose: Cow-dung, in particular, is most beneficial when buried *in a dry* soil; but when laid *on a wet* soil it answers but little purpose. In the mean time, if the meadow happens to be bare and unfrozen, as is often the case, the cattle will indeed have the chance of picking some dead grass, but at the expense of destroying the roots, and of poaching the soil with their feet, which produces an additional injury to the meadow.

If the ground will admit, the barn ought to be about so far distant from the house, and in such direction from it, as to preclude all danger of fire being communicated from the one to the other, by the means of the most prevalent high winds.

The farmers of the elder parts of Pennsylvania build very large barns in general, and to obviate the consequences of the hay or grain heating, in a large mow, four poles or pieces of timber are set up in middle, so as to form within them a square space of about three feet. The poles are braced by cross pieces at certain distances. Through the aperture thus made, the extra moisture in the hay or grain has a chance to escape, so as to prevent its being mow-burnt. Their barns are usually built of stone, and in the walls a large number of small holes are made for the admission of air. Their cattle are chiefly all housed, and their dung is under cover when thrown out of the stables, to prevent its being injured by the rains. The roofs of the barns are usually painted to preserve them against the weather.

The floor of the barn ought to be kept tight, so that the grain cannot fall through in threshing, and for this purpose it should have a layer of thin boards under it. It is most advisable also, to have a place set apart in the barn for the purpose of storing away the grain after it is threshed. The bins for the grain should be made of hard plank to prevent the rats and mice eating through them, and should have lids which can be fastened down with padlocks. A row of narrow bins with different apartments for various kinds of grain may be placed very conveniently along the side of the floor where the horse-stable is placed, so as to be partly under the manger.

BARN-YARD. The practice of having a barn-yard on a declivity is a bad one, as in this way very much manure is washed away without essentially benefiting the adjoining grounds. The yard should be level, and lowest in the middle, in order to prevent the escape of much fertilizing liquor, that will otherwise run off from the dung during heavy rains. It should be cleared in the Spring of the dung made during Winter, and if the milch-cows and other cattle are to be kept in it at night during Summer, much manure may be made in it by carting in rubbish of various kinds, together with suitable earths to mix with the dung of the cattle and absorb their stale.

The yard should also have a high close fence round it, as well for securing the cattle as for breaking off the winds, and in order to make the most of the dung, the cattle should be kept constantly in the yard during the season of foddering and have a well close adjoining to supply them with water. The stiffer the soil of the barn-yard the less manure will be lost by the stale and wash soaking into the earth, and for this reason some have taken the trouble to cover the whole with a thick layer of clay.

BEAN; (Vicia.) There are a great variety of beans, some of which are best adapted for field husbandry and others for culinary purposes. For the former, the English or Windsor bean is the best for strong clays and other rich soils, and the little white bean for those which are light and dry. They are each cultivated in the drill method, and ploughed and hoed like other hoed crops.

The English bean is to be sowed early as a little frost will not hurt it. When they have grown to the height of about three feet, and incline to become too tall, the tops should be broken off. After gathering the first crop the stalks are to be cut off close to the ground, and a a growth of suckers will rise and afford another green crop late in the fall.

The little white bean is to be pulled before the fall frosts and to lie on the ground to dry and ripen. The haulm of beans should be saved for winter food for sheep, as they are very fond of it.

For culinary purposes, the Canada bean, which is a bush bean, ripens soonest, and is therefore to be preferred for an early supply; the pods, however, become unfit for eating when the bean has attained its size. Of those which have vines, the case-knife bean, the cranberry, and the thousand for one, so called, are very good. The short bean, as it is called, is also much esteemed on account of the pod being good to eat when the bean is full grown. Mr. Deane says, the best manure for beans which have vines is hog's dung with a mixture of ashes.

When beans are cultivated in a climate which are not natural to them, they will degenerate; and, therefore, fresh supplies of seed should be obtained from that country to which they are best adapted.

BEER. *To make Spruce-Beer.*—Boil some spruce boughs with some wheat-bran till the water tastes sufficiently of the spruce; strain the water and stir in at the rate of two quarts of molasses to a half barrel; work it with the emptyings of beer, or with yeast if you have it; after working sufficiently bung up the cask, or which is better, bottle its contents.

To make Molasses-Beer.—Take five pounds of molasses, half a pint of yeast and a spoonful of powdered ginger, put these into a vessel, and pour on two gallons of scalding hot *soft* water; shake the whole till a fermentation is produced; then add of the same kind of water sufficient to fill up your half barrel. If the cask be greater or smaller than this, the component parts must be in proportion. Let the liquor ferment about twelve hours, then bottle it, with a raisin or two in each bottle.

If honey instead of molasses be used, at the rate of about twelve pounds to the barrel, it will make a very fine beverage after having been bottled a while.

To make Beer with Hops.—Take five quarts of wheat bran and three ounces of hops, and boil them fifteen minutes in fifteen gallons of water; strain the liquor; add two quarts of molasses; cool it quickly to about the temperature of new milk, and put it into your half barrel, having the cask completely filled. Leave the bung out for twenty-four hours, in order that the yeast may be worked off and thrown out, and then the beer will be fit for use. About the fifth day bottle off what remains in the cask, or it will turn sour if the weather be warm. If the cask be new apply yeast or beer emptyings to bring on the fermentation; but if it has been in this use before that will not be necessary.

Yeast, particularly the whiter part, is much fitter to be used for fermenting than the mere grounds of the beer barrel; and the same may be observed in regard to its use in fermenting dough for bread.

To recover a cask of stale Small-Beer.—Take some hops and some chalk broken to pieces, put them in a bag, and put them in at the bung-hole and then stop up the cask closely. Let the proportion be two ounces of hops and a pound of chalk for a half barrel.

To cure a cask of ropy Beer.—Mix two handsful of bean flour with one handful of salt and stir it in.

To feed a cask of Beer.—Bake a rye-loaf well nutmegged; cut it in pieces and put it in a narrow bag with some hops and some wheat, and put the bag into the cask at the bung-hole.

To clarify Beer.—For a half barrel take about six ounces of chalk, burn it, and put it into the cask. This will disturb the liquor and fine it in twenty-four hours.

It is also recommended in some cases to dissolve some loaf-sugar and add to the above ingredients.

BEES. The product of these is almost entirely clear gain, as their honey and wax is principally extracted from flowers without injuring them. Rural economy is incomplete where the yearly supply which may be derived from bees is wanting; the expense of occasionally attending them is but trifling when compared with their products; and that attention can scarcely be called labor but rather an amusement.

In every hive or swarm of bees there are two sorts beside what is called the *queen bee.* She is distinguished by being larger, and of a brighter red than the rest. She is said to be the leader of the swarm and to lay the eggs in the cells for new broods, which consist of thousands every year. The other kinds are the drones which have no stings, are the darkest colored, and are supposed to be the males; and the honey or working bees, which are much the most numerous.

3

The bee-house should be at a proper distance from places where cattle are kept, or where horses are tied; from hog-sties and every other place where filth is collected. It should be open to the south, with the other sides close. Let it stand leaning forward a little with the front part of the roof projecting over considerably to prevent southerly rains from wetting the hives. These should be kept dry, clean, and warm in winter; not so warm however as to tempt the bees abroad in warm winter days. The species of swallow called martins will destroy bees, of course no harbor should be afforded these birds.

One method of managing bees, as recommended by Mr. Deane, is as follows: Three hives of the same dimensions, say ten inches in heighth, each, and fourteen inches in diameter each way, are to be placed one on the top of the other. The two undermost ones are to have square holes in the tops, about three inches in diameter, and covered with a sliding shutter. Let each hive have also a place of entrance two or three inches long and a third of an inch high. The square holes in the two lowermost are to be open. The bees will fill the uppermost hive first. When this is full, which can be ascertained by weighing it in a cool morning when the bees do not stir, take it off and carry it into a room with a window open to the morning sun, and as this enlivens the bees they will fly off to their accustomed place and commence their labors in storing the second hive, which should then have the hole in its top closed. When this is filled the same process is to be repeated; but when they have filled the last hive, let it remain for the winter stock of provisions for the swarm.

In taking out the honey from the hive, which should be done speedily, let those bees which are found unable to fly be thrown into a tub of water, out of which they can crawl again, and they will soon recover their wonted activity and go after their companions.

In this way there is no necessity for the process of fire and brimstone for getting rid of the bees—a procedure equally cruel and destructive to their race.

Another method of taking the honey without killing the bees, is as follows: When the hive is filled with honey, take it in the night and turn it bottom upwards, and set an empty hive of the same size with its bottom exactly on the bottom of the other: Let there be one or two cross pieces within the empty hive for the bees to light on: Then take a stick and strike gently on the sides of the full hive, and the bees will leave it and ascend to the upper one. When they have all got into this, take it off gently and set it where the full hive stood, and the bees will go to work again as before. This is the method usually practised in France.

But, perhaps, the following management is the best : Have a hole in the top of the hive, covered with a shutter, as before described. When this is filled, which is to be known by the bees lying inactive about its mouth, open the hole above and set a small hive on the top, into which they will ascend and fill it with the purest honey, without any mixture of the bee-bread. When full, take it off as before directed and place another in its stead. The bees in the full hive will soon fly off to the old one, and the swarm will recommence their labors in filling the empty one again. When full, take it away as before, and set the empty one in its place. These upper hives should hold about seventeen pounds of honey when filled, and such the swarm will usually fill three times in a season. The honey in the lower hive is to remain for their winter food.

To preserve bees from the worm or butterfly, which has lately proved so destructive to them.—About the first of May, raise the hives up and strew some fine salt under the edges which will drive the worms away. A writer in a late Morristown paper, says, that he has tried this for two years with complete success.

It is sometimes advisable to feed bees when their stock is exhausted. If this be near the close of winter, motives of interest alone will dictate the measure ; but if they are found destitute more early, then their destiny must be averted from motives of compassion. And is the industrious insect that toils incessantly for us during summer, unworthy of pity in the hour of distress? It should be remembered, for it tends to soften and ennoble the heart, that when even a little bee perishes with famine, it " feels a pang as great as when a giant dies."

Honey is the most natural food for bees. It is to be conveyed into the hives by very small troughs, and the food is to be given to them daily until they are able to provide for themselves. Toasted bread soaked in strong ale is also good to give them, as they will consume the whole of it.

Sometimes it is advisable to join two small swarms together. This, says the last mentioned author, is done by stupifying them with the smoke of the dried mushroom which is commonly called *puff-ball*. It is first to be compressed and then dried in an oven, till it will retain fire. The hives intended to be joined are to be placed with their bottoms over those of two empty ones—a piece of puff, set on fire, is placed under each full hive so that the smoke will ascend into them— and, when the bees have become supified, let the full hives be knocked gently on the sides and the bees will fall into the empty ones in a torpid state, when the queen-bee of one of the swarms must be search-ed for and killed. The two swarms are then to be put together, mixing them well, and dropping them among the combs of the hives they are to inhabit. The door of the hive is then to be covered with a cloth so that they cannot get out.

The second night after their union, remove the cloth in the dusk of the evening, and the bees will sally forth; but on account of the approaching night they will soon return. Keep them confined for three or four days longer, letting them out in the evening as before, and then the cloth may be removed.

Sometimes the bees which are owned by one, will be found carrying off the honey from the hives belonging to another, to their own dwellings, and in that case, the bees of the emptied hives are always found to follow. Whether this be a matter of conquest on one side, or of consent on the other, is difficult to say; but where the owner of the deserting bees finds this to be case, which is to be known by the sudden desertion and emptying of his hives, perhaps his best remedy is, to remove his remaining swarms to another neighborhood for that season, or to change his stock of bees.

It should be added, that many disbelieve either the existence of the queen-bee, or that one, and one only, is to be found in every swarm.

BEET ; (*Beta.*) There are varieties of beets, but the best are the red, and the redder the sweeter. Sow them early, if the soil be not very rich, but they may be sown later where it is strong. The soil should be well mellowed to a good depth. A soil naturally mellow is best for them. The larger they grow the farther they should be set apart, even to the distance of twelve inches. The seeds generally come up double, but should be separated while young, otherwise both roots will be small and sometimes twisted round each other. Those taken out may be transplanted, yet they will make but short roots. Beets should be kept clear of weeds till the leaves covering the ground prevent their further growth.

The roots should be dug up before any severe frosts; none of the fibrous roots should be taken away, nor should the tops be cut close. In this situation they should be boiled to prevent any loss of their juice. In winter they are best kept in sand, and they should not be suffered to freeze, as this makes them tough and unfit for use.

In Europe this root is now applied to the purposes of making sugar and ardent spirits; the knowlege of which uses is probably calculated to confer on it a great additional value.

Some of the most enterprising English farmers are in the practice of raising beets for feeding and fattening cattle.

BOG-MEADOWS. Where these are not a turf, but a mere loose black dirt and can be drained sufficiently, having then a sufficient depth, they make valuable lands, particularly for the purpose of raising hemp. The drier this land can be laid the better. When this earth is carted out upon upland it is found a good manure; and upland, particularly gravel and sand, when carted into bog-meadows is almost equally beneficial. Prodigious great crops of herdsgrass have been raised on them when thus manured with upland earth; and if this be so beneficial for grass, why not equally so with hemp? It would seem, that not only grass and hemp, but many other productions, such as Indian corn, potatoes, cabbage, carrots, beets, turnips, parsnips, and perhaps, almost every grain but wheat, might be cultivated to great advantage on well drained bog-lands, where they had been previously well manured with upland earths. The Indian corn, however, must be such as has been long cultivated in a more northerly climate, and of course, ripens so soon as to escape the early frosts which prevail in bog-meadows. Hops are cultivated to great advantage in these lands.

The method of draining these lands effectually, is, first to run a ditch through the middle, and draw off as much of its waters in this way as possible. Where the meadow is very wet and miry, you commence at the *lowest* part of the ground where you design its outlet to begin, and from thence carry the ditch into the meadow, sinking it all the way as you proceed, as low as will barely give the waters a current to run off; and the deeper this ditch can be sunk the better. You then run a ditch proportionately deep all round the edge of the bog, for the purpose of cutting off all the springs. Then cross ditches are to be made, in number and size proportionate to the extent of the bog and of the size of the middle and surrounding ditches. Generally speaking, the deeper and larger your ditches, the fewer cross ditches you need have.

It should be remembered, that bog lands will settle down very much after draining, for which a due allowance ought to be made in regard to the depth of the ditches. Sometimes it may be found, that there will, after draining, be too thin a layer of bog dirt above the clay on which it is bottomed to be of much value; and foreseeing this, it ought in some cases to deter the proprietor from going to the expense of draining the swamp, particularly if it be covered with a thrifty growth of timber.

See further, article DITCHES.

BOT-WORMS. The manner in which these are produced is this: An insect somewhat resembling a bee in its head and neck, having a long crooked tail, may be seen during the months of autumn, almost constantly flying about horses, and in the course of a few weeks will fill their hair, particularly about the breast and legs with great numbers of its nits. Whenever the horse itches in any part, he applies his teeth for the purpose of scratching; in doing this he loosens some of these nits, and they are received into his mouth, from whence they pass with his food into the stomach, and from these the bot is produced. Experiments which have been communicated by Mr. Livingston put this matter out of doubt.

To kill bots in a horse, pour a quart of rum down his throat. This will make them loose their hold of the maw, and they will be carried off with its contents. Repeat the dose as often as may be found necessary. A few doses of linseed oil, one pint each time, will also quickly effect a cure.

See also *Burtet's Farriery* for his method of cure.

BUCK-WHEAT; (*Polygonium.*) The product of this grain is quite uncertain, owing to the degree of heat prevailing during the time it is in blossom. If there be much warm weather at this time, the grain will not be well filled. The proper time to sow it is when the chesnut trees are in full blossom. This is the rule in those parts where chesnut trees grow. Perhaps the time when herds-grass first begins to blossom, or a little sooner in more northern climates, might afford a more general rule for farmers in every part of the country.

A crop of buck-wheat is very easily raised; it requires but little ploughing, and with the aid of a little gypsum will grow year after year on a poor piece of land, provided it be suitable to the use of gypsum. It is pretty good to fatten hogs, to feed horses and fowls; but its peculiar excellence is for the purpose of making cakes, which, while warm, are more generally liked than any other kind of bread.

About half a bushel, or less, is sufficient seed for an acre. Sometimes a crop of rye is sown with the buck-wheat, and in this way a tolerable crop of each may usually be obtained; perhaps fifteen or twenty bushels of buckwheat and ten bushels of rye to the acre. This is considerable for the small quantity of labor laid out; but the rent of the land ought also to be brought into the account of profit.

BULL. *See* article NEAT CATTLE.

BURN-BAKING. A method of manuring stiff clay lands. It is performed by paring off the sward in pieces about eighteen inches long, a foot wide, and two or three inches thick; these are set on their edges, leaning against each other, to dry, which in good weather requires about three weeks. They are then laid up somewhat in form of ovens, with their mouths to a common windward side, having a hole in the top of each for the smoke to pass off. In a dry day when the wind blows into the mouths, they are set on fire with straw, and if they burn too briskly some earth must be thrown on to deaden the fires. At the end of about three days they will be completely burnt through, and then the burnt earth is spread over the ground and ploughed in with a shoal furrow.

See further article WEEDS, for another use of BURN-BAKING.

For cutting up the sward in squares for burn-baking—a roller with sharp iron rims round it, at suitable distances, is to be used. As the roller passes over the ground the rims sink into it sufficiently deep. The ground is first to be cut one way with this implement, then with another implement, resembling a wheel plough; it is cut into squares by crossing the direction of the roller, and the squares are at the same time severed underneath by a broad thin share for the purpose, and are turned over in the manner of turning over sward ground. They are then to be set up as before directed.

Mr. Young, the late famous agriculturalist of Great-Britain, recommends burn-baking, where it can be easily performed, as highly beneficial to cold, stiff, and clayey soils.

BURNT CLAY. This is a good manure for clay and other heavy soils In "*The Complete Grazier*," it is also recommended for light soils. The method of preparing it is as follows:

In the first place dig your clay in spits of the size of bricks and let them be well dried in the sun: Take small billets of wood, or faggots of brush, and pile them up in the form of a sugar-loaf three or four feet high; then pile your spits of dried clay closely round this, leaving a hole on side to kindle the fire and another in the top for the smoke to pass off: Surround the pile again with two more enclosures of the spits of clay, and then kindle the fire: When it has gotten well on fire stop up the holes with clay, and the innate heat will so fire the mass, that wet clay may be thrown on in great quantities. Care must however be taken, not to lay it on so fast, nor so closely, as to put out the fire, as in that case you must begin anew. By raising a stage round the pile you may throw on clay till you get it as high as you please. The pile must be watched day and night till fully burnt.

Farmers possessing clay lands will do well to make experiments of this manure. From ten to twenty loads of it is a suitable dressing for an acre.

BUTTER. For curing butter take Dr. Anderson's recipe as follows: " Take two parts of common salt, one of brown sugar, and one of saltpetre; beat them together so as to blend them completely, and apply one ounce of this to every pound of butter; work it well into the mass and close it up for use." This will cost about a cent per pound more than by curing butter in the usual way; but its peculiar excellence is, that butter thus cured will keep sweet for two or three years, and its taste is much superior to that which is cured in the common way. It must not, however, be used sooner than a month after it has been laid down, as it does not fully acquire its rich marrowy taste until about that length of time. Butter cured in this way and laid down for winter use, will then be found worth at least twenty-five per cent more than that which has merely been cured with salt alone.

Dr. Anderson condemns the practice of keeping milk in leaden vessels, and butter in stone jars, as communicating to the milk, and to the butter a poisonous quality extremely injurious to the human constitution.

To prevent the rancidity of common salted butter, Mr. De Witt very judiciously recommends making it into rolls, and keeping it in a pure brine in a cask with a lid and dasher, somewhat similar to the common churn. The dasher is for the purpose of keeping the rolls under the brine, which is effected by means of a cord tied at one side of the vessel, run over the head of the handle of the dasher, and then tied down at the opposite side. The brine does not penetrate the butter, and therefore may be made strong; and, to keep it pure it may be occasionally heated, and the scum taken off, which will clarify it.

Country merchants, who take in butter, by attending to this, may preserve all their spring and summer butter sweet for the fall market.

To make the finest butter, take the *last* fourth part of the milk of each teat of the *best* cows for making butter and make it by itself. The first part of the milking, which contains much the least and the poorest of the cream can be made into inferior butter, or used for other purposes.

Butter made in the month of May is observed to be the best for keeping.

C.

CABBAGE; *(Brascia.)* There are many sorts of this plant, such as the common white and red cabbage, the Dutch and Scotch, the Savoy, the winter-green globe, the brocoli, the borecole, the Battersea, the turnip-cabbage, &c. The oil called rape-oil is made from the seeds of the borecole, or *rape*, as it is sometimes called.

In Great-Britain the cultivation of cabbages is a part of field husbandry, and they are used for feeding and fatting cattle in the fall and during winter. Our winters are too severe for this; but for fall use we might raise and feed them to advantage.

Cabbages require a soil made rich, but the kind is not so material. Mr. Young makes mention of good crops raised in red sand. Rich swamp lands, well drained, are good for them. They will grow yearly on the same ground, and they exhaust the soil but little. For field culture the plants are to be set in rows four feet apart and about two feet from each other, and ploughed and hoed like other hoed crops. Transplanting is the most advisable method, though the seeds may be planted at first where they are designed to grow. Strewing soot, ashes or lime round them, while young, will assist considerably in keeping off the insects which usually attack them. Where they are liable to become club-footed, by reason of worms which eat into their roots, a small trifle of salt strewed round them is good.

When cabbages are fed to milch-cows, the decayed leaves must be taken off, or they will impart a bad taste to the milk and butter.

Where a field-crop of cabbages is to be raised, or an early crop for the table, the seeds for the plants should be sown very early in the spring; where the crop is designed for fall and winter use the seeds may be sown later; but as the proper time for this must still depend on the climate, it is a matter that is best learned by experience.

Cabbages for winter use should be pulled in dry weather, and be well dried before they are put into the cellar. Let them be hung up in the cellar with the heads downwards. The cellar should not be too warm or they will soon rot. They may also be kept well during winter, by cutting off the heads and laying them away in a cask filled with snow and keeping them in a cold place.

But for the spring supply, let a trench be made in a dry soil and line it with straw; set the heads in closely together with the roots upwards; cover them with straw, and then with earth, piled up as

4

steep as possible.   In this manner they will keep till May, and may occasionally be dug out as they are wanted.

The turnip-cabbage, so called, on account of its large bulb above ground, is a perenniel plant, and will withstand the severity of our climate.   It is good for table use in spring and does not grow spongy when old.   Its culture was highly recommended by the Bath Society in England, as an article of profit for feeding sheep and other cattle in the spring.   By Sir Thomas Bevor's communication to that society, it appears, that he kept twenty-four bullocks and one hundred sheep, for three weeks, on two acres of this plant; the value of which keeping he estimated at a sum equal to about sixty-five dollars.   This was in the year 1770.

This plant is to be sown and cultivated in the manner most proper for turnips.   It is left in the field all winter, and in the spring the cattle are to be turned in to eat of it at pleasure.   As sheep can eat the closest, they are to have the last feeding.

CALVES *See* article NEAT CATTLE.

CANKER.   *See* article FRUIT TREES.

CANKER-WORM. *See* article INSECTS.

CARRIAGES.   Some of the best British farmers principally use one horse carts, instead of waggons, on their farms.   Mr. Young particularly recommends them for this purpose, as being on the whole more convenient and cheaper.   In Ireland the wheel car is almost universally used on farms and for transporting on the highways.   On these, one man is found sufficient to drive four cars; the horses being under good command, and follow each behind the other.   Each horse draws from ten to twenty hundred weight, acccording to the state of the roads; for it is found that one animal drawing by itself in a car or cart, can as easily draw eight hundred weight, as two can draw twelve hundred weight when put together in a waggon.   The reason of this is obvious; in a cart the horse carries a part of the load on his back; and in drawing, his exertions are not baffled by the jostling and unequal exertions of another.   Carts are, however, more easily upset in bad roads than waggons.   Another objection against them is, that they press too heavily on the horse or oxen when going down hill, particularly when carrying a top-heavy load; and they incline to tilt up behind when going up hill with such load.   These defects are, however, easily obviated by a contrivance fixed in front of the box, for the purpose of raising its fore end when going down hill, and of sinking it when going up, so that in either case the centre of gravity of the load will not be materially altered from what it is on level ground. A cart contrived and used by Lord Somerville, in Great Britain, answers this purpose in part. Another contrivance of that nobleman's is, a wooden bar placed on the outside of each wheel, just above the hubs, so that when going down hill the bars are drawn by each end against the sides of the wheels so strongly as to impede their motion, and thus prevent the load pressing forward with more force than is convenient.—A description of the means by which these several operations are performed is here omitted, because they are, perhaps, nearly as easily imagined as described. Any one wishing to test their efficacy, need not be long at a loss for the means.

The cart wheels made use of by the above nobleman and others are of cast iron, being about three feet in diameter, with a rim about four inches broad; the spokes are flat, and broadest where they join the hub and the rim, so as to give them most strength where most is wanted. If any part of the wheel happens to break by a too violent concussion, it can be mended again with wrought iron, when it will be as strong as ever. The axletree is of wrought iron. Such a cart may last an age, with good usage, and the cost of them is not so great as that of carts made of wood. Probably they would, however, be found too brittle on stony lands; though their strength will be found very great if cast of the best metal to be had for the purpose.

In the construction of the body of the cart, the essential points are to fit it for the purposes for which it is mostly to be used; to place so much of it before the axletree as that, when filled, about a fifth of the weight of its contents will rest on the horse; and that it be so contrived as to be tilted up to empty its load.

The improvements above mentioned for regulating the centre of gravity of the load, and for impeding the progress of the carriage in going down hill, may be equally well applied to our ox carts.

The waggons generally used in this country, whether for one, two or more horses, are, perhaps, as convenient as those to be found elsewhere; all that is particularly insisted on is, that according to the experience of the best British farmers, the one horse cart should be preferred to the waggon on smooth well cultivated farms, as being cheaper, and more convenient for most uses.

Whether the wheels of carts be made of wood or of cast iron, the rims should be as much as four inches broad; by this means they sink less into the earth, and therefore run more safe and steadily. Their being low, and placed pretty wide apart, also renders the cart less liable to upset.

Carriages should be constantly shielded from the weather when not in use; the summer sun cracks and shrinks the wood, and wet weather tends imperceptibly to decay it, and to waste the parts which are of iron by rust.

For the best method of seasoning timber for carts, waggons, &c. see article TIMBER.

Waggons and carts may be made to run at least one fifth easier, by having iron rollers in the boxes—this at the same time saves the trouble of tarring the axletrees. A plan has been patented for waggon boxes with rollers, which has the rollers held at equal distances by having each end fixed in a rim or ring, so that as the rollers run round in the inside of the box, the ring turns with them, and thus prevents any friction by the rollers getting out of their places. If four or five dollars a year can be saved by the easy running of a carriage, by being enabled to carry, perhaps, a fifth more at a load, it is well worth while to be at the additional expense of four or five dollars in the first instance to fit the carriage for this purpose.

CARROT; *(Daucus.)* There are few articles of culture more profitable than that of carrots. They will yield, with good cultivation, from six hundred to a thousand bushels an acre. Allowing them to be worth nineteen cents a bushel for the purpose of fatting hogs and cattle, and taking 700 bushels as the average produce of an acre, this amounts to 133 dollars. Allowing what would be equal to 40 days labor to an acre to raise and gather them, which, at 75 cents a day for hire and boarding, would amount to 30 dollars; and then allowing 10 dollars an acre for the rent of the land, this would leave 93 dollars the clear profit of an acre.

Carrots require a mellow soil, into which they can easily penetrate deeply. They will grow very well on one which is moderately rich, provided it be well and deeply mellowed. A fertile sand, a sandy loam, a dry warm loam, or a fertile gravelly loam, are each suitable for them, with proper manuring and cultivation. The ground ought to be ploughed till it is perfectly mellow, and as deep as possible, not less than a foot in depth, if you expect the best crops. The land should be perfectly free of stones. The best way is to plough but one way—not to cross plough—for this is only necessary in rough hard ground, for breaking clods and other obstructions to the plough; but for the mere purpose of mellowing land, cross ploughing is not more efficacious than constantly ploughing one way. In this way where you make the parting furrow, you begin the next time to make the back furrow, and thus you keep the depth of the earth that is stirred by the plough equal, which is essential to the equal growth of carrots. The ground ought to be ploughed in this way in the fall, and then but little will be requisite to prepare it in the Spring; after ploughing in the Spring it ought to be finely harrowed, and then it will be fitted for the reception of the seed.

The sowing is performed either in the broadcast way or the drill. In the former, the seed is covered with a rake instead of a harrow, to prevent its being covered too deep. The first hoeing being gone through, after they have arrived to a suitable size, the ground is all harrowed over; and they are then to be gone over again, for the purpose of uncovering those which the harrow may have covered: this is also a proper time for thinning them where they are too thick— they are to be thinned so as to stand from about four to six inches apart. They may, however, be thinned after this, when they have got to some size; and then those which are pulled out may be given to the hogs, as they are very fond of them, and will readily eat both roots and tops. As soon as they have got so large that the tops will cover the ground, they will stop the further growth of weeds. For neat cattle and hogs they cannot be too large, and therefore ought to be sown as early as the fore part of May if the ground and season will admit; they will, however, do very well when sown as late as the latter end of May, and such are the best for culinary purposes.

The hoe which is proper for working among them is the garden hoe; it must be sharp for cutting weeds, and about four inches wide; and on the other side of the handle is fixed four small prongs, similar to those of a dung fork, for the purpose of stirring up the ground.

The method of drilling, or sowing in rows, would be much the best, were it not for the tediousness of the operation of getting the seeds into the ground. The seed must be dropped into the rows by hand, unless some drill machine can be devised by which to commit them to the earth more rapidly. This, probably, might be done, notwithstanding the seeds are so badly shaped for that purpose. If they were first rubbed smartly together, so as to make them of rounder shape, then made wet with lye or brine, and dried with gypsum, and this repeated till the seeds should become encrusted, they might then probably be managed successfully in a small hand drill machine, which may be easily contrived for the purpose.

The first hoeing of drill rows, after ploughing between them, requires considerable hand labor, after which it may be performed almost entirely by the horse hoe or cultivater. (*See* articles HORSE

Hoe and Cultivator.)   The rows are to be thinned, so that the carrots when grown will be about an inch apart.

The best way to keep carrots through the winter for family use, is to bury them in dry sand.   In this way, they may also be kept for feeding out to horses, hogs, sheep, &c. and a cellar for the purpose might be made in a side hill, covered with earth, and otherwise fortified against the frost, to be sufficiently warm for that purpose.

Many farmers in G. Britain, where farmers in general understand the means of making the most of their lands much better than we do, sow yearly ten, twenty, thirty acres or more, of carrots, for fatting cattle or swine, &c.   Such are the farmers that grow wealthy there; and such would rapidly acquire wealth here, where wealth is so much more easily acquired.

For the best method of boiling carrots for feeding to hogs, &c. *see* the article Swine.

CATERPILLARS.   *See* article Insects.

CATTLE.   *See* articles Ass, Foals, &c. Goats, Horse, Mares, Neat Cattle, Sheep and Swine.

CHANGE of CROPS.   By a judicious change of crops land can be yearly applied to the most profitable uses of which it is susceptible. At the same time the food requisite for different plants being somewhat different either in kind or quantity, can be extracted with less injury to the soil where the extraction is equal—that is, where by one kind of crop certain given quantities or kinds are extracted, and different quantities or kinds by another.

Some plants will grow yearly on the same soil; others again will not.   Flax, for instance, so exhausts that food which is necessary to produce it, that it will not grow to perfection on the same ground oftener than about once in six or seven years.   Wheat sown yearly on the same ground will degenerate; and perhaps the same may be said of oats and barley.   Rye, on the contrary, will grow yearly for twenty years or more on the same soil, without materially injuring it.   Corn will also grow yearly, but it greatly exhausts the soil.   The same may be said of buckwheat.   Potatoes, carrots, parsnips, beets, and perhaps all kinds of grasses, require little or no change of soil, and do not materially exhaust it.

The propriety of changing crops arises partly from convenience and partly from necessity.   When we have raised a crop of potatoes, for instance, we know that we can raise a succeeding crop equally good on the same ground.   But here we study convenience; we want to raise a crop of flax or barley, and this ground is the best prepared for such purpose, while at the same time another piece will do equally well for potatoes. On the other hand, when we have raised the crop of flax, we are under the necessity of taking another piece of ground for the next crop; and for the same reasons we change, yearly, the grounds on which we raise our wheat, oats and barley. It may, therefore, be properly said that changing crops is partly a matter of convenience and partly of necessity, and that these two causes combining serve to give a direction to that course of cropping which no good farmer will resist.

But though a change of crops is in general the best management, it is not such in every case. If we have got a piece of ground well fitted for raising carrots, and we find the culture of these more profitable than any thing else we can apply to that ground, it would not be advisable to apply it to a less profitable culture, and be at the trouble of fitting another piece of ground for raising this root; unless it should be found that the ground became exhausted for its culture, and that a change was on that account necessary. The same may be observed with respect to the culture of onions, parsnips, beets, &c.

The best changes of crops must depend much on the soil. In a fertile sand, sandy loam, gravelly loam, or other dry warm soil, it is as well to begin the first year with corn and potatoes, or perhaps potatoes alone, first ploughing in all the barn dung made that Spring; the second year corn, which will then receive the greatest benefit from the rotten dung and the previously fermented state of the soil; the third year, barley, and clover sown with it; the fourth, clover; the fifth, clover, one crop, and then the sward, after the clover has grown considerably again, well turned over, and harrowed in with wheat; the sixth, wheat, sown as before mentioned, with clover; the seventh and eighth, clover; and then the sward torn up again in the fall for potatoes the next year.

If the lands are a cold loam or clay, which are too wet for wheat, I should advise to break up in the fall, and in the Spring cart on all the barn dung, and plough it in well, and harrow the ground; then plant it with potatoes in rows, on the top of the ground, about four feet apart. When the potatoes are laid, a light furrow run close along each side of the rows will cover them. When they have got to a proper height, run a furrow on each side of the rows, turning it against them, and complete the dressing with the hoe. In due season give them another such dressing. By this time the earth forming the rows will be thrown up so high that it must be sufficiently dry, and have every chance of producing the greatest degree of fermentation, and of course will afford the best chance to produce as good a crop of potatoes as such soil is capable of producing.

When the potatoes are dug, which may be chiefly performed by the plough being run through the rows, first on each side and then in the middle, throw up the ground again in high ridges of two furrows on each side, and so let it lie during the winter. The next Spring plough it all level at first, and harrow it fine, then ridge it again by throwing up two furrows against each other, at the distance of four feet apart, and plant your Indian corn on the tops of the ridges; and then with proper attention in ploughing and hoeing it, when the ground is not too wet, a good crop of Indian corn may be raised on ground, which, when planted in the cold unfermented state of the soil, and receiving no immediate assistance from the crude state of the barn dung, would scarcely produce a crop worth gathering.

After the corn is taken off, by again ridging the land for the winter frosts, and then levelling it in the Spring, and ploughing it well in dry times, you may fit the soil for a good crop of oats, or perhaps barley or summer wheat, if the lands lie in the more northerly part of this state. With this crop it must be seeded down—not with clover, for this will winter-kill in such soils—but with herdsgrass, which it will produce well for several years. After this grass has failed, tear up the sward, and go through the same process of culture again. This, or something similar, is about all the change of crops that can be had to any advantage on such lands.

Such lands, by being hollow drained, become dry enough for wheat and clover, and are then generally excellent for cultivation. Farmers, therefore, whose lands are all of this description, ought to commence hollow draining, and as they progress they will find themselves enabled to raise crops of wheat superior to those which are raised on soils naturally dry. (*See* article HOLLOW DRAINS.)

There are other courses of crops that may be most suitable for different soils, and perhaps variations may be made to advantage in each; all of which are calculated to exercise the judgment and skill of the experienced farmer.

CHANGE OF SEEDS. Most plants are found to degenerate to a certain degree, unless their seeds are frequently changed. This has been attributed to their cultivation in climates where they are not indigenous. But this can hardly be the sole reason; for it is found that most plants will be improved by having the seeds brought from the east to the west, and *vice versa*.

Providence, in making so large a world as this, seems to have designed that there should, nevertheless, be a common acquaintance among the nations which inhabit it. They are invited abroad for conveniences which their own climates do not furnish; they are impelled to a general intermixture, from a knowledge that it is beneficial; and the benefits to be derived from a change of seeds are probably only in furtherance of the general design of a community among nations.

But we are as yet much in the dark as it respects the best changes of seeds, and from what parts of the world they should be brought, to produce the greatest crops. Ought not this to become a matter of more general concern? The Irish farmers sow our flaxseed, and find great account in it. Would their flaxseed be equally beneficial when sown here? I have known flaxseed brought from Long-Island and sown in Orange county, which produced nearly double the crop which the common seed there produced. Spring wheat brought from Canada and sown here, (Herkimer county) greatly enhances the crop, but soon degenerates. Siberian wheat yielded largely in this country for a while. The seeds of apples brought from Europe will produce trees larger than our own. For roots it is generally supposed that seeds brought from a more southerly climate are best. Indian corn brought far from that quarter will be in danger of ripening too late; that brought far from the north will ripen too early for a large crop. On the whole, the farmer should make his changes as judiciously as possible, and in most instances he will then find the product of his crops greatly increased.

CHEESE. For making this article take the following directions: Make your milk blood warm, and put in your runnet, but no more than will just make the curd come. Add an once of fine salt to so much curd as will make a cheese of fifteen pounds, and in that proportion for a greater or less. Stir the curd till it is gathered; put it in a strainer, and with your hands work out all the whey; then lay it in a clean linen cloth, put it in the hoop, and covering it with the cloth, put it in the press, and let it stand there two hours; then take it out, rub it over with fine salt, put it in another dry cloth, and put it in the press eight hours; then take it out again, put it in another dry cloth, and put it in the press again, where it is to remain till the next cheese is ready. When taken out of the press, put it in brine twenty-four hours, and let the brine have as much salt-petre in it as will lie on a shilling. Some little additions of salt and salt-petre must be occasionally made to the brine, and let it be cleansed as often as necessary, by heating it and taking off the scum. When you take the cheese out, dry it with a cloth; bind it round with a long string to make it keep its shape, which must be kept round it for some days, and let it be daily turned on the shelf for two months. .

Let the evening milk be put with that of the morning; and to make the best cheeses, let none of the cream be taken away. If the evening milk, however, be skimmed, and added to that of the morning, it will make tolerable cheese. Skim-milk cheeses are also made, but they are not worth much.

But no good cheese can be made unless the runnet be good. *See* article RUNNET.

The room where cheeses are to be kept for drying should be dark, to keep out flies; and to prevent these from depositing their eggs in the cracks of the cheeses, let them be smeared over with a mixture of salt butter and tar. To give them a fine colour, let a little annatto be put in the milk; this is harmless—but beware of colouring them with any thing that is poisonous.

CHURN. The best churn is the oblong square, which is turned on two pivots by a crank. The pivots are not placed in the centre of the two ends; but one is placed at one side of the end, and the other at the opposite side of the other end, so that the churn is suspended *diagonally* on the pivots. This, when it is turned, gives the milk a violent motion from one end of the churn to the other, while at the same time it turns very easily. The churn ought to be about of the following proportions: One that is three feet long ought to be one foot wide one way, and about nine inches wide the other way, so as to form a *flat* oblong square. The pivots are made of iron, and are rivetted on the outside. A square hole is made on one side for letting in the milk and taking out the butter; and a square piece is made exactly fitted to fill up the hole, which is fastened down to its place by a little iron bar across it, with staples at each end. .

Oak is generally preferred for churns, as pine is apt to communicate something of its taste to the butter.

CIDER. To make the best cider there are several requisites.—— The apples should be of one sort, and of the best kind. They should be perfectly sound, ripe and clean. Those which are shook from the trees by a gentle shaking are best; and all knotty, wormy and rotten ones should be rejected. Such as are not of this prime rate may be made into common cider.

Let the apples thus selected be spread on a floor, raised from the ground, with a cover over it, and the sides enclosed. Here they are to lie for the purpose of sweating, by which their more watery parts are thrown off. Let them lie here about four or five days when the weather is dry and warm, but longer when wet and cool, and let them then be dried, by exposure to the sun, and ground immediately in a clean mill. Some prefer having the seeds broken in grinding, as imparting a more agreeable taste to the cider. Let the vessels which receive the cider be perfectly sweet and clean, for without this the best juice will be spoiled. New casks, or those which have just been emptied of brandy, are the best. The manufacturers of wine take great pains to have their casks clean, and commence the cleansing for months before they are to be used.

For cleansing casks, let them be first washed perfectly clean, after they are emptied of cider, and bunged up tight. Before they are to be used again, take at the rate of a pint or more of unslacked lime for a barrel, put it in, and pour in three or four gallons of hot water, or more for a larger cask; shake it well, and while the lime is slacking give it some vent, lest it burst the cask. Let it stand till cooled, and then rinse it with cold water. If it still has any sour smell, repeat the operation till it smells perfectly sweet. The effect of this is, that the lime destroys all the acidity which may be in the cask.

The first and the last running of a cheese should be put in a cask by itself, as it is not so good as the rest. In pouring the cider into the cask, let there be a strainer of coarse cloth in the bottom of the funnel to keep out the pumace. After the casks are filled, the next process is the fermentation, and this is a matter of some nicety.

There are three fermentations—the vinous, the acid, and the putrid. When the first ceases the second begins, and when that ceases the third begins. The first is only necessary for cider, and care must be taken to stop all further fermentation as soon as this is over. This is known by the liquor ceasing to throw up little bubbles to the top. Then too all the pumace is raised up, and if suffered to remain there, will again sink to the bottom and render the liquor turbid. Let this time then be carefully observed, and let the liquor then be drawn off, not too closely, and put into other clean casks, or bottled, and closed tight, and set away in a cool cellar. Let a gallon of French brandy be added to every barrel.

But to further improve it, let it undergo a further operation, as follows: As you draw off the cider from the first casks, put it into fresh ones, filling each about three quarters full, and set them away till winter; at which time let them be exposed to the frosts until one half, or even two thirds of the contents of each are frozen; give the liquor some vent while freezing; draw off the unfrozen part, bottle it, or put it in clean new casks, and set it away in a cool cellar, and let it remain there for two or three years, and it will then nearly equal the best wines.

If it should require clarifying, let it be done with isinglass; or it may be leached through a tub of powdered charcoal, which will render it very clear; but the tub should be covered close to prevent any evaporation of the spirit. To clarify it with isinglass, pour into each vessel about a pint of the infusion of about sixty grains of the most transparent of this glue in a little white wine and rain or river water, stirred well together, after being strained through a linen cloth. This viscous substance spreads over the surface of the liquor, and carries all the dregs with it to the bottom.

Some boil cider in the spring, for summer use; but the practice is a very bad one, particularly when boiled in brass kettles. If any boiling be ever proper for cider, it must be as it comes from the press. This is the proper method of treating water cider, or that which is extracted from the pumace after the cheese has been pressed. The pumace is put into casks in the evening, with a due proportion of warm water thrown on it, and in the morning it is made into a cheese, and pressed off again, the liquor is then to be boiled till all the scum has risen and been skimmed off, and then it is to be put away in casks in a cool cellar, and treated like other cider. It ferments but little, and makes a pleasant drink for the next summer, if bottled, or otherwise kept well. Perhaps this would be a good method of treating all cider.

Cider may be kept for years in casks without fermenting, by burying them deeply under ground, or immersing them in spring water; and when taken up the cider will be very fine.

A drink called cider-royal, is made of the best running of the cheese, well clarified, with six or eight gallons of French brandy, or good cider brandy, added to a barrel; let the vessel be filled full, bunged tight, and set in a cool cellar, and in the course of a twelvemonth will be a fine drink. If good rectified whiskey be used, instead of brandy, it will answer very well.

A quart of honey, or molasses, and a quart of brandy, or other spirits, added to a barrel of cider will improve the liquor very much, and will restore that which has become too flat and insipid. To prevent its becoming pricked, or to cure it when it is so, put a little pearl-ashes, or other mild alkali, into the cask. A lump of chalk broken in pieces, and thrown in, is also good. Salt of tartar, where the cider is about to be used, is also recommended.

To refine cider, and give it a fine amber colour, the following method is much approved of. Take the whites of six eggs, with a handful of fine beach sand, washed clean, stir them well together; then boil a quart of molasses down to a candy, and cool it by pouring in cider, and put this, together with the eggs and sand, into a barrel of cider, and mix the whole well together. When thus managed it will keep for many years. Molasses alone will also refine cider, and give it a higher color, but to prevent the molasses making it prick, let an equal quantity of brandy be added to it. Skim-milk, with some lime slacked in it, and mixed with it, or with the white of eggs with the shells broken in, is also good for clarifying all liquors, when well mixed with them. A piece of fresh bloody meat put into the cask, will also refine the liquor and serve for it to feed on.

To prevent the fermentation of cider, let the cask be first strongly fumigated with burnt sulphur, then put in some of the cider, burn more sulphur in the cask, stop it tight, and shake the whole up together; fill the cask, bung it tight, and put it away in a cool cellar.

To bring on a fermentation, take three pints of yeast for a hogshead, add as much jalup as will lie on a sixpence, mix them with some of the cider, beat the mass up till it is frothy, then pour it into the cask, and stir it up well. Keep the vessel full, and the bung open, for the froth and foul stuff to work out. In about fifteen days the froth will be clean and white; then, to stop the fermentation, rack the cider off into a clean vessel, add two gallons of brandy, or well rectified whiskey to it, and bung it up. Let the cask be full, and keep the vent hole open for a day or two. By this process, cider that is poor and ill tasted, may be wonderfully improved. Let it be refined by some of the methods before described.

To cure oily cider, take one ounce of salt of tartar, and two and a half of sweet spirit of nitre, in a gallon of milk, for a hogshead. To cure ropy cider, take six pounds of powdered allum and stir it into a hogshead; then rack it off and clarify it.

To colour cider, take a quarter of a pound of sugar, burnt black, and dissolved in half a pint or hot water, for a hogshead, add a quarter of an ounce of allum to set the colour.

Cider-brandy mixed with an equal quantity of honey, or clarified sugar, is much recommended by some for improving common cider; so that, when refined, it may be made as strong, and as pleasant as the most of wines.

Cider has been made in Great-Britain, of such superior quality as to command a price of sixty guineas a hogshead. If such can be made there, it can also be made here, where our climate in general is more favorable for the production of apples of the best qualities.

CLAY. The basis of this earth is alumine. A quality peculiar to clay is, that by reason of its alumine, it contracts when dried or heated, and expands again when moistened. A clayey soil therefore is always to be known by its cracking open in dry weather; and the more clayey, the wider will be these openings.

Where the soil is very clayey, and at the same time wet, it is worth but little for the plough, though it may be good for mowing, or pasture; but if the adhesion of the soil be destroyed by proper manures, and it be laid dry by hollow draining, it then becomes a fine soil for most productions.

See articles MANURES, and HOLLOW DRAINS.

Some nicety is requisite as to the proper time for ploughing this ground. If it be too dry it will not crumble; and if too wet, the ploughing will only render it more compact. The hard clods are easiest mellowed by the plough after they have been merely wet through with a gentle rain.

See further article EARTHS.

CLEARING OF LANDS. But little need be said on this subject, as he who has to undertake the clearing new lands will acquire more knowledge from practice of the best methods of subduing our heavy forests, than from any essay on the subject. He will find that the essential point is to put his shoulder to the wheel, and persevere undauntedly; and in a few years he will find his exertions amply compensated by the pleasing scenes and profitable improvements which shall have been made around his dwelling.

When new settlers first go into the woods, they have to spend much valuable time in hunting up their oxen and milch cows, which, for want of an enclosed pasture, have to run in the woods; and to remedy this as soon as possible, I would propose the following: About the first of June, take a suitable piece of ground, cut out the bushes, and all the small growth of timber which shall be under a certain size, say a foot over at the but; pile all the brush round those trees which are left standing. In a dry time, in the month of August, set fire to them, and the fires will kill the trees left standing; then pile and burn what lies on the ground, which is soon done, and in due season harrow in a crop of wheat or rye, and in the following spring sow the ground over with herdsgrass. The crop of wheat or rye, sown in this way, will be nearly as good as if the timber were all taken off; and the year following the ground will afford the requisite supply of pasture and hay. When the limbs of the standing trees begin to rot and fall off, cut the whole down, and let them lie there; as the pasture will not be injured, but rather eventually benefitted, by the trees lying and rotting upon it. This method of killing trees by fire, is however, only recommended where they are such as cannot be killed by girdling; such as beach, maple, bass-wood, &c.

New settlers, who will take this method of providing a supply of pasture and hay, will always find their account in two ways; it is turning the grounds to immediate profit, with the least possible expense; and the surplus of hay and pasture will demand an extra price; as those articles are always scarce during the commencement of new settlements.

CLIMATE. All seeds are to be planted, or sown, at such time as is suitable to the climate. In northerly climates, or in very elevated situations, the spring and autumn press closer upon each other, and there the spring crops must be planted, or sown, later, and the fall crops earlier than in more temperate climates. The right time for planting and sowing, must, therefore, be ascertained by the judgment of the farmer, founded on due experience, and a knowledge of the climate in which he lives.

Climate depends greatly on *altitude* as well as *latitude*. This is no where more strikingly exemplified than on the sides of Mount Ætna. When, at the base of that mountain, the peasants are reaping their spring crops, on its highest cultivable parts they are busied in sowing the same crops; and at its extreme point of elevation is perpetual winter. The highest lands which lie between the Mohawk and Black river, in this state, are not fifty miles north of Albany; yet the climate on this height, is at least six degrees of latitude colder than at that city.

From a knowledge of these facts, it is obvious, that the same productions will not thrive equally well in all places, under the same degree of latitude, even though the soil be the same; and, knowing this, it becomes necessary for the farmer to regulate his system of farming accordingly.

CLOVER; (*Trifolium pratense.*) White clover is a very fine grass, affording the sweetest pasture and hay, but the product is too small, when compared with red clover, which is nearly as sweet, to be worth cultivating.

The almost universal use of red clover upon dry upland soils, is, it would seem, an indication of its superiority over most other grasses; but, it certainly never can be made to yield so great a clear profit as Lucerne, where this grass is cultivated in a suitable soil and climate.

One excellence of red clover, is, that it is the only grass which can with advantage be turned under by the plough, and thus, with one ploughing only, ensure a good crop of wheat, or other grain. The crop, however, will be best where the clover is mowed, and not fed off by cattle. Another good quality is, its superiority over almost all other grasses, in mellowing and enriching the soil. It derives most of its nourishment from a considerable depth, and like all tap-rooted plants, it exhausts the land but little, while at the same time, when ploughed under, it forms a good green dressing for the soil.

Green clover is a good food for swine during summer; and clover-hay, when boiled, is also found to be a good food for them during winter. Mr. Livingston makes mention of a farmer at Rhinebeck, who fed his hogs during winter with no other food but boiled clover, and that they were kept in good condition. The clover used for them was preserved by being salted, a quart to a load. It was cut and left in win-rows about six hours, then put into small cocks. The next day, about noon, these were opened; towards evening they were rode home, and laid away with salt, which kept it green and juicy all the year.

See further, article Swine.

The quantity of red clover seed, to be sowed to the acre, is about ten pounds, and none but clean seed ought to be sown.

The best crops with which to sow clover, are barley, oats, and spring wheat. It is, however, frequently sown in the spring on winter wheat, or rye; but in this way it often happens that the seeds do not grow, owing to their not being covered. This difficulty may, however, be obviated, by giving the ground a brushing, by dragging a large bunch of bushes, tied together, over it, where the land is rough; or by giving it a light harrowing where it is smooth; either of which methods, but particularly the latter, will be a benefit to the growth of wheat or rye. It may also be sown with winter wheat, or rye, in the fall; but there is danger in that case of its being killed by the succeeding winter.

Clover yields two crops in the season, if the land be in good heart; unless it be in the northerly parts of the state, where the second growth will generally be too small to mow to advantage, and is, therefore, best to be fed off.

When you wish to let the clover go to seed, take the second crop; or, where you cannot have two crops in a season, pasture it till some time in May, and then let it grow up to seed, which will of course be late. The reason for doing this is, that in the first crop in each season, very little seed is to be found. A machine has been invented for gathering the seed, which runs through the clover, while standing, somewhat similar to a comb running through hair, and the heads are nipped off by a sharp edge, and fall into a box made for the purpose. Keeping a growth of clover for seed injures the roots more than mowing; and, therefore, the seed crop ought to be the last that is taken from any one sowing. Clover is only a biennial plant; the third year the crop is little or nothing.

Cattle, when first turned into a luxuriant clover-field, either of white or red, sometimes become *hoven*, as it is called; that is, so expanded with wind as to die, unless relief be afforded. The cure for this consists simply in stabbing them with a sharp pointed knife, with a blade three or four inches long, between the hip and the short ribs, where the swelling rises highest. This will let out the wind, and if it gathers again, open the hole afresh with the knife, and repeat this as often as may be necessary. The wound will soon heal of itself.

See article GRASSES.

COMPOSTS. *See* article MANURES.

COWS. The marks of a good cow are these; the forehead broad, the eyes black, the horns large and clean, the neck long and straight, the belly large and deep, the thighs thick, the legs round with short joints, and the feet broad and thick. Red cows are said to give the best milk; though the black ones are said to bring the best calves, which is, however, doubtful. But the cow that gives milk the longest time between the periods of her calving, is generally best for profit or for family use; provided, the quantity and quality of her milk be equal to that of others. Just before calving, a cow should be well fed; and if she calves in winter, her drink should be a little warmed for a day and night afterwards. If she does not clean well after calving, give her a pail of warm water, with some ashes in it. Those that calve pretty early will yield most milk in the season.

The times of milking ought to be regular, and as nearly equi-distant as possible. Where the feeding is full, it is found that milking three times a day, during the summer season particularly, will increase the quantity nearly one third. In that case, the first milking ought to be by sunrise, the second about one, and the latter about seven or eight o'clock in the evening. Omitting to milk cows regularly, at least twice a day, tends very much to dry them. Sometimes one or more teats of a cow may be diseased, but this does not affect the milk of the rest.

Cows are certainly very profitable. Allowing one to give only six quarts a day, for forty weeks in each year, and this is not a large allowance, her milk, at two cents per quart, will amount to upwards of thirty-three dollars; which is probably sufficient to purchase her, and pay for a year's keeping.

See further articles, CATTLE, CREAM, DAIRY, &c.

CRAB-APPLE-TREE; *(Pyrus Coronaria.)* This is a genuine and distinct species of the apple; it grows in all parts of North-America which have been explored, from the Atlantic as far west as the Missisippi; its blossoms are remarkably fragrant; its fruit small, possessing, perhaps, of all others, the keenest acid. It makes an excellent vinegar, and the cider made from it is much admired by those who profess to be connoisseurs in that article. The European crab-apple is a very different fruit from this.

There are no varieties of fruit of the crab-apple tree. Every tree bears nearly equally well and pretty plentifully. It is believed, that this fruit is well worth cultivating.

CREAM. Pans, or trays, for holding milk, to raise the most cream, ought to be broad and shallow, and the milk in them ought not to be more than three or four inches in depth. Tin and wood are the best materials for making these. Some line wooden trays with lead; but this is a bad practice, as lead may sometimes be dissolved by the acid of the milk, and then it is poisonous. Wooden trays ought to be well scalded, and dried in a cool place, as often as new milk is put in them, to prevent the wood from absorbing too much of the acidity of the milk, and thus coagulating the new milk before the cream has time to rise; for cream will not rise after the milk has become coagulated.

If new milk be kept as warm as when it comes from the cow, no cream will rise on it; but when sufficiently cooled, the cream separates from the rest and rises to the top. In order then to effect this to the best advantage, the new milk should be made as cool as possible, and the cooler it is thus made, the more suddenly and effectually the cream will rise. The cooler the cellars, therefore, in which milk is kept, the better. To set milk-pans, made of tin, in beds of salt, would, no doubt, be useful, where the cellar is too warm; and to set all milk vessels on a floor which is constantly covered with cold spring water, is also an excellent plan, and where it can be done, ought never to be omitted.

Most of the cream comes last from the cow in milking. The last half pint of milk that can be got, by milking the cow dry, contains as much cream as the first quart, or perhaps three pints; and for this reason, cows ought always to be milked as clean as possible. The quantity of cream will also be greater, if the milk of each cow be strained into a pan by itself, as soon as possible. The practice of pouring the milk of the cows together, while milking, and letting the whole stand till nearly cooled, is a very bad one, as, in this way, much of the cream will not afterwards rise.

CUCUMBER; *(Gumoumis.)* These are a cold fruit and hard of digestion, yet pleasant to the taste. They are rendered more wholesome by pickling; though the taste of a pickled cucumber must be considered far inferior to those which are fresh when properly prepared for eating. This is best done by slicing them, and then putting them in cold water for a while, which renders them more easy to digest.

Cowper in his " *Task*," in describing the method of raising cucumbers in hot-beds, directs that after " two rough indented leaves" are produced, " a *pimple* that portends a future sprout," on " the *second* stalk" is to be pinched off, to prevent its growth; and this, he says, will make the other branches grow more strong and be more prolific.

The soil for cucumbers cannot be too rich, nor too well cultivated, to raise a great crop. A spot well manured with fish, or other flesh, will produce a great quantity. Hog's-dung is also very good for them.

See also article RADISH, for a good manure for them.

Take a tub and fill it half full of stones, and with as much water; over this lay some straw, and fill the tub with the richest earth; plant this full of the seeds, and guard the plants well while they are subject to insects, though they will be much less subject to them in this way; spread some brush round the tub for the vines to run on, and in this way a great crop may be raised. The water in the tub must be constantly replenished by a tube from the outside, which will keep the soil in the tub sufficiently moist to keep off insects from the plants.

See article INSECTS.

CURRANT; *(Ribes.)* There are a variety of currants, including those called gooseberries. (*See* article GOOSEBERRY.) The black currant, which grows in the swamps in this country, is greatly improved by cultivation, says Mr. Winterbotham, and affords a wine equal to Port when it has age. It is also an excellent medicine for a sore mouth and throat. When bruised and steeped in whiskey, or other spirits, it is also excellent for colds and for bad coughs arising from pulmonic complaints. They are to be steeped a fortnight or more, then strain the liquor, bottle it, and put it away for use. The red and the white currants are most common here, and each make good wines, though the white is thought to make the best. Currants are the most useful of all the small kinds of fruit-trees, and for making wines they are very profitable.

After pressing out the juice for making wine, let the seeds be dried and sown late in the fall, or early in the spring, on fine light earth, and from these, new varieties may be had; some of which may be found very fine and much superior perhaps to those in common use. Some may be found to ripen early, others late, which are qualities particularly desirable for family uses.

Currants are easily propagated from cuttings, which is the usual method, or from layers or slips.

See articles LAYERS and SLIPS.

As soon as vegetation has commenced, take the strongest and straightest shoots, but not such as are suckers, and set the ends pretty well in the ground, in order that they may have sufficient moisture; and, let them be watered if the weather be very dry after planting. They will soon take root, and the next season will begin to bear. They should then be kept carefully pruned, and should not be suffered to run too high. They should be kept clear of suckers, as these draw much of that nourishment which is requisite for the fruit. The ground about them should be occasionally hoed, to keep it clear of weeds and grass.

Currants will do very well even on light sandy soils; but perhaps, the best soil for them is a good mellow sandy loam. With proper culture, however, they will grow pretty well on almost any soil that is not too hard and poor.

Mr. Forsyth gives some very minute directions for pruning currants, and applying his composition to the wounded parts; but in this instance, as in some others, he probably carries his theories to extremes. Whatever may be the case in Great-Britain, where fruit is not so easily raised, it is believed that the above general directions, if pursued, will ensure good crops of currants in this country, which appears to be very natural to their growth.

To make Currant Wine.—Take currants fully ripe, at the rate of one gallon for each gallon of water; bruise them fine in the water; strain the whole through a cloth, and add two pounds and three quarters of good brown sugar to every gallon of currants and water thus mixed together; stir it well, and when the sugar has dissolved, put the whole into a clean cask, filling it full and leaving a good vent hole open. When the fermentation is over, stop it up tight, and in six months it will be fit for bottling or for use. Like other wines, however, it improves much by age.

Probably molasses, well clarified, might be made to answer instead of sugar; and, probably, honey, or a due mixture of it, would be better than either.

An acre planted with currants, and well cultivated, would probably yield, on an average, a quantity of fruit sufficient to make a thousand gallons of wine yearly. The expense of making this wine does not exceed fifty cents a gallon, and the wine, after having a little age, is worth treble this money.

A currant-garden should be set with the bushes in rows, about eight feet between each, and about three feet between each bush, with intervals of proper width and at regular distances for passing across the rows. Planting currants on the south side of a wall will make them ripen more early, and they will ripen later when planted on the north side.

CUTTINGS. These are twigs of trees cut off and set into the ground, where they will take root and grow. They should be taken from young thrifty trees.

Cuttings of currants, grape-vines, willow, Lombardy poplars, &c. are made to grow without any difficulty; those of quinces are not so easy, and those of the apple-tree are still less so. Let those which are most difficult to grow be set as deep as twelve inches; those less difficult six, eight, or ten, as the kinds may require. Let them be cut and set in the spring, as soon as vegetation has commenced, and perhaps earlier than this is best for those which are most difficult to grow. Let them be frequently watered when the ground is dry. The twigs used for this purpose should be of good straight growth, but not such as are suckers.

Apple-trees raised in this way will not grow so large as those raised from the seeds, nor will they be so long lived; but in this way as in grafting, the choicest selections of fruit can be made.

Where cuttings are to be kept some time before setting in the ground, let the cut ends be kept in moist earth and soaked in water, before they are set.

See further article SLIPS.

SCIONS: Twigs cut off for grafting. They should be taken from young thrifty trees, but not from sprouts or suckers. Let them be of

the ends of limbs of the former year's growth.   Cut them just before
the buds begin to swell, and keep them in a moist place with the cut
ends in moist earth till the time of grafting.

D.

DAIRY. The business of the dairy requires close attention. The
milkings, in order to be most profitable, should be three times a day ;
the first at day-light ; the second at noon ; and, the latter at twilight.
This will very considerably increase the quantity of milk given in a
day from any number of cows.

In order to ascertain which cow's milk is the best, as yielding the
most cream, let the milk of each be put by itself, and their products of
butter will then determine the point.   The quantity of milk afforded
by each should also be taken into consideration.

See further articles, BUTTER, CHEESE, CHURN, COWS, CREAM,
NEAT CATTLE.

Dr. Anderson recommends wooden vessels as being the most wholesome for holding milk ; but that if tin pans be used, they should be
washed, every time they are emptied, with warm water in which a little salt has been dissolved, and should be kept clean by scouring ; and
to prevent acidity in wooden vessels they should in like manner be
scoured and cleansed with hot water.   Leaden vessels he condemns,
as is mentioned under article BUTTER.

The dairy requires two apartments—a clean cool room in the cellar
for the milk, and a dark room above ground for drying and keeping
the cheese. Many farmers, however, confine their attention to making
butter alone, and in that case a good cool cellar is the essential requisite.   Let the milk be set on the ground, for it is the coolest part of
the cellar in summer and the warmest in winter.

If milk be kept in tin pans, and set within earthen ones, of a texture
so porous, so that the water in them will gradually exude, this will impart a great degree of coolness to the milk. The water in the earthen
pans should surround those holding the milk.   If the outer pan were
made of stiff leather, it would answer the same purpose.

DEW. "An experiment," says Mr. Livingston, "has been made to ascertain the difference between dew water and rain water, by puting an equal quantity of each in different vessels, and setting them in the sun to dry away; the result was, that the sediment or settlings of the dew water were greater in quantity, blacker, and richer, than that of the rain water."

Dew is, therefore, fertilizing; and, this is the reason why lands will be most benefited by being constantly ploughed when the dew is on them.

See article FALLOWING, &c.

DITCH. This is either for enclosing grounds to serve in the place of other fencing, or to carry off superfluous water. When made for a fence, it ought to be four feet wide at the top, one, or less, at the bottom, and about two and a half deep, with the earth all thrown out on one side, and banked up as high as possible. This, however, is but a poor fence, unless a hedge of some kind be planted on it; or, unless it be raised higher by posts and rails, or boards; or, by stakes and wicker-work; and this, where cedar can be had for the purpose, makes a good durable fence.

See article HEDGES.

To drain swamps, ditches ought to be of size and depth proportionate to the extent of the swamp; or rather let them be proportionate to the quantity of water to be carried off. Those round the edges of the swamp ought to be so placed as to receive all the water from the springs which commonly run in on every side; or, if convenient, they should be so placed as to cut off the springs, by receiving them into the ditch. When a very wet swamp is to be drained, the months of August and September are the best for performing this labor, as the ground is then driest, while at the same time the water will not prove troublesome by its coldness. The proper proportions for these kinds of ditches are to be three times as wide at the top as they are at the bottom, and a little more than half as deep as they are wide. If they are not thus sloped they will fall in; owing to the heaving of the ground by the frosts. To prevent their falling in, it is advisable to sow some strong rooted grass on the sides of the ditches.

See further, article BOG-MEADOW.

DIVISIONS OF A FARM. If a farm be nearly square it may sometimes be advisable to have a wide lane through the middle, and lots laid off on each side; or, if it be more oblong, a wide lane on one side may be advisable, and the lots laid off to it. No certain directions can, however, be given on this head, owing to the different shapes, soils, &c. of farms. A lane of this kind may often be the more eligible where it can take in some spring, or other living water, as in that case, every field becomes accessible to the water at all times, by leaving open the gate of that which is in present use in pasturing.

Lots for tillage should always be square, or at least of equal sides; those for mowing or pasture may be irregular without any inconvenience.

DRESSINGS. A dressing differs from a manuring only in this, that the former is intended merely for one crop, while the latter is intended for several. Some dressings, such as gypsum, ashes, salt, &c. &c. are to be laid on the soil; others again, such as composts, &c. are to be slightly buried in it, and mixed with its surface.

DRILL: An instrument for sowing seeds by opening furrows at proper distances, and of proper depth, dropping the seeds and covering them all at one operation. It may be drawn by horses, or by hand, according to its size, and the use to which it is to be applied. A single drill plough is successfully used for planting Indian corn in rows. Mr. Rutherford makes mention of one used in New-Jersey for sowing wheat in rows thirteen inches apart, which is drawn by two horses, with which a man can drill in about eight acres per day. The cost of it is about eight or ten dollars. He adds, that where the seed is drilled in with this machine, the crop will be much larger, and at the same time less seed is requisite.

The land on which the drill is used should be entirely clear of stumps and stones; and on such lands the farmer may find great account in making use of these machines. Particular descriptions of them are here omitted, because it is difficult to describe them so as to give the reader an adequate idea of their construction. The spirited farmer who is anxious to test their efficacy may easily inform himself of the construction of the different kinds in use.

DROUGHT. As a country becomes cleared of its timber, it becomes more liable to droughts; and these will be more or less severe according to the climate. That which is naturally cool and moist, such as that of Great-Britain and Ireland, will seldom, if ever, be affected by too much dry weather; while that in which the summers are hotter, and of course, the atmosphere dryer, will often suffer much on this account. In most parts of Spain, the fields are parched up by the middle of summer; but before this the crops are all harvested. In this country, droughts are never so severe, nor so universal, yet partial ones are often experienced, much earlier, and long before the crops have come to maturity. This is an evil, and all the farmer can do, is to make the best possible provision against it.

Generally speaking, nothing is better calculated to ward off the effects of droughts than good cultivation, by ploughing sufficiently deep, and effectually, and manuring well. Ground that is well mellowed to a proper depth will stand a drought much better than that which is ploughed shallow and left in clods; and that which is well manured will retain more moisture than that which is poor. Again, ground which is thus well prepared and manured, shoots forth its crop so rapidly, that the ground is soon covered and shaded from the heat of the sun, and for this reason, retains its moisture longer. The same may be observed of mowing lands.

Gypsum is also an antidote to droughts; and fortunately, it suits the soils best which are most affected in this way.

Another way to avoid the effects of droughts, is, to cultivate swamp lands more extensively, in raising such productions as are most liable to receive injury in this way. Such lands, when well drained, and duly mixed with proper earths, or other manures, may undoubtedly be rendered excellent for almost every summer crop which is liable to be injured by too much dry weather. Wet lands also, which have been hollow-drained, will stand a drought much better than in their original wet state.

In pastures, planting some kinds of trees in different parts, is beneficial in preventing the effects of drought; and the best for this is the locust; as it will increase the pasture, serve for shade, and eventually yield much valuable timber and fuel.

See article LOCUST.

DUNG, DUNGHILLS, &c. *See* article MANURES.

E.

EARTHS. Chemists by analysing the matter which forms the Earth, find it to contain several *primitive* earths, some of which are called *alkaline* earths, and some, earths simply. The former are barytes, strontites, lime, and magnesia; the latter are silex, alumine, zircon, glucine, and ytria.

It is unnecessary to describe these earths minutely, or to say any thing of any other than those which commonly enter into the composition of soils. These, says Mr. Davy, are principally silex, alumine, lime, and magnesia. In addition to these, other substances are found soils, such as animal and vegetable matter in a decomposing state, certain saline compounds, and the oxyde of iron.

Of lime, something has already been said. (*See* article LIMESTONE.) Lime is but seldom found in its purity; it is generally combined with other earths, and with acids. Limestone, marble, chalk, marle, &c. are mixtures of lime with other earths, combined with carbonic acid. Gypsum, or sulphate of lime, is a mixture of lime with other earths, combined with sulphuric acid; and, when lime is combined with phosphoric acid, it is called phosphate of lime. Lime, in its pure state, is infusible, but is readily dissolved in acids, or in 680 times its weight of water.

Magnesia is a pure white earth, very friable, light, and spongy, and is always combined with other substances. Alumine is the basis of clay, and serves to endue it with the peculiar characteristic of contracting when dried, and still more when heated, and of expanding again when moistened.

Silex, or flinty earth, is mostly exhibited in the form of white or crystalline sand. There are also calcareous sands, and silex is sometimes mixed with these. Calcarious sands are soluble, with effervescence, in muriatic acid.

Animal decomposing matter exists, says Mr. Davy, in different states, according as the substances from which it is produced are different. It contains much carbonaceous substance, and may be mostly resolved, by heat, into this, together with carbonic acid, volatile alkali, and inflammable aeriform products. It is principally found in lands that have lately been manured.

Vegetable decomposing matter is likewise various in kind, and contains more carbonaceous substance than animal matter. It produces no volatile alkali. It forms a large proportion of peats; abounds in rich mould; and is found in greater or less quantities in all lands.

The saline compounds found in soils are rarely to be discovered, and are principally muriate of Soda, (common salt,) sulphate of magnesia, (Epsom salt,) and muriate, and sulphate of pot-ash, nitrate of lime, and the mild alkalies.

The oxyde of iron, (rust of iron,) is found in all soils, but most in yellow and red clays, and yellow and red silicious sands.

The same combinations of earthy matter may be productive of very different degrees of fertility in different situations, and in different climates. Thus a sandy soil under the equator is barren from its want of retaining a sufficiency of water for the climate, while the same soil in a cool moist climate would be found sufficiently retentive to be productive. A stiff clay, again, which under the equator would not be too retentive of moisture for fertility, would be found barren from its wetness in a cool moist climate. But let the sand in the hot climate have a close understratum of stiff clay, or the clay in the cool climate a close understratum of loose sand, and they would each be rendered fertile.

Mr. Tillet, in some experiments made on the composition of soils at Paris, found that a soil composed of three eights of clay, two of river sand, and three of the parings of limestone, was very proper for wheat.

Mr. Davy mentions a very fertile corn soil from Ormiston, (England,) which contained, in an hundred parts, eleven of mild calcarious earth, twenty-five of silicious sand, and forty-five of finely divided clay. It lost nine in decomposed animal and vegetable matter, and four in water, and afforded indications of a small quantity of phosphate of lime. He attributes its extreme fertility to the presence of the phosphate, as this is found in wheat, oats, and barley, and is probably part of their food. Soil from the lowlands of Somersetshire, which is famous for producing wheat and beans, without requiring any manure, he found to consist, one ninth of sand, chiefly silicious, and eight ninths of calcareous marle, tinged with iron, and containing about five parts in the hundred of vegetable matter. This contained no phosphate, or sulphate of lime, and he supposes its fertility owing principally to its power of attracting vegetable nourishment from water and the atmosphere.

By analysing the finest soils in this country, and comparing the results with those which are poor in the same neighborhood, we might ascertain the deficiencies of the latter, and thus in many instances be enabled to apply the remedy with much more precision and effect.

ELDER. These are extremely offensive to almost all insects, and are therefore good to spread round plants when they are liable to their attacks.

See article INSECTS.

ELM ; *(Ulmus Americana.)* A beautiful tree to plant near houses and elsewhere. It grows pretty rapidly and is very long-lived. There are three varieties, the white, the yellow, and the red elm. The two latter are the best timber for any kind of use, and the latter in particular is very durable.

ENCLOSURES. Throughout the most of France and some other parts of Europe, the arable and mowing lands are not fenced, but lie in common, while the lands on which cattle are usually kept are enclosed.

This method of husbandry has some advantages, and it has its disadvantages ; much is thereby saved in the expense of making enclosures ; but when cattle are to be fed on uninclosed grounds, as must sometimes be the case, they must be watched, to prevent their straying away, or getting into mischief. This, says Mr. Livingston, is generally done by the women ; they may be seen at all times during the season of pasture, sitting in the fields employed in spinning, while the keeping of the cattle within their proper limits does not require their immediate attention.

It may be difficult to determine whether this method of farming may not, on the whole, be as good as any, in a highly cultivated and thick settled country. Be this as it may, those countries which have adopted this method will hardly ever be found to change, owing as well to the inconvenience of producing, throughout a whole country, so radical an alteration, as to the difficulty of overcoming prejudices, which are almost inseparable from an ancient and hereditary custom.

EXPERIMENTS. There is no way of making improvements in farming but by experiments. If the farmer is informed of, or has conceived a different and better method of culture, or management, in any branch of his farming, he is to test the goodness of that method by experiments; and if these prove successful he may congratulate himself on having performed an act which is serviceable to his country and honorable to himself.

Perhaps it would be well, if some institution was devised and supported at the expense of the state, which should be so organized as would tend most effectually to produce a due degree of emulation among farmers, by rewards and honorary distinctions conferred on those who by their successful experimental efforts and improvements, should render themselves duly entitled to them.   It might also be advisable to have two or three experimental farms in different parts of the state, under the direction of suitable superintendents, who should have the profits of the farms to themselves, and who should be excited to a degree of emulation by a reward given yearly to that superintendent which should be found the best entitled by his superior culture, and by the success of his experiments, when duly authenticated, and published yearly for the benefit of community.   Something like these might cost considerable at first; but might eventually be made the means of greatly enriching the state by improving its agriculture.

F.

FALLOWING of LAND.   Lands may be greatly recruited by a summer fallowing, and also, by a winter fallowing; as by these methods, particularly the former, sufficient time is given to recruit and enrich the soil by frequent ploughings and harrowings.   All kinds of soils, however, do not derive equal benefit from fallowings.   A very rich soil, and a light sandy one, require little more than to be sufficiently mellowed for the reception of the seed; but all others which are naturally more or less sterile, or have been exhausted by too frequent cropping, may be greatly recruited by frequent ploughings and harrowings.   Mr. Tull, an ingenious farmer of Great-Britain, was of opinion, that lands could be made and kept rich by the mere operation of the plough and harrow; that dung, or manure, only served to produce a greater fermentation in the soil; and, that this could be as well effected by frequently stirring it.   This is perhaps in a great measure true, but not wholly so.   Undoubtedly in what are called the harder or stiffer soils, frequent ploughings will do wonders, not only in preparing the ground for a single crop, but also in fertilizing the soil.   Take, for instance, a field of any stiff or hard soil, which with the common culture of ploughing three times and harrowing twice, will yield a crop of ten bushels of wheat, or rye, to the acre; let this same field be broke up early and give it ten ploughings, and it will then yield twenty bushels an acre, and the land will afterwards be richer and much freed from weeds by this culture.   Here, then, by the seven extra ploughings the farmer gains ten bushels an acre— Will this pay him?   The expense of these seven additional plough-ings, allowing a man and two horses to plough two acres a day, and putting this at two dollars, would cost seven dollars; and for this he gets ten bushels of wheat, or rye, in the field, and his lands made more valuable by the extra ploughings.

The farmer will find nearly the same advantage in winter fallow-ing as in summer fallowing, particularly in the stiffer soils, where the ground ought to be well mellowed in the fall, and thrown up in ridges or large furrows for the operation of the winter frosts; as these will as-sist much in mellowing and fertilizing it.

Summer fallowing is, however, merely recommended, generally, for exhausted lands; but by no means as part of a general system of good farming, where the land is in a proper state for high cultivation and a rotation of fruitful crops.   The farmer, if his fields are exhaust-ed, may begin to recruit them by summer fallowings, and frequent ploughings; but he should do more than this; he ought to persevere in enriching them by gypsum or other manures, and clover, until he has rendered them truly fit for complete cultivation.

Ploughing early in the mornings, while the dew is on, is much the best; as the fertilizing qualities of dews are then absorbed in the soil, which are afterwards evaporated by the heat of the sun.   (See article Dew.)   A farmer cannot, however, always wait to have all his lands ploughed while the dew is on, though it may be well to do as much of it then as possible.   When coarse barn dung is to be applied to a fallow, it ought to be carted on in the spring, so that it may be well mixed with the soil by the ploughings; but where composts are ap-plied it should be done just before sowing, and then be well mixed with the soil, but not buried deep in it.

Green sward land intended for spring crops should always be broken up pretty early in the fall, and if it be wet, or a stiff soil, let it be cross ploughed and thrown up into high narrow ridges, in order to lie dry, and be mellowed and fertilized by the winter frosts.

FALSE QUARTER.   A rift or chink in the hoof of a horse from top to bottom.   The inner side of the hoof being the thinnest is most liable to it.   When it becomes troublesome to a horse, Gibson directs, that the cleft be pared out to the quick; then annoint the hoof with a mixture of tar, honey and suet, melted together, and lay a pledget, dipt in the same, along in the cleft. Then bind up the hoof as tight as possible, by winding rope-yarn closely round it from top to bottom. The shoe should previously be taken off. The wound should be opened and drest every third or fourth day, and to prevent any inconveniency from this, let the cleft be held together at the bottom by a thin plate fastened on for the purpose.

It is however very difficult, and often impossible, says this author, to effect a cure in an old or a diseased horse.

FARCY. A disease in horses similar to the scurvy among men, and is caused by confining a horse too long to dry meal. It is known by small tumors appearing on the head and other parts of the body. Turning the horse to fresh pasture will effect a cure in the first stages of the disorder; but where it has become more inveterate by long standing, Gibson directs, that the horse be bled, moderately purged, and then, that doses of antimony be given him.

FARMERS. Originally those were called *farmers* who took lands upon rent; while freeholders and those who owned farms themselves, were called *yeomen* or *gentlemen* farmers. But here we apply the term generally; every man who cultivates a farm, whether he owns it, or has a freehold estate in it, or merely rents it, is called a farmer. We do not consider the mere circumstance of owning a farm sufficient to dub the owner a gentleman; neither do we consider the condition of him who is obliged to hire lands of others to cultivate for a living, so low as to be on that account precluded from that rank. Farmers here being generally lords of the soil they cultivate, have reason to be thankful that their lots are cast in pleasant times and places; and that their condition is not that which too generally prevails throughout Europe. There, it is at best but as tenants in common socage; and descending from this to the lowest state, as in Poland and Russia, is that of mere slavery; being attached to the soil, liable to be sold with it, and under the despotic control of their landlords or masters.

But though the farmer here has attained his proper standing, let him not suppose, that in all cases the mere holding and occupying a large farm will either contribute to his profit or to his consequence as a farmer. If he has hands sufficient within his own family to carry on the necessary labors of a large farm, it is well; but if he has to hire all his laborers for this purpose, he must be industrious and farm on the best plans, if he makes as much as ought to be the just reward of his exertions. Owing to the circumstance that the most industrious young men who are destitute of property are in the habit of going off to new countries to procure new lands for themselves, the price of labor is so high, that the utmost must be made of it, if the farmer expects a good profit; and hence is derived an additional reason why farmers should study to improve their system of farming.　But by no means let those be discouraged who are ambitious to excel in farming on a large scale, for when ably conducted, farming largely has usually been found to yield most clear profit to the acre; but those who have but little help within their own families, and at the same time do not feel sufficiently ambitious to drive the business with vigor, are advised not to trouble themselves with large farms; rather let them sell these and buy small ones, which they can sufficiently cultivate with their own resources of labor, and put out the surplus money at interest.　When we see a farmer attempting to cultivate a farm of two or three hundred acres, with one or two hands; and, as is usual in such cases, merely running over his fields without deriving much from them, the reflection must naturally arise, how much better it would be for him to sell his large farm, purchase one of half, or a third of its size, cultivate that well, and then from the interest of the surplus money he might derive an annual income, which could be yearly added to the principal, and thus enable him to grow rich in a few years; while with his large farm he might toil all his life-time without making any material addition to his estate.

These remarks are, however, more applicable to farms which are naturally arable lands, than to those soils which never fail of yielding plentiful crops of grass and an abundant supply of pasture; and such lands greatly abound in the western and northerly parts of this state. On such lands the farmer may turn almost his whole attention to rearing cattle, raising little more grain than is sufficient for his family, and as many hands are not requisite in this case, except in mowing time, the labor necessary for a large farm may be performed with less expense, and at the same time to advantage; but not with so much clear profit to the acre as may be derived from most of the same lands if made arable, and brought under the most approved cultivation.

As this method of farming affords abundance of manure from the dung of the cattle, it enables the farmer to cultivate a small piece of ground to the utmost advantage.　He may raise a few acres of the necessary roots for feeding his cattle, and the same of grain, and have the produce of each as great as it is possible for the soil to yield.

See further articles, SOILING, NEAT CATTLE, &c.

FENCES.　Poor fences are productive of incalculable mischief to the farmer.　By these his crops are constantly liable to be destroyed and his cattle learn to become habitually unruly. One unruly creature will learn others to be so; and thus the farmer, with his poor fences, finds his cattle, instead of being profitable, to become productive of unceasing losses, and, what follows of course, of unceasing vexation. When the farmer is conscious, that he cannot even sleep in peace, on account of the danger of his cattle destroying the fruits of his labors, he cannot be said to enjoy that tranquillity which ought to be the reward of the sweat of his brow. Rather, therefore, let him make his fences what might be generally deemed more than sufficiently high and strong, than too low and weak. This, if it be an error, is erring on the safe side—on the side which secures the fruits of his labors, and promotes his tranquillity and happiness.

Log fences are often made on new cleared lands where rail timber does not sufficiently abound, and these the farmer will of course make of the most durable logs which his new cleared land affords. White pine log fences are very good, and will last twenty years without any essential repairing. Clear white pine timber may, however, be split into rails, which are very durable. All kinds of wood will last much longer in rails where the bark is peeled off.

What are called worm fences are made with most ease, but require more timber than some other kinds. If, therefore, timber be scarce, post and rail fences, set in a bank, made of the earth of two small ditches thrown up together, ought to be preferred, where good durable posts can be had. If the posts are too small to have holes made through them, the rails may be flatted at the ends and fastened to the posts with spikes, or with wooden pins well secured. Post and rail fences, without these ditches on each side, are very good where the soil is dry, and the same may be observed of board fences; but where the soil is wet, the posts will be thrown out by the frosts. In all cases the posts ought to be set at least two feet in the ground. Red cedar is best for posts. Locust, chesnut, butter-nut, and black walnut are also good. Good oak will also last pretty well. Burning the ends of the posts which go into the ground, so as to make them black, will make them last longer.

For hedge fences, *see* article HEDGES. For making stone walls, *see* article STONES.

FERMENTATION. Ground is in a complete state of fermentation when the adhesion of its particles is destroyed; when it is in a soft puffy state, so that when pressed down it will expand again. It is to be brought to this state by frequent ploughings, or by ploughings and manurings together.

8

When ground is in the highest fermentation, it is then in the best state for growing of plants; and the more effectually the fermentation is kept up during the time in which the plants are growing, the greater will be their growth.

Frosts have great effect in preparing for a state of fermentation in stiff soils, when thrown up during winter, in such manner as to lie dry. (*See* article FREEZING.) Moderate rains, succeeded by warm sunshine, have also a similar effect on such soils.

During the summer season a proper state of fermentation is only to be produced in the soil when it is neither too wet nor too dry. Ploughing, however, when the ground is very dry, if not so good for producing a state of fermentation, is nevertheless, good for killing all weeds and grass, with which the soil may be infested.

FERN, OR BRAKES; (*Polypodium.*) This weed grows in some cold loamy soils in the northern parts of this state; but it appears to be easily extirpated by tilling the land. In the northern parts of Europe, it is in many places troublesome and difficult to subdue. They however esteem it much when made into manure, as it contains a large portion of salts. In some parts of the north of Europe they burn it, and gather the ashes, which, being wetted with water, are made into little balls and dried in the sun, and are then esteemed to be nearly as good as soap for the purposes of washing.

FLAX; (*Linum.*) Such crops of flax as are usually raised do not pay for the labor bestowed on them. This must be owing to bad management. As this is a crop that the farmer must raise, if he has any regard to domestic economy, the means of raising it to advantage should be duly attended to.

A good method of raising a great crop of flax, is as follows: Summer-fallow a piece of ground of suitable soil, and give it six or eight ploughings and harrowings during the summer, so as to destroy all the seeds of weeds. (*See* article SUMMER-FALLOWING.) Apply your manures during the first ploughings, unless they be composts, or top-dressings; at all events let the soil be eventually made rich enough for hemp. The next spring mellow the ground well again by two or three ploughings, harrow it, and sow, of well cleaned seed, at the rate of about three bushels to the acre, and harrow it in lightly. Give the ground a top-dressing of about four bushels of fine salt to the acre, and also some gypsum, if the soil be suitable. Let the crop be sown about the first of May, or as soon as the ground can be effectually prepared after vegetation has commenced. By this method of culture, and with a proper change of seed, five or six hundred pounds of flax may be expected from the acre, of a fine quality. This is probably about the best culture, and all deviations from it, by less expensive methods in preparing the ground, will, generally, be much for the worse. Ground may, however, be pretty well prepared for a good crop by previous hoed crops which have been well manured, particularly if pains be taken to prevent any weeds going to seed in the fall. Weeds are the enemy of flax; and no good crops can be raised on ground that is full of their seeds, even though it be sufficiently rich and well prepared.

See further article, FOLDING OF LAND, for a proper method of preparing the ground for flax.

In addition to the requisites of a rich earth, free of the seeds of weeds and well mellowed, for obtaining a good crop of flax, another requisite is, that the ground shall not have borne flax for as much as seven years previous to the time it is to be sown with this crop. Almost every soil that is sufficiently dry for a proper degree of fermentation, may, by being well prepared as above directed, be made to yield good crops of flax, unless the soil has too little moisture, as may be the case with dry gravelly and light sandy earths. Gypsum will, however, very materially assist in supplying these earths with a due degree of moisture.

But a very essential point in raising great crops of flax is to have frequent change of the seed.

See article CHANGE OF SEEDS.

The quantity of seed sown should be proportioned to the strength of the soil. Flax of good length, but coarse, may be raised on a soil which is far from being rich, if it be well mellowed, clear of weeds, and sown with not more than three pecks of seed to the acre. I have seen 450 pounds raised from one bushel of seed sown on better than an acre and a half of ground. Such flax is, however, not so well fitted for very fine spinning. Where the stalks stand so thin as to branch at the roots they also branch widely at the tops; and, though more seed is in such case to be expected, still the lint will be less in proportion and of a coarser quality.

If flax is to be water-rotted, it should be pulled as soon as the blossoms have fallen off; and at this time the coat of the stalk is stronger than afterwards. The ground also which produces the crop is less exhausted than when the crop has stood until fully ripe. If it is to be rotted on the ground it should stand until nearly ripe, and then the seed can be saved, which is a matter of some consequence. That which is designed for affording seed for sowing again, should have the seeds ripened most before pulling.

The process of water-rotting flax, which is almost wholly practised in Ireland, is very similar to that of water-rotting hemp, and the same precautions are requisite. (*See* article HEMP.) Probably the method of rotting by boiling, as mentioned there, might be found equally proper for flax. The method common in this country, of rotting on the ground, is so well known, that it is useless to say any thing of it farther, than that the flax should be spread thin and evenly, and that it should be turned over when about half rotted, otherwise the under side will be more rotted than the upper.

Flax that is harsh may be softened in the manner directed for hemp. That which is rotted too much may be restored to its strength by keeping it a few years.

It is a very nice point to give flax the proper degree of rotting. If rotted too much, its strength is impaired for present use, and it wastes more in cleaning; and, if rotted too little, a great addition of labor is requisite in fitting it for use. That which is coarse will rot quicker than that which is fine; these should, therefore, be kept separate while rotting, in order that the latter have longer time for this purpose. The short and the long should also be sorted, as it is inconvenient to have them mixed in dressing.

In some parts of Europe the dressing of flax is a business carried on by itself, and water machinery is generally used for the purpose. Many kinds of labor are accelerated by being divided into different branches; as it is found that those following a particular branch become more expert in it, and of course can perform the labor better, and at the same time cheaper.

The farmer perhaps would do well to make more of a business of raising flax when he becomes engaged in it, by raising enough in one season to last him two or three years; he would then have a greater inducement to go more spiritedly into the most approved method of cultivation, from the conviction that cultivating it in the most complete manner, and pretty largely at a time, is the only way to make the business profitable.

Particular care should be taken to have the seed perfectly clean, and also to sow it evenly. This is best effected by first sowing one half of the seed over the whole ground, and then the other half crosswise. It should be sown in a calm time.

FLOODING OF LANDS. Where swamp land is to be cleared, and it can be flooded, by making a dam at the outlet, at a small expease, it is a matter of economy to attend to this, as in this way its growth of wood can be completely killed. This may also be performed on lands after they are cleared, for the purpose of killing the grass, if it be bad, in order with more ease to introduce a better kind, or a better system of culture. Flooding also serves, in a greater or less degree to enrich the land; though this depends chiefly on the kind of water with which it is flooded. If it contain a rich sediment it is good, but if destitute of this it is of no use.

See article IMPROVING OF LANDS.

FOALS, OR COLTS. To raise the best colts, the first step is to procure the best breeding mares, then put them to the best horses, and give the colts good keeping, particularly during the first winter after they are weaned. The proper time for weaning is the beginning of foddering time; and then they ought to be put in a stable by themselves, kept on good hay, and fed regularly twice a day during winter with oats, or some other nourishing food. The next summer they ought to have a good dry pasture.

Colts are frequently spoiled by poor keeping at the time they require the best; and this, as this is the case with all other young animals, is during the first winter. After this they do not require better keeping than is requisite for other horses. If colts be not well kept the first winter they are very apt to get stunted, and of this they never wholly recover. If farmers would pay more attention to keeping their colts in the best manner, as well as a due attention to the selection of breeding mares, and of horses for covering, we should soon find the breed of horses in our country much improved.

FODDER AND FODDERING. Much chaff and straw, that is often thrown away, may with a little pains be made good fodder for cattle, by being mixed with green corn stalks, or with hay not fully dried, and sprinkling a little salt throughout the whole. In this way the moisture and much of the sweetness of the stalks, or hay, is absorbed by the straw and chaff, and with the addition of the salt, the whole mass is converted into good fodder. Cattle will also eat straw or chaff very well, after having some brine sprinkled over it.

Salting all fresh hay when put up, is a great addition to it, as it renders it more nourishing to cattle, and of course will go further in keeping them. A respectable farmer of this county, (*Herkimer*,) who keeps a large stock of cattle, says, that by adding eight quarts of salt to every ton of hay, he is certain that a ton thus salted, will go as far as a ton and a quarter that has not been salted. At the same time, hay may be put into the mow, when salted, in a much greener state than without it; and when taken out will be found almost as green and apparently as fresh as when first stowed away.

Hay which is stored in narrow mows, or on scaffolds, will keep well with less drying than that which is put into large mows.   To prevent hay from damaging in a large mow, some recommend a barrel or a stuffed sack to be placed in the center, and gradually raised as the mow is raised; this forms an opening in the middle through which the steam of the heated hay can pass off, and thereby prevent it from being mow-burnt.   Another method is to put the driest hay in the center, and the wettest nearest the outsides.

See also, article BARN.

Meadows which produce wild grass ought to be mowed very early, and the hay well salted down, and in this way cattle will eat it nearly as well as herdsgrass.

Stacking of hay in meadows, to be fed out there, is a poor plan; as the meadows are often in this way much injured by the treading of the cattle; and even when this is not the case much hay is generally wasted, and the dung of the cattle turns to little or no account. The farmer ought always to have sufficient room in his barn, and hay houses, to hold all his hay; or if he has not this he ought to stack his hay adjoining his barn, and then it can be easily thrown in at once when his barn is emptied.

Foddering should not be commenced till it is really necessary, for when the cattle have been taught to expect it they will neglect their other feeding.   Fodder at first in the mornings when the frost is on the ground.   Neat cattle should not yet be housed but horses should. In cold rains they should however be sheltered, as these are more hurtful than cold weather.

The meanest fodder should not be dealt out first, but leave this for severer weather.   If the stock of fodder is too scanty for the stock of cattle, don't pinch them in the forepart of the winter; they can better endure scanty living when they have become hardened to the rigors of the season.

Some farmers feed their straw entirely to some of the hardiest of the young cattle, and for this purpose keep them by themselves, without suffering them to taste any other food, by which means they will keep tolerably well; but perhaps the better way is to lay aside the straw, when threshed, with some brine sprinkled over each layer, so as to give a degree of saltness to the whole mass, and after it has lain a while, to occasionally feed it out to all the neat cattle.   This will answer in place of salting them, and at times they will eat this food with a good relish.

It should be remembered, that cattle ought not to be kept constantly on salted fodder, for in that case they grow tired of it ; a change of food, sometimes salt, and sometimes fresh, is best.

Too much fodder should never be laid before cattle at once ; rather let them have a little at a time, and be fed the oftener. By constantly breathing on their food it becomes less palatable, and for this reason they will eat that which has been exposed to the open air and winds, after they have rejected it in the stable.

Cattle which run out during winter should have a shelter, and a rack under it to hold their fodder. By this means most of their dung being dropped under the shelter, will be preserved from the rains, and will on that account be much better than that which has been more exposed.

Cows that are near calving should not be confined to their stalls, but each should have a separate apartment and be kept without tying.

Horses keep best on well cured clover hay, though herdsgrass and some others are very good for them. If they are to be fed with Indian corn, or other hard grain, it should be well soaked, boiled, or ground, before it is given them. They may be kept in good order by feeding them with raw potatoes or carrots, washed clean, though they would be more nourishing if they could conveniently be fed on them when boiled.

See further, article NEAT CATTLE.

FOLDING of LAND. Folding sheep on fields which are ploughed up for fallow land, is a very good practice; as in this way the land receives all the manure that is made from their dung and urine, without the trouble of any previous preparation, or carting, &c. But folding sheep on small pieces of ground, says Mr. L'Hommedieu, will do the sheep as much injury as it will benefit the land. The reason of this seems to be, that for sheep to lie on ground on which they have previously lain and dunged for several nights, becomes hurtful to them for pretty much the same reasons that they are injured where too many of them are placed together in one pen during winter ; their own breath and the smell of their excrements are injurious to each other. But where they are folded in a larger field, they choose a fresh place to lie down every night, and in this way eventually go over the whole field. It is said, that in this way, one hundred sheep will, in one season, sufficiently manure a fallow of eight acres for a good crop of wheat. The manure thus made, should be frequently ploughed, or harrowed under, to prevent much of its evaporation.

Folding cows, &c. on land, can only be done to advantage on small pieces of ground designed for cabbages, turnips, &c.; for if put into a large field, they will almost always lie down on nearly the same spot.

See article MANURES, for an advantageous method of folding cows, &c.

A low spot of grass ground, which is inclining to bear coarse wild grass, will be much helped by folding sheep on it, to the injury of the sheep, however, and so will a dry spot by folding cows on it.

When ground is folded for raising turnips, instead of sowing this crop the first year, let it be frequently ploughed, in order to kill all the weeds, and sown early with flax the next spring, and then with turnips, after the flax is taken off. Great crops of flax may in this manner be raised, and by again mellowing the ground, after the flax crop, a very good crop of turnips may be raised.

FOOD OF PLANTS. Every seed contains a plant in embryo; when it has acquired its full size and shape it is then a perfect plant. In the mean time it derives from the air, the earth, and from water, certain food which nourishes it and causes it to grow to maturity.

From the air it absorbs hydrogene gas and the septous principle, or azote; and for this reason will grow most thrifty in large cities, or in the vicinity of animal putridity. Let any putrid decaying flesh be laid in a field of growing plants, and those which are nearest to the putrid matter will grow much faster than those at a distance, because those nearest have a greater chance of absorbing the impure air emitted from it, than those growing farther off.

See further, article AIR.

From the earth, plants derive some of their component parts, as discovered by chemical analysis; such as earth, salts, oil, &c. and from water, whether mixed with the earth, or otherwise, they imbibe the juices or sap, which is so essential to their existence.

See article SAP.

Some manures, it would seem, operate by attracting matter which is food for plants; such as gypsum, which is supposed to attract nitre and moisture. Ashes afford salts and attract nitre. Other manures again afford, in part, the food of plants, and at the same time assist them in obtaining more from the earth by opening it for the more easy extension of their roots: such as barn dung and manures of that kind. Others, perhaps, assist directly in supplying food; such as salts, blood, putrid flesh, &c. Others again merely serve to open earths which are too solid to admit the roots in search of food; such as sand, rotten wood, saw-dust, &c. applied to clays. And, lastly, clay applied to sand, assists in part, by supplying additional food, and partly by enabling the soil to retain a sufficiency of water to supply plants with the requisite proportion of this article.

Some plants extract their food principally from the air; some mostly from air and water, and others principally from the earth. The hyacinth, and many other plants will grow well with air and water, without the assistance of earth. But generally speaking, plants require the united assistance of air, water, and earth; and from these they extract that food which is requisite to bring them to perfection.

Some plants require most of one kind of food from the earth, and some another. Tap-rooted plants, again, derive their nourishment from a greater depth, while those with fibrous roots merely extract from the surface. Hence, the earth, as the common parent of plants, may become exhausted in continually producing some kinds, while it may still be well fitted for the production of others; and hence, in some instances, arises the necessity of a change of crops.

See article CHANGE OF CROPS.

FOREST. Every farm ought to have a piece of woodland, or forest, sufficient for fuel and other purposes. Raising timber for the purpose of fencing, will not often be found advisable; farmers must eventually depend on making stone walls, or hedges, for the purpose of enclosing their lands. But wood and timber sufficient for fuel, for building, for carriages, and implements of farming, cannot be dispensed with. Of these the farmer will always find it most advantageous to keep the requisite stock himself, and not rely on others for purchasing it. Nor is it advisable to have his woodland separate, and at a considerable distance from his farm; unless it be in parts of the country where part of the lands are too valuable to be kept in wood, and other adjacent parts are only fit for that purpose.

When the farmer is clearing up his farm, he ought to reserve for woodland, that part which is least adapted for tillage, or for grass. Land which is swampy with a thin soil over a sandy bottom; that is rocky and hilly; or that is dry, poor, sandy, or very gravelly, may do well for woodland, while it would answer but poorly for tillage.

The quantity of ground to be set apart for this purpose must depend on the size of the farm; the quality of the soil of the woodland; the nature of the climate; and, frequently, according to the demand or market for wood; for in some cases, it may be found more profitable to keep tolerable good land in wood than in any other cultivation. Of the natural growth of wood, it will require as much as twenty acres, or more, to keep two fires, according to the common method of using wood for fuel; but it is a very easy matter to have sitting rooms warmed, and all the cooking and other apparatus of the kitchen so contrived as not to require more than one third of the wood that is commonly used.

See article WARMING OF ROOMS.

To thicken a forest, or to prevent its becoming too thin, cattle should be kept out of it at all seasons. Acorns ought also to be planted in every part that becomes destitute of growing wood. If woodland be suffered to become so thin that the sun can get in and cause the ground to be covered with a sward of grass, this will prevent the further growth of young timber; and in this way the ground eventually becomes stripped of all its growth. This, however, is not the case with the locust, as it encourages the growth of grass amongst it, and in this situation grows very rapidly. Perhaps the farmer will find, when he is reduced to the necessity of planting wood for fuel, that this tree will answer his purpose best.

See article LOCUST.

The Lombardy poplar, also grows very rapidly, is easily raised from cuttings, and when cut and dried, will answer tolerably well for fuel.

The easiest method of raising the locust, is as follows: Plant, in the first instance, about fifteen or twenty trees on an acre; when they have got to be twelve or fifteen feet high, and their roots well extended, run straggling furrows through the ground, and wherever the roots are cut with the plough, new trees will start up, and soon stock the whole ground with a plentiful growth. This tree has been but lately introduced into general use in France; and it is said to be there valued more than any other which is cultivated in that country.

Where wood is raised merely for fuel, it may be suffered to grow as thick as it will; it becomes sufficiently thinned of itself as it grows larger; but where oak, or any other trees are to be raised for timber, they ought to stand further apart, in order to have their growth rapid, and of course, the timber firm and durable.

If woods are old and decaying, the better way is to cut all off as you want to use the wood, and let an entire new growth start up, which will grow more rapidly.

Much poor exhausted lands in this country should be planted with forests, to supply the waste of wood that is constantly encreasing.

For raising oaks, which are an essential article, let the acorns be ploughed under, with a shoal furrow, in the fall; or they may then be buried in a bed of earth, and after they have sprouted in the spring, planted as before, at the distance of about a foot from each other. They may also be planted in the sward, at the depth of about two inches, by digging little holes for the purpose. Let the weeds be kept down till the young growth of the forest shall have overpowered them. The strongest plants will keep down the weakest, and thus sufficiently thin the trees as they increase in size; but where a growth for timber is intended, let the weakest be cut away to give more room for the strongest, after they have attained some considerable size. Let no cattle be admitted into the forest until the trees are beyond their reach: and, at no time whatever, where young successive growths for fuel is intended.

FOUNDERING OF HORSES. We usually say that a horse is foundered, when his legs and feet have become stiffened and sore, by eating too large a quantity of hard grain at once. The best remedy for this, is exercise by riding; and in addition to this let the bits of his bridle be wound round with a rag, into which let as much human ordure be put as it will hold. Put this into his mouth, and let him chew upon it while riding him, and in due season repeat the dose, if necessary.

But there is a disorder of the feet of horses, in which they are also said to be foundered. This is a painful disease; the horse affected with it draws himself up in a heap and is loth to move. It is occasioned by standing in cold water, after being heated with exercise, or sometimes even by standing still in the stable several days after exercise, sometimes by bad shoeing, or by bruises on the legs.

In this case, if a remedy be not speedily applied, a gathering will take place in the feet, and the hoofs will be cast off; by which the use of the horse will be lost for some time. The remedy is to slit the hoofs open from top to bottom, so that blood will follow pretty freely. In order to cure these wounds again, apply tar, turpentine and honey, melted together, with a fourth part of the spirits of wine. Let pledgets made of tow, be soaked in this, and then laid in the chinks, and the foot bound up. These are not to be opened for two days; and then let fresh applications be made every day till the channels in the hoofs be grown up.

If the sole of the foot is also drawn, it must be served in a similar manner. A piece of leather should be laid over the sole, and the whole foot so bound up with strong bandages, that the applications may not be displaced.

FREEZING. Every hard stiff soil when thrown up in ridges in the fall, and mellowed by the frosts, receives thereby an essential addition to its fertility. A winter's frost is not however always sufficient to mellow the largest clods; these should, therefore, be broken in pieces in the fall, in order to derive full benefit from the frosts.

A farmer of New-Jersey, some years since, trench-ploughed an exhausted field of stiff soil in the fall; cross-ploughed a part of it, and in that part broke the lumps to pieces. In the spring the field was all ploughed equally and sown with barley and clover. The part on which the most labor had thus been bestowed was in fine order when sown, and yielded about thirty bushels an acre of barley; the other part was still in lumps, the frosts not having been found sufficient to mellow them entirely, and the product of barley was only about twenty bushels an acre. The same difference was afterwards observed in the clover.

But this field, with this stratum of crude earth thrown uppermost, would have yielded little or nothing the next spring, and until mellowed and fertilized by summer suns, had it not been mellowed and fertilized by winter frosts.

Another benefit derived from freezing is, that it serves to restore all soils to a due state of sensibility to the operation of heat.

Heat is the stimulant of soils; but, as is the case with all stimulants, the longer it is applied without intermission, the less powerful it becomes; particularly in the production of grasses and other plants which are natural to northern climates. Thus, a degree of heat which in the fall will not be found sufficient to make those plants grow, will make them grow rapidly when applied to them in the spring. In this respect, therefore, freezing, which is only the absence of heat, serves as a kind of restorative to the soil and refits it for the reproduction of those plants. Thus freezing is a fertilizer of stiff soils, and a restorer of all, by renewing their sensibility to the effects of heat.

When plants have been frost-bitten, while growing, they may be restored by sprinkling them plentifully while in the frozen state with brine, or with water containing a solution of sal ammoniac, which is better.

FRUIT-TREES. Mr. Forsyth's essay on these has been justly esteemed for its originality and research. It is, however, a production best calculated for the country where it was written; and even there, perhaps, some parts of it may be found more pleasant in theory than profitable in practice. His composition for curing defects in trees, and restoring old decayed ones, and the method of preparing it shall be first noticed, and is as follows:

Take a bushel of fresh cow-dung, half a bushel of lime rubbish from the ceilings of old rooms, which is best, or pounded chalk, or old slaked lime will answer, half a bushel of wood ashes, and a sixteenth of river sand; sift the three last articles fine before they are mixed; work them well together by beating, &c. so as completely to mix them: Then reduce the mass to the consistence of thick paint, by mixing with it a sufficient quantity of urine and soap-suds, so as that it can be used with a brush. A good coat of this is to be applied to the naked wood where a limb is cut off, or the wood otherwise laid bare, and the powder of wood ashes and burnt bones is to be sprinkled over this and gently pressed down with the hand. When any of the composition is left for future use it is to be covered with urine to preserve it from the atmosphere which injures it.

With this composition Mr. Forsyth restores old rotten decayed trees to a flourishing state. In order to do this, all the rotten and dead part of the tree is first cut away and scooped out, quite down into the roots, till you come to the live wood, and then smoothed, and the edges next the live bark rounded off. Then the composition is laid on with a brush, and covered as before directed, with the powder. As the bark on the edges grows over this covered wood, it works off the composition and supplies its place, till at length the bark of the two edges meet and grow together. If the growing bark should raise up any flakes of the composition, so as to expose the wood, let them be pressed down with the finger some rainy day when the composition is pliable. Where a tree would be too much weakened by cutting away all its dead wood at once, cut only a part away next the edges, and as the bark covers this cut away more. Where limbs are cut off let the stumps be pared smooth and the edges rounded, before the composition is laid on. He says, this should always be applied where-ever a limb is cut off, in order to preserve the tree from rotting at such places.

He makes mention of many old decayed trees, some of whose trunks were rotted away two-thirds, and half of the roots gone, which he restored to a sound flourishing state by the process above described. It is, however said, that some who have tried the experiment in this country have not been successful; but whether this may be ascribed to a want of skill in the performance, or to a difference in climate, is perhaps not well ascertained. Perhaps the composition ought to be varied in its materials, so as to be better adapted to the greater degree of heat and dryness which prevails in our atmosphere. He also makes mention of shaving off all the cankery bark of old stunted trees, then scarifying the remaining bark, where they were bark bound, and covering the whole with his composition, which produced a surprising alteration in their growth.

In lieu of the above composition, the following has been successfully used about Albany for healing the wood, and for covering the stock in grafting : Take two parts of bees-wax, one of rosin, and one of hogs-lard ; melt them, and blend them together : It must be made soft enough to put it on with the hand ; and let it be laid on thickest round the edges and thinly in the middle. If it becomes too soft during the heats of summer let a little powdered rosin be sprinkled over it.

Mr. Forsyth's method of *heading down* trees, in order to renovate their growth, and to procure a new set of straight thrifty bearing limbs, is as follows : First take off one or two of the principal limbs, just above an *eye ;* let them be cut slanting downwards, with the sides where the eye is the highest : Pare and round off the ends of the stumps, and cover them with the composition : Presently, sprouts will start out from the eyes, which are to be trained and pruned for new bearing limbs. When these have grown a little, cut off more of the limbs, and go through the same process with them, and so on, till they are all taken off. Thus, a new set of thrifty limbs are given to the tree, which will be better bearers than the old. The new growths soon cover the stumps so as to leave only a slight cicatrix. He speaks of heading down some trees at once, and particularly recommends the heading down of all young trees while in the nursery, by taking off the whole trunk a little above the ground, and in the manner above directed, which he says will greatly improve their future growth, and make them better bearers. He mentions, particularly, some young oaks, that he thus headed down, which afterwards grew more than as fast again as those which were not.

He also describes a method of pruning the limbs at their bearing ends. This is to take off the most prominent twig, when it has become *tired* of bearing, close to the next lateral branch, and then this shoots forward and becomes the bearer ; when this has in like manner become tired of bearing, the limb is to be taken off, back at the next lateral branch, and the next shoots forward again, and so on. This may be a good plan to keep trees in the dwarf state, which is so much practised in Great-Britain; it being necessary there to raise much of their more tender fruit by the sides of walls, made very high for the purpose, round the fruit-gardens, and there the keeping of some kinds of fruit trees in the dwarf state, is the more necessary.

Fruit-trees are subject to a disease, called the *canker*. It occasions the bark to grow rough and scabby, and turns the wood affected to a rusty brown colour. It will sometimes kill the tree, if not remedied in due season.

This disease may arise from various causes; from bad pruning; from dead shoots left on the tree; from frosts killing the last year's shoots, &c.

The diseased parts are to be entirely cut away, till nothing but sound *white* wood remains; or if the disease be merely in the bark, the outer bark must be cut away, and if the inner bark be also affected, which is to be known by its exhibiting small black spots like the dots of a pen; cut all away that is thus affected, and let the composition be applied, as before directed.

Fruit-trees, of the stone kind, are frequently diseased with *gum*, which arises from bad pruning, bruises, and other causes. The diseased parts are to be cut away, and the composition applied as before.

Thus much for Mr. Forsyth. Those who are anxious to be more intimately acquainted with this author, will do well to purchase his book. In the plates annexed to it are exhibited many specimens of his ingenuity.

If fruit-trees be suffered to run much to suckers, these will greatly injure their bearing. Let them, therefore, be kept clear of these. All straight upright shoots from the limbs of trees, should also be taken away, for these bear no fruit; though in time their lateral branches may bear some. Lateral branches are always the bearers, and such branches as do not bear, only serve to rob the bearing branches of their requisite nourishment, and should therefore be taken away. The trees should also be cleared of all dead and decaying branches, and of all cross branches that rub against each other.

Young apple, and plum-trees in particular, are apt to get covered with what are usually called *lice*, being an inanimate substance resembling an insect, of the colour, and somewhat of the shape of a grain of flaxseed, but narrower. Where the bark is thickly covered with these the growth of the tree will be very much impeded, and sometimes it will be killed, if they are not removed. They are to be scraped off with a knife. Moss ought also to be scraped off, as it greatly injures the growth of the tree.

For keeping off moss, lice, and every thing else that should be kept off from young apple, and some other fruit-trees, it is a good plan to white-wash their bodies, and principal limbs, every spring, with a mixture of lime and water; or, perhaps, Forsyth's composition, before mentioned, would be equally good. He, however, recommends for this purpose, a mixture of old urine and soap-suds. Where young fruit-trees stand in sward ground, the sward should be cut away from about them, and the ground about their roots loosened every spring.

It is found, that the seeds of the apple, and probably all other fruit-trees, which are brought from Europe, here, will grow larger than those of our own. Probably, this is merely the effect of a change of seed, if so, our seeds sown there might produce the same inequality. Be this as is may, it is by no means certain, that the largest fruit-trees are the most profitable to the acre; as the larger they are, the more ground each must have.

See further, the articles which treat of the various kinds of fruit-trees.

FULLER'S THISTLE; *(Dipracus.)* The heads of these are used for raising the knap on fine wollen cloths. From their present scarcity in our infant manufactories, they command a great price, and are, therefore, worthy of attention.

Sow the seeds at the rate of about a peck to the acre, about the first of May, on ground properly prepared by ploughing and harrowing. Keep down the weeds by hoeing, and let the plants stand about a foot asunder; all the rest are to be cut away. Hoe them as often as the weeds rise. The heads do not form until the second summer. When they are fit to cut, which will be about the first of August, let them then be cut, tied in bundles, and dried, under cover, or in the open air, according to the state of the weather.

The heads have sold in our woollen factories for a cent a piece, and sometimes double that price. An acre, at this rate, would amount to several hundred dollars.

G.

GARDENS. These are distinguished into the flower garden, the fruit garden, and the kitchen garden. I shall say nothing of the flower garden, for farming has nothing to do with flowers; but the fruit and kitchen gardens are somewhat more substantial.

It is best to have the fruit and kitchen gardens in the same enclosure; but the plan, too often observed, of blending them together in too great a degree, ought to be avoided. Fruit trees which make considerable shade, must be injurious to the growth of vegetables in the same neighbourhood, and ought therefore to be cultivated by themselves. Such fruit trees, however, which make but little shade, as grapes, currants, quinces, &c. may be very agreeably intermixed with the growths of the kitchen garden.

For the Fruit Garden, *see* articles FRUIT TREES, PEACHES, APRICOTS, QUINCES, &c. &c.

A kitchen garden well stored with vegetables is highly important to the farmer, as the use of these supercede the necessity of consuming much meat, a practice equally inconsistent with economy and with good health. When we perceive that the food of the cottagers of Ireland is principally milk and potatoes; that these are a race of people which are healthy, robust, well made, with strong, quick and ardent powers of mind;—and when we perceive that those savage nations, which, for want of other food, are obliged to subsist entirely on fish or other meat, are generally the most stupid, squalid and ill made, we certainly cannot draw very favorable conclusions in favor of eating great quantities of flesh.

It is advisable to have a close high fence round your kitchen and fruit gardens. This in the first place renders every thing within it secure from pillagers, and also serves to keep out fowls. Another benefit consists in keeping off the strong cold winds of the spring, which are very injurious to the young plants, and also to the fruit, which is then about putting forth.

Dung that is old, and destitute of the seeds of weeds, ought only to be used in manuring a kitchen garden, and the ground ought not to be ploughed, but deeply dug, for all vegetables which root deeply in the ground. Nothing further need be said with regard to the kitchen garden, than that a loose mellow soil, with a southerly exposure, is the best; that it ought to be kept rich; that as fast as weeds rise, they ought to be extirpated; and that no weeds ought to be suffered to go to seed within the garden.

If the garden be of a wettish, or stiff soil, it will be greatly benefitted by being thrown up into high ridges in the fall; at the same time this will assist some in destroying the seeds of weeds, but particularly in destroying insects which may be breeding in the soil.

GARGET. *See* article NEAT CATTLE.

GERMINATION OF PLANTS. By experiments made by Mr. Humbolt, in 1793, it was found that seeds which require thirty hours to germinate in common water, could be made to germinate in six hours in *oxygenated muriatic acid gas* mixed with water; and by adding " the stimulus of *caloric* (heat,) to that of the oxygene, he was enabled still more to accelerate the progress of vegetation." He took the seeds of garden cresses, peas, French beans, garden lettuce, mignonette; equal quantities of which were thrown into pure water, and the oxygenated muriatic acid, at a temperature of 88.° Fahrenheit. Cresses exhibited germs in three hours in this acid, while none were seen in the water till the end of twenty-six hours.

By means of this stimulant, seeds which were more than an hundred years old, were made to vegetate; as were other seeds which had been kept for thirty years at the botanical garden at Vienna, which had resisted every other means used for that purpose.

The application of this may be found useful in planting Indian corn, as it will be sooner out of the way of birds and squirrels; and, when the first planting has failed, or when birds, &c. have pulled up the corn, this method would greatly accelerate the growth of a second planting. It is also useful for many kinds of garden seeds which have been kept over one year. Probably, the seeds of the American thorn might, also, in this way, be made to vegetate readily, and that hemp-seed might thus be made to grow after the first year.

Another method of making old seeds germinate more readily, is, to immerse them in water, nearly boiling hot, for the space of half a minute, then suddenly cooling them by exposure to the air, and sow them when the soil is well warmed by the sun. If sown, however, when the earth is cold, they will rot in the ground.

GIGS. Little tumors, or bladders, filled with matter, found in the mouths of horses. The cure is effected by slitting them open, and then washing them with salt and vinegar.

GLANDERS. Commonly called the *horse distemper*. It is always accompanied with a discharge of matter from the nostrils, and a swelling of the glands under the throat and tongue. When the bones in that part become carious, it is generally incurable; and this may be known by the bad smell which is produced in such cases. The treatment recommended in Gibson's farriery, for this disease, while in its first and second stages, is to make use of purges, diaphoretics, and rowelling in the hinder parts. I imagine, that rowelling in the breast will answer the same purpose.

See article ROWELLING.

To clear the nostrils, Gibson recommends passing the fumes of burnt brimstone, or burnt leather into the nose of the horse, and after the matter has been discharged, to syringe his nostrils with brandy, or red wine. Afterwards, he says, a small quantity of *Unguentum Egyptianum*, dissolved in oil of turpentine, may be injected through a large pipe for the purpose of cleansing the ulcerated parts.

GOATS. These animals are hardy and rather more prolific than sheep. The kids are apt to poison themselves by eating laurel, if they can find it. These are excellent for the table, and even the old ones are tolerable good eating, and are generally well filled with tallow. The milk of the goat, of which they give a greater quantity than any other animal of their size, is good to mix with that of cows in making cheese. It is also much esteemed in consumptive cases. Their skins are much more valuable than those of sheep, being nearly as strong as that of the deer.

Goats are very useful on new farms, as they serve effectually to destroy all sprouts and bushes. They are peculiarly excellent in destroying shrub-oak bushes, as these are naturally hard to subdue.

GOOSE. *See* article POULTRY.

GOOSEBERRY ; *(Ribes Grossularia.)* This species of the currant requires about the same soil and culture, that is required for the common red or white currant.

See article CURRANT.

A very good wine may also be made from the gooseberry, and varieties may be produced of this plant, by sowing the seeds in the same manner as is mentioned of currants. Mr. Forsyth observes, that by mixing up a rich soil to plant those in that have been raised from seed, and by watering and thinning the fruit, they have grown much larger than any ever before seen in England. He further observes, that great attention should be paid to the early and late sorts; that where they run up to long naked stems they should be *cut down*, which will make them throw out good bearing shoots, and in that case his composition must be applied. There are other observations made by Mr. Forsyth, on the culture of this plant, which are here omitted, as not being considered of any material consequence.

GRAFTING. Mr. Forsyth describes several methods of grafting :—

As, first—*Grafting in the rind*, which is proper only for large trees.

Secondly—*Cleft-grafting*, which answers well on small stocks or limbs, and has been mostly practised in this country :

Thirdly—*Whip-grafting*, or *tongue-grafting*, which is also proper for small stocks only, and as Forsyth says, is the most effectual of any and the most in use in Great-Britain :

Fourthly—*Inarching*, or *grafting by approach*. This is done where the stock to be grafted on, and the tree from which the graft is taken, stand so near together, that they may be joined.

Forsyth says, that grafts, or scions, should be cut off from the trees before the buds begin to swell ; that they should be laid with the cut end downwards, and buried half their length in earth, having the tops covered with litter to prevent their drying too much ; that they should be all of the growth of the former year ; that they should always be taken from healthy, fruitful trees, for if taken from sickly ones, the grafts often partake of the distemper ; that if taken from young luxuriant trees, they may produce luxuriant shoots, but will not be so productive as those taken from fruitful trees ; that those which are taken from lateral, or horizontal branches are to be preferred to those of the strong perpendicular shoots ; and that none should be taken from the sprouts of trees.

Mr. Forsyth prefers the *whip-grafting* for common cases, but for these, Mr. Deane prefers the *cleft-grafting*. This, he says, is most commonly practised in this country and is attended with success. It is done on the stocks in the nursery, or on the small limbs of trees. The proper season for it is just before the leaves begin to open. The head of the stock must be cut off sloping, and a slit made sloping the opposite way, deep enough to receive the scion, which should be cut like a wedge, with the outside thicker than the inner. The rind of the scion must exactly join the rind of the stock. The slit should be opened by a wedge of hard wood ; the scion should then be gently put in its place and the stock closed. After this, the whole must be daubed round closely with a mortar made of a mixture of loam and fresh horse-dung, so as completely to exclude the access of air ; and this mortar must be surrounded with a winding of tow, or old cloths, to prevent the rains washing it away. The scion should be covered nearly to the top with this mortar; and it should also extend two or three inches downwards round the stock.

In place of this mortar, Forsyth recommends a plaister made of pitch, turpentine and bees-wax, which is in like manner to be daubed closely round, so as to exclude the external air. The mortar, however, if well made, and well applied, will answer very well. It should be composed of fine loam, not clay, because clay will contract and crack open when dried.

Whip-grafting is performed by cutting off the head of the stock sloping, then making a notch in the slope from the upper part downward, a little more than half an inch deep, to receive the scion, which must be cut with a slope upward, and a slit made in this like a tongue, which is to be inserted into a slit made in the slope of the stock, and the scion is then set in, so that the rinds of each join exactly together. The scion is then fastened by a ligature to keep it steady, and then surrounded with mortar, or the plaister, as before.

Grafting in the rind is performed by cutting off the stock square; slitting down the bark a small distance, and raising it up, so that the end of the scion may be inserted between it and the wood: The scion is made with a shoulder, cut in about half its thickness, and the other half is sloped off gradually, so as to give it the form of a wedge; the cut side being flat and the bark side untouched. This wedge or tongue, is inserted under the bark, with the shoulder fitted to the stock; the raised bark is then pressed close and bound round, and the plaister is applied, as before mentioned. It is usual, in this case, to insert three or four scions in one stock.

See further, articles INARCHING and INNOCULATING, for the methods of performing these operations.

GRAIN-HOUSE, or GRANARY. If the farmer thinks proper to build a grain-house, which is very useful for Indian corn in particular, the best method of keeping rats and mice out of it, is to set it on blocks, covered with flat stones, large enough to project four or five inches beyond the blocks, on every side. To prevent the blocks from rotting at the bottoms, they ought to be set on stones, raised a little above ground. It is a good plan to have a grain-house and carriage, or waggon-house built together; the upper part for Indian-corn, and other grain, and the lower part for waggons, carts, ploughs, &c. &c.

Some farmers make provision for a place to keep their Indian-corn in their barns, which is a pretty good plan. The place for this is a floor, raised on a second set of beams, which rest on posts set in the beams, next below the plates of the barn. In the middle of this floor is a hole, through which a tackle is suspended, and the corn is raised in baskets and spread a proper thickness over the floor. Such a floor in an ordinary sized barn would probably contain three hundred bushels. At the proper season, the corn is thrown down on the barn floor, and there threshed out with flails, or with a threshing-machine, which is better, and is then cleaned and put into bins made for the purpose on one side of the barn floor. (*See* article BARN.) The bins must be made tight, of hard plank, sufficiently thick to prevent the rats from gnawing through them; and the lid to each may be fastened down by a clasp secured by a padlock. This plan is equally good for keeping wheat and other grain. If the grain which is put into these should heat, it can be shovelled out upon the floor, and there stirred about until it is sufficiently dry to be returned into the bins. The method of ascertaining whether grain has become heated in the bin, is to run a stick to the bottom; let it remain there for a quarter of an hour; and if in that time there be any heat in the grain it will be communicated to the stick.

If grain be kept long in sacks, its heating may be prevented by frequently turning them first on one end, and then on the other.

GRASSES. Some of these are best calculated for moist or wet soils, some for dry, and some for the different climates in which grass is cultivated. Some again are best for pastures and some for mowing. The different kinds which are most valuable are here noted, together with their proper soils, &c.

MEADOW CATSTAIL, *Timothy Grass*, or *Herdsgrass*, *(Phleum Pratensis,)* is the grass most used for hay in the northern states. It is also erroneously called *fox-tail*, but this is another grass. The catstail has a long head, somewhat resembling the tail of a cat with very fine seeds; the fox-tail has a short bushy head more like the tail of a fox with coarser seeds. In other respects they have considerable resemblance.

Catstail grows best in a rich *moist* soil; but it will grow well for a few years in a rich *wet*, or in a rich *arable* soil. In the rich wet soil it gradually lessens in product, while at the same time it gives way to wild grasses. In the rich arable soil it gradually fails by reason of the ground becoming bound and the sward thickened with other grasses. Probably if it were well torn with the harrow every spring, and not too closely pastured in the fall, and none in the spring, it would grow well for many years in such soil. By close pasturing in the fall, it is apt to be torn out by the roots, and by cropping it again in the spring, it suffers greatly. It will yield one half more when not pastured at all, than when pastured closely in the fall and again in the spring. In the richest soils, and when not pastured, upwards of four tons may be had from the acre in a season at two mowings. Cattle are not quite so fond of it in pastures as they are of clover, but when made into hay they eat it very readily. It is not so much a fertilizer of land as clover; on the contrary, it binds, and somewhat exhausts the soil. It is perennial, and will last beyond the memory of man, if not destroyed by close pasturing. The proper time for mowing it, is, when it is in blossom, or a little later.

From the trials made in Great-Britain of this native American grass, it is however asserted by Mr. Curtis, to possess no excellence which is not possessed in an equal degree by the

MEADOW FOXTAIL; (*Alopecurus Pratensis.*) This grass is much cultivated in Great-Britain. It is an early grass and vegetates with such luxuriancy, that according to Mr. Curtis it may be mowed three times a year. The British graziers consider it as one of their best grasses, particularly for larger cattle. The soil best suited for it, is moist meadow-land, or that which is occasionally overflowed, though it will grow well on almost any soil except those which are very wet, or very dry. Linnæus states it to be a proper grass for grounds which have been drained.

It is perennial, and yields abundance of seed, which is easily gathered. The seed is, however, sometimes liable to be destroyed by an insect.

MEADOW FESCUE; (*Festuca Pratensis.*) Is an early, hardy, perennial grass, and grows well on almost every soil; good for hay or pasture; produces abundance of seed, which is easily gathered. Mr. Curtis says, it has a great resemblance to ray-grass, but is superior to it for forming meadows, as it grows longer and has more foliage. It blossoms about the middle of June.

DARNEL, or RAY-GRASS; (*Lolium Perrene,*) Is good for an early supply of pasture, as it starts very early. It grows to the height of about two feet and blossoms the latter end of May. Horses are extremely fond of it when made early into hay; and for race horses, particularly, has been found preferable to any other hay. It is, however, apt to run too much to stalks in most soils, and then cattle dislike it in pastures. A natural sort of ray-grass is mentioned, as having been lately cultivated in Great-Britain, which is much superior to the sort usually cultivated there.

CRESTED DOG'S-TAIL; *(Cynosurus Cristatus,)* Is good for upland pastures, and is a wholesome food for sheep. It forms a thick turf, and blossoms about the middle of June. It abounds with seed, which is easily gathered; but care should be taken, that it be fully ripe, as otherwise it will sometimes fail to grow. It is suitable for dry, sandy soils and will not thrive in wet meadows.

MEADOW-GRASS; *(Poa Pratensis,)* Will flourish well even in the driest soils, and will endure drought better, perhaps, than almost any other grass. It makes fine hay and is fit for early cutting. It is also good for early pasture. It yields plenty of seed, but this is difficult to sow on account of their filaments causing them to adhere to each other. To remedy this, it is recommended to put them in newly slaked lime, to separate them, and then to be rubbed in dry sand.

VERNAL *or* SPRING GRASS; *(Anthox Antiem Odoratum,)* Is a very early grass for pasture and grows in almost every situation, though not equally productive in each. It is an odoriferous grass and is recommended by some to be sowed with other grasses, in the proportion of about one eighth for meadows. It is not very productive.

MEADOW SOFT GRASS; *(Holcus Lanatus,)* Grows well on any soil, not too dry and barren. It is best calculated for sheep in pastures. It is injurious to horses when made into hay, by producing a profuse discharge of urine, and general weakness, which may, however, be readily removed by a change of food. It is not a very early grass.

SHEEP'S FESCUE; *(Festuca Ovina,)* Grows well in dry, sandy soils, is very good for sheep, as they are fond of it, and soon fattened with it. It is perennial and flowers in June.

HARD FESCUE; *(Festuca Duricuscula,)* Flourishes in almost every situation, wet or dry, and blossoms in June. It grows luxuriantly at first, often to the height of four feet, but it soon becomes thin and disappears after a while. It is best for mixing with some other grasses.

ANNUAL MEADOW GRASS; *(Poa Annua,)* Is in flower throughout the summer. Cattle of every kind are fond of it. It is recommended for milch cows, on account of its affording butter of a very superior quality.

ROUGH-STALKED MEADOW-GRASS; *(Poa Trividlis,)* Resembles the preceding in its appearance and in flowering, but is best suited for moist or wet meadows. It is very productive and good for pasture or hay. It is, however, liable to be injured, says Mr. Curtis, by severe cold or excessive drought.

FOWL MEADOW-GRASS; *(Poa Avaria, Spicalis Subbifloris,)* Was first discovered in a meadow, in Dedham, and was supposed to have been brought there by water-fowls, says Mr. Deane. It is an excellent grass for wet meadows, and has been known to yield three tons to an acre in a season. It remains so long green, that it may be mowed at any time from July till October. It makes very good hay for horses, and neat-cattle particularly.

FLAT STALKED MEADOW-GRASS; *(Poa Compressa,)* Flourishes in dry soils, and flowers from June to August. Dr. Anderson esteems this as the most valuable of all the *Poas.* It forms a fine turf, and imparts a delicate flavor to the flesh of sheep and deer, which animals are very fond of it.

SILVER HAIR-GRASS; *(Aira Caryophyllea,)* Is most suitable for sandy lands, and is recommended by Mr. Stillingfleet for sheep-walks, on account of the fineness of the mutton of those sheep which are fed on it. It flowers in July. Mr. Stillingfleet applies the same remark to the waved mountain hair-grass, *(aira flexuosa,)* which grows in heaths and barren pastures, and is in flower from June to August.

CREEPING BENT-GRASS; *(Agrostis Stolonifera,)* Grows in moist lands, and is a good food for cattle. It grows with such luxuriance as to suppress the growth of moss and other weeds.

TALL OAT-GRASS; *(Avena Elatior,)* Flowers in June and July. It grows very large and coarse and makes a pretty good hay, though horses are not fond of it. In point of excellence, Mr. Curtis ranks it next to foxtail. In pastures it should be closely fed. It yields plentifully of seed. No doubt, a little salt applied to the hay made of this grass, when laid down in the mow, would be a great improvement to it.

Mr. Muhlenbergh, of Pennsylvania, recommends this grass very highly as one of the best he had cultivated. It would probably answer well for soiling, as it starts very early and grows very late.

YELLOW OAT-GRASS; *(Avena Flavescens,)* Is also a coarse grass, which thrives in meadows and pastures, and on hills of calcarious soil, where it flowers in June and July. Though tolerably sweet, it is less relished by cattle than the *poas,* and *fescue* grasses; though Mr. Curtis says, it promises to make good sheep pastures.

YARROW; *(Achillea Millefolium,)* Is highly recommended by Dr. Anderson, as being one of the most valuable plants growing in Great-Britain. It thrives well on moist loams and on the driest soils, and will be found green when other grasses are parched with drought. Every kind of cattle are fond of it. The seeds are gathered in October. It flowers in June and July.

11

RIB-GRASS; *(Plantago Lanceolata,)* Has been considerably propagated in Yorkshire, (Great-Britain) where it is held in estimation. It is best adapted to rich sands and loams, and on poor sands it answers tolerably well for sheep. It is not liked by horses, and is bad for hay, on account of its retaining its sap. It is said by Baron Haller, that the richness of the milk in the celebrated dairies of the Alps is owing to the cows feeding on this plant and the lady's mantle, *(alchemilla vulgaris.)* Its seed is plentiful.

COCK'S-FOOT; *(Dactylis Glomerata,)* Is a coarse grass and grows with luxuriance. It suits all kinds of soils but those which are very wet or very dry. It is recommended by Mr. Pacey, who says it affords an abundant crop; springs early; yields abundance of seed; makes excellent hay; and is very permanent. It flowers in June. Where it grows on rank soils, however, or in coarse patches, cattle will not eat it.

BLUE DOG'S-TAIL GRASS; *(Cynosurus Coerulius,)* Is the earliest of all the British grasses, and flowers a fortnight sooner than any other. It is, however, not very productive, but may be useful in sheep pastures, in high rocky situations where there is but little soil.

Of Aquatic Plants which are useful in Cultivation, are the following:

FLOTE FOXTAIL; *(Alopecurus Geniculatus,)* Grows in meadows on the Severn, where other good grasses are expelled by reason of wetness and inundations. It is a good grass for hay and flowers in May and June. It is recommended for newly reclaimed morasses and lands recovered from the sea.

FLOTE FESCUE; *(Festuca Fluitans,)* Will grow in still wetter grounds than the *flote foxtail*, or rather may be said to be amphibious, growing as well in the water as otherwise. It flowers in June, and is a constituent part of the celebrated Orcheston meadow in Great-Britain. Horses and cows are very fond of it. It springs early, and promises to be useful for the same purposes as the last mentioned grass. The Chedder and Cottenham cheese owe their excellence principally to this grass, and to the

WATER HAIR-GRASS; *(Aira Aquatica,)* Which is further said to contribute much to the fine flavor of the Cambridge butter. It generally grows in the edges of standing waters, and flowers in June and July.

REED MEADOW-GRASS; (*Poa Aquatica,*) Is one of the largest and most useful of the British grasses, and forms much of the riches of Cambridgeshire and other counties in England, where draining meadows by wind machinery is carried on. It is good for pasture and hay, particularly for milch cows, though it is not relished so well by horses. It is strong and well suited to low places which are liable to be inundated. It grows to the heighth of six feet, but should be mowed when about four feet high. It may be mowed several times in a season. It grows plentifully in the marshes of Sandusky Bay, River Raisin, Detroit, and elsewhere, round the westerly part of Lake Erie, where it is the principal reliance for pasture and hay. The French farmers there cut it, and bind it in bundles, when dried, which seems to be similar to the management of it in the parts where it is cultivated in Great-Britain.

In addition to the Natural Grasses here enumerated as worthy of culture, are several Artificial Grasses, or Vegetables which are cultivated as such, among the most valuable of which are the following :

LUCERNE; (*Medicago Sativa.*) This grass was introduced from France into Great-Britain, about sixty years since, and is very highly esteemed for *soiling*, though it makes good hay, if cut while quite green. Mr. Livingston has made considerable trials of it in this state, and the products have, in some instances, been greater than those mentioned by British writers. With the best cultivation and plentiful manuring, from six to nine tons of hay, per acre, may be had in a season of this grass. Twenty pounds of seed are requisite for an acre, if sown in the broad cast, or six pounds if drilled. If cultivated in the latter way it is to be ploughed and hand-hoed three or four times in the season; but perhaps the broadcast is the more profitable culture here where labor is high. Mr. Young recommends it to be sown with oats; first sowing and harrowing in that grain, and then sowing or drilling in the Lucerne, and covering it lightly with a light harrow. Others, however, advise, that the ground be previously well prepared by deep, frequent and effectual ploughings, and that the seed be sown by itself; and as it is essential that the ground be well seeded, perhaps this is the better way. Mr. Livingston sowed it in the fore part of September, after a crop of early potatoes, and found it to answer very well. If the ground be prepared for it by summer-fallowing it may be sowed at this time. The essential points in preparing the ground are, first,

to manure it well, and then to have it frequently and deeply ploughed, and well cleared of the seeds of weeds.   A dry loam, sandy or
gravelly loam, rich sand, or other good dry soil, is suitable for it. It is
said to grow well in the coldest climates; but those which are mild
are most suitable for it.   It is a very early grass, endures drought well,
and grows very late. Probably our dry warm summers are more favorable to its growth than the cool moist ones of Great Britain, and that
for this reason greater crops of it may be raised here.   Where ground
has been well prepared for a crop of flax this grass might be sowed to
advantage immediately after that crop.

See article **FLAX.**

During the first season of its growth the product will not be so
large as afterwards; in this season too, when cultivated in the broad
cast, it is most infested with weeds, which are most easily destroyed
by frequent mowings for the purpose of soiling.   The mowings may
be as often as the grass will fill the scythe.   During this season too,
it will be much hurt by being pastured; but after this, it may be fed
without injury.

Sometimes this grass becomes diseased and turns yellow; in such
case, let it be mowed immediately, and it will then start as fresh and
green as ever.

Mr. De La Bigarre says, that after this grass has stood two or three
seasons, it should be well harrowed early in the spring; and if the
roots are considerably torn by the operation they will not be injured.
This should be repeated every second spring afterwards, and at these
times the ground should previously have a good top dressing, which
will be well mixed with the soil in the operation of harrowing.   The
dressing should not be of barn dung, but some manure, or compost,
free of the seeds of weeds.   Bog dirt, bog marle, mud, &c. are good
for this purpose.   Let gypsum also be applied every spring, but not
before the harrowing, as this manure should never be buried in the
soil.

Mr. Young, of Great-Britain, makes a computation of his expenses
in cultivating an acre of this grass in the drill way; and after deducting the expenses and rent of the ground, tythe, and rates, he makes
the clear profit 9*l*. 18*s*. 4*d*. sterling.   Mr. Livingston has also made
a similar computation of some cultivated by him in the broad cast,
the result of which was not very far different, though the value of the
crop was in this case set much lower than that put upon it by the
former gentleman.

This grass lasts about ten years, when the ground should be ploughed up, and it will then be found very rich, as the crops do not materially exhaust the soil.

It is believed, that for soiling, in particular, this ground will be found more productive and profitable than any other, where the highest cultivation and a suitable soil are given to it, and where the climate is suitable for its growth. Mr. Young says, that for fatting bullocks, and for pasturing swine, this grass may be very advantageously used. Where it is made into hay, let it be cut while quite green, and made without much shaking about, as the leaves fall off considerably when dry. A little salt added to it when laid down in the mow, would no doubt be a great improvement.

SAINTFOIN ; (*Hedy Sarum Onybrychis,*) Will grow very well on dry stony soils, that are unfit for any good cultivation, and will produce on the worst lands a ton of hay, beside considerable after-math, in the season. On good dry lands the product will be much larger. It may be used for soiling during the forepart of the season and mowed for hay in the latter part. The hay will fatten horses considerably, as is said, without the aid of oats. It increases the quantity of the milk, and some say of the cream also; while the butter is improved in its colour and flavour.

Saintfoin requires a soil free of the seeds of weeds, as for Lucerne, and the ground should be well mellowed by deep ploughings. The seed may be sown with the drill, or in the broad cast ; three bushels being allowed to the acre in the former method, and at least four in the latter. The seeds should be *fresh* and sown early in the spring. Those which have a bright husk, a plump kernel, which is bluish, or grey without and greenish within, are the best. It is believed to be the better method to sow from one to three bushels of this seed, with about five pounds of common red clover to the acre ; as the clover serves to keep down the weeds till the saintfoin has become well rooted. The seeds may be sown with oats or barley.

During the first season of its growth no cattle should feed on it, nor should sheep during the second season. At the end of six or seven years, and afterwards, the ground should have such top-dressings and harrowings as is directed for Lucerne, and let gypsum be also applied every other spring.

If the first season for mowing proves wet let the crop be left for seed. It is at no time to be cut before it is in full bloom.

BURNET ; (*Poterium Sanguisorba,*) Is mostly used for early sheep feeding, though it may be advantageously used for soiling cattle, as it is hardy—is little affected by drought or frosts—and will even vegetate in moderate winter weather.   If reserved for hay, it must be cut early, or it will become too coarse.   It requires a dry soil, and may be sown with the drill or broad cast.   It is essential to have good seed, for which purpose a proper spot for raising it should be selected. When a crop is designed for seed, let the ground be fed till sometime in May, otherwise the grass will be too rank for seed.   These should be gathered while moist with dew, and threshed out in the barn as soon as they can be dried there.   They may be sown any time before August, after the ground has been well prepared.   The following season the crop is to be kept clear of weeds by the harrow, and after that, it will grow so strongly as to keep down all other growths.

CICHORY; *(Cichorium Intibus,)* Commonly called wild succory, has been but lately cultivated; but on poor blowing sands, and weak dry soils, Mr. Young thinks it superior to any other plant; and, that if sown with burnet and cock's-foot, it will form a layer for six or seven years, far exceeding those made of trefoil, ray-grass and white clover. It grows more luxuriantly than burnet, Lucerne, or saintfoin, and may be often cut for soiling during the summer; twice during the first season, and three or four times afterwards, or every second month till October.   It may be made into hay, which is coarse, but tolerably nourishing; its principal use, however, is for soiling and for sheep-feeding, as it is less injured by close feeding than most other vegetables.

Mr. Young advises it to be drilled at the distance of nine inches on poor lands, or twelve where the soil is richer, after the soil has been first duly mellowed.   In this case it will be greatly improved by an occasional scarifying.   It may also be sown with oats in the broad cast, but for soiling it is best sown alone in the fore part of the season and lightly harrowed in.   It produces plenty of seed which is easily gathered.

SPURRY; *(Spurgula Arvensis,)* Has been considerably cultivated in Flanders, on account of its growing very late in the fall, and even during winter, and affording good food for sheep and cows.   Cattle are very fond of it.   It flowers from July to September, and is best suited to sandy and other dry soils.

THE BUSH VETCH; *(Vicia Sepium,)* Is said to shoot earlier in spring than any other artificial grass; it grows late in autumn, and in Great-Britain, retains its verdure through the winter. Mr. Swayne states the amount of its produce, per acre, to have been about twenty-four and an half tons of green fodder, equal to about four and an half tons of dry hay. The culture of this plant was long since recommended by Anderson, but the principal difficulty seems to be in collecting the seeds, as the pods burst when ripe, and thus scatter them before they can be conveniently gathered. Dr. Withering also observes, that the seeds are often destroyed by the *larvae* of a species of *catelabus*.

TARES; *(Vicia Sativa.)* Of these there are two varieties, the *winter* and *spring* tares. Mr. Livingston made some trials of the latter, which were not very successful.

The spring tare is to be sown as early in the spring as the ground can be well prepared, and the winter tare early in September, each at the rate of about eight or ten pecks to the acre, broad cast, or about half that proportion for the drill. Each kind is good for feeding cattle of every description, particularly the winter tare, which, in Great-Britain, comes into use just as the turnip crop is exhausted. This plant is not proper for making into hay, being greatly injured by wet weather and requiring more than common pains to dry it. The seeds of the different kinds must be carefully kept apart, as they cannot be distinguished from each other.

THE BROAD LEAVED VETCH, *or* EVERLASTING TARE; *(Lathyrus Latifolius,)* Was long since recommended by Dr. Anderson as promising to afford large crops of hay and grass, It is eaten eagerly by cattle, and often grows to the heighth of twelve feet.

THE TUFTED VETCH, *or* TARE; *(Vicia Eracca,)* Attains considerable heighth and produces abundance of leaves. This sort and the *wood vetch* *(vicia sylvatica,)* which rises from two to four feet high, are said to restore weak or starved cattle sooner than any other vegetable known.

THE STRANGLE VETCH; *(Lathyroides,)* Has been strongly recommended by Mr. Amos, as affording a tender and agreeable food for sheep.

Of CLOVERS, *the most valuable kinds which are known and cultivated, are the*

TREFOIL, *or* COMMON RED CLOVER; *(Trifolium Pratense,)* Which is commonly cultivated in this state. It grows well on all dry soils. About ten or twelve pounds of seed are requisite for an acre. It is sown in this country with barley, oats, or spring wheat, when that article is raised; or it may be sown with winter wheat in the fall, if the land be dry and warmly exposed; or in the spring, when it should be lightly brushed or harrowed in.

The product of this grass, when well manured, may be four tons to an acre, at two mowings. It is peculiarly excellent for forming a lay for a crop of wheat; which may be sown to great advantage on the clover sward, when properly turned under. All kinds of cattle feed and thrive well on it, eithes in pastures, when soiled on it, or when when fed on the hay. For feeding swine with the hay, however, it should be well saved, early cut, and steam-boiled before it is given them, and in this way it will keep them in good condition through winter.

See article SWINE.

RED PERENNIAL CLOVER, *or* COW-GRASS; *(Trifolium Medium,)* Is cultivated in Great-Britain, in almost every kind of good upland soil, even in heavy clay lands. It is to be sowed in the spring with oats, barley, &c. It is also usual to sow it there, as well as the commen red clover, with the crop of flax. It rarely succeeds when sown by itself. It produces abundance of seeds which are easily collected.

HOP CLOVER; *(Trifolium Procumbens,)* Grows naturally in Great-Britain, in dry meadows and pastures. It is recommended by Mr. Amos for laying down land to grass, by mixing it with the clover last mentioned, and the

WHITE CLOVER; *(Trifolium Repens.)* This grass grows spontaneously on dry uplands in this state, after they have been manured with gypsum, or with bog marle, &c. It is a very sweet grass for pasture or hay, but not very productive. It is generally short-lived, but may be made to last longer by passing a roller over it; for where the stalks come in close contact with the ground, new roots will start and descend into it. It is cultivated in Great-Britain for sheep pastures and for other uses. It is most useful in mixing with other grasses for the purpose of thickening the growth at the bottom, and thus increasing the product.

After having said thus much of each particular kind of grass, something remains to be said of them in general.

It may firstly be observed, that in laying down lands to grass of every kind, the work should be done effectually. The ground should be made mellow and fine; the seed should be clean and good, and sowed evenly and plentifully, and lightly covered, and the ground made perfectly smooth, particularly where it is intended for mowing or soiling.

The graziers of Great-Britain in laying down their grass lands, make use of much more seed than is usual in this country. Whether they use more than is profitable, experiments alone are competent to determine. Let one rod square of ground, properly prepared, be laid down with a given quantity of seed; another square rod with a greater quantity, and another with a still greater; then carefully gather and weigh the product of each square rod separately; and if that which has most seed has an increase of product sufficient to pay for the extra seed, and about thirty per cent more, that quantity of seed may be most advisable to give the ground. In the same way it may be ascertained how far it is profitable to sow the ground with different kinds of grasses, in order to increase the product of the whole. This is a matter that is much attended to in Great-Britain, as will be seen by the following directions of Mr. Young and Mr. Tollet, for laying down particular soils to grass. Thus, Mr. Young directs for an acre of clay land, the following grasses and proportions of each:

Of cow-grass, 5 pounds; trefoil, (common red clover) 5 do.; dog's-tail, 10 do. and of fescue and foxtail, 1 bushel.

For an acre of loam, of white clover, 5 pounds; dog's-tail, 10 do.; ray, 1 peck; fescue 3 do.; foxtail, 3 do.; and of yarrow, 2 ditto.

For an acre of sand, of white clover, 7 pounds; trefoil, 5 do.; burnet, 6 do.; ray, 1 peck, and yarrow, 1 bushel.

Mr. Tollet directs, that for an acre of such dry light soil as is adapted to the culture of turnips, the following proportions of seeds be given:

Of smooth stalked poa or meadow-grass, 6 quarts; ray-grass, 4 do.; dog's-tail, 6 do.; yellow oat-grass. 4 do; cock's-foot, 2 do.; vernal-grass, 1 do.; cow-grass, 3 do.; white clover, 2 do.; rib-grass, 2 do.; and of yarrow, 2 ditto.

Again, for such soil, as is of the moister kind of upland, he allows, for an acre, of foxtail, 6 quarts; rough stalked poa, 6 do.; meadow fescue, 6 do.; smooth stalked poa, 4 do.; ray-grass, 2 do.; vernal-grass, 1 do.; cow-grass, 3 do.; white clover, 2 do.; rib-grass, 2 do.; and of yarrow, 2 ditto.

For firm low lands, liable to be overflowed, he allows of foxtail, 2 pecks; meadow fescue, 2 do.; rough stalked poa, 2 do. ray-grass, 1 do.; vernal-grass, 1 quart; white clover, 2 do.; cow-grass, 2 do.; and of rib-grass, 2 ditto.

Where the water lies longer, he directs the composition to be as follows:

Of rough stalked poa, 2 pecks; foxtail, 2 do.; meadow fescue, 2 do.; flote foxtail, 3 quarts; and of flote fescue, 4 ditto: And, for situations still more wet, the following: Of rough stalked poa, 2 pecks; foxtail, 2 do.; flote foxtail, 1 do.; and of flote fescue, 1 ditto.

The above are given merely as specimens of the quantities of seeds advised to be apportioned to different soils, and of the several kinds which are deemed most suitable to each, in Great-Britain. Our summers being warmer, and our atmosphere less moist, it does not follow, that the same sorts of grasses, or the same proportions and quantities of the seeds of each, would here be found most proper in similar soils. These are matters that are proper subjects of enquiry with the ingenious and experimental farmer. Generally speaking, it is believed, that the British farmers and graziers give their grounds more seed than will be found necessary in this country, whatever may be the case in Great-Britain.

GRAVEL. The principal difference between gravel and sand is, that the latter is chiefly a collection of very minute pebbles, and the former is merely pebbles of a larger kind.

Soils may be more or less gravelly, and where they are little else but gravel, they are worth but very little for tillage. Where they are but moderately gravelly, they may be very good for most productions. What are called gravelly lands, generally speaking, are lands of a middling quality; they will, however, produce good crops with the aid of gypsum, and the more gravelly the soil, to a certain extent, the greater will be the effect of this manure upon it. Poor dry gravels are much helped by carting clay upon them.

GREEN-DRESSING. Turning under a growth of green vegetables for the purpose of manuring the soil. Buckwheat is much used for this purpose. Sow it in May, about half a bushel to the acre; and when in blossom, run a roller over it, exactly in the way that it is to be ploughed under. After it has been all turned under, let it lie about twenty days, or a month, by which time it will be rotten, and fit to be ploughed again to receive the grain intended to be sown. To increase the growth of the buckwheat, and of course the quantity of manure, let a little gypsum be strewed over the ground, if it be suitable to that manure. Even to wet buckwheat intended to be sown, and then strew on it as much gypsum as will adhere to the grains, will make the growth of it considerably larger.

A green dressing may be useful to a crop of wheat where the land is summer-fallowed, and at the same time is in poor heart. Lands, however, which are suitable for gypsum, are most easily recruited by the free use of that manure and red clover; but where the soil is not assisted by that manure, or where it cannot be procured on reasonable terms, green dressings may be found a useful part of husbandry.

GREENS. Pot-herbs, proper for boiling when young and tender, for food in the spring.

Spinage, sown in the fall, affords a plentiful supply of these; so will the common turnips, French turnips, kale, &c. But the farmer ought to supply himself, in addition to these, with at least one good bed of asparagus. (*See* that article.) The plant which is commonly called poke-weed, is a very fine green when it first starts up in the spring, and until it gets to be about a foot in height. It might be well to keep a small patch of ground sown with it, as, after it has once got into the ground, it will start up every spring from the roots. The same may be said of the tops of the plant which is commonly called milk-weed, which are also very fine.

The *caltha palustris*, or marsh-marygold, growing abundantly in marshy places, makes an excellent green in the spring of the year.

GREEN SCOURING. A disease to which sheep and bullocks are often subject. It is cured by verjuice; a wine glass full for a sheep, a pint for a bullock. Verjuice is the juice of the English crab-apple. Our crab-apple is of a different kind. The juice, however, of sour unripe apples of the common kinds may answer in place of verjuice.

GRIPES. A disorder of the cholic kind with which horses and sometimes horned cattle are troubled. It generally proceeds from wind pent up in the stomach or bowels, and is caused by a high state of costiveness. Horses and horned cattle have been known to have the dung within them so hard and dry, that it could not be voided without assistance, and this assistance is by clearing it out by hand. After it has in this way been principally cleared out, clysters are to be administered which will open the passage and of course give vent to the wind.

See further, article NEAT CATTLE for the particular treatment of the disorder in them.

GROVES. These are both ornamental and useful. To plant heights of ground, the sides and tops of which are generally not very good for tillage or pasture, adds much to the beauty of a landscape; and is at the same time highly useful, as it regards the quantities of firewood which may be produced from such spots. Planting rows of trees along highways is also pleasant for shade to the traveller and profitable to the owner of the soil. The same may be observed in regard to lanes and to passages from the highway to the mansion-house. Sugar-maple trees, planted round the borders of meadows, and some straggling ones in them, are very pleasant and profitable, as they do no injury to the growth of the grass. Wherever trees can be planted in pastures and along fences, without doing injury to the growths of the adjoining fields by their shade, this part of rural economy ought never to be omitted.

The shade of some kinds of trees is much more hurtful to the growth of plants than others. " I planted maize," says Mr. Livingston, " on the west side of a young wood, consisting of oaks, poplars, a few chesnuts, and a large mulberry somewhat advanced into the field; the shade made by the rising sun, extended nearly across the field, and was not entirely off until about ten o'clock; I remarked, that as far as the shade of the chesnut reached, the corn was extremely injured; it was yellow and small; the conical shape of the morning shade from particular trees might be traced a considerable extent, in the sickly appearance of the plants; the black oaks were likewise injurious, but less so than the chesnuts; the poplars very little so. Near the mulberry-tree, the corn was covered by its shade for a very long time every morning, and though not so large as that which had more sun, maintained a healthy appearance."

The shade of the black-oak is particularly hurtful to the growth of wheat; that of the locust is, on the contrary, beneficial to grass grounds; and that of the sugar-maple does but little injury to the growth of grain and none to grass.

GYPSUM. *See* article MANURES.

H.

HARROWS AND **HARROWING.** In regard to shape, the three-square harrow is as good as any; but let it be long and narrow for stoney or stumpy grounds, and wider where the ground is smooth. The essentials for a good harrow, are, to have long heavy teeth, made of iron, and pointed with steel at the ends. Where the land is rough there ought to be fewer teeth than where it is smooth. The teeth of the harrow for rough ground ought to be set slanting a little backward, so that it will not get fastened on the stones, roots, or stumps; and, on the contrary, where it is used for smooth ground they ought to be set slanting considerably forward.

In stoney rough grounds, harrowing cannot be performed to so much advantage, but on smooth grounds, and every farmer ought to make his grounds smooth, two or three good harrowings may be as good as a ploughing. Harrowing ought to be performed on wet ground, in a dry time, and in the middle of the day. On dry lands it is best to harrow in the mornings while the dew is on, and when the ground is moderately dry. It ought to be harrowed before seeds are sown; otherwise they will be buried of unequal depths and will come up in rows; most of the seeds being in that case thrown into the bottoms of the furrows.

On furrows of green sward turned under, the harrow must be loaded with more than its common weight, which in all cases ought to be pretty heavy, and run lengthways with the furrows. Where seed is sown on ridges, the harrow ought also to be run lengthways. Perhaps, in such cases, it is best to let the land remain in the furrows, as it is left by the plough; the seed, in such cases, being usually ploughed in.

Harrowing meadow lands, where they become bound, or where they become cold and mossy, is of essential service to them, and will make them produce much more largely the following years. The best time to do this is in the spring while the ground is soft. If the meadow be too wet, however, for spring harrowing, it ought to be done in the drier part of the fall; and, in such case, if a dressing of horse, or sheep-dung, mixed with sand, be laid on previous to the harrowing, it will be of essential service.

Harrowing wheat and rye in the spring is considered by European writers to be very beneficial; but doubtless this ought to be done very carefully; and, it is advised by some, that a roller be afterwards passed over the ground to fix the plants which may have been disturbed by this process.

See also, article SPIKY ROLLER.

HARVESTING. In addition to the wheat and rye-harvest, in this country, we have the Indian corn harvest.

A general rule, as it regards wheat and rye is, that the earlier each are harvested, and before the grain has become hard, the whiter the flour will be, and the thinner the skin of the grain; but the whole weight of the product will be a little less than if the grain be harvested later. Probably all that is gained by late harvesting is an addition to the skin of the grain.

When a severe blight or rust has struck wheat or rye, it must be cut immediately, even if the grain be in the milky state, and it must lie on the ground, but not so close as to injure the heads, until such time as the stalks have become dry and the grain somewhat hardened. Then it ought to be bound up and put in shooks, and carted in as soon as it is sufficiently dry. It ought to be observed, that the later wheat and rye are cut, the easier it will thresh; but at the same time there is greater waste by the shelling of the grain in harvesting and carting it in.

As soon as Indian corn is ripe, it should be harvested; but while the stalks have any greenness, the crop cannot be said to be fully ripe. If the corn is merely topped in the field, not all cut up by the roots while green, it is advisable to gather the ears, cart them home, and husk them out by night; by which means time is saved, and by which also, the husks may be saved, which are very valuable for fodder for cows, &c.

If Indian corn be killed by a frost, it ought to be immediately cut up by the roots, before the leaves have had time to wither, and set up in shooks, having the tops tied together, to keep out the rains. In this way the ears will ripen in the same manner as when left to ripen on the stalk. This, in most cases, is a good practice where no frost has injured the crop; as in this way the field is cleared of the corn in time to plough and sow with wheat, and at the same time all the leaves and stalks are saved for fodder.

HAY-MAKING. If a meadow is to be mowed twice in a season, the first crop ought to be cut earlier than where mowed but once, in order that the roots may recover immediately and be ready for vegetation afresh. Where the grass is cut later the vegetation of the roots stops for some time. The grass, however, which is thus cut early will not be so heavy as that which is cut later, as it will shrink after cutting, but the roots will not be so much exhausted, and will afford a larger crop the next time of cutting, or the next summer, if cut but once in a season.

The best time for cutting herds-grass, where but one crop is cut in the season, is when the seeds of the grass have formed, but before they have become fully ripe; but as farmers cannot cut all their hay in a day or two, it is necessary they should begin before this time, that they may not end too long after it. The same time is also proper for cutting clover; or rather when a part of the heads begin to turn brown. Fowl-meadow or bird-grass, may be cut much later, without being hurt by long standing. I have seen wire-grass mowed on the clay lands of Coxackie in the month of October, for the first time in the season, and it then made tolerable good hay. Lucerne, on the contrary, must be cut while entirely green, otherwise it will make but poor hay: The same may be observed of all wild swamp grasses, and of the high coarse grasses which grow every where on the vast prairies that extend through the western parts of the territory of the United States.

For hay-making, it is essential to have dry weather; and the prospect for this ought always to be an object of attention with the farmer. Frequently the change and full of the moon produces an alteration of the weather, either for the better or the worse; but there is no certainty in this. As a general rule, the weather between the change and the full may be expected to be the best. Sometimes rainy spells of weather last for weeks during hay-time, and during such spells it is sometimes as well for the farmer to let his grass stand untouched, until the indications of the weather become more favorable.

See article WEATHER.

Some methods are recommended for making hay which are more tedious and more expensive than the common method, and on that account, so much the worse, if in other respects they are better. But where labor is scarce, time is every thing, in " making hay while the sun shines," and that method in which it can be made with most expedition, ought to be preferred. The best plan, therefore, is, for the farmer to be at his mowing betimes in the morning; cut down as much as possible by nine or ten o'clock, by which time the dew will be off; then spread the mowed grass evenly, and about twelve turn it over where it lies thick ; in the afternoon rake it into winrows, shake it up lightly, that it may be better exposed to the air ; towards sundown make it into neat small cocks and let it remain so a day or two; if it be not then sufficiently dry, shake it out again on a small space of ground, and turn it over till it is dried ; then cock it again, if necessary, and as soon afterwards, as possible, draw it in.

But in order to save much trouble in drying hay, the application of from four to eight quarts of salt to the ton is recommended : it is found that hay thus salted, can be well saved in a much greener state, and at the same time the benefit which the hay derives from the salt is more than fourfold its value.

The method, also, of having a hole in the middle of large mows, may be found well worth attention, on account of its obviating the necessity of so much labor in drying hay, that is to be stowed away in such mows.

See article BARN.

General Smith, of Suffolk, makes use of a *horse-rake*, for raking in his smooth mowing grounds, which, with one man, a horse, and a boy to ride the horse, will gather hay as fast as six men in the ordinary way. The rake is about ten feet long ; the teeth about two feet ; and at right angles from these are some upright slats of the same length, set at the lower end, into the piece into which the teeth are morticed, and into another light slender piece at the top. The teeth, when in operation, run along the ground nearly horizontally, with the points a little the lowest, so as to run under the hay, and as they take it up the upright slats retain it till the rake is full, when the man who follows it behind, turns it over, and thus empties it in a row ; then lifts it over the hay, thus emptied, and sets it in beyond it, and so it proceeds on till it is again filled, and the same process is again repeated. When one strip across the piece is thus raked up, the horse is turned round, and another strip is raked in the same manner, emptying the hay at the ends of the last heaps raked up, so that in this way winrows are formed. When it is thus raked into winrows, it is dragged up by the rake into bundles, large enough for making into cocks.

Those who make use of smooth ploughing lands for mowing grounds, or have smooth meadows, will do well to attend to this labor-saving implement.

HEDGES. Mr. De La Bigarre, recommends that the white mulberry be used for making hedges, as it answers well for this purpose, and has the peculiar advantage of affording food for silk worms, which may be either raised on the hedges, or the leaves may be gathered to feed them. (*See* article SILK WORMS.) For wet lands, however, willow should be used for making hedges.

If the hedge be made of thorn, let it be our own thorn, for the English is apt to be killed by the winters in this state. The difficulty in making the seeds of our thorn vegetate, it is believed, can be easily overcome by their being put in hot water, or in muriatic acid gas, mixed with water. *See* article GERMINATION OF PLANTS.

For raising thorn, mulberry, and willow, *see* those articles.

Mr. L'Hommedieu says, if apple seeds, in the pomace, be strewed along and buried in the top of the bank of the ditch made for the hedge, and kept from the cattle, until they have attained sufficient strength, they will answer very well for this purpose: and as the cattle will be constantly biting off the young shoots, it will make the hedge grow more bushy, thick and strong.

In dry lands hedges may do very well without ditches; and in this way they are now made in the middle states, of English thorn, which can endure the winters there. But where the soil is wet, or spongy, the thorn should be set in the bank of a ditch, and no doubt it would be equally necessary for the mulberry. Willow in such grounds perhaps would not, in any case, need a ditch, as it is natural to wet grounds. Mortimer directs that the hedge consist of two rows, a foot apart, if no ditch be used.

Where ditches are used, probably the better way in general is to have two small ones, with the bank thrown up between them. Mr. Miller directs that the sets of thorn, when planted out, be of the thickness of a goose-quill; that they be planted when newly taken up, with their tops cut off about six inches above ground; and that they be bedded in the richest mould dug out of the ditch. Where two rows are set together, let each plant be put at the distance of about a foot; but where there is only one, they should stand closer. They should be hoed and kept clean of weeds during summer, says this author, and after having one summer's growth, they should be cut off early next spring at the distance of about an inch from the ground, which will make them send out strong shoots, and help their growth. This is agreeable to Forsyth's plan of *heading down*.

See article FRUIT TREES.

When the hedge is eight or nine years old, it should be plashed, by cutting them half through and weaving them together, trimming off superfluous branches. This should be done early in the spring. The

young hedge is to be protected from cattle, by another fence, until it
has grown sufficiently strong to form a fence of itself.   After twenty
or thirty years some occasional repairs may be necessary, by setting
young plants in the place of those which may have died out.

For making white mulberry hedges Mr. De La Bigarre directs that
the plants when set should have a year's growth, and be cut off as before directed ; that their roots be taken off, and that they be set five
inches apart, and eighteen inches deep, in a ditch dug for the purpose,
and the earth thrown in upon them again.   The depth he recommended for setting the plants is evidently too great, and the distances
between them too small, unless they are to be afterwards thinned as they
grow larger.   He also directs that the shoots be cut off the following
spring a little above ground, in order that they acquire more strength,
and shoot forth more branches; and then they will form a pretty
good hedge the third or fourth year, and at last grow so thick as to be
impassable by any cattle.   He says the branches must be twisted and
woven together much earlier than those of thorn.   The young plants
when set out are to be kept clear of weeds, and protected from cattle,
as before directed.

Mulberry hedges may also be made from slips or cuttings, taken
from mulberry trees, and in that case they should perhaps be set as
deep as Mr. De La Bigarre recommends for sets.

Hedges may be made of other trees than those above named; such
as white-oak, elm, hickory, birch, &c.   In all cases the hedge should
be made of such growth as is suitable to the soil; and this growth
should be raised in a soil similar to that in which it is to be planted.

Where timber is scarce, the farmer will find that hedges are cheaper than rail or other wooden fences.   When hedges are once made
they are very durable, need but little repairs, and the expense of making them is not very great.   Those farmers, therefore, whose farms
are growing scarce of rail timber, ought to get into the method of
making hedges.   They will find too, that a well made hedge is a
much better protection for their crops, than such wooden fences as are
usually made.   They are, however, not so good to keep out hogs ;
but these should always be kept in inclosures made for the purpose.

HEMP.   This plant requires a mellow dry soil and the richer the
better.   It turns to but little account where the soil is not sufficiently
fertile.   It will grow year after year on the same ground, and it is not
so exhausting as some other crops.   If the soil be sufficiently rich, it
is the surest of any crop; it is subject to no diseases ; severe droughts
do but little affect it; and cattle will not touch it.   From two to

three bushels of seed are requisite for an acre; two, where the soil is middling, and three where it is very rich.

Where the soil is not naturally very strong, some advise having two fields for this culture, which are to bear crops alternately; while the one is bearing a crop the other is preparing for the next season, by ploughings and manuring. This is productive of an extra expense for the rent of the land, &c.; but as very large crops is the essential point in making the culture very profitable, two years rent of the land may be found but a small drawback in the amount of the profits. If, for instance, two acres can be made to produce a ton, which shall bring three hundred dollars in the market, and half that amount be allowed for the expense of preparing the ground, and raising and cleaning the crop, the surplus profit would be but little lessened by deducting the extra year's rent of two acres.

To enrich the ground during the alternate years, perhaps, two successive green dressings of buck-wheat, ploughed under, might be found of considerable service.

See article GREEN DRESSING.

In this case, the first growth might be ploughed under in the summer and the latter in the fall. If barn-dung is to be added, let it be ploughed under in the spring; but if compost, not until the next spring, when the seed is about to be sown for the crop of hemp, and then let it be well mixed with the surface of the soil. Gypsum will also help the crop, if the soil be suitable for that manure.

Let the ground be well mellowed by repeated ploughings in the spring for the reception of the seed, and let it be harrowed before the seed is sown, and then harrow the seed in. It should be sown pretty early in the spring, but not before the ground has sufficiently dried and can be put in ample order. The seed should be buried of as even a depth as possible, in order that it may all start equally; otherwise a part of the plants will outgrow and keep down the rest. When sown as early as above directed, it will be fit for pulling, or cutting, about the first of August, the time for which being known by the falling of the flowers and withering of the leaves.

The male plants of hemp bear the flowers and the female plants the seed. A sufficiency of the latter are to be left for seed, and these will require about six weeks further time to ripen; the ripeness being known by the seed turning brown. The seeds may be gently beat off the stalks when dried; or they may be taken off by a coarse kind of comb made for the purpose. The female hemp which has stood to ripen the seeds, requires a longer time to rot than the male, and when dressed is harsher.   The better way is to sow some hemp, thinly, by itself, for seed, and then the rest of the crop may be all pulled or cut together.

In the bog-meadows of Orange county, the hemp is cut close to the ground with an instrument made for the purpose; but in uplands which have any little stones in the way, it is best to pull it.   In cutting, or pulling, each one takes a swarth wide enough to spread the hemp as he goes along.   When sufficiently dried, which in good weather will require about a week, it is to be gathered in bundles and bound with straw, and carefully stacked in the field till about Christmas.   It is then to be carefully spread on the snow, and then by being covered with other snows, it will be bleached and improved in its colour.   When the snows dissolve in March, it will generally be found sufficiently rotted; and is then to be taken up and set in small loose shooks in the field.   When sufficiently dry it is to be broken with a coarse break, then carried to the barn to be again broken with the common flax break, and then dressed in the manner of flax, but more gently, as it will waste with hard beating.

The above is the Orange county method; but the hemp may also be rotted in the fall, and then dressed out agreeably to the above directions.   It may also be water-rotted, which is to be done shortly after it is pulled, and about five days are generally requisite for this purpose.   When sufficiently rotted in this way, a small handful may be pulled asunder with a little exertion; and then it must be taken out very carefully, so as not to injure the coat, and dried.   The water in which it is rotted should not run rapidly, as such will wash away the coat.   Let the sheaves be laid lengthways across the stream, and sunk completely under.   Standing water is good for rotting; but unless the hemp be once turned while rotting, that which lies uppermost will be rotted most, owing to the water near the surface being warmer than that below.

A new method of rotting hemp has been communicated by M. Bralle, as follows:

Put fifty pounds of hemp, in the stalk, into a vessel filled with water, sufficient to cover the hemp, and previously heated as high as 200 degrees of Fahrenheit, and into which has been mixed at least one pound of good soft soap; take away the fire, and let the hemp remain in the vessel two hours; then take it out and cover it with straw, so that it may cool gradually; the next day, spread it evenly on a floor, and run a heavy roller over it several times, which serves to break it; spread it out on the grass for five or six days to bleach; then take it up, dry it, and clean it. By this management, it is stated, that one fourth more of cleaned hemp may be obtained than by rotting in any other way; the hemp is much softer, stronger, of better quality; and the process of cleaning is much less expensive.

To make this method of cleaning hemp profitable, it must be made a separate business and carried on extensively. Wooden vessels may be used for boilers, and the boiling performed by steam, in the manner described under article SWINE. If a larger quantity of hemp be put into the boiler, the soap must be proportionate, and more must be added, as more water becomes necessary.

The seed for a crop of hemp must be of the last year's growth; that which is older will not readily vegetate.

See article GERMINATION OF PLANTS for the method of making old seeds vegetate.

Some kinds of birds are fond of this seed, and must, therefore, be kept from it when sown.

If hemp be suffered to stand after the right time for pulling, the stalks of the male wither and blacken, and then the coat is but of little value. Where hemp grows too long for dressing, it may be cut in two without any injury.

Hemp may be made a substitute for flax for all ordinary purposes; but in that case, it must be softened by steeping it over warm water, or lye; and after it is dried again, beating it till it is perfectly soft. The steeping is performed by placing it on sticks, within the vessel, over the water. The steam-boiler, just mentioned, might be applied to this purpose.

No very particular directions are here intended to be given in regard to preparing the ground for hemp, by manuring, &c.; all that will be insisted, is, that plenty of manure must be applied, evenly to the soil, of such kind as is suitable to it, and that the ground must be effectually ploughed.

See article NEW HUSBANDRY for a good method of preparing ground for hemp.

HERDS-GRASS, *see* article GRASSES.

HESSIAN-FLY, *see* article INSECTS.

HIDE-BOUND. Horses often become hide-bound when they are poorly kept, and badly used. In this case the animal grows poor, his skin sticks to his ribs, and small boils break out on his back. A method of treatment opposite to that which the horse has received will generally restore him; that is, keep and feed him well, work him moderately, and loosen his skin by oiling it, and using the curry-comb frequently, but not too harshly.

HILLS AND VALLEYS.   It is found that more rain falls in the valleys than on the hills.   The reason of this is, that in the valleys the drops of rain having farther to fall, of course come in contact with, and absorb more of, that vapor with which even the driest atmosphere abounds.

If a goblet filled with cold water be set in a warm asmophere, this vapor will presently adhere to its sides in the form of water, and in the same way it adheres to the drops of water in their descent.

In this, as in every thing else, the wisdom of the Creator is displayed.   The temperature of the valleys being warmer than that of the hills, more moisture is required, and more is given them.   Hence, too, the reason why many plants which require much heat, grow best in valleys; they have the requisite degree of heat, and at the same time a proportionate degree of moisture.   But as all grasses which are indigenous require only the heat of the hills, they grow as well on them as in the valleys: a good general rule, therefore, is, *the valleys for tillage, and the hills for pastures.*   Two other good reasons for this are : firstly, when hills are kept in tillage they are generally more or less washed by the heavy rains, by which much of the best of soil is carried off; and secondly, they are always more or less inconvenent for ploughing, and generally still more difficult for carrying any heavy manures upon them.   The above rule, however, is not to be applied to hills of large extent and moderate descent ; it is, in strictness, merely applicable to broken hills and declivities.

HOE AND HOEING.   Where the hoe is to be used in rough or stony ground, it must be made stronger and narrower; where the ground is light and mellow, it ought to be broader, and may be made lighter.

Hoeing, generally speaking, ought to be merely the finishing work of the plough or horse-hoe.   Where it is used merely by itself, the work is more laborious, and less effectual, as the hoe merely passes over the surface of the ground.   It is, however, of great use in killing those weeds which the plough or horse-hoe does not touch, and in duly distributing the fresh earth in its proper place near the plants. Where the plough is not used, the hoe is indispensable.   (*See more on this subject in treating of crops that require hoeing.*)

HOGSTY.   A good sty is of the utmost importance in fatting hogs ; nor is it less important for keeping them in winter, as the more comfortably they are kept the less nourishment they require.

The sty should be proportioned in size to the number of swine it is to contain. One of sixteen feet by twelve is probably sufficient for eight fatting swine. It should be divided into two apartments; that in the rear, which should be about six feet wide, should be close and warm for the hogs to lie in. Here they should have a constant supply of dry litter when the weather is cool, for it is an essential point to keep them comfortable. The front part of the sty, which would then be about ten feet wide, should have the floor descending to one side for the urine to run off, and in order that the lower side may be repository of their excrement; and on this side should be an opening wide enough to scrape it out. The trough should be on the upper side, covered with one or more lids; and upright pieces should be set before it, at such distances apart as that one hog only could put his head between any two of them, in order that while feeding, the weaker animals should be protected against the stronger. The whole should be covered with a roof; for it is essential that they be protected from storms while they are in the outer or feeding apartment.

According to the foregoing, if sixteen hogs are to be kept or fatted in the sty, it should be thirty-two feet long and twelve wide, and in that case there might be a sleeping apartment at each end. These apartments should again be subdivided, in order that, for the quiet of the animals, particularly in fatting, too many may not be forced to lie together. It would probably be best also to divide the feeding apartment; for too many hogs kept together are not apt to enjoy that peace and quiet which is necessary to their fatting well. Posts should also be set up in the sty for the hogs to rub themselves.

If thirty-two hogs are to be kept or fatted, then, perhaps, the better way is, to have two stys, of the dimensions last described, placed together, with a roof over the whole, and a passage between them for purpose of carrying food to the troughs.

The upper part of the sty, or some part of it, may be appropriated to storing the different articles of food which are intended for feeding or fatting. It would be well also to have the steam-boiler under the same roof. For a description of this, *see* article SWINE.

If a part of the roof extended considerably beyond the sty, it would afford a convenient cover for forming a heap of compost from the dung of the swine.

HOGS. *See* article SWINE.

HOLLOW DRAINS. These are made for the purpose of laying lands dry which are naturally too wet; and the operation at the same time tends greatly to fertilize the soil, and render it well fitted for many kinds of culture for which it was unfit before.

In making these drains regard must be had to the shape of the land; and for this purpose the leading ones must be carried in such direction that the smaller ones will naturally run into them. The descent of the drains ought not to be too rapid; and therefore, where the ground is considerably descending, let them be carried in an oblique direction. The smaller ones are to be placed about twenty or twenty-four feet apart, and to be dug about four feet deep upon an average, minding to have the descents in the bottoms uniform. The width of them need not exceed fourteen inches at the top, and ten at the bottom. After they are thus dug they are to be filled about half full with stones which weigh from one to twelve pounds, and these are to be covered with a layer of quite small ones, that will serve to fill up the chinks, so that when the earth is thrown on, it cannot fall down among the stones below. Then throw on the earth that was before thrown out, reserving the best for the top. The main leading drains are to be of a width and depth proportioned to the extent of ground from which they carry off the water.

Sometimes lands may require hollow draining which are so shaped as to have no natural outlet for the waters to pass off. In such case let a hole be dug in the lowest part of the land, if it be upland, sufficiently deep to find a loose coarse sand, or gravel, if such can be found at a reasonable depth. When the hole has been thus sunk to the sand or gravel, fill it up with stones as before mentioned, and run all the drains into it, and here the waters will sink away into the sand or gravel.

Where stones cannot conveniently be had to fill hollow drains, it is said by some English writers that cutting the bottoms of the small drains very narrow, not more than four inches wide, and cutting the top of the ground into proper sized chunks, with the sward on it, so that where these chunks are wedged into the bottom of the ditch, with the grass downwards, there will be left a cavity below them sufficient to carry off the water; this will sufficiently answer the purpose of hollow drains for forty years. Others advise that, in place of these chunks, large rolls of twisted straw be laid in the bottom. Others again advise that coarse gravel be used for the purpose.

Large tracts of lands in Great-Britain, which, before they were hollow drained, were too wet for grain, or even for good grass, are said by Mr. Young and other British agriculturalists, to have become so

Well fitted for the plough and for grass as to be considered lands of the first rate. It would be desirable that some of our more opulent agriculturalists, stimulated by successful experiments of this kind beyond the Atlantic, would make suitable trials of this method of improving our cold wet lands, in order to ascertain whether in this country, where labor is higher, this improvement would be warranted by its expense. I think that in most cases it would.

HOP; *(Homulus.)* This plant requires a rich mellow soil, well prepared by digging or deep ploughing. Bog-meadows are good for raising it.

The plants are raised in hills, six or seven feet apart where the soil is not very rich, and at a greater distance where it is richer. In the spring, when the plants begin to shoot, take cuttings from branches which grow from the main root; if of the last year's growth, the better, and these are known by their white appearance. Let each have three or four buds; bury them lightly in the hills, with the buds uppermost; allow two or three sets to a pole, and three poles to a hill. For making the hills, first dig round holes about three feet in diameter, a foot in depth, and deeper if the soil will admit it, fill up these with the earth thrown out, well mixed with old compost, if the soil be not already very rich.

The first year the hills are not to be poled, but the ground in this, as in all succeeding years, is to be kept mellow and free from weeds by ploughings and hoeings. As the vines rise this year, let them be slightly twisted together on each hill, and let the hills be raised a little by hoeing in some earth round the vines.

Early in the spring the second year, and always after this, the hills are to be opened, and the sprouts or suckers cut off within an inch of the old root; but that must be left entire, as well as those shoots which incline downwards, to form new roots. Some manures should occasionally be added, of composts formed of sea sand, marle, ashes, &c. with other ingredients, such as rotten hog dung, &c.

The poles should never be too long, as the vines never begin to bear much till they have got to the ends of the poles. Set them so as to form a triangle, with one point to the north, and let them meet together at the top. Poles of ten feet are long enough for the first year; after that they are to be fifteen, eighteen or twenty feet long, according to the strength of the ground, but never so long as that the vines cannot go somewhat beyond their tops.

14

About the first of September, or as soon as their colour is changed and they emit a fragrant smell, they are to be gathered. If gathered later, the vines will bear more the next year, but the present crop will not be quite so good.

When the poles are drawn to be picked, cut the vines asunder three or four feet from the ground; for cutting lower while they are green weakens the root by too great a flow of sap.

The best way to dry them is on kilns, and this is necessary where large crops are raised; but they may be dried in the sun, or on floors under cover, though these will not be so well flavored as when well kiln-dried. When kiln-dried, let the heat be steady and moderate, for if it turns the hop brown it will be injured. Let them lie about six inches thick, and be frequently turned while drying. The seeds will crackle a little when bursting, and then the hops are sufficiently dried.

Before they are bagged they should be laid in a heap, about four days, to sweat and grow tough, and if covered with blankets awhile they will be the better. The bags are to be of coarse linen cloth, about eleven feet long, and about two and a half yards in circumference, and should contain about two hundred and fifty weight of hops. The thicker the bag the better they will keep.

To bag them, a hole is made through an upper floor, to which the open bag is suspended; the hops are thrown in, in small quantities at once, and trod down as hard as possible, for the harder the better. When full, sow the bag up as tight as possible. Mind to make four handles to the bag, one at each corner; they are made by tying a handfull of hops in each corner, so as to form knobs, which may easily be held in the hand.

The best poles are those which will last longest. Chesnut is on this account to be preferred. They are to be laid under cover while not in use. Each pole should have three vines, and all above this should be broken off in the spring.

A hop garden, says Mr. Young, will last almost for ever by renewing the hills that now and then fail; but the better way is to grub it up and new plant it about every twenty-five years.

Mats made of the splinters of ash, will answer as well as those made of hair, for the purpose of being used in kilns for drying the hops.

The seed of the hop is the strongest part, and therefore they should always be grathered so soon as that these will not fall out in gathering.

The long white hop are most esteemed, as yielding the greatest quantity and being the most beautiful. Care should be taken to have the hops all of one kind, for if there be differents sorts some will probably ripen before others.

Some say that the hills in the hop yard should be covered with manure every fall, to preserve the roots from the frosts; but this may probably be the suggestion of those who are often so minutely nice that their practice is not warranted by the expense. Experience, however, is the best guide in these matters.

The culture of hops is very profitable. At the price they command in this country, an acre of them, well cultivated, will amount to two or three hundred dollars, and the expense to the acre of raising them will not be found more than one hundred. Nor need the farmer be fearful of a want of market for them, as they are always a good article for exportation if not wanted at home.

HORN DISTEMPER. See article NEAT CATTLE.

HORSE. The marks of a good horse are, a high neck, full breast, a lively eye, a strong back, stiff dock, full buttocks, ribs reaching near to the hips, good hoofs, and a good gait.

Something has already been said of colts, and of the manner in which they ought to be treated while they are acquiring their growth. (See article FOALS.) The next point is to treat of them as horses; and here a matter of the first consequence is, to break them well.

The common method of forcibly breaking them is absurd in practice, and often dangerous to him that undertakes it. In this case, as in most others, gentle means are best. First let a young horse be tamed by leading with a bridle; then saddle him, and lead him about smartly so as to make him trot; then put weights in the saddle, adding more and more till he carries the full weight of a man. If he be very fractious, lead him with another horse. After he has been broke to leading well, and carrying burdens, let him be gently mounted, while some person holds him, and rode about in a ploughed field, with another horse before him if necessary, until he learns to go by himself.

In teaching a young horse to draw, the same gentleness should be used; first putting him with a gentle horse that is true to draw, then loading him lightly, and gradually heavier, till he has learned, like his fellow, to exert his utmost strength.

Horses should have a dry pasture, and a good shade in it. Mr. L'Hemmedieu makes mention of a horse which was always kept in a

dry poor pasture of wild grass, and yet was always fat; and the reason assigned for this was, that the horse, for want of water, learned to
feed at night, when the dew is on, which renders the grass more
nourishing.

The best method of keeping working horses in Summer, where it
can be conveniently done, is to *soil* them, that is, to feed them in stables, cutting and carrying in grass to feed them.   The grass should be
cut and carried in during the morning, while the dew is on.   They
should also have a yard adjoining the stable, in which they may run
at large at times.   This practice is a great saving of pasture land;
the horses will keep much better, and they are always at hand for
service.   *See* article SOILING, &c.

Clover, whether green or dry, is considered one of the most nourishing grasses for horses.   When grain is given them, let it be either
ground, well soaked or boiled.

A horse should never be exercised so severely as to make him
sweat profusely; or if he should, let him be well covered until his
skin and hair be dried, and in the mean time thoroughly rubbed
down.   He should at all times be kept clean, and his skin curried,
but not too severely.

A very common error with farmers is to keep more horses than
they want, and to keep them all but poorly; but the reverse of this
can only be called economy.   Keep but few horses, and keep them
well.   On a stock or dairy farm of a hundred acres, two horses, if
properly kept, are sufficient; and double that number is enough on a
farm of the same size that is kept under the plough; or rather, on
such farm, two horses and a yoke of oxen may, perhaps, be found advisable.

When a horse is on a journey, he should be fed with hay and provender, and not turned out to grass at evening, for his joints to be
stiffened by the dampness and cold of the night, after the warm and
severe exercises of the day.   To prepare him for a journey, he ought
also to be previously kept to hay, with provender, and have moderate
daily exercise, in order that his fat may become more solid, and of
course his body better enured to fatigue.   He ought also to be shod
some days before hand, in order that the shoes may become easy to
his feet.

It would be desirable to have a remedy for the dryness of hay, so
as to render it a more agreeable food for horses.   Set a basket of snow
before a horse while at hay, and he will take a mouthful of hay and

then of snow, alternately; which shews that something is needed to
supply the waste of saliva which is absorbed by the hay while eating.
In summer, horses might have water constantly before them, but the
coldness of winter precludes any substitute but snow, unless something of this kind should be found in feeding plentifully with carrots.
These they are fond of, and it is found that they will keep them as
well as oats, and fatten those that are lean. Some other kinds of
roots would, perhaps, answer equally well, particularly when steamed.
It is chiefly what may be called a comfortable state of existence, or a
freeness from suffering, which occasions a horse to grow fat; and
therefore, the less they suffer from thirst, from want of agreeable food,
or comfortable stabling, or from too severe exercise, the easier they
may be kept in good order. These things are apt to be little attended to ; and in this way animals entrusted to our care, which it is our
duty to make comfortable while they exist, are often neglected, and
left to suffer.

A disorder has for some years past been gaining ground among
horses in Pennsylvania, and is extending to those of this state;—
this is, an excessive watering or running at the mouth, which prevails
mostly during the middle and latter part of the growing season, and
tends to weaken and impoverish these animals exceedingly. The
disorder seems to follow the culture of clover, where the lands have
been manured with gypsum. Probably the luxuriant growth of the
clover on which they have been used to feed, is the remote cause of
the disorder. If so, either a change of grass, or a change in the manner of keeping the horses, or both together, would no doubt remove
the disorder. Let the farmer whose horses are thus afflicted pursue
the method of *soiling* during the growing season, and let their food be
Lucerne, or some other good grass for that purpose, and it is believed
this will be found an adequate and very profitable remedy. *See* articles GRASSES, SOILING, &c.

When the teeth of an old horse meet together they project out-
ward, so as nearly to form a right angle ; those of a young horse meet
almost perpendicularly; those of the middle age are a medium between the former and latter; so that the age of a horse can be very
nearly ascertained by attention to these circumstances. The lips
also of a young horse are firm and hard, and his mouth is very fleshy
within the palate. The lips of an old horse are soft and flabby, and
easy to turn up, and his mouth is lean above and below the palate,
and seems only to have the skin over the bones. The teeth of the

young horse are usually short, those that are old usually long—though these signs are not always certain. The eye of an old horse usually appears sunken, that of the young more full. The ends of the teeth of a two year old horse have no black spots; at three, they have two of these in the two middle under teeth; at four, they have four such spots; at five, they have six, each front tooth then having one; and at six these spots disappear in the four middle teeth, and are only seen in the two next the tusks, which at the age of five make their appearance. Those well experienced in these matters have other signs by which they can judge pretty nearly of the age of a horse after he has passed six years, but not with certainty.

See further, article MARES. For the diseases of horses, *see* articles BOT-WORMS, FALSE-QUARTER, FARCY, FOUNDERING, GIGS, GLANDERS, GRIPES, HIDE-BOUND, LAMPAS, POLL-EVIL, SCRATCHES, SPAVIN, STAGGERS, STRAIN, SURFEIT, TUMOR, VIVES, ULCER, WHEEZING, WINDGALL and YELLOWS.

When horses, by long journeys or otherwise, have the skin rubbed off their backs, let a little dry white lead be occasionally sprinkled over the raw flesh, which will soon heal the sore. Persons on journeys ought always to carry some of this article with them for this purpose. When the withers of the horse are wrung, and swelled by means of bad saddles or otherwise, the swelling may be allayed by washing the part with brine, or with salt and black soap mixed together, applied to the swelling. Any restringent, such as alum beat up with the white of eggs, is also good.

HORSE-HOE. This is a kind of plough invented by Mr. Tull. It differs from the one horse plough, in having shafts like those of a one horse carriage, and the plough is regulated in a great degree by the shafts, so that much depends on the steadiness of the horse. Its being but little used, would, however, seem to favor the opinion that it is no better than the common one horse plough.

I.

IMPROVEMENT of LAND. This is to be effected in various ways and by various means. Some lands are naturally sterile from the want of moisture ; some from having too much of this ; some from being destitute of certain ingredients in the soil, and some from being too rough and stony for any profit in tillage.

In the southern states, too, there is much land that has become sterile by severe cropping with tobacco and Indian corn, and by being left bare have washed much into gullies by the rains.

Many dry, sandy and gravelly tracts may be converted into a state of fertility by the addition of clay or marle to the soil. *See* article MANURES. There are also particular grasses that flourish in very dry soils, which would enable the farmer successfully to pursue the soiling system of culture in such lands. *See* articles GRASSES, SOILING, &c. Where such soils are, however, at the same time very broken, perhaps the culture of the locust would be found the most profitable to which they could be applied. The mulberry might also be cultivated in the lower and richer parts. *See* articles LOCUST and MULBERRY.

Where lands are too retentive of moisture, and at the same time not too level nor too steep, they may be greatly benefitted by hollow drains. *See* article HOLLOW DRAINS. Where they are flat meadows, marshes or morasses, they are to be laid dry by open drains. *See* articles BOG-MEADOWS and DITCHES. Where they lie too low for any draining of this kind, they are either to be raised by the means of *warping*, or the water is to be raised out of the ditches for the purpose of being thrown back into the river, ocean or elsewhere, from whence they came, by the means of wind machinery. In this manner a large proportion of Holland has been redeemed from the ocean ; and considerable tracts in Cambridgeshire and Lincolnshire, in England, have in like manner been made very productive for grass. In this case, the ditches, which are to be large and proportioned to the extent of the tract drained off, are to be run to that point where it is most convenient to raise the waters out of them by wind-machinery, to be carried off. But in order to this, a dyke, or bank, is first to be raised round that part of the land adjoining the side from whence it is overflowed; or if it be an island, it is to be banked all round. The bank is to be of a height and thickness suitable to the weight and turbulence of the waters it may at times have to encounter from without. It is advisable to plant the outside of these banks with the shrub willow, which grows along the banks of the lowlands of many of the small rivers of this country; but by no means should such banks be planted with trees of large growth, as these are liable to be upset by the winds, and might thus do great mischief by letting in the adjacent waters.

The method of raising land by the means of *warping*, as it is called in Great-Britain, where it has been successfully practised, is a modern agricultural improvement. Along the banks of rivers low tracts are frequently to be found which are constantly overflowed, either by the usual tides or by the floods of the spring. If the waters of such rivers have considerable sediment, the method of warping is calculated to retain that sediment, and thus to raise the land on which the sediment settles, so as eventually to make it sufficiently high and dry for growing all kinds of vegetables. In this way considerable has been done on the banks of the Don, the Ouse, and the Trent, in Great-Britain. The low land which is thus to be raised, has, first, a dyke, or bank, made round it, as before described, to keep out the neighboring water, except where it be necessary to let it in. When it should be let in, that is, when it has considerable sediment to deposit, the floodgate is raised, and after all the sediment of the water has settled, it is let off, and a new supply of muddy water is again taken in at the next tide, or at the next flood. Where this operation can be constantly repeated at every tide, its effects will of course be much the most effectual, or will fill up the enclosed land more rapidly. Mention is made in "the Complete Grazier" of lands in Great-Britain being raised two feet by this operation in a short time. The land thus made, too, is of the best quality, being similar to the finest intervale. No doubt many extensive marshes on our tide rivers, and others, might in this way be converted into the finest lands. But this plan appears to be admirably calculated for filling up the swamps on the Mississippi, by letting parts of its turbid stream through the levees, during the season of high water, into the back grounds, when properly embanked, and letting the water off again into the bayous or elsewhere, after its sediment has been deposited.

Soils which are naturally destitute of the necessary ingredients to promote vegetation, are mostly of the turf or pete kinds. They, however, abound but little in this county, or at least but seldom to any great depth. They appear to be principally masses of woody and vegetable matter mixed together, and only decomposed to a certain extent, owing probably to a want of sufficient heat; for if these earths be mixed with lime in composts, they will then undergo a complete decomposition, and thus be rendered good manure. They mostly abound in low wet morasses.

Where such land is laid sufficiently dry, and exposed to the sun, the surface, by being frequently stirred, will undergo that further decomposition which serves to endue it with fertility, by making it more tenaceous of moisture; but it is most effectually helped by the addition of sand or gravel carted on it, which renders it suitable to the production of many kinds of good grasses. If such lands can be flooded with waters which have a sediment to deposit, by the method of *warping* before mentioned, this will most effectually ameliorate them. Mention is also made of land of this description being very successfully cultivated for grass in Great-Britain, by the improved method of irrigating meadows which is practised there. *See* article WATER.

The clearing of lands which are full of rocks and stones is sometimes a matter of no small difficulty, and in some instances it may be advisable to calculate whether the additional value of the land, when cleared, will warrant the expense. Lands may be very stony, and yet of considerable value for pastures, or for fruit or other kind of trees. *See* article STONES.

The southern planter finds himself in possession of large tracts of worn-out lands, which, when abandoned to commons, are termed *old field*. These, perhaps, do not yield him six cents an acre by the year. How shall he renovate these lands, and thus restore beauty, plenty and fertility, to that portion of country where nature has been most profuse in her benefits, but which have been blasted by the hand of man?

There is nothing more easy. Let the planter change his system of culture. Let him turn his attention to the rearing of a due proportion of cattle, to afford him the means of making manures. Let him keep his grounds well stocked with clover, Lucerne and other suitable grasses; attend to the soiling culture, before mentioned, where his grounds are suitable; be diligent in manuring; plough often and well, and he would soon find that his now barren wastes would bloom with fresh and increased verdure. Those grounds, however, which have become too much washed and deeply gullied, should be planted with locust and other good wood. In short, it is believed that the soiling husbandry in particular is amply calculated, in a very profitable manner, to change into a state of high fertility the most exhausted tracts in the southern states.

The improvement of a country, not only by bringing its waste and barren tracts to as high a degree of productiveness as they will bear, but by adding the highest additional fertility to the better parts, is the foundation of its wealth and prosperity. The greater the *clear profits* which are derived from the lands, the greater is the wealth of a country. Farmers with large tracts of lands which yield little more than the value of the labor bestowed on them, as is but too often the case in some parts of this country, are, properly speaking poor—their condition is but little better than that of the laborer who earns his daily bread. With the best culture, a little land is sufficient to make the farmer comfortable; but with such culture as is frequently to be found, his troubles are often proportioned to the extent of his grounds. The best culture is a source of rational pleasure; the worst, of unceasing vexation. The highest improvement of a country is, then, properly a source of happiness, as well as of wealth, to its inhabitants.

In the highly cultivated country, as much less ground is requisite for the support of each family, they are brought closer together; thus much labor is saved in their necessary intercourse. The distances, also, to the necessary places of resort are proportionately shortened, and thus much is saved in all the usual purposes of transportation and travelling. Such are some of the most prominent advantages resulting from highly improving a country.

INARCHING. Sometimes called grafting by approach. It is the joining of two young trees together, that stand sufficiently near each other for that purpose. A part of each, of the same length and width, is to be cut away, so that when the trees are brought together, the pared edges of the rinds will exactly join. A tongue should be made in the one, and a slit in the other to receive it; to keep the parts from slipping, they are to be bound firmly together, and coated with wet loam, or otherwise, as is directed in article GRAFTING. After about four months they will be so well joined that the top and bottom of either part may be taken away at pleasure; so that in this way the top of one tree may be set on the stock of another. Let the parts taken away be cut pretty close and sloping, and cover the ends with Forsyth's composition, or with a coat of wet loam.

This operation is to be performed in April or May, and is commonly practised upon myrtles, jassmines, walnuts, firs, pines and other trees, that will not succeed by common grafting. Forsyth, however, observes, that the trees thus reared will be weakly.

INDIAN CORN; (*Zea.*) This plant is a native of this country, and seems to be adapted to every part of it that is tolerable to be inhabited. There is but one species of it, though many varieties, owing perhaps principally to the variations of climate. It requires a warm summer, and this is afforded even beyond the most northerly parts of our territory. It is a very valuable grain for almost every purpose; its great increase when properly cultivated, and the trifle that is required for seed, must ever render it a favorite of the poor, as well as an article of profit with the wealthy. The praises of "*the hasty pudding*" have been deservedly sung; and surely those at least whose "bones are made of Indian corn," will readily assent to the eulogiums of the poet on the cheap, yet delicious, meal which this pudding, with milk, affords. It is to be hoped that our farmers will never so far ape the fashions of the proud and wealthy, as to acquire a taste sufficiently vitiated to reject the hasty pudding; as it is believed that a proper proportion of this diet is as well calculated to raise a fine, hardy and comely race of men and women, as perhaps any other whatever. The author of "The Wealth of Nations" observes, that those of the Irish whose principal food is potatoes and milk, are the handsomest and best made of any people in Great-Britain: but in point of taste the hasty pudding is very far superior—and is probably better calculated to nurture rising generations of the first order, such as, with proper culture, will be better fitted to be " the lords of human kind," than those who arrogantly assume this pre-eminence.

In Kentucky, and elsewhere on the rich lands of the Ohio, a hundred bushels of Indian corn are frequently raised to the acre. This has also been done in this county, (Herkimer)—but so great a crop in this northern climate is not to be expected, unless on some chosen spots, and where the best cultivation is bestowed. Two very large crops which were raised near the city of New-York some years since, deserve, however, to be noticed, as specimens of what good culture is capable of producing in this state. Mr. Stevens, who raised the largest of these crops, each being the product of three acres, ploughed his ground three times, and previous to the last ploughing carted on 700 horse-cart loads of street manure. He planted his seed in double rows, about eight inches apart, and the seeds were set, diagonally, the same distance from each other: between each of these double rows was left a space of five and a half feet. During the season the crop was suckered three times, and the intervals were repeatedly ploughed, and kept clear of weeds by hoeing and hand weeding. His product was 118 bushels to the acre; and it would probably have been greater, had not a thunder-storm injured it, by blowing most of it down at the time the ears were sitting.

Mr. Ludlow, who raised the other crop, had 98 bushels to the acre. He, however, carted only 200 loads upon his three acres. He planted his seed in single rows, which were four feet apart, with the grains set eight inches asunder. Probably the reason of this crop being less than the other was on account of less manure having been carted on; as it is doubtful whether planting in double rows is better than planting in single.

From all this, it appears that a greater quantity of Indian corn can be raised on an acre than any other grain; and considering its nutrimental qualities, it may safely be said that, next to rice, a given piece of ground cultivated with this grain will support a greater number of people than that which is cultivated with any other grain whatever.

The proper soils for this grain are the sandy, sandy loam, gravelly loam, and rich red, or dark coloured earths, which have no clay in them. Stiff clays are very unfit for this crop, and cold or wet loams are not much better unless well managed. *See* article CHANGE OF CROPS for the best method of managing such soils.

Where sward land is intended for Indian corn, it should be broken up in the fall; and if it be a stiff or wettish soil, it should be thrown up in high narrow ridges by a second ploughing. In the spring the ground should be well mellowed with ploughing immediately before planting. Whatever fresh barn dung is to be applied, should be ploughed in. Planting in rows, agreeably to the methods before described, is best, as in this way about one sixth part more can be raised from the acre. As soon as the plants have got to the height of six or eight inches, run a furrow, with a one horse plough, as close to the rows as possible without injuring the roots, turning the furrows from the plants; then immediately turn the furrows back again, so as effectually to mellow the mold into which the roots are shortly to extend. Let this ploughing be of a good depth—the hoe is to follow and complete the dressing. In due season the plough is again to be applied, running the furrows farther from the plants, and turning them towards them, which is again to be followed by the hoe. After this another hoeing should be given, for the purpose of extirpating all the after-growth of weeds, which in old ground are apt to spring up; but any further ploughing, unless at a considerable distance from the rows, will be found of little use to the roots; and the stalks, which are now very tender, will be easily broken.

In raising this crop, the essential points in tilling the ground are, to keep it mellow and clear of weeds; and, therefore, ploughing immediately before planting, and then again stirring all the ground that can be stirred, by first ploughing closely from the rows and then back to them, answers the purpose of mellowing most effectually. As the roots extend into the ground thus mellowed, that part only into which they have not yet extended can, with any benefit to the roots, receive any further mellowing from the plough.

It is essential to have this plant started well; because if it gets stunted at the outset by the cold rains, it seldom gets the better of this during its whole growth, particularly if the soil be not perfectly suitable to it. To prevent this, it is advisable to apply some stimulants to the plants at that time; and the best for this purpose are bog dirt, marle, dug out of bog swamps, ashes and gypsum. The latter ought, however, to be preferred on all soils to which it is suitable, because it is cheap and easily applied.

Where a soil is wettish, it ought, after being well mellowed, to be thrown up into ridges, by having two furrows thrown up against each other at proper distances, and on the top of these ridges let the seeds be planted, the planters carrying their rows crossways of these ridges.

Where furrows are made for planting they ought to be shallow, not more than half the depth of common ploughing. It would be as well to have no furrow at all, but merely to harrow the ground smooth before planting, and then to plant in rows, by a line or mark drawn along the ground by hand, with an instrument made for the purpose. A more complete method, however, is to drill in the seed, by a light drill plough that may be easily made for the purpose. One of this description may be drawn by hand; and may be so contrived as to make a small furrow about two inches deep, drop the seeds at proper distances into the furrow, and cover the seeds, all in one operation. —These methods, however, are for ground that is entirely clear of stones.

If this crop be harvested too early it will lose much by shrinking. It is also found by experiments, that where it is topped at the usual time, the crop will be considerably less than if it stand without topping. If, therefore, it be topped at all, it ought not to be done before the grains have hardened. It is believed that the best plan is to cut up the stalks by the roots some days after the usual time for topping, and set it up in shocks to harden. In this mode the ears derive the same nourishment from the stalk which they do when it is left standing. A large additional quantity of valuable fodder is thus saved, while at the same time the ground is cleared of its incumbrance, so to be ready for sowing a crop of wheat the same fall. The additional labor of husking out the corn in this manner is very trifling. The shocks are to be of such size as can be conveniently tied together at the top by bands of straw, in such manner as to keep out the rain.

The best and soundest ears should be selected for seed, rejecting the grains which grow near each end. In order to accelerate the growth of the crop, it is sometimes advisable to soak the seed in water a little warm, for about twenty-four hours. Another method is to pour boiling water upon it, let it stand on it about half a minute, then cool it as soon as possible, and plant it before it dries. In this manner the seed will come up much sooner; but if there should be cold rains immediately after planting, there is danger that it will not come up at all. *See* article GERMINATION OF PLANTS, for a safe method of quickening its growth.

If the seed be smeared all over with tar, and then have ashes or gypsum sprinkled on it sufficient to render it fit for handling, and be then planted, neither birds nor squirrels will touch it. In this case, however, it is necessary first to soke it sufficiently to make it vegetate; as without this the coat of tar will keep out the moisture, and prevent the seed from sprouting.

The proper time for planting depends on the climate. In this state, however, from the twentieth of May to the first of June is about the best time. The old Indian rule, which perhaps is the best, is to plant when the leaves of the oak tree have grown to be as large as a squirrel's foot.

A change of seed is advisable with this grain as with all others, but a change of seeds grown on different soils is perhaps the most requisite. Changes of this seed ought rather to be from east to west, or from west to east, allowing the climate to be the same, than from north to south, or from south to north. If it be carried from the south too far to the north, the crop will be large, but will not ripen before the frosts; and if carried from the north too far to the south, it will ripen earlier than is requisite, but the crop will be small. But it must be remembered that climates often depend on altitude as well as on latitude. Where this crop is raised on bog-meadows, which are always subject to early frosts, the seed should be brought from the northward, in order that it may ripen before the frosts.

Of the varieties of this plant, those which have the longest ears and the largest grains will yield most; but farmers, in many situations, must have regard to that kind which ripens earliest, whether the most productive or not.

The practice of making very large hills to this crop while growing is unnecessary. The principal point in hoeing is, to destroy all the weeds, drawing at the same time a little fresh earth round the stalks while young. There ought, however, to be sufficient of earth eventually drawn round to support the stalks. The growth of suckers is injurious to the crop, and ought to be either pulled up, or bent down to the ground and covered with earth sufficient to kill them; and this is believed to be the better way, as by this means the principal stalk is not injured by wounding. It is said that sprinkling some gypsum on the silk of the ear will make it fill to the very end.

Indian corn will grow many successive years on the same ground; but it is never advisable to plant it more than two years successively, as it is a crop which exhausts the soil. Like some other crops it cannot be overdone by manuring, but on the contrary the richer the soil the greater will be the clear profit; and if the ground be left too rich for wheat or barley, it can be put to the more profitable culture of hemp.

This plant may be gradually habituated to a more northerly or southerly climate. For instance, take the Virginia corn and plant it one or two miles farther north every summer, and by the time it has got into Canada it will be the small Canada corn, and *vice versa*.

INOCULATING, or BUDDING. This, says Forsyth, is the best method of grafting most kinds of fruit, particularly stone fruit.

He observes that this operation is best learned by practice, but gives directions for performing it, as follows: Provide a sharp penknife, with the end of the handle flat for raising the bark; prepare your slips intended to be inserted; choose a smooth part of the stock, five or six inches above the ground for *dwarfs*, for *half standards* about three feet, but for *standards* about six feet; cut horizontally across the stock about an inch in length, and from that slit the bark downwards about two inches, so as that the incisions be in the form of the letter T : Don't cut so deep as to wound the stock. After having cut off the leaf from the bud, leaving the foot stock remaining, you make a cross cut about half an inch below the eye, and with your knife slit off the bud, with part of the wood to it, in form of an escutcheon; pull off with your knife that part of the wood which was taken with the bud, observing that the eye of the bud be left, for those that lose their eyes in stripping should be rejected. Then, having gently raised the bark of the stock, insert the bud; place it smooth between the rind of the stock and the wood; and having fitted it in as exactly as possible, wind the whole closely round with bass mat made soft by soaking in water, (soft rope yarn will perhaps answer as well) beginning at the under part of the slit and proceeding to the top, minding not to bind round the eye of the bud, which should be left open.

In three or four weeks you will perceive which have taken, by their appearing fresh, and then the bandages round these should be loosed. In April following, cut off the stock, sloping, three inches above the bud; fasten the shoot proceeding from the bud to the stump of the stock for the ensuing season, and the next season take off that stump close above the bud.

The time for inoculating is, from the middle of June to the middle of August, or rather at the time when the bark raises easily, and the buds will come off well from the wood. The most general rule is, when you observe the buds formed at the extremity of the same year's shoots, for then they have finished their spring growth. Cloudy weather, and mornings and evenings, are the best for the operation. Forsyth says, the slips or cuttings to be used for budding should not be thrown into water. He adds, that all trees of the same genus, which agree in their flavor and fruit, will take upon each other. All the *nut bearing* trees will therefore grow on each other, and the same may be observed of all the *plumb bearing* trees, including the almond, peach, nectarine, apricot, &c.

To the foregoing directions, which are also those of Mr. Miller, Mr. Forsyth has added drawings, which are calculated better to explain the process of inoculating.

INSECTS. Immense numbers of these prey upon the labors of the farmer, against the ravages of which it is in most instances difficult, or impossible, to provide adequate remedies. Such, however, as have been discovered shall be here noticed, as something is said of different kinds of insects.

It may be firstly observed, that the leaves of the elder, (*Sambucus nigra*) are extremely offensive to all insects as long as the leaves remain green—the dwarf kind is said to be most offensive. Elder leaves may, therefore, be considered as an antidote in regard to insects, as far as its use can be rendered practicable or profitable.

In treating of insects, we shall begin with

CANKER-WORMS. These are insects of the species of the miller, which, about eighty years since, made their first appearance in the oldest settled parts of the New-England states, and were called canker-worms because they produced an effect upon apple trees similar to that produced by *canker*. *See* article FRUIT-TREES.

One of the most effectual methods to prevent their ascending the trees, which the female does early in the spring to deposit her eggs, is that which is found equally effectual in preventing the ascent of caterpillars, that is, to fasten a strip of sheepskin, with the wool outwards, round the body of the tree. This, it is found, is a barrier which they cannot pass, as in attempting to climb over the wool, they lose their hold and fall down. Another method is, to fasten a strip of oiled paper round the tree, with the lower edge projecting out an inch or more, and slanting downwards, which edge they cannot pass. These strips must be closely fitted round the tree to prevent their passage between them and the body. Dr. Mitchill recommends scraping off the shaggy parts of the bark, in order to deprive them of places of safety from birds, and of shelter from storms. In addition to this, let the bodies and the large limbs of the trees be white-washed with lime and water, or with a mixture of old urine and soapsuds, as is recommended by Mr. Forsyth for keeping off all insects. The urine is to be saved in vessels for the purpose.

CATERPILLARS. The above directions for keeping canker-worms from trees, are equally applicable to these insects.

When a nest of these is formed, run a pole into it, twist it round till the nest and its contents are wrapped round the pole, and bring the whole down and kill the worms. Let this be done early in the morning, when the worms are all in the nest. If any escape this operation, repeat it when they have rebuilt the nest.

Where the nests have been suffered to remain till the insects have left them, young broods for the ensuing year will, the next spring, be found on the trees in the chrysalis state, under the shelter of a dry curled leaf or two, bound with filaments like cobwebs; these should be searched for and destroyed.

16

It is said that caterpillars will take shelter under woollen rags, when put on trees where they resort, from which they can be easily taken and destroyed.

GRUBS. Large maggots, produced from the eggs of a certain species of the butterfly, very injurious to corn by eating its roots. They are said to produce the beetle. Frequent ploughings will nearly destroy them.

TOP, or SPINDLE-WORMS. White worms resembling grubs, found in the central hole which is formed by the leaves of Indian corn; and they there eat off the stem which forms the top of the plant. They are mostly to be found near barn-yards, and in rich spots. They are discovered by their excrement appearing on the leaves.—— Sprinkling the corn with a weak lye of wood ashes will extirpate them.

BLACK-WORMS. Ash coloured worms, with black stripes on their backs. When full grown they are of the thickness of a goose-quill, and about an inch and a quarter long. They hide in the soil by day, and commit their depredations by night. They eat off young plants above ground, and frequently endeavor to draw them under. It is said that manuring the ground with salt will drive them from it, and that lime and ashes will also have nearly a similar effect.

RED-WORMS. These are slender, about an inch long, with a hard coat, and pointed head. They eat off wheat, barley and oats, above the crown of the roots; and they also eat through turnips, potatoes, &c. No adequate remedy known, unless it be lime and soot, and effectual summer fallowings, which destroys them by depriving them of food.

PALMER-WORMS. About half an inch in length, with many legs, and very nimble. They give to apple trees the same appearance that the canker-worm does. Mr. Deane says, that great numbers of them appeared in the year 1791, in Cumberland, (Massachusetts) and eat off all the leaves of the trees, except the membraneous parts, but that next year they disappeared. They let themselves down from the trees by threads, similar to the spider. No remedy known.

TIMBER-WORMS. The smaller kind merely eat into the sap of wood, and turn it into powder post, as it is commonly called. Felling timber about the middle of winter, the time it has least sap in it, will obviate this difficulty.

The large boring worm takes its residence chiefly in pine timber. They are hatched in the cavities of the bark, and being small when they enter the wood, they grow larger as they proceed, till their boring may be heard at a considerable distance. If the trees be scorched in a light flame, says Mr. Deane, or steeped in salt water, it will destroy these worms, or prevent their entering the wood.

The same author also makes mention of formidable armies of worms which, in the year 1770, over-ran the county of Cumberland about the middle of July. They stripped the vegetables of their leaves, leaving only the stems—were extremely voracious—moved in apparent haste, and all in the same direction—crawled over houses, &c. unless they found an entrance. Other parts of the eastern states have since experinced their ravages.

The best security found against them was, to stop their course by trenches, having their sides leaning over, out of which they could not climb after they had got into them.

HESSIAN FLY. Well known for its ravages in wheat. Remedy: Immerse the seed wheat ten or fifteen seconds in boiling hot water; cool it suddenly; dry it, with lime or gypsum sprinkled upon it, and sow it immediately. This process will assist its growth, in addition to its killing the nits of the fly, which, by a good glass, are said to be discernible near the sprouts of the grains that are infected. This remedy stands well attested by several publications, and is believed to be effectual.

This insect appears to be now on the decline, and its duration will probably be found to be temporary. Though we have given it a German appellation, it is very doubtful whether it ever was known in Germany, or any other part of Europe.

MAGGOTS. Troublesome to the roots of cabbages, and to turnips and radishes. Let the ground have a previous manuring with salt, which it is believed will be effectual; if not, let some brine, about as strong as sea water, be sprinkled once only about the plants; for if repeated it will probably be found hurtful to them. Or perhaps a better way is, to apply a weak brine more than once. Let it be done just after a rain.

YELLOW STRIPED BUG. Formidable to young plants of cucumber, squash, melons, pumpkins, &c. while in the seed leaf. Water made bitter by bruising tansy in it, and sprinkled over the plants, will keep off this insect; but this must be frequently repeated, particularly after rains. Green elder leaves are also very useful in this case. Sprinkling soot over the plants while the dew is on is also good; but must be repeated after every rain. Gypsum is also recommended for this par-pose. It is advisable to plant a great many seeds in every hill, and then some of them will stand the better chance of escaping the ravages of these insects.

TURNIP FLY. This eats the seed leaves of the young turnip plants, and thus destroys them. One remedy is, to sow the ground thickly, partly with old and partly with new seed, which will come up at different times, and thus a part of the one or of the other will stand a chance of escaping. Gypsum, soot and tansey water, applied as before mentioned, is good. Elder leaves, frequently dragged over the ground after the plants are up, is also efficacious. Some advise to sow some tobacco plants with the turnip seed, or rather to set some of the plants where the seed is sown. Smokes made to the windward side will help to keep off this insect; and rolling the ground after sowing, is also recommended, but this must be done where the ground is very smooth. The benefit derived from this consists in compressing the surface of the ground, so as to afford fewer hiding places in it for these insects. It is also advisable to let ducks into a turnip field, as these will destroy the insects without injuring the young plants.

GARDEN FLEA. Very destructive to young cabbage plants while in the seed leaf. Remedy: Elder leaves, gypsum, soot and tansy water, as before mentioned. Soap-suds is also good to be sprinkled over them.

LICE. These infest cabbages, &c. They may be extirpated by smokes, particularly of tobacco, but the frosts generally destroy them.

WEAVEL. A little black bug, very destructive to wheat, either in barns or graneries. On thrusting your hand into a bin of wheat infested with them, considerable warmth will be felt; but as they are usually collected together, every part of the heap or bin should be examined.

They may be destroyed in a close apartment by fumigating it with burnt sulphur for about twelve hours. But Mr. L'Hommedieu's method of extirpating them is believed to be the best. Having found his bin of wheat full of weavel, he emptied the bin, white-washed the inside, and then returned the wheat into it, sprinkling a handful of fine unslacked lime over every four or five bushels thus returned, and five or six handfulls was sprinkled over the whole. In ten or twelve days the weavel had wholly disappeared. When the wheat was used, he winnowed it, which took out the lime.

Weavel may be sifted out of wheat by a seive, which will let them pass through and retain the wheat.

GRASSHOPPERS. Prodigious quantities of these are some years generated in upland mowing grounds. Upland pastures do not produce so many, owing probably to the feet of the cattle destroying many before they are brought forth. Low wet meadows or pastures seldom produce many of them. The only known remedy against them, and it is sometimes very inadequate, is to destroy them by raising large flocks of turkies and other poultry, which feed on them.

LICE on cattle, and TICKS on sheep, may be added to the above catalogue of destructive insects. Where colts and young neat cattle become lousy, by reason of poor keeping or otherwise, the lice are to be destroyed by oiling the creature, or washing it with a decoction of tobacco; and then they should have better keeping to prevent a return of the lice. And where sheep become full of ticks, which will sometimes kill them if not removed, the ticks are to be destroyed by a fumigation of tobacco smoke. *See* article SHEEP.

J.

JAUNDICE, *see* articles OVERFLOWING OF THE GALL, and YELLOWS.

JERUSALEM ARTICHOKE; (*Helianthus Tuberosus.*) This is a hardy perennial plant, with a large bulbous root. The stalk grows to a considerable height. It is cultivated by the roots, in the manner of potatoes. The roots are particularly useful for feeding swine when boiled, and are said to very productive. One cultivator found its produce to be about four hundred and eighty bushels to an acre, without manure. Another raised between seventy and eighty tons from an acre. They will grow well in almost any dry soil, even if it be poor. When cut, and ground in a cider mill, they make good food for horses, with the addition of a little salt. Mr. Legaux, of Springmill, (Pennsylvania) raises this root from Dutch seed, and has had them eight and nine inches in diameter. He says they are easily kept through winter in the ground, nothing being requisite further than to dig a trench round them to prevent the water injuring them.

K.

KILLING of BEASTS. But little need be said on this subject, as butchering is only to be learned by practice. But the cruel manner in which butchering is often performed is deserving of some animadversion. The killing of beasts for our use is lawful, but surely it is not so to torture them. He who, in the act of taking the life of an unoffending creature, deals not the stroke of death with mercy—must either have become callous from inveterate habit, or in feeling must be of little higher grade than the animal against which his hand is raised,

---

L.

LAMPAS. An excrescence in the roof of the mouth of a which hinders him from feeding. Young horses are most liable to it. It is cured by applying a hot iron, made for the purpose, to the swollen parts. Care must be taken, says Gibson, not to penetrate so deep as to scale the bone that lies under the upper bars of the mouth, for this would be very injurious to the animal.

LAYERS. Trees and shrubs that yield no seed in this climate, and which cannot be propagated by slips or cuttings, may nevertheless be propagated by layers. The manner of doing it is as follows : Take shoots of the last year's growth, bend them to the earth, and bury them half a foot deep in a good mellow soil; fasten them with hooks to prevent their rising, and bend the tops so as to bring them above the surface. A slit upwards should be made in that part of the twig which lies deepest, or a wire drawn tightly round it there, to prevent the sap from mounting too fast. Let the ground be covered to keep it moist, and let it be watered if necessary. When the twigs have struck root they may be cut off in the spring and transplanted into the nursery.

The time for laying evergreens is July or August, and October for deciduous trees. Many herbaceous plants may also be propagated in this way.

LICE. *See* article Insects.

LIMESTONE. If sulphuric, nitrous or muriatic acid, be laid on stone which has lime in it, an effervescence will be produced, by which means limestone can always be known.

Limestone is the last of the stony incrustations of the earth, and appears to have been formed before " the dry lands appeared." Chemists suppose it to have been formed from shells, such as those with which many parts of the bottom of the ocean now abound in prodigious qantities; and the skeletons of fish and other aquatics, often found in this stone, would seem to confirm this opinion.

Some limestone is principally combined with argillaceous, some mostly with silicious earths; and some is found to contain a large proportion of magnesia. The former is generally known by its hardness and smoothness of surface when broken, and is the least calculated to benefit a clay soil. The silicious limestone is the best for clay, and is more soft and rough when broken. That which contains much magnesia makes what the English farmers call *hot* lime, and is of much less value as a manure, as magnesia is found to be destructive to vegetation.

" The magnesian limestone," says Mr. Tennant, " is easily distinguished from that which is purely calcarious, by the slowness of its solution in acids, which is so considerable that even the softest kind of the former is much longer in dissolving than marble. It has also frequently a chrystalized structure, and sometimes, though not always, small black dots may be seen dispersed through it." (*See* Henry's Chemistry for the most accurate method of ascertaining the presence of magnesia in limestone.)

LOAM. This earth has the greatest resemblance to clay, of any other, but is not so solid and compact, nor does it shrink and crack open as clay does when dried: It is of different colours, but that which is of a deep or pale red, or brownish yellow, is the best. That which is of a pale colour, and is hard and slippery when wet, is poor. Frequently what are called loams have a little clay in them. Probably clays and loams are nearly the same earths; with this difference, however, that clays have more or less of *alumine*, of which loams are destitute.

Loams are generally cold and wet, and in their natural state are more or less covered with moss, particularly in the colder climates. Some, however, are dry and very natural to grass, and will in their natural state produce good crops of most kinds of grain, Indian corn excepted. This is a soil which, whether cold, wet or dry, will pay well for manuring it, particularly with horse and sheep dung, and other warm manures; but where it is wet, it is most effectually mended and fertilized by hollow draining. *See* that article.

LOCUST; *(Robina.)* This is a very valuable tree for cultivation, as it will grow well on any poor barren sand hill, and indeed in every kind of dry soil, where the climate is not too cold. A sandy loam or gravelly loam is best suited for it. It will cause grass to grow on the poorest soil; so that ground planted with these trees answers the double purpose of forest and pasture. The trees will acquire a very considerable size in fifteen years, and in about twenty-five years are full grown. The timber is excellent for the trunnions and knees of vessels, for cogs for mills, and for many other purposes where hardness and durability are required. For posts for fences it will last fifty or sixty years, and for firewood it is also excellent. On the whole, considering all the good qualities of the locust, it may be accounted the most profitable which the farmer can cultivate. *See* article FORESTS for an easy method of cultivating this tree.

It is said that immersing the seeds of this tree for half a minute in boiling hot water, and then cooling them before planting, will make them sprout very suddenly, and grow two feet high the first year.

LOMBARDY POPLAR; *(Populus.)* This tree acquires its full size in about twenty years, by which time it will contain half a cord of wood. It is grown at present merely for ornament; but when fire-wood becomes necessary to be planted, probably this tree may be thought worth cultivating for fuel. It will not, indeed, make fuel equal in quality to that of the locust; but as it grows faster, its inferiority of quality may perhaps be compensated by the rapidity of its growth. It must, however, be dried before it will be fit for fuel, as in its green state it will not burn to any advantage. It is easily raised from slips or cuttings, and will grow on almost any soil.

In France and Italy this tree is cultivated and trimmed up for beams and other timber for buildings; but probably it will grow larger in those countries than in this state, as the climate there is more friendly to its growth.

LUCERNE. *See* article GRASSES.

M.

MANGEL WURZEL, or SCARCITY ROOT; (*Beta Altissima.*) This species of the beet is very highly esteemed in many parts of Europe for feeding milch cows. It imparts a fine flavor to the milk and butter. For fatting cattle it is thought not to be so good as carrots, parsnips, potatoes and turnips. Its abundant foliage, says the compiler of "The Complete Grazier," may be given with much advantage to horses, sheep, cows and swine; but for the two last, the leaves should be separated from the roots, as these animals will not eat them fresh from the plants. They are not subject to the depredations of insects. The seeds of this vegetable should be dibbled, in the month of April or May; in the manner of the common beet, but at greater distances apart.

MANURES. A knowledge of the efficacy of different manures, to what soils they are most suitable, and the means of making the most of each, is worthy of the particular attention of the farmer.— Lands are seldom so rich but it may be a matter of gain to increase their fertility; and few tracts are so poor but, with proper tillage and manuring, they may be made the residence of plenty.

Manures are composed of all those substances which either directly or indirectly supply plants with their requisite food, by means of

17

which they are enabled to expand and come to maturity. *See* article FOOD OF PLANTS.

In the first place, different earths will serve to manure each other. Thus clay is a fertilizer of a light sandy soil, and sand is equally a fertilizer of clay. Where clay lands are in grass, the sand should be laid on as a top dressing; but where they are ploughed, it should be well mixed with the soil for the purpose of destroying its adhesion. Sand which has been washed down in roads and elsewhere is best. Where clay is applied to a sandy soil, it should be carted on in the fall, and spread evenly over the ground, that the frosts may pulverize it before it is mixed with the soil in the spring. The better these earths are mixed in the respective soils, the more sensible and immediate will be their effects; but their principal excellence is, that they are calculated permanently to improve the soils to which they are applied. Stiff loams are also in the same way assisted by sand, and sand again by these; but neither in so great a degree as in the former cases. Generally, it may be observed, that all light dry soils are improved by being mixed with heavy earths, and *vice versa*.

Sand and fine gravel will greatly fertilize the soil of bog-meadows, and this earth again is a very good manure for all upland soils, but best for those which are light and dry. It is peculiarly excellent for Indian corn when applied to the hills, and is very good for flax, hemp, and most other summer crops. Like gypsum, it is friendly to the growth of white clover. When applied to upland grasses, it should be laid on a top dressing. Every kind of black mud, from ponds and swamps, answers a somewhat similar purpose, though if the mud be stiff and clayey it should only be applied to a light dry soil.

The different sorts of marle found in bog-swamps are also excellent manures for all upland soils. These earths are usually found at the depth of from one to three feet from the surface, and are either of a white, grey or brownish colour. The former is the most efficacious, and the latter the least so, their strength being in proportion to the quantity of carbonate of lime which they contain. It is best to mix these earths with the mass of black earth or bog dirt that forms the upper stratum, in order to reduce their strength; and when thus mixed, a load of even the weakest kind is more efficacious than two of common barn dung. Their operation as manures is similar to that of gypsum, having little or no effect when first applied to wheat and rye, but by its afterwards covering the ground with a thick growth of white clover, it is then rendered fit for producing largely of these crops. The same may be observed of the bog dirt. Like this, too, they are peculiarly excellent for Indian corn and all summer grain, and a less quantity is sufficient. They may be used as top dressings or otherwise.

The upland marles are good manures for sandy, gravelly and other dry soils. They are also valuable in proportion to the quantity of carbonate of lime which they contain. Mr. Young mentions the tract of country lying between Holkam and Houghten, in England, having been converted into good farming lands, which formerly were so light and poor as to be kept only for sheep walks. This was effected by digging up the marle, which was found to lie at some depth underneath, and manuring the soil with it, at the rate of about one hundred loads to the acre.

This kind of marle is merely a clay, with sometimes a mixture of fine sand, having a greater or less proportion of carbonate of lime in it, and the more the better. It is generally of a bluish colour, and like other marles is to be known by the effervescence it occasions when dropped into vinegar, or other stronger acid. The greater the effervescence the better the marle. (See Henry's Chemistry for the means of ascertaining how much calcareous earth any marle contains.) Upland marle should be carted out in the fall, and spread as directed for clay. The other kinds should be thrown up in a dry time in the fall, and may be carried out in the winter or other time when the ground is sufficiently firm to go upon.

Ashes, as a manure, are found to be more efficacious in some parts of the country than in others; generally most so when applied to lands near the ocean. The Long-Island farmer can afford twelve cents a bushel for even leached ashes, while in Herkimer county they are suffered to lie untouched about the pot-asheries.

Ashes generally answer the most valuable purpose when applied to Indian corn, particularly where the soil is not suitable to this plant. Where the soil is wet, cold, loamy or clayey, the plants are apt to get stunted by the cold rains which usually fall after planting, and then the ashes serve to supply the natural deficiencies of the soil till it becomes fertilized by the summer suns. But where the soil is natural to the growth of this plant, and there is no danger of its being stunted at its outset, perhaps it may be better to apply the ashes later, so that the plants may derive the greatest assistance from this manure while the ears are setting and forming.

Ashes should generally be used for top-dressings; their salts lose nothing by exposure to the air, and soon find their way into the soil.

Soot is much more efficacious than ashes; beside salts, it contains oil. The soot of coal is esteemed equally as good as that of wood. It is used for top-dressings, and requires about forty bushels for an acre. When applied to winter grain, it should be sown in the spring; and the same may be observed of ashes. Coal soot particularly is very good for meadow lands which have become sour and mossy. This manure can, however, only be had in considerable quantities in the vicinity of large towns.

Of salts which serve as manures, the principal are, the common sea salt, salt-petre and alkaline salts. To the latter, the virtue of ashes as a manure is principally owing. Salt-petre should be dissolved in water, in which the seeds should be soaked before sowing or planting. Instances are mentioned of its good effects on Indian corn—the seeds thus soaked started much quicker, the plants grew faster and larger, ripened earlier, and produced more than those whose seed had not been thus previously managed. Mr. Johnson mentions a very striking difference produced in a crop of wheat where the seed-wheat of part of the field had been thus soaked, and part had not—the former being near a fourth larger than the latter. The farmer should, therefore, test the effects of salt-petre, by soaking every kind of seed in it before sowing; and then, by comparing the products with other parts of his fields where the seed had not been thus prepared, he can more exactly ascertain for what seeds, and in what soils, its effects are most evident. Let him try it on wheat, rye, barley, and on Indian corn in particular. Let the seeds be soaked about twenty-four hours, and those of wheat and rye be dried with lime, those of barley and corn with gypsum.

Sea salt is a good manure for almost every soil that is not too wet or too near the ocean. Too much at once, however, is hurtful; three or four bushels to an acre is probably sufficient at a time. Let it be made fine, and sown in the broad cast way. It is particularly recommended for flax, though perhaps its effects are nearly the same on most plants. When applied to wheat and grasses, it should be sown in the spring.

Lime is much used as a manure in Great-Britain and other northerly parts of Europe where the summers are cool, and of course where there is much soil that is cold. Where the summers are warmer, and therefore the soil generally warmer, it is believed that lime is not in general so efficacious as a manure. It should be applied to soils, or in composts, immediately after it has slacked.

Mr. Livingston is of opinion that the effect of lime as a manure consists principally in imparting heat to the soil. Others have maintained that its use is in supplying plants with carbonic acid, (fixed air) with which it abounds, and which is found greatly to assist their growth. But if this were the case would it not have nearly the same effect on light warm soils that it has on those which are cold and clayey? Even in Great-Britain lime is never applied to warm, sandy and gravelly lands. If, however, the farmer has any cold, loamy or clayey lands, and has limestone at hand, he ought to make accurate trials of the efficacy of this manure; but where this is not the case, it is most probable that in this country he can generally apply his time to more advantage in procuring other manures. In stiff clays it is, however, believed that lime will be found particularly useful in destroying the adhesive quality of the soil. (See further, article LIME-STONE.)

Probably if lime could be easily impregnated with a due proportion of sulphuric acid it would then be as efficacious as gypsum. "One hundred parts of gypsum," says Mr. Chaptal, "contain thirty of sulphuric acid, thirty-two of pure earth, and thirty-eight of water." "If it be kept in a fire of considerable intensity in contact with powder of charcoal, the acid is decomposed, and the residue is lime."

"Gypsum is found in the earth in four different states: 1. In the pulverulent and friable form, which constitutes gypseous earth, fossil flour, &c.—2. In solid masses, which constitute plaister stone—3. In stalactites, and—4. In determinate crystals of different forms."

"The colour of gypsum," continues the same author, "is subject to a great number of varieties, which are the signs of various qualities relative to its uses. The white is the most beautiful; but sometimes it is grey, and in this case it is less esteemed and less valuable. The several states of the oxydes of iron, with which it abounds in greater or less quantities, constitute its rose coloured, red, black and varieties."

For all light, hard and dry soils, which are not too near the ocean, this is an exceeding cheap and valuable manure, and its use has tended greatly to equalize the respective value of soils, by enabling the farmer to render those which are light and sterile almost as productive as those which are naturally rich. From one to two bushels is a sufficient dressing for an acre for a year or more. It is generally best applied to red clover, by which means the soil is afterwards well fitted for other crops. It is excellent to apply to young plants of Indian corn, about a tea-spoon full to each hill. It is perhaps more or less a stimulant to every kind of plant, except wheat and rye, and when sown on these it has no very sensible effect; but it afterwards covers the ground with a fine sward of white clover, which is an indication that it has enriched the soil, and fitted it for a better succeeding crop. A rich sward will always afford a good crop of wheat or rye. In order, therefore, for the farmer to reap immediate benefit from this manure on his poor fallow ground, let him apply the gypsum to it early in the spring, and by the first of June following it will cover the field with a fine growth of white clover; then let the ground be broken up and well ploughed, and a good crop of wheat or rye may be expected, perhaps nearly double the amount which the field would have produced without the gypsum. The field will also be left much richer than it was before the gypsum was applied. Gypsum has no sensible effect when sown on herdsgrass.

The farmer should keep a due supply of this excellent manure, if his lands are suitable for it. He will find that, with proper management, every bushel that he applies to his soil will yield him double, treble, and even fourfold its value, according to his soil, and the price which his gypsum costs him.

Mr. Livingston says, that in travelling through Flanders he found that pyrites were used as a manure, particularly for grass lands, at the rate of about six bushels to the acre. The seed grain is also covered with it, as it is with gypsum in this country. This stone is sufficiently impregnated with sulphur to burn when dry, and this is the method there used to reduce it to powder. For this purpose it is laid in heaps, and when it has become red with burning, the fire is extinguished; for if it burns longer it becomes black, and then the quality is not so good. After the burning it is easily reduced to powder; and as a proof of its great value as a manure, he observes it is carried forty and fifty miles into the country on the backs of asses.

Mr. Livingston is of opinion that the sulphuric acid in this, as well as in gypsum, is the fertilizing principle; that in this slow combustion this acid is absorbed in the burnt earth, while the inflammable matter is dissipated; and that the union of the alkali and the acid forms a salt not unlike, in its chemical relation, to gypsum, or perhaps one that is more soluble, more impregnated with the acid. Referring also to a circumstance mentioned by Duhamel, where this acid being scattered over weeds, with the view of destroying them, only made them grow with additional vigor, he observes, that probably if it were diluted, and applied to the soil, or mixed with wood ashes, and applied in that way, it might answer the purpose of gypsum. And in order to find an acid that would be cheaper and better, as being already composed of a constituent part of vegetables, he observes that the pyro-ligneous acid may be obtained at a trifling expense, by converting wood into charcoal, and condensing the vapor; as the charcoal would of itself repay the expense of the operation, particularly where wood is cheap.

Mr. Livingston further observes, that he has seen pyrites on his own estate, and advises that experiments be made of this earth. It is to be laid in beds about four feet thick, and while burning should be stirred with a rake. When cooled, pound it fine and sift it. If the earth should prove too inflammable, he advises to give it a mixture of lime, which, by the process of burning, would be converted into gypsum; or wood ashes would be found useful. If the pyrites be in lumps it must be reduced to a coarse gravel before burning.

A due attention to the recommendation of Mr. Livingston on this subject might be productive of very beneficial results, as no doubt many parts of the interior of this country may be found abounding in pyrites which are destitute of gypsum.

Pulverized stone coal, says Mr. Muhlenbergh, is a good manure for most soils. Four hundred pounds are sufficient for an acre. Pulverized charcoal is also said to be good, and the same is said of pulverized slate, limestone, and shells of shell fish. The latter are also good to be ploughed in whole in a dry soil, for the purpose of increasing its moisture.

Burnt clay, good for cold stiff soils. *See* articles BURNT CLAY and BURN-BAKING.

.Every part of animal substances can be converted into good manure. The flesh, in decomposing, discloses abundance of azote and miasma; and some of the constituent parts of blood are alkaline and sea salts, oil, air, water, &c. all of which are essentially the food of plants. The bones, when powdered, are good as a top-dressing; and even the shavings of the horns, and of the hide when curried, are good in composts, or when buried in light soils. The flesh should be spread over the ground to rot, and be ploughed in. The blood is best used in composts.

Of vegetable manures, those which are either ploughed down for green-dressings, or are otherwise buried in the earth while green, are much more efficacious than when dried, especially if long exposed to the weather. *See* article GREEN-DRESSING. Such may, however, be useful when brought into cow-yards and there mixed with the dung of the cattle, by which means they absorb much of the stale and juices of the excrements that would otherwise be lost. For this purpose almost every kind of plant, whether green or dry, is more or less useful.

Of the contents of the barn-yard, horse dung is the worst, and sheep dung is much the best, as a manure. If the former be suffered to lie long in a heap it will be spoiled by its own heat, which is to be known by its white mouldy appearance; and therefore should be applied to the soil as soon as possible. It is most suitable for cold, wet and stiff soils, and the same may be observed of sheep dung; though this will greatly assist any soil. Cow dung is best for light dry soils. Every kind of barn dung is much injured by being suffered to lie exposed to the rains, and therefore should be kept as much under cover as possible. It should be carted out in the spring, and immediately buried in the soil for a crop of Indian corn or potatoes, in order that the seeds of weeds which it contains may be destroyed by the hoeings and subsequent ploughings. Or if any part of the dung be retained in the barn-yard for making composts, it should be that which is under cover; and if this be the horse dung let it be immediately mixed with some cooling earths which are fit ingredients for composts.

These may be made of every ingredient that can be gathered together that is calculated to manure the soil for which it is intended. Clay, sand, mud, lime, peat, &c. may therefore be parts. To these may be added the scrapings of the back-yard, turfs on which cattle have long dunged, old rubbish of buildings, earth that has been long covered, banks of rich earth that have been thrown up by the plough against fences, and generally all rich earths that can be spared. On the heaps of composts should be thrown all the soap-suds, dish-water, meat-brine, urine, water that has run from dung, and generally all the filth that is collected in and about the house and barn.

Composts should be frequently stirred up from the bottom, in order that a due degree of fermentation may eventually pervade the whole mass; and when it is in this state of fermentation it should be carted out, spread evenly on ground well prepared, ploughed in very lightly, and well mixed by the harrowings which cover the seed that is at the same time to be sown.

A heap of compost of this kind may be made to advantage near the dwelling-house, for the purpose of receiving from it the additions that may be afforded there. Another may also be made adjoining the hog-pen, to receive all its contents; for hog dung is an excellent manure for all dry soils.

These heaps of compost will be the better to be slightly covered, so as to admit no more rains than will serve to keep them in a proper degree of moisture. If properly prepared, they will be found much superior to equal quantities of raw barn dung; and if proper pains be taken very considerable quantities of them may be made every year.

An excellent method of making a large quantity of manure with little trouble, is as follows: In the spring enclose a piece of ground, say ten rods long and two wide: Have the two end fences so that they can be speedily removed at pleasure, to plough the ground more easily. After ploughing it with a cleft furrow, turn the milch cows and other young cattle upon it every night. After they have saturated the surface, plough it with a gathering furrow; and so on alternately, at intervals, until the ground is completely saturated with their stale and dung. Then cart it off, and apply it as before directed for composts.

By first carting earth and rubbish into the barn-yard, the same process of making manure may be carried on there; but this requires an additional carting, which greatly enhances the expense. It is usually better to make these yards in suitable places, and drive the cattle into them after the cows are milked. They may be made in the field intended to be manured. Sheep, however, should never be shut up in this manner, as it will be found more hurtful to them than the advantage gained by their manure is worth. Perhaps the same may be observed of horses. Let a slight shed be made in a sheep pasture, and under this cart a layer of sand or other earth; the sheep will resort to this for shade if it be the only one in the field. As they saturate the earth thus carted in, bring in more and spread it over the other; as this becomes also saturated, let more be brought in, until the mass is raised so high as to render it necessary to cart it off to manure the soil, as before directed. The same process may be carried on in the sheep-pen, during winter, to nearly equal advantage. The earth becomes in this way so fully saturated with the urine and excrements that it becomes very good manure; for it should be remembered that the stale of cattle, and generally all urinary matter, possesses very fertilizing qualities, and should never be suffered to be lost for want of something to absorb it. Human urine is, however, much superior as a manure to that of brutes, and is excellent for grass when sprinkled over it. The stale and manure of horses and other cattle, might in part be saved during the warm summer days in the manner above directed for sheep.

The reader will find the most effectual and complete method of making the most of the manure which is usually lost in summer, under article SOILING.

The method recommended some years since by the *Society of Improvers* in Scotland, for making use of the ridges which are apt to gather along side of the fences in fields which have been long ploughed, shall be here noticed. First plough the ridge deep with a cleaving furrow, then cart on a layer of stiff clay, then a layer of barn dung, then another of clay, and on the top of the whole a layer of lime, and cover the whole over with ploughed earth from each side, and let it lie a spell. After a while enter it with a deep cleaving furrow, and in this way plough it to the bottom; then go over it again with gathering furrows, until the whole is thrown up in a high ridge, and in this situation let it again lie to ferment. Repeat this process of cleaving down and ridging up, at proper intervals, until the whole mass is well mixed and fermented, and then cart it out as a compost manure for the soil, at the rate of about fifty loads to the acre.

The farmer may easily follow the directions here given, or he may vary from them in regard to the component parts, so as to fit the compost for the soil for which he intends it; and no doubt in many instances it may be done to great advantage.

Mr. Davy, in his Memoir to the Board of Agriculture in England, after mentioning the different results of analyzed earths which were found extremely fertile, observes, that " in supplying animal or vegetable manure a temporary food is only provided for plants, which is in all cases exhausted by means of a certain number of crops; but when a soil is rendered of the best possible constitution and texture with regard to its earthy parts, its fertility may be considered as permanently established. It becomes capable of attracting a large portion of vegetable nourishment from the atmosphere, and of producing its crops with comparatively little labor and expense. *See* further, article EARTHS.

When manures of the common kinds are to be applied, let them be laid on pretty plentifully, and generally for that crop which needs them most. They should be applied evenly to the soil. It is but too common to see dung scattered thickly round where the heaps were laid in carting out, while the ground farther off has little or none on ; but this is miserable management. All kinds of dung, in composts or otherwise, should be mixed with the soil as soon after carting out as possible, as they lose much by drying and evaporation.

It should, however, be remembered, that soils may be overcharged with composts or raw barn dung. Too much of even composts in a sandy soil tends to overheat it, and thus lessen instead of increasing its moisture; and too much in clays tends to produce too rank a growth. Raw barn dung may, however, be buried plentifully in clays, where its fermentation will be so slow as not to produce too great degree of fertility. In sand, however, it is otherwise. Composts, or raw barn dung, is much more efficacious to the growing plants when laid in the drills where they are planted than when mixed generally with the soil; but as this requires much more labor and expense, and as the ground becomes hardened by carting on the manure, it is doubtful whether any thing is, in general, gained by the practice.

MAPLE. *See* article SYCAMORE.

MARES. Those which are kept for breeding are only here to be noticed.

Mares should not be suffered to breed till after they are four years old. They should be free from distempers, lest their colts inherit them. They should be of good colour and size, well made, strong and spirited, with bright prominent eyes. If the mare have any defects, don't put her to a horse having the same. About the first of June is the proper time to put her to horse, and every ninth day afterwards till she refuses to take him.

Mares with foal should be housed pretty early in the fall, and be well kept till foaling. They should not be ridden swiftly, nor put to drawing or carrying burdens, for a month or two before foaling. The smell of a hide newly taken off will make a mare lose her foal. When about to foal they should be kept in a yard by themselves.

It is very desirable to have the breeding mares cast their colts after the likeness of the horse, as in that case their own form and qualities are not so essential. They should also give plenty of milk, in order that the colts have a good first summer's growth. A further and very essential requisite is, that they should be sure in being got with foal every year, in order that the owner may not be disappointed in his expectations of profit.

Good breeding mares are profitable; but those not possessing the above qualities had better be kept for some other use. Pastures which are wet, and bear coarse grasses, are usually applied with more advantage to keeping breeding mares than to any other purpose.

MARLE. *See* article MANURES.

MEADOWS. All mowing lands are properly meadows; but when we speak of these in general, we mean low moist grounds, which in their natural state are best fitted for the production of grass.

Many pieces of land of this description which bear nothing but coarse wild grass, might be made the best of lands by hollow-draining and manuring with sand or other proper manure. This will render them fit for the plough, and well suited for the production of the largest crops of grass. Three tons of hay to the acre, beside fall pasturing, or perhaps a second crop, may be had from such pieces of land after being thus improved. Such land would then be worth two hundred dollars an acre, while perhaps in its natural state it would not be worth thirty. Farmers should study their own ease, pleasure and profit, by fitting a small piece of meadow so as to yield them a sufficiency of hay. An acre, at two mowings, can be made to yield four tons of hay, and at this rate ten acres would yield sufficient for a hundred acre farm. The greater ease, and saving of expense, in gathering forty tons of hay from ten acres of fine smooth meadow, instead of perhaps twenty-five acres of rough meadow, ought of itself to be a sufficient inducement for the farmer to improve a part of his meadows, so as to answer in place of the whole.

Meadows may be pastured in the fall without much injury, but not closely. The after-growth of grass should never be too shortly eaten, but a part should be left to cover the roots during winter. Good meadows are often spoiled by close feeding in the fall; and in addition to this many farmers practice feeding them in the spring, until such time as the upland pastures have grown. By this means the meadow is poached, and the roots of the grass torn to pieces, in such manner that not more than one half of the crop is to be expected that might be obtained by pasturing moderately in the fall and none in the spring. By this bad management, too, all the best grasses are eaten out, as cattle will eat these the closest; or being more tender, they are destroyed by the feet of the cattle; and in the mean time the wild grasses usurp their places, to the great injury of the meadow.

Where a meadow is quite wild it should be mowed rather before the grass has attained its full size, and in this way it may yield a toierable good second crop; while each crop, by being mowed while very green, and by adding a peck of salt to every ton, may be converted into good fodder. By mowing wet meadows very early, the grass may be out of the way before the heavy rains which often fall in the month of July. Meadows which are entirely of wild grass are much less liable to be injured by close pasturing and the treading of cattle than any other; the treading of such grass will not essentially injure it, and cattle are never disposed to eat it very closely.

For destroying moss in meadows, *see* article Moss.

MELON. Seeds brought from the southward produce the best melons, and the seeds should occasionally be renewed by a fresh supply from that quarter. Mr. Miller says they should be three years old before planting, and that those which will swim in water should be rejected. The ends of the runners, and the fruit last formed, says Mr. Deane, should be taken off, in order that the fruit first formed may have more nourishment, grow larger, and arrive to greater perfection.

A sandy loam, with a southern exposure, is best for melons. A good manure to be put under them when planting, is an old compost made of good loam and the dung of neat cattle or swine. The Canteloupe is the finest tasted melon.

METHEGLIN. A hundred pounds of honey is generally used to make a barrel of this liquor, but Mr. Deane says he found ninety pounds to answer very well. It improves considerably by age, and becomes as strong as common wines. The liquor is made thus : Take of honey and clear water, in the proportions above mentioned, and boil them for an hour; when the liquor is cool barrel it, adding some ginger, cloves and mace, though it will answer tolerably well without these. Some yeast must be put in the cask to ferment it. Let it have a little vent while fermenting, but close the vent as soon as most of the fermentation is over. It will be improved by being bottled after five or six months.

MILDEW. Mr. Young says that when the wheat-stem has a particular cast of a bluish green, it is then affected with mildew.

Mr. Marshal directs that as soon as wheat is discovered to be struck with mildew it should be cut, and that this serves to *prevent* the *effects* of the mildew; that wheat may be thus cut three weeks before the usual time of harvesting.

The grain in this case will be smaller than usual, but will make much better flour, and the quantity will be greater, as the skin will then be found very thin. If the grain has attained its full size, though only in the milk, it is sufficient; it receives that nourishment from the stalk which serves to mature it. The green stalks of the wheat must be sufficiently dried before stacking, and when carted in they will be found bright and clear of the mildew, and will make good fodder.

Mildew is probably owing to a revulsion of the sap in the stalks of the wheat, occasioned by cool nights, when the atmosphere has become cooler than the earth, which in that case forces the juices upward too fast, and thus bursts open the stalks; as they are perhaps more easily split than those of any other plant whatever. The knowledge of this, however, points to no practicable preventive of mildew; all that can be done is to counteract its *effects*, as above directed.

MILLET; *(Panicum.)* The stalks and leaves of this plant resemble those of Indian corn, though much smaller. It grows to the height of about three and four feet. A sandy soil suits it best, and it should be sown in drills, about three feet apart. The plants should stand about six inches apart in the rows after hoeing. It will produce as large crops as Indian corn, and bears drought admirably well. A crop of it sown thick, and mowed green, is excellent fodder.

"This grain, (says Mr. Deane) is a good food for fowls and swine; for the latter it should be ground into meal. Some mix it with flour in bread, but it is better for puddings."

MOSS; *(Lichen.)* There are various kinds of this; some grows on trees, on stones, on the shingled roofs of houses, on the surface of the ground; and some of a very minute kind, which is commonly called *mould*, on the surface and in the crevices and cavities of almost every substance which is wet or moist.

Moss is particularly injurious to the growth of trees and of grass. Its growth is encouraged on fruit trees, where the soil is either too cold and wet, too sterile and dry, or too thickly planted. Where the soil is too cold and wet, the best remedy is hollow-draining, and manuring with sand, sheep dung, and other manures suitable to the soil. Where it is too sterile and dry, dig away the earth from about the roots, and supply its place with a mixture of earth and mud from ponds or creeks, or some other rich earth, that is better calculated to retain moisture. Where the trees stand too thick, cut part of them away, rub the moss off the rest, and apply Forsyth's method of *heading down* if necessary, making use of his *composition* to preserve the wood. *See* article FRUIT TREES.

Where moss prevails in grass ground, apply a heavy sharp iron-toothed harrow to it, scarify the top of the soil till it is somewhat raw, strew some seeds of herdsgrass, or other good grass, over it, and give it a good dressing of a mixture of sheep dung and sand, or other warm manure that is suitable to a cold soil. This is for grounds sufficiently dry; but if the moss be occasioned by too much wetness in the soil, although the above method may prove beneficial for a while, yet nothing short of hollow-draining will ever prove effectual for any considerable length of time.

By experiments, says Mr. Deane, it is found that the common yellow moss is a good manure for potatoes. It would seem to be best, however, when mixed with stable dung, or rather laid on top of it. It is said to be very good to mix with lime in composts, as the lime is best calculated to dissolve the oil which it contains; and oil is known to be an ingredient in the food of plants. It is also recommended to be mixed in dry sandy or gravelly soils, for the purpose of enabling ███ to retain a due degree of moisture.

MOWING. This being a laborious employment, it becomes necessary for the mower to husband his strength to the best advantage. For this purpose, the first requisite is to have a good scythe, of proper length, if the mowing ground be not too rough, well hung on a light stiff snead, so that the scythe will not tremble as it goes through the grass, having the edge of the scythe to face the nib which is held in the left hand, and to keep it well ground and well whetted. As much art is requisite in keeping a scythe in the best order, as there is in learning to mow well.

The sneads most commonly used are bent in a twisted shape; but some use a snead which is nearly in the shape of a half circle, and the latter are always preferred by those who have become used to them. They take a wider swarth with the same extension of the arms; a larger cut, and therefore may be slower; require less stooping; and from the position of the body which is requisite to enter the point of the scythe into the grass, being more twisted round to the right, requires little more than bringing the body to its natural posture to carry the scythe through.

Mowers should always be at their work betimes in the morning, so as to have half their days's work performed before the heat of the day; and then they can afford themselves a resting spell during the most sultry hours. By this means, too, the mowed grass has a longer time for drying during the day.

Where mowing grounds or meadows are of perfectly smooth surface, as they ought always to be, particular pains should always be taken in mowing to cut the grass as close to the ground and as evenly as possible. Mr. Young remarks, that grass will never thrive well that is not mown quite close; and the loss in the crop where this is not done is very considerable, "as one inch at the bottom weighs more than several at the top."

MOWING GROUND. We generally apply this term to arable lands that are laid down to grass. But little is necessary to be said under this head further than what has been said under articles GRASSES and MEADOWS. This may, however, be observed of all grasses which are not biennial, that where the ground becomes bound it is good husbandry to tear it well with a sharp iron-toothed harrow before manuring, and in this way to mix the manure with the soil as much as possible, particularly if the strength of the manure be such as is calculated to evaporate by drying and exposure to the air. It may also be further observed, that it is a waste of money to lay down to grass lands which are exhausted by severe cropping, unless they are of such nature as can be recruited by gypsum, or some other similar top-dressing. Generally, if lands be poor, and cannot be assisted by gypsum, they ought to be recruited while under the plough, not while under grass.

Ground that is full of small stones may be fitted tolerably well for mowing by passing a roller over it after sowing; but the better way is, to gather the stones into small heaps and carry them off, and they will then be of no further trouble in future crops. It is almost unnecessary to add, that all grass grounds should be laid down smoothly, by being well harrowed after sowing.

MUD. *See* article MANURES.

MULBERRY; *(Morus.)* This tree is well worth raising; not only for its fruit, and great use in feeding silk worms, but also for its timber and for fuel, as it grows very rapidly, and is generally well adapted to our climate. It grows well in a deep dry soil that is moderately rich. It may be raised from the seeds, or by cuttings or slips. *See* further, articles HEDGES and SILK WORMS.

MUSTARD; *(Sinapis.)* This plant requires a soil sufficiently strong for turnips. Let the ground be well prepared, by ploughings and harrowings early in the spring, and sow, of well ripened seed, at the rate of two quarts to the acre. When the plants are a few inches high, thin them so as to stand about ten inches apart, and destroy the weeds with the hoe. When the lower seeds are ripe, the middle seeds green, and the top of the plants in blossom, cut them with a sickle, bind them in moderate sized sheaves, and put these in small stacks for a few days. In this situation the green seed will soon ripen. Carry the sheaves to the barn, having a large cloth under them, to prevent wasting, and in a few days they will be fit for threshing.

The ground for raising this plant should be previously well cleared of weeds.

N.

NEAT CATTLE. All tame animals which are fed in pastures, are properly cattle; but to distinguish the cow-kind from others, they are usually called *neat cattle*.

Of these are various breeds, which appear to be original and distinct, though perhaps climates and soils may have done something in producing these varieties. The most obvious of these is the *Galloway*, or *polled* breed, as they are called in Great-Britain, or the cattle without horns. Other breeds in that country, where, perhaps, the greatest variety is to be found, may be well worthy of notice.

1. The original or wild race of that country. Colour invariably white; horns tipped with black; end of the ears, inside and outside, reddish; black muzzles; flesh fine and well tasted.

2. The *Devonshire breed*, said to be in part descended from the above race; colour, light red, with a light dun ring round the eye; thin face; thin skin; hips wide; tail quite low; rather small boned; horns turning upward; the cows yield good rich milk; oxen good for draught and fatten early.

3. Dutch, or short horned breed; hide thin; horns short; tails set high; colour, red and white nearly mixed; tender constitutions; fatten kindly, and yield large quantities both of milk and tallow.

4. *Lancashire breed*, with straiter horns than those of any other, spreading widely and extending forward; large and square built;

19

fore-quarters deep; milk not abundant but rich; the animal hardy. From an intermixture of this breed with others, Mr. Bakewell obtained his *Dishley* breed, which are remarkable for fatting very easily and upon the most valuable parts; though they yield but little milk or tallow, when compared with some others.

Considerable pains have been taken to introduce bulls of this, or similar breeds, into this state, without any apparent knowledge of the uses to which the calves from such bulls were to be applied. It should have been understood, that such breeds are not so well fitted for milch cows as for fatting cattle, and in England are raised for that purpose.

5. *Highland breed*, or *Kyloes*, with horns turned upwards; colours, various, chiefly black, though sometimes brindled or dun; hair long and close; bodies well shaped; best suited for cold mountainous countries; good for milk, and kind to fatten.

6. *Polled breed*, before mentioned; shaped like the Devonshire breed, though rather shorter; hides moderately thick; hardy, and fatten kindly on the best parts; flesh good, and well mixed with fat; oxen good for draft. A variety of this breed of cows called the *Suffolk duns*, are excellent for the dairy. These are small, lean, big-bellied, and of a dun colour.

7. *Aldernay*, or *French breed*; small; light red; smooth neat horns; tender constitutions; rich milkers; flesh good.

8. *Welsh breed*, chiefly black; small, with horns thick, and turning upward; well shaped; vigorous, and well calculated for labor.

Our cattle mostly resemble those of the Devonshire, but evidently we have mixtures of various breeds; so much so, that no specific characters can be given them. We have also the polled breed distinct by itself; though sometimes they are found mixed with others.

Mr. Livingston observes, that black cattle are uncommon in France, but almost universal in South Holland and Brabant; that the butter made in the latter countries is much inferior to that of the former; and hence he concludes, that the butter of black cattle is inferior to that made from cows of lighter colours, which is agreeable to the common received opinion.

"A perfect cow," says the compiler of "*The Complete Grazier*," "should have a broad smooth forehead; black eyes; large clean horns; thick skin; large deep body; strong muscular thighs; large white udder, (*yellow* is better,) with four long elastic teats, together with every other token requisite in a bull, allowing for the difference of sex. They should also be young; for milch kine are not good for breeding after they are twelve; though they will often live much longer if kept well and free from diseases."

Heifers generally arrive at the age of puberty when they are eighteen months; though instances have occured where they have brought forth calves before that time. The better they are kept the sooner they will breed. If, however, they breed so early, they should be highly kept; for otherwise, they will be apt to be stinted in their subsequent growth. Mr. Bakewell used to keep his Dishly breed of heifers from the bull until the age of three; but Sir John Sinclair attributes to this their often missing being with calf. It is believed to be best to follow nature's law—let them go to the bull as soon as they feel the inclination.

Breeds of cattle are usually much improved by crossing or mixing different kinds together; and it also seems essential, that there should be no pro-creation between animals which are nearly related. Let there be little or no consanguinity between the bull and the cow which is put to him. This seems to be agreeable to the laws of nature, and among men, is strikingly exemplified in the degeneracy of the race where the peasantry of some small secluded districts constantly intermarry with relatives; or where the pride of families has served to preclude a due intermixture with others.

But in the best breeds of all animals, some of their young will always be found more promising than others; among cattle, therefore, where a selection is to be made, pains should be constantly taken to select the most promising for raising, provided they are brought forth in the proper season; and this for calves should be early in the spring. Those brought forth late will not so well endure the succeeding winter; and, if heifers, will usually go to the third year, before they are with calf, while those which were earlier calved, will usually bring forth a year sooner.

In the selection and improvement of breeds of cattle, a due regard is to be had to the uses for which they are intended. Thus, if the best milch cows are desired, select from the breeds of those which are known to be the best for that use; that is, admitting the size to be equal; those which yield the most of such *cream* as makes the *best* butter in any one year, are generally to be preferred. This is to be ascertained by keeping the milk of different cows separate, and then the quantity and quality of their products can be easily determined. The size of cows is not so material; as, it is found that all cattle eat nearly in proportion to their respective sizes: What would be necessary to feed one of the large Lancashire breed of cows would be nearly sufficient for two of the Alderney breed, before mentioned; while the milk of the two latter, would, probably, nearly double that of the former   There is hardly any breed of neat cattle but what are sufficiently large for milch cows, if well kept; for it should be remembered, that all cattle will grow much larger, if well kept, than if kept poorly, during the winter season particularly.

In Great-Britain, much pains have been taken to select breeds which should unite the two most valuable qualities, of being the best for milking, and the kindest to fatten; but hitherto such breed is said not to have been found.   Sir John Sinclair, however, observes, " It is probable, that by great attention a breed might be reared, the males of which might be well calculated for the shambles, and the females produce abundance of milk, and yet when they reached eight or nine years might be easily fattened."   He further adds, that some of the English and Scottish breeds have nearly reached this point of perfection.

If the object of the farmer or grazier be merely to raise cattle for fatting, then, perhaps, some of the larger breeds may sometimes be best.   In large towns particularly, a piece of a mammoth ox, when highly fatted, seems more desirable, and will usually command a greater price, than an equal weight of equally good beef of a small animal. The Dishly breed, before mentioned, are highly esteemed in Great-Britain for this purpose.   The most essential points, however, in a breed for fatting cattle are, that they grow rapidly, in order that they may soon attain their full size; that they are of comely shape, for this will usually enhance their price with the butcher; that they keep easily and fatten kindly, and on the *best parts*, as the English graziers say; and that their beef be tender, sweet flavored, and well mixed with fat.

In this country but little has been done in the way of raising cattle which are only intended for fatting.   Our working oxen are usually bought up at the age of seven or eight years for the purpose.   For the best breed of working oxen, therefore, due attention should be had as well to their possessing the foregoing requisites for good fatting cattle, as to their being strong, hardy, quickpaced, and good for the draft.

The signs of a good ox, says Mr. Deane, are, thick, soft, smooth, short hair; short thick head; glossy smooth horns; large shaggy ears; wide forehead; full black eyes; wide nostrils; black lips; thick fleshy neck; large shoulders; broad reins; large belly; thick rump and thighs; straight back; long tail, well covered with hair; and short broad hoofs. The best colors are brown, dark red, and brindled.

Young steers which are intended for labor should be early yoked and taught to draw; for if this be delayed till they have attained considerable growth, they are more difficult to break. They should be moderately worked at first with old oxen, till they have acquired sufficient strength, and become enured to labor.

If yokes be used, let that part which rubs against the breast and neck of oxen be rubbed with tallow, when worked much in wet weather, to prevent soreness.

When an ox is eight years old he should be turned off to fatten; and to promote his fatting, let a little blood be then taken from him. If kept longer his flesh will not be so good.

Lord Kaimes observes, that among cattle, the strongest rules and claims precedence by taking the lead; that if the strongest ox be not therefore first unyoked he is apt to be unruly while his fellow is letting loose.

At the age of four years, all neat cattle have one circular ring at the root of their horns, and one additional ring yearly thereafter. When, however, they become quite old these rings become so indistinct as no longer to be separately perceptible.

For the bull, the finest looking calf, possessing as nearly as can be judged, the foregoing requisites for a good ox, should be selected, and from the finest of the breed which he is intended to propagate; and he should not be suffered to go to a cow until he has attained a good growth. Suffering young, or dwarfish, or ill looking bulls to go to cows, only tends to degenerate the breed; and, in the two former cases, the cow by being served with such, frequently misses having a calf.

The bull should have good keeping, so that he may be in prime condition when he is put to cows. When he is about eight years old, if he grows cross and mischievous, he should be castrated and turned off to fatten. Bulls may be broke while young, and worked, and then they prove much less refractory.

In regard to calves, those which are brought forth early, are best for raising, as they will endure the first winter better; and, if heifers, will generally be with calf a year sooner than those brought forth late.

The most promising calves should be selected for rearing, for the uses intended, and the rest fatted and killed. In fatting such, Mr. Deane advises, that they be taken from the cow the next day after they are calved, and let them have only two teats of the cow to suck during the first week, three during the second, and all during the third and fourth; and in this way, he says, they will be fatter in the end than if they had all at first. The teats which are not given them should be previously milked.

In Holland, calves are fatted in coops or pens made for the purpose. These are merely narrow boxes with bottoms of lattice work, just so wide as to admit the calf to lie down, but not to turn round, and sufficiently high to stand up in. They hold but one calf at a time, which is kept in darkness. When it is to be fed, a small hole is opened in front, just large enough to put its head through, which it readily does, being attracted by the light, and the pail of milk is then presented to it to drink. A lump of chalk is also hung up by the door for the calf to lick at. The box or pen is to be kept sweet and clean. In this way, says the compiler of " *The Complete Grazier*," they fatten much faster than in any other.

Whether calves are kept for fatting, or for rearing, feeding them three times a day is much preferable to feeding them only twice; but whether fed twice or thrice a day, the times of feeding should be regular, and as nearly equi-distant as possible.

Dark coops or boxes, something similar to those above described, are also provided by some of those who make a business of fatting calves for market, in the vicinity of the large towns in England, where they are treated in a manner similar to that above mentioned. Fresh litter is constantly provided for them to lie on, and particular attention is paid to their cleanliness. The use of the chalk is for correcting the acidity of their stomachs. Pains are also there taken to have calves brought forth at different times during winter for fatting, as the veal then commands a great price. They are kept five or six weeks before they are killed; and a little before killing, and also, when about four weeks old, they are plentifully bled; taking as much away as they can well bear, which is usually about a quart at each time. The principal use of the bleedings is to give a superior degree of whiteness to the veal. Keeping them in dark places tends to keep them quiet, so that they do not fatigue themselves by too much exercise. They are fatted with various kinds of food beside milk, as that is in such places too valuable to be much used. The most common articles used are chopped turnips and potatoes, grains, bran, sweet hay, &c. No doubt, a little flaxseed broth, mixed with hay tea, would be an excellent addition.

In regard to the best food for rearing of calves, the method pursued by Mr. Crook, as mentioned in "*The Letters and Papers of the Bath and West of England Society*," deserves to be mentioned. In 1787, he purchased three sacks of linseed, value 2*l.* 3*s.* (equal to about nine dollars,) which lasted him three years. One quart of seed was boiled in six quarts of water for ten minutes, to a jelly, which was given the calves three times a day, mixed with a little hay-tea. Thus he was enabled to rear in 1787, seventeen calves; in 1788, twenty-three; and in 1789, fifteen, without any milk at all: And he states, that his calves throve much better than those of his neighbors which were fed with milk. Thus, it seems, that less than eighteen cents worth of flaxseed, with a trifle of hay, is sufficient for one calf. Linseed-oil cakes, when pulverized and boiled, make an equally good broth, or jelly.

The above is nearly similar to the directions of Mr. Clift of this state. He directs, that after the calf has been fed for a fortnight upon sweet milk, give it skim milk, mixed with an equal or larger quantity of flaxseed broth or jelly, and let it be given to it milk warm. Enough jelly may be boiled at once for three or four days; but if the weather be warm, it will spoil by souring. With this drink, Mr. Clift says, calves will thrive as well as if fed on sweet milk. For learning a calf to drink at first, the best method is, to let it suck your finger with its nose in the milk.

Mr. Budd, of Massachusetts, directs to take the calves from the cows when three days old, and feed them with gruel composed of one third barley and two thirds oats, each ground fine, and the mixture sifted. A quart of this gruel is to be given to each calf morning and evening. The gruel is made by taking one quart of the flour, and twelve of water, and boiling them together for half an hour, and is to be given when milk warm. In about ten days after commencing the feeding, tie up and suspend a bundle of sweet hay in the middle of the pen where the calves are kept, which they will eat by degrees. A little of the flour put into a trough for them to lick, is also of service. Feed them till two months old, increasing the quantity as they grow larger. Half a bushel of the above mixture is sufficient for one calf. The communication of the above method, obtained for Mr. Budd the prize from the agricultural society of Massachusetts.

When calves are put into pasture, it should be such as is dry and sweet. White clover is the best for them; red clover or trefoil is also good. Mr. L'Hommedieu recommends, that there be no water in the pasture, but sufficient of shade. The effect of this is, that the calves learn to feed at night, or when the dew is on, and lie by in the day; and as grass while wet with dew is believed to be most nourishing, they will, in this way, thrive much better than those which have free access to water; for this, it is contended by Mr. L'Hommedieu, tends to stunt them and make them pot-bellied. Probably the better way is to give them a little nourishing drink, at certain times, when the dews fail, or at mid-day when the weather is very warm.

When the weather is pleasant, after being put to pasture, the males may be castrated and the females spayed, if they are designed to be raised for fatting.

During the first winter, calves should be kept in a comfortable place; and have plenty of good fodder and a little Indian meal, or other nourishing food. They should have shelter earlier than larger cattle, as they cannot so well endure the first approach of cold weather.

Although calves until a year old should have the best of keeping, let it not be supposed, that they will afterwards thrive well with very indifferent keeping. It is but too common for farmers to turn their young growing cattle into poor pastures of stinted growth, or into woods where there is not sufficient for them to eat; by means of which their growth is retarded, and what is sometimes worse, they learn to become habitually unruly, from the constant temptation they are under of breaking into fields where there is plenty.

In the first settling of new countries, the extensive woodlands may afford plenty of good food for young cattle; but the woodlands of old settled countries afford but little food that is well calculated for their nourishment and growth. In such cases a few cattle are sufficient to overstock the woods, so as to leave them little to eat, excepting what is obtained to the great injury of the young growth of timber. Growing cattle, if their pastures be not of the best, should nevertheless have plenty to eat of that which is middling good, and the same may be observed in regard to their winter food; they should have plenty of such fodder as they will eat freely, and they should be well sheltered from the severity of the weather. When exposed to cold rains in winter, they are frequently more injured than when exposed to much colder snow storms. From each of these they should be sheltered, as well as from the cold winds. In short, the better and more comfortable young cattle are kept, the larger and more rapid will be their growth; and although middling good keeping will answer, they will do better with better keeping.

The keeping of cows in such manner as to make them give the greatest quantity of milk, and with the greatest clear profit, is an essential point of economy. Cows are in general very poorly kept in this country. By better keeping they would afford more clear profit. Give a cow half a bushel of potatoes, carrots, or other good root, per day, during the six winter months, beside her hay, and if her summer feed be such as it should be, she will give nearly double the quantity of milk she would afford, if only kept during winter in the usual manner, and the milk will be richer and of better quality. The carrots, or other roots, at nineteen cents per bushel, amount to about eighteen dollars. The addition of milk, allowing it to be only three quarts per day, for three hundred days, at three cents per quart, amounts to twenty-seven dollars. It should be remembered too, that when cows are thus fed with roots, they consume less hay. They are also less liable to several diseases, which are usually the effect of poor keeping.

The feeding of milch cows, cattle for fatting, and for labor, with roots and cabbages, is a very prominent part of the employment of the British graziers, and of farmers who attend to the dairy. For this purpose, fields of turnips, cabbages and carrots are yearly raised, and fed out to the cattle during the fall, winter and early spring. Beets, potatoes, and the Jerusalem artichoke, are also found to be good for this purpose.

Our winters, however, being much severer than those of Great-Britain, renders the feeding of cattle with roots, &c. less practicable than it is in that country. It is more suitable to the climate of the states south of Pennsylvania. Much more, however, might be profitably done in this way, even in winter, than is generally imagined. If the farmer, or grazier, were first to provide himself with a cellar or apartment under ground, sufficiently large for storing away his roots, and sufficiently warm to prevent their freezing, with a place in it also, for a *steam-boiler*, for steaming the roots, he would then find but little difficulty in dealing out this food to his cows, &c. even in the coldest weather. In this case, however, they must be kept in stalls, with troughs suitable for this kind of food. Nor is there any additional expense in this; as it is well ascertained that this is the most economi-

20

cal method of keeping milch cows, working, and fatting of cattle, as well during winter as during summer. In winter, as they can be kept warmer, and more comfortably, less fodder is requisite to keep them well and much less is wasted.

See article SOILING for the reasons why stall feeding is also to be preferred in summer.

See also, article STABLE, &c.

For a description of a *steam-boiler*, see article SWINE.

If milch cows be pastured in summer, they should have the best or first feeding of each pasture lot.

See article PASTURE.

See also, article GRASSES, as it respects those which are best for pastures.

They should have plenty of water and that which is good. It is also good for them to have plenty of shade to which they can retire during the heat of the day. They should be kept quietly, not suffered to be worried with dogs, or by having stones or clubs thrown at them as is but too common; nor should they be forced to travel too far, by having their pastures at too great a distance; for these are all matters which are essential, in order to their giving the greatest possible quantity of milk.

In regard to milking and the proper treatment of the milk, see articles DAIRY, CREAM, CHURN, BUTTER, CHEESE, &c.

When cows are kept very fat they will not give so much milk. The proper state to keep them in, during winter and summer, is that in which they are usually found when fed in good pastures during the latter season. On the contrary, where they are suffered to grow poor during winter, and particularly about the time of calving, their milk will be greatly lessened in quantity during the following season. If they are plentifully supplied with food as nutricious as that of green grass, they will usually give plenty of milk until very near the time of calving.

Some cows are naturally barren, and this is said to be always the case where a male and female calf are brought forth together; the male in such cases is perfect, but the female is incapable of propagating.

Particular attention should be paid to cows in regard to their keeping for some weeks before calving. They should have plenty of good hay, and other succulent food, such as roots of the kinds before mentioned, or cabbages with the decayed leaves taken off; or, if in the growing season, they should have plenty of good sweet pasture, or other good green food. The day and night after a cow has calved, she should be kept housed, and her drink should be lukewarm when given to her. Let her be kept up for three or four nights thereafter, so as not to be exposed prematurely to the cold or dampness of the atmosphere, for this tends greatly to weaken her. If she does not clean well after calving, Mr. Deane directs to give her a pail of warm water with some wood-ashes in it. Particular attention should be paid to this, for if the after-birth be suffered to remain in the *uterus*, it will become putrescent, and the smell will sometimes communicate an infection among other breeding cows. They will also sometimes incline to eat the after-birth, which should be prevented.

For cleansing the cow, the directions in " *The Complete Grazier*" are, to put about three quarts of water over the fire, and when warm, stir in as much oatmeal as will make a strong gruel ; stir it till it boils ; then stir in a quart of ale, or two of table beer, and a pound of treacle, and give it to the beast when lukewarm. This will also prevent their taking cold.

To regulate the state of the body, give a mash of bran, wetted with warm water. Where the udder is hard, it should be milked three or four times a day ; or the calf should be allowed to suck at pleasure ; and care should be taken that it sucks all the teats, for when any of these are sore the cow will sometimes prevent their sucking them. If the kernel of the udder is hard, the hardness may be removed by rubbing it three or four times a day.

The natural position of the calf in the *uterus*, is, with its forefeet and head foremost ; the forefeet lying parallel on each side of the head, and the back uppermost. When found in any other position, it is unnatural, and the extraction of the calf then frequently requires more than ordinary skill. I have known them safely extracted by fixing a hook with a cord to it, in the under jaw of the calf, and gently drawing them away. If the flesh of the cow be torn in the operation, it should be carefully sewed up, and if afterwards swollen, washed with warm milk and water. If the cow disowns or refuses to lick the young calf, a little salt sprinkled upon it will have the desired effect.

Sometimes, cows, from abusive treatment, violent exercise, or that unnatural appetite, called *longing*, slink their calves ; and in such case they should be carefully treated, and kept warm and clean till they recover. If they exhibit previous symptoms of this, it may frequently be prevented by bleeding them two or three times.

It would be a great improvement of our husbandry, if our farmers and graziers, stimulated by the example of those in Great-Britain and elsewhere, would enter largely into the culture of roots and cabbages for feeding milch cows and fatting cattle; as the business when well conducted is very profitable. In Norfolk, and other countries of Great-Britain, great quantities of turnips are raised and mostly used for fatting. During the fall they are put into carts and scattered over the stubble of the last harvested wheat-field, and pains is taken to scatter them over every part of the ground successively, in order that each part may have equal benefit from the manure thus bestowed on the land. The turnips are raised with an iron instrument fixed to a handle; on the other side of which instrument are edges set crossways to cut each root in four pieces as they are raised. After the cattle have eat their allowance, which should be no more than they can eat at once, they should have some hay given them. Part of the crop of turnips are also gathered and stored away for winter feeding, and some are left in the ground for spring feeding.

Other farmers and graziers, again, feed their fatting and other cattle, in stalls, where cabbages and roots of different kinds are fed out to them; and this is believed to be the most economical way. These various articles of food are much more efficacious by being steam-boiled.

For the various roots, &c. to serve as articles of food, see articles CARROT, PARSNIP, POTATOE, JERUSALEM ARTICHOKE, MANGEL-WURZEL, BEET, TURNIP, TURNIP CABBAGE, CABBAGE, &c.

In stall-feeding, as well as in soiling, great attention should be paid to the comfort and cleanliness of the cattle. Dr. Anderson says, they should not only be kept clean and well littered, but they should be curried daily in the manner of horses, and that they will fatten much faster, and keep better for this. He also says, that particular attention should be paid to their having pure water, and such as they are fond of. It is obvious, that if such water be not given to cattle, they will not drink as much as they want, and will, therefore, remain in a suffering condition, which is repugnant to good keeping or easy fatting. They should also have water often, so as not to be at any time suffering for want of it. Dr. Anderson states, that he knew a man who attained great opulence by attending strictly to these matters, particularly to the important point of having a continued supply of the purest water for his milch cows; nor would he suffer the animals to put a foot in it, or even to be tainted by their breath.

In addition to the various roots there used for feeding and fatting cattle, meal of different kinds is used to advantage, either when mixed with steamed or saw chopped roots, or with chopped hay, or straw. Instead of wasting the straw, as is but too common here, it is all saved, and used for littering, and for chopping up with straw-cutting machines, for the purpose of mixing with other food, and thus a great saving is made of hay. It would also be a great improvement to chop up our corn-stalks in the same manner. The kinds of grain which might be used here to most advantage for grinding up and mixing, as before mentioned, are probably Indian corn, rye, and buckwheat. Machines are also used in Great-Britain for grinding different kinds of grain by hand, with which a man may grind a bushel or more in a quarter of an hour.

In addition to the above articles for fatting and feeding are the grains of breweries and distilleries, and the refuse or wash of starch factories, which, as they are all in a state of acidity are considered by some to be the better on that account for fatting. Mr. Young particularly recommends, that all meal should be in a state of fermentation before it is fed out. The grains of breweries, &c. may be kept during summer in vats under ground, being first well trod down, and then well covered with a sufficient depth of earth. Oil cakes are also of great use for fatting, and for feeding to cows before calving, for the purpose of increasing their milk. It however makes the beef which is fatted solely with it, of a loose flabby texture, which is not so agreeable. Flaxseed broth, or jelly, is also much recommended for fatting. It is made by putting about a quart of flaxseed to seven of water, and then let stand about forty-eight hours; after which it is to be boiled gently for two hours, minding to stir it frequently, lest it burn. After it is cooled, it is to be mixed with meal, bran, or cut straw, and fed out at the rate of about two quarts a day to each beast, and it is said to make a great saving in the article of food.

It is stated in " *The Complete Grazier*," that an intelligent farmer of this country, but of what part is not mentioned, tried fatting with turnips from October until February, and that his cattle rather lost flesh; but that on his substituting hay, chopped potatoes, and Indian meal mixed together, they soon fattened. Probably a difference in climates may produce different results in regard to roots which are used for fatting. But as the cattle in question were fed entirely on turnips, which might have produced too great a degree of laxity or scouring, it is probable, that had the turnips only constituted the same proportion of food which the potatoes did, they might have proved equally nourishing. In regard, however, to raising the different articles for feeding and fatting, those should be cultivated which yield most in the different soils and climates of this country; and which at the same time, are found most efficacious for fatting, or in producing the most, and the richest and best flavored milk.

On the experimental farm of the Marchioness of Salisbury, (Great-Britain,) parsnips are preferred, as well for feeding as for fatting; and for the latter use are esteemed almost equal to the oil-cake. The milk of the cows fed with them, is also very plentiful, rich, and well tasted. Next to the parsnip, is, perhaps, the carrot. Mr. Young states, that four bullocks, six milch cows, and twenty working horses were fed a few years since at Partington, in Yorkshire, for above five months with carrots, which were the produce of three acres only, and with no other food than a little hay during that time. He adds, that the milk was excellent in quality and flavor; and that the refuse or waste, with a small quantity of other food, fatted thirty swine.

The hay used for feeding and fatting is greatly improved by the addition of a little salt. Mr. Darke, of Breedon, (Great-Britain,) says, that by adding only eight pounds of salt to a ton of flooded mouldy hay, he found that his oxen did better on it than others which were fed on the best.

The proprietors of the Bolingbroke distillery, near London, says the compiler of "*The Complete Grazier*," have erected stalls for fatting about three hundred and fifty head of cattle at a time. The stalls are paved with brick, and great attention is paid to keeping them clean. The food for fatting is the wash or grains of the stills, and hay, and occasionally, chopped oat or barley-straw. The hay or straw is given twice a day, that they may ruminate as usual; and they have as much grains as they can eat. In general, they come readily to this food; though some are four or five days before they become fond of it. They are usually fatted in about sixteen weeks. The grains are conveyed to the stalls in tight bodied carts, made for the purpose, and turned into vats fitted for their reception. Others again, practice chopping the hay and straw fine, and mixing it with the grains in the vats, and letting the mass lie two or three days, in order to give the taste of the hay to the whole. The cattle thus kept, afford great quantities of excellent manure. Particular attention is paid to their littering, in order, that when done eating, they may lie down and repose comfortably; for comfortable and quiet repose, as well as cleanliness, is deemed essential to their speedy fatting.

It would seem, that the saccharine parts of vegetables contribute very essentially in fatting, and for this reason, molasses has been successfully used in the West-Indies for fatting the poor old worn out oxen that are used there. About half a pint is given them twice a day, mixed with other food for this purpose.

A beast will eat more in a cold day than in a warm damp one; and therefore, where messes are dealt out in stall feeding, regard should be had to this circumstance when the food is such as may cloy the cattle, and thus weaken their stomachs; for in that case they are liable to fall back until the tone of the stomach is recovered. Regularity in the times of feeding, and that those times be as nearly equi-distant as possible, are also essential points to be observed.

The quantity of food to be given to fatting cattle should be in proportion to the weight of each. An ox will eat a little less than a fifth of his weight per day of cabbages, and about a third of his weight of turnips, beside a little dry food to counteract the super-abundant moisture of the roots. For middle sized animals from a bushel to a bushel and a half of brewers or distiller's grains, with some dry food, will be consumed in a day. About a sixth part of the animal's weight, with the addition of some dry food, is the proper allowance, per day, of carrots or potatoes. About a pound of powdered oil-cake, and another of hay, for every hundred weight of the animal, is the usual allowance per day of this food; but the quantity of the former is to be gradually increased as the fatting progresses, until it is one half more than at first.

It is stated in the work last mentioned, that every load of hay and litter given to beasts fatting on oil-cake, will make seven loads of dung; and, that one load of this is more efficacious, as a manure, than two of common barn dung. It is also there stated, that Mr. Moody littered forty-five oxen, while fatting, with twenty waggon loads of stubble, and that the product of dung, when rotted and fermented, was six hundred tons. Another trial is also there mentioned, of Mr. White, who tied up thirty-six cows and four horses, and while they ate fifty tons of hay and had twenty acres of straw for litter, made three hundred tons of rotten dung, in good order for the land.

In addition to gathering stubble for the purpose of littering, our farmers may supply themselves with ample quantities of dry leaves every fall; as they may be easily raked up and gathered in the woods, for the purpose. Mr. Livingston makes mention of his having used this substitute, in his valuable essay on sheep.

It may not be amiss to observe, in concluding our remarks on feeding and fatting, that as the larger English breeds require richer pastures for thriving well than the smaller, many of the best English graziers have latterly preferred the best selections of the latter, as being on the whole most profitable.

When a beast is well fatted, outwardly, it is indicated by its plump and comely appearance; its skin on the lowermost ribs will feel *kindly* and *mellow*, as the English graziers say—that is, soft and yet firm to the touch; the part where the tail is set on, will feel plump and soft; and the *natch bones*, as they are called, which lie on either side of the root of the tail, will feel loose and well covered. When also the cod of the ox, or the navel of the cow feel thick, round and plump, and the hips are well covered, these are indications of their being well lined with tallow.

As the grazier is usually less skilled in judging of the weight of live cattle than the butcher, Lord Kaims advises selling them by weight. This may be done in a manner very similar to that commonly practised for weighing loads of hay. The beast is to be suspended by being put in a box made for the purpose.

The weighing of cattle, Lord Kaims well observes, is also useful in order to ascertain whether each beast fattens in proportion to the value of the food bestowed on it; as it may, in some instances, be best to dispose of such as do not.

The four quarters, says Lord Kaims, are about half of the whole weight of the beast when alive, and when its belly is moderately full; the skin is about the eighteenth part; the tallow about the twelfth; the remainder is composed of the head, feet, tripe, blood, &c. which offals never sell by weight, but in proportion to the weight of the beast. With a knowledge, therefore, of these particulars, and of the market price of the beef, tallow, skin, &c. the farmer or grazier can ascertain what his beasts are worth when alive.

By weighing fatted calves when alive, says the same author, and deducting eight pounds from every twenty, the remainder will prove to be about the weight of the four quarters.

The diseases of neat cattle are various: and frequently new and uncommon diseases occur. A farmer in this vicinity, (*Herkimer,*) informs me that he lost eleven head during the last winter, (1813,) by a new, and till then, unknown disease. When his cattle were attacked with this disorder, it was indicated by small protuberances appearing round the neck; and after the beasts died, some of these were opened, and were found to be full of worms or maggots. Probably, if these lumps or protuberances had been opened and cleansed, when they first appeared, the cattle might have been saved.

A disorder prevails among neat cattle in the northern parts of this state, which is usually termed the *hoof-ail*. It has ruined many hundred cattle in this county. It would seem that the feet of the cattle first become diseased, and then they are frozen during the course of the winter, after which they are of no further value except for their skins.

There is probably something in certain soils which is calculated to injure the feet of cattle in the fall, and thus render them more liable to the frosts of winter. In Herkimer county, those cattle which are kept on farms of moist rich soil have been most liable to this disorder; and it is believed, that such as are fed on sandy, sandy loam, or gravelly farms, have seldom suffered in this way. Probably it would be found, that pursuing the soiling husbandry, feeding the cattle with plenty of rich food, as has been before directed, and keeping them well littered in warm stables, would at once be the most profitable and effectual method of avoiding this disorder.

In the spring, our cattle which have been poorly kept through the winter, are subject to a wasting of the pith of the horn, which is usually called the *horn distemper*. It is sometimes in one horn only and sometimes in both. The indications of the disease are coldness of the horn, dullness of the eyes, sluggishness, want of appetite, and a disposition to lie down. When the brain is affected, the animal will toss its head, groan, and exhibit indications of great pain. To cure the disease, bore a hole with a small gimblet in the lower side of the horn, about an inch from the head, and the corrupted matter in the horn will run out. If this does not complete the cure, Mr. Deane directs, that the horn have a mixture of rum, honey, myrrh, and aloes thrown into it with a syringe; and that this be repeated till the cure be effected. Probably warm water thrown in would answer just as well; as the essential point seems to be to cleanse the horn of the corrupted matter.

Another disease, to which our poorly kept cattle are subject in the spring, is commonly called the *tail sickness*. In this case the tail becomes hollow and relaxed. The cure is effected, says Mr. Deane, by cutting of a small piece of the tail, which will be attended with a small discharge of blood; or when the hollow part is near the end, cut a slit in it one or two inches long and this will effect a cure.

21

The *gripes* or *cholic*, is mostly troublesome to young cattle. When attacked with it, they lie down and rise up incessantly, and keep striking their horns against any object that presents. It is attended either with costiveness or scouring. In the former case, they are to be treated with purgatives, and in the latter with restringents. To stop the purging, give them half a pint of olive oil sweetened with sugar; or a quart of ale mixed with a few drops of laudanum, and two or three ounces of oil of sweet almonds. To promote purging, give them five or six drachms of fine Barbadoes aloes, and half a pint of brandy, mixed with two quarts of water-gruel, in a lukewarm state. These are the directions of " *The Complete Grazier ;*" but it is believed, that other purgatives and restringents would answer as well. In either case speedy attention to the beast is necessary, in order to prevent an inflammation of the intestines, which must prove fatal.

The *scouring* is known in neat cattle by the frequent discharge of slimy excrement, loss of appetite, loss of flesh, increasing paleness of the eyes, and general debility. The beast should be immediately housed and put to dry food, and this in the early stages of the disease, will generally effect a cure. Should it, however, fail, it is directed in the work last mentioned, to boil a pound of mutton suet in three quarts of milk, till the former is dissolved, and give it to the beast in a lukewarm state; or, in obstinate cases, boil half a pound of powdered chalk in two quarts of water, till it is reduced to three pints; add four ounces of hartshorn shavings, one of casia, and stir the whole together; when cold, add a pint of lime water and two drachms of the tincture of opium; keep the whole in a corked bottle, and after shaking it before using, give one or two hornsful two or three times a day, as the nature of the case may require. Sometimes, however, this disease proves incurable.

Cattle sometimes become *hoven*, as it is termed, owing to eating too much when first turned into rich pastures, to swallowing potatoes, or other roots without sufficient chewing, and to other causes. The stomach of the animal becomes distended with wind, and if a vent for this cannot be afforded the beast must die.

The usual remedy is to open a hole with a sharp pointed knife, with a blade three or four inches long, between the hip and the short ribs, where the swelling rises highest, and insert a small tube in the orifice, till the wind ceases to be troublesome. The wound will soon heal again.

But some of the English graziers have adopted an improved method of obviating this complaint; this is by providing a flexible tube, with a knob at one end ; the tube with the knob-end foremost, is run down the throat of the beast into its stomach, and then the confined air escapes through the tube. The operation is repeated if necessary. The tube for a large ox should be upwards of six feet long, as that is about the length requisite to reach to the bottom of his stomach.

The method recommended by Mr. Young for curing this complaint, is, to take three fourths of a pint of olive-oil, and a pint of melted butter, or hog's-lard, and pour this mixture down the throat of the beast; and, if no favorable change be produced in a quarter of an hour, repeat the dose. For sheep, about a gill should, in like manner, be given, and the dose repeated, if necessary. Mr. Young asserts this to be a specific which will not fail of a cure in half an hour.

To prevent this disorder, cattle should not be turned at first with empty stomachs into rich pastures; nor should they be allowed to feed on potatoes and some other roots, without their being first cut in pieces. Where a beast, however, happens to get one of these in its throat, which cannot be forced down, take a smooth pliable rod and make a knob on the end, by winding and tying rags round it, and run this down its throat into the stomach, which will force all before it into that receptacle.

The *staggers* are easily known by the drowsiness, lethargy, and staggering gait of the animal. This disorder is sometimes occasioned by plethora, or fullness of blood, and sometimes it is seated on the brain; in which case it is incurable, unless by trepanning. In the former case, the remedy is to keep the beast housed and bleed and purge it sufficiently.

For wounds of cattle, *see* article WOUNDS.

The *overflowing of the gall*, which is also sometimes called the *yellows* or *jaundice*, is known by the yellow tinge in the mouth and eyes, and sometimes the whole body assumes a yellowish cast. The nose is dry; the udder of the cow becomes swollen, and yields but little milk, which also becomes yellow and curdled on being boiled, and sometimes the fore teeth become very loose.

The beast affected with this disorder should be housed and have two or three gentle purges ; then give it, twice a day, a pint of beer in which has been infused, for three or four days, about an ounce to each quart of the filings of iron, and a small quantity of hard soap. Let the beast be well kept during the time with warm messes of bran, and other nourishing food, to which some olive-oil, or other purgative medicine should be added, if the beast be costive.

For curing this disorder, Mr. Deane directs, to take an egg and empty it of its white, retaining its yolk, and fill the cavity with equal quantities of soot, salt, and black pepper; draw out the tongue of the beast, and with a smooth stick push the egg down its throat. Repeat this two or three mornings, and he says, it will seldom fail of a cure.

Sometimes, however, this disorder does not yield to the power of medicine, but at length turns to the *black jaundice*, which is incurable.

The disorder called *red water*, or voiding bloody urine, it is believed, has seldom or never prevailed in this country. Its attacks are mostly on young beasts, which in that case are seen leaving the herd and exhibiting frequent ineffectual attempts to void urine.

The British practice has been to house the beast and give it two doses of glauber-salts, of a pound each, in two succeeding days; but this practice is condemned in " *The Complete Grazier,*" and instead of purgatives, strong decoctions of Peruvian or white-oak bark and alum, are recommended to be given, in such quantities, and at such times, as the violence of the disease may require.

The *pantasie* is known by the panting or heaving of the animal's flanks, which is accompanied with trembling and a decay of flesh. House the beast, and give it, every six hours, during the continuance of the chilly symptoms, a quart of warm strong beer, in which a table spoonful of laudanum, another of ground ginger, and two of the spirits of hartshorn have been infused. The beast should be fed on sweet hay, and well littered. Its drink should be warm water, with a little nitre dissolved in it, if there be symptoms of fever. As it gains strength, let it out in the middle of the day, until such time as it has fully recovered.

The *inflammation of the liver* is indicated by fever, difficult breathing, a swelling near the shorter ribs, and in cows, a remarkable distension about the womb. Cattle affected with this disorder will never fatten. It is sometimes hereditary in certain breeds; in which case, it is incurable. In the work last mentioned, it is recommended to house the beast, bleed it profusely, and give it the following medicine in a tepid state, viz :

Saltpetre and glauber's salts, of each two ounces; Venice treacle, mithridate and white ginger, pulverized, of each one ounce; let these be boiled in three pints of water, in which may be gradually added, one gill of oil of sweet almonds, the whole being stirred together. This is sufficient for one dose, which should be repeated the succeeding day.

Warm messes of bran should be the principal diet of the beast till it has recovered.

The *inflammation of the lungs* is known by a shortness of breath, and a painful cough. The animal looks dull; the skin is hot and harsh; and a copious discharge of thick ropy phlegm issues from its mouth. House the beast, bleed it plentifully, and give it a dose composed of the flour of sulphur, balsam of sulphur, syrup of colt's-foot and oil of sweet almonds, of each an ounce, blended together. If the above treatment produces no visible alteration in eighteen hours, repeat it. Probably any other purge would answer as well as the above. Let the beast be kept comfortable and have some exercise every day till it recovers.

The *locked-jaw* is similar to that in the human frame, is caused by similar means, and requires a similar treatment. If the beast be hardy opiate frictions, and dashing on of cold water is recommended. If it be of slender constitution, opiate frictions and warm fomentations of the part affected is directed. As the beast cannot swallow, let gruel be poured down its throat with a horn till the disorder is removed.

The indications of *colds* in cattle, to which they are mostly liable in the spring, are hollowness of the flanks, roughness of the coat, heat of the breath, and running at the eyes. House the beast, keep it warm, and if it be very feverish, bleed it pretty freely, and let its drink be warm, and have some nitre dissolved in it. Expose it to the air, at first, in the middle of pleasant days, when recovering.

Cattle are sometimes poisoned by eating poisonous plants, or by being bit with mad dogs, &c. In the latter case, if the wounded part be cut away shortly after the bite, and then be kept open for some time, it is, perhaps, the only effectual remedy. Dr. Crouse's prescription for curing the bite of mad dogs, as made public in pursuance of a law of this state, is believed by many to be effectual, and is certainly worth the trial. It is believed, that any medicine which is very strongly anti-spasmodic, if given plentifully, and in proper season, will counteract the effects of the bite of mad animals.

For the bite of rattle-snakes and most other vipers, a plentiful dose, and repeated when necessary, of olive-oil, has been found effectual in most cases.

Other diseases of neat-cattle, it may not be amiss to mention, which have, at times, prevailed in particular places. Some years since, a very fatal disease, which principally attacked calves in the fall, and yearlings in May and June, and sometimes older cattle, prevailed in

Connecticut. It was called the *mortification*. Those in the best condition were most liable to it. Its symptoms were an aversion to move, a swelling most commonly in the region of the kidney, but sometimes in the shoulder, leg, flank, or side, &c. ; and in a short time the beast died with little pain, but with a very fœtid smell. On examining the swellings, they were found to contain a jelly and black blood. The cause was ascribed to fulness of habit, and a too sudden change from indifferent pastures into such as are very rich. Bleeding was recommended as a preventive. No cure was discovered.

A disease, something similar to the above, prevailed, about sixty years since, in the north of England, which was commonly called the *black quarter*. Bleeding was found a preventive ; but in very few instances was a cure effected, after the beast was seized with the disorder. This was ascribed to too much succulent food when given to beasts of full habit.

It would seem, generally, that cattle in a plethoric state, when overfed with rich food, or when too suddenly surfeited with it, are suddenly indisposed and carried off before relief can be given. There are, however, epidemics among cattle, as well as among men, the precise causes of which may oftentimes be difficult to ascertain. Generally speaking, it is believed, that among the horned race either plentiful bleeding, or purging, or both, will be found a preventive, and in most instances, a cure, of the maladies which are usually most fatal to them from too full habit.

When oxen are long and hardly drove in muddy roads, particularly where the soil is calcarious, they are liable to a soreness between their claws. This will make the beast lame ; and when discovered, the part should be cleansed and healed with some proper ointment. Sometimes, from inattention to this, the part becomes horny ; in this case, the hard parts must be cut away and the wounded flesh cured.

A general indication of health in neat cattle is a moist or wet nose, and when this is found dry, it is a certain symptom of disease of some kind or other.

Cows have some diseases which are peculiar to them, such as those attendant on calving, and such as affect the udder, &c.

The udder is divided into as many apartments as there are teats, so that if one or more of these are diseased, this does not affect the rest. The milk of one teat may be good and that of another bad. The udders of cows may be injured in various ways, and swellings and inflammations are the usual consequence. These must be removed, or the beast will be in danger. Mr. Deane, speaking of hard swellings in the udder, which he calls the *garget*, recommends making a rowel or seton in the dewlap, and inserting therein a piece of the root of *mcchoacan*, as large as a nutmeg, with a string fastened to it, so that it may be drawn out when the cure is effected ; and this, he says, will cause a revulsion of the humor in the udder into the orifice in the dewlap, where it will be discharged. When the cure is effected, the piece of root is to be drawn out by the string. Probably a common rowel placed in the breast or dewlap, would answer the same purpose. Where hard tumors have formed, the compiler of " *The Complete Grasier*" recommends, to take of common hemlock, (*conium maculatum,*) dwarf or round leaved mallow, (*malva rotundifolia,*) and common millilot, (*trifolium millilotus,*) of each a handful, and boil them in water ; with this wash the tumor, after it has opened ; the water to be as warm as the beast can bear it ; and after thus cleansing the part, cover it with a plaister of basilicon ointment. The following is also recommended in the last mentioned work, in obstinate cases of ulcerated udders ; take gum ammoniac, gum galbanum, castile-soap, and extract of hemlock, of each one ounce ; form them into eight bolusses, and give one every morning and evening. It is observed in the same work, that internal remedies are always necessary where the udder and teats are considerably inflamed, and for this purpose another internal medicine is mentioned, viz : Four ounces of nitre mixed with a pound of common salt ; give two table spoonsful of this, powdered in a gallon of thin water-gruel, every three hours.

Where the inflammations are less violent and exhibit no symptoms of increasing rapidly, it may answer to anoint the udder frequently during the day, with fresh butter ; or with a salve made of an ounce of castile-soap, dissolved in a pint of sweet milk over a gentle fire ; or with an ointment made with the juice of the leaves of the thorn ; mixed with hogslard ; or the tumor may be anointed with a little mixture of camphor and blue ointment ; and let about half a drachm of calomel be given, in a hornful of warm beer, if the malady increase.

Where the teats are only sore, they may be washed with soap-suds, and rubbed with an ointment made of white-lead and goose-grease, or fresh butter would perhaps do as well.

The proper position for the calf to lie in the calf-bed has already been mentioned ; where, therefore, it is not presented in this position, at the time for its birth, and by reason of this the cow cannot deliver her burden, it becomes necessary, if possible, to place it properly. Where this cannot be done, the method of extracting it by a hook fixed in the under jaw, as before mentioned, may be frequently successfully practiced. Sometimes the hind parts of the calf are foremost; and in this case it is best to extract it in that position, by proper force used for the purpose. Whatever assistance, however, may be requisite in these cases, it should be given with care and judgment, minding to hurt the cow as little as possible.

Another impediment to calving, as noticed in the last mentioned work, is owing to a part of the natural passage becoming of so horny or firm a texture, that it will not yield or distend. When on due examination this is found to be the case, insert a sharp pointed penknife with the forefinger to the back of it, to guide it correctly, and with this carefully cut the horny circle through, which will immediately give the animal the requisite relief, if proper assistance be also given. In this case, as in others where the passage is wounded, or torn, it should be bathed with a pint of camphorated spirit of wine, injected with a syringe; the beast should be housed and kept moderately warm, and well and dryly littered, and be fed with wholesome nourishing food, and with drink a little warmed.

The *falling down of the calf-bed* frequently happens after a laborious birth; though some cows are naturally disposed to this disorder. Where this is apprehended, it is directed in the last mentioned work, that the cow should be carefully watched, and the placenta, or cleaning, removed without effusion of blood; after which the operator may gently replace the calf-bed, taking care not to withdraw his hand till the former begins to feel warm. The following draught may then be given: Of bay-berries, pulverized gentian-root, and corriander-seeds, each an ounce; of aniseed and juniper-berries, each two ounces; together with half a pound of treacle, and the whole put into three pints of strong beer. After this, it is advisable to lead the beast gently down a hill, if one be near, which will assist much in placing the calf-bed in its proper place, and render the application of stays to the womb unnecessary. Where the calf-bed, however, comes down, and no immediate aid can be had, the parts exposed should be laid on, and kept covered with a linen cloth; and when replaced, bathed with a mixture of new milk and spirits; after which the above treatment may be pursued.

Some cows have a peculiar shape of the hinder parts which tends to produce this malady; and in such case, it is perhaps difficult to prevent it, unless it can be done by keeping their hinder parts higher than usual, while confined to their stalls, about the period of gestation.

The *puerperal fever* is caused by taking cold while calving. Cows thus affected should have housing and good treatment, as has been directed in other cases, and the head should be placed highest, in order to assist the natural discharges. In other respects they should be treated as in cases of violent colds, except that no blood should be taken, unless, perhaps, in violent cases, and then only at the commencement of the disorder.

Close attention should be paid to cows, as well as to the females of other kinds of cattle, about their periods of gestation. They often then stand in need of some skilful aids, which, if rendered in due season, may save their lives; and which if not thus afforded, may be of essential loss to the owner.

Calves are also liable to some diseases, and in some countries, to such as do not prevail in others. In this, it is believed, they are subject to but few. One, however, which frequently attacks them is *looseness* or *scouring*. It is sometimes caused by their having the milk of the dam too soon; sometimes by too frequent changes of the milk which is given it. One method of cure is to stint the animal of its food, and give it once or twice while fasting, a hard boiled egg, mashed fine and well mixed with its milk. Another directs that powdered chalk, mixed with wheat flour, and made into balls with gin, (brandy would seem to be better,) be given the animal as a safe medicine.

Calves are also liable to *colds*, in which case they should have a treatment similar to older neat cattle.

In the foregoing observations, which are rather miscellaneous in point of form, no attention has been paid to the various terms which many English farmers and graziers apply to cattle of different kinds, ages, and conditions, further than such terms are usual in this country. We have plain English enough for every purpose of this kind; and there is no need of farmers having a vocabulary for cattle, consisting of barbarous words, which none but themselves would be likely to understand.

NEW HORSE-HOEING HUSBANDRY. In the year 1731, Mr. Tull, an ingenious farmer of Great-Britain, published a book under this title, and afterwards further supplementary essays on the same subject, the object of which was to introduce a new system of husbandry, particularly in the culture of wheat. His method is this: The ground is ploughed into ridges of about five, six, or seven feet wide, and then smoothed with the harrow; then the seed is sown in straight lines by a drill in small furrows, about two inches deep; two of these furrows being placed together at the distance of about nine inches, with an interval between these and the next two of about two feet; so that a horse-hoe, or a horse-plough can be run between them. As the seeds are dropped by the drill-plough, they are covered by little harrows, which are fastened to the plough, and follow after it. The horse-hoe has already been mentioned; it is the invention of Mr. Tull; but I imagine the one horse plough is just as good. After the plants of wheat have got to a proper size in the fall, the horse-hoe, or plough, is run close to the plants, on each side of the double rows, and the furrows are turned from them; and thus, Mr. Tull says, the growing grain should be left during winter; it being, by this process, laid so dry, that it will be in no danger of being thrown out of ground by the winter frosts.

Early in the spring the earth is to be turned to the rows, then in May, from them, and in June to them again. Some weeds which will rise between the double rows and round the stalks, must be taken out by hand.

This culture, Mr. Tull says, is equally well applied to barley, and some other kinds of grain. For barley, it has been found to answer very well here; but for wheat, in particular, it will not answer. It makes this grain grow so rank and thrifty, and continue so much beyond the usual time in the green state, that it generally becomes blasted or mildewed. Probably the same fate would, in some measure, attend this kind of culture with regard to rye, if a culture so expensive could, in this country, be afforded to that grain.

Mr. Tull's leading principle is, that frequent ploughings have the same effect on lands as manuring; and this, in general, is believed to be correct though not equally in all soils; that by this constant ploughing or horse-hoeing, the lands will be sufficiently and constantly manured; that soils not very rich can, in this way, be made to produce very large crops; and what is sometimes important, they can thus be made to produce the same crops every year; as the ground is ploughed up again as soon as the grown crop has been harvested.

Although the husbandry of Mr. Tull will probably never come into general use in Great-Britain, where, from the coolness of the summers it will always answer best; yet, the drill plough, and the method recommended by him, of ploughing among plants, are each founded in an accurate knowledge of good husbandry, and the latter will ever be found best in the cultivation of many plants; such as beans, Indian corn, carrots, cabbages, potatoes, &c. ; and, no doubt, barley, and probably, some other kinds of grain may in this manner be successfully cultivated.

Mr. Dean says, he has cultivated barley in this way and never had less than forty bushels to the acre.

NURSERY. It is not advisable to make a nursery on too rich a spot, because if the trees be afterwards transplanted into poorer ground they will not thrive so well. It is better that the change by transplanting, be from a poorer to a richer soil. A gravelly loam, or sandy loam, should be preferred for a nursery.

Let the ground be ploughed very deeply, early in the fall, and be well mellowed; then lay the seeds, or stones, along in straight rows, and let them be laid plentifully, in order that enough may come up. The next year they are to be thinned, so as to stand at proper distances, and the ground is to be kept hoed, and clear of weeds and grass. After they have had one summer's growth, they may be cut off near the ground for grafting.

See article GRAFTING.

Inoculation, may also, at this growth, be successfully performed on them.

See article INOCULATION.

They should afterwards be kept clear of weeds and grass, by hoeing among them, until they are transplanted.

Where snows fall deep, they are apt to bend down the young trees, and make them crooked; the best remedy for this, is, to drive down stakes, proportinate to the height of the young trees, and tie them to these in such manner, that the bark will not be injured by the string, nor by rubbing against the stakes. This is to be done after grafting them.

Some sow the seeds, or stones, on a small spot, and afterwards plant them out in the nursery. This may be best for stone fruit; but for apple-trees, sowing the seeds in the pumace is the easiest method, and answers as well as any ; and for other seeds, or for acorns, if oaks are to be raised in a nursery, the above method will answer very well.

Many trees are propagated from the slips, or cuttings, such as the Lombardy poplar, mulberry, and others.

For raising apple-trees in this way, *see* article SLIPS.

O.

OAK; *(Quercus.)* European writers mention many more species of the oak than we have in this country. We have the *live-oak*, which is a native of the southern states; the *black-jack*, which is found in the middle states; the *black-oak*; the *chesnut-oak*; the *shrub-oak*; and the *red-oak*, of which botanists reckon three varieties; the *red*, the *yellow*, and the *swamp-oak*. All the different species, except the two first, are to be found in each of the states.

The white-oak, which grows in moist uplands, is generally of the most rapid growth, and the firmest timber; and, therefore, such grounds ought to be chosen for cultivating it, as it is the oak that is generally preferred for cultivation.

For an approved method of cultivating it, *see* article FORESTS.

The oak is also cultivated in nurseries, and then transplanted at pleasure.

Mr. Forsyth, in speaking of those which are raised in nurseries, says, it is a generally received opinion, that when an oak looses its tap root in transplanting, it never produces another; but this he found to be a mistake. He transplanted a bed of oak plants into a fresh bed, cutting off the tap roots near the small fibres shooting from them; the second year afterwards he *headed down* one half of the plants, and the other half he left to nature.

For his method of *heading down*, *see* article FRUIT-TREES.

During the first season, those which were headed down made shoots six feet in length, and covered the tops of the old stems, leaving only a slight cicatrix, and produced new tap roots upwards of two feet long.

The others which were not headed down, did not grow to one fourth of this length. He further says, that when the former were eighteen feet high, the latter were only five. This case is cited by him as a striking instance of the superiority of his method of *heading down* over the common method of managing trees.

His method of curing, or restoring old hollow and diseased trees, which are partly dead, is also generally applicable to the oak.

For the method of doing this, *see* also article FRUIT-TREES.

The farmer who finds his stock of good oak timber growing more scarce, should turn his attention to the means of replenishing his farm with this valuable timber. When planted on little heights and declivities, he may find the growth of oaks ornamental to his farm, as well as profitable, by raising its value; and it may afford him much pleasure, in his more advanced years, to observe their increased dimensions, while in his mind he rolls back the wheels of time to that period when they were but acorns in his hand.

The bark of the white oak is best for tanning. The inner bark of it when reduced to a powder, and administered in the manner of the Peruvian bark, answers nearly the same purpose, but the doses must be larger.

The juice of the galls of the shrub-oak, is excellent for making the best ink, and is also a component part in black dies. They are formed by an insect's depositing its eggs in the tender rind of the twigs of the tree; and through the wound thus made, this black juice oozes, and forms a tumor, sometimes as large as a walnut, in the heart of which the young insect is to be found.

OATS: *(Avena.)* The clear profit which can be obtained from a crop of oats is at best but small. They exhaust the soil, and render it unfit for bearing a good succeeding crop of wheat. Their principal recommendation is, that they are an excellent food for horses, particularly in travelling, being of a loosening nature, while most other grains are binding.

Carrots and potatoes may be made good substitutes for oats; and of these, an acre will produce an abundance, without essential injury to the soil.

Oats, like most other kinds of grain, require the ground to be pretty well prepared and to be in good heart. It is a mistaken notion, that they will do well with indifferent culture. If the ground be suitable for gypsum, that manure applied to the crop will greatly increase it. Two bushels are generally sowed to the acre, but whether so much seed be necessary, is doubtful. I have seen very heavy crops raised, where but one bushel to the acre was sown.

A moist soil and a moist climate is best for oats; in order, therefore, that they may not be cut short by the early droughts which frequently prevail, it is advisable to sow them as early as the ground can be well prepared. They will, however, do very well when sowed late, provided they have moisture sufficient during the heat of summer.

Oats, like most other grains, will degenerate, if the seed be not frequently changed.

OLIVE; *(Olea.)* This tree is famous for the production of oil. It thrives well in Italy and the southern parts of France, and it is believed, it would grow well in some of the southern states. The winters here are too severe for it. We have, however, a plant which is said to be an excellent substitute.

See article SUN-FLOWER.

It has been found, in France, that immersing the olive fruit in vinegar, before pressing out the oil, will improve the quality, and add a tenth more to the quantity.

ONION; *(Allium.)* In the northern parts of this state, onions may be raised on soils which are suitable, at the rate of 500 bushels to the acre, and perhaps more. They require a warm, rich, mellow soil; and if it be somewhat sandy, it will be the better. They will grow year after year in the same soil.

To prepare the ground at first for this crop, it is well to plough it in the fall, but not deep. It is said, that they will grow well, yearly, on the same soil, without ploughing or digging, but by merely loosen, ing the ground to the depth of two inches by a heavy iron rake. Be this as it may, the-ground ought to be well mellowed on the top, and then marked out into beds about four feet wide; then with the end of a stick draw lines across the beds, about ten inches apart and strew the seeds evenly along in these, and cover them over by hand. They may also be sowed with a little hand drill. For fear the seeds may not all come up, it is best to sow them pretty thick, and if they come up too thickly, they can afterwards be thinned. Some plant them in holes, about ten inches distant from each other, in straight rows, each way like hills of corn, putting about eight seeds in each hole. This method is attended with the least trouble in weeding, as the weeding hoe can be run each way between the bunches while growing, though it is believed, that the other method will give the greatest product.

After the plants have come up, all that is requisite is to be vigilant in destroying the weeds by the hoe and hand-weeding, as often as they appear. It is essential to keep the weeding hoe well ground, as it will not cut off the weeds unless it be kept sharp. Its edge should be of well hardened steel.

When the stalks have become dead and dry, the onions will have ceased to grow, and then they should be pulled, and laid on the ground some days, to dry and harden, before they are carried in. Those which have thick necks and the bulbous part small, and are commonly called *scallions*, may as well be left in the ground during the winter, as they will continue green till that time; they will stand the frosts, and the next spring will grow in their places to be good onions; or they may then be taken up and set in a bed made for that purpose. At all events, they are good for nothing without a second year's growth.

There is a kind of onion, which, instead of bearing seed, bears bunches of small onions on its top, and these being preserved and set out the next year, grow to be large, and their tops again bear the small ones. Probably these are best calculated for more southerly climates, though they grow very well in this.

In the fall, after the onions have been dried, and the tops cut off, they are to be carried in and spread over a floor; and, at the commencement of cold weather, put into casks, and set in a place where they will not freeze. A little freezing, however, will not essentially injure them. The place where they are kept, should not, at all events, be too warm and moist, as this will cause them to rot. If they be kept where they are somewhat frozen, they should not be disturbed in their frozen state; but the better way is, not to suffer them to be frozen, but to keep them in a temperature a little above the freezing point.

Those which are shipped from New-England, for market, are usually tied up in wisps of straw, and if they be hung up in this way, they will, perhaps, keep longer than any other. If they incline to sprout, sear the roots with a hot iron, which will stop their growth.

To obtain seed from the onions, plant them in the spring in beds, about nine inches apart. Take the largest and soundest for this purpose, and keep them clear of weeds while growing. When they have come to a head, tie them loosely to stakes drove down for that purpose; otherwise they will fall to the ground, and then the seeds will not come to perfection.

Soot is said to be the best manure for this root, and ashes are also said to be good. If dung be used, it should be such as is well rotted, and in which there is no seeds of weeds.

Some practice beating down the tops when the onions have acquired a pretty good size, for the purpose of making the roots grow faster; but it is doubtful whether this be any service to them.

ORCHARD. Farmers often make use of their most level pieces of land for planting their apple-orchards, but this is sometimes bad management, as such grounds should be reserved for the plough. Uneven grounds ought rather to be applied to this purpose, if the soil be good. The best soil is a fertile sandy loam, or gravelly loam. A fertile sandy soil will do much better than a stiff soil, though it be ever so rich.

The first step toward making a good orchard is to prepare a nursery of the best grafted fruit, of such kinds as are suitable to the different uses to which they are to be applied. Cyder being the principal, the scions for grafting should be taken from trees which have the following qualifications; that bear every year and plentifully, of apples that ripen in the right time for making this liquor, and which are mellow, of a rich juice, and make a fine tasted cider. Trees possessing all these qualifications in the highest degree, are not perhaps to be found in every orchard; but they should be sought after; and, wherever found, they alone should be used for obtaining a supply of scions. The mere grafting indiscriminately from other trees, without any regard to the goodness of their fruit is of no use to an orchard. Trees may be found which yield, on an average, forty bushels of good cider apples every year, which is sufficient to make five barrels of cider: Sixty of such trees may stand on an acre, and would give three hundred barrels of cider; which is, probably, ten times the product that is usually obtained from that extent of ground. Say, however, that trees can be selected, which, after they have grown to a good size, will, on an average, each yield, yearly, twenty bushels of apples; this will be sufficient to shew the vast importance of grafting from the best selected fruit-trees, in preference to planting orchards in the common way.

It is well for the farmer to have four or five different kinds of cider apples in his orchard, and some that ripen sooner than others, in order that he may have more time allowed him for making all his cider; but it is believed to be much the best not to mix different kinds of apples together in making it.

See article CIDER.

The same pains ought to be taken in the selection of scions from proper trees, to afford yearly, a sufficient stock of winter apples. The like attention should be paid to having a proper selection of early apples for summer use.

Some very fine apples, of different kinds, for cider, and other uses, are extensively cultivated in New-Jersey, which may be found well worth the attention of the farmer in procuring scions from the different trees.

In planting an orchard, it is advisable to set the trees pretty closely; and if they are found, when they are well grown, to be too close, the poorest ones may be then taken down to afford more room for the rest. The distance, therefore, of from twenty to twenty-five feet, between the trees, will not be found too close at first. For the first five or six years, the ground should be well manured and cultivated with hoed crops; taking care to have the rows of trees in a line with the different rows of these crops, so as to be out of the way of the plough. The ground about the roots should be kept clear of grass and weeds, and the plough should not come so near as to injure them. A strong growth of grass immediately round every kind of young fruit-tree, is injurious to their growth, and therefore, should never be suffered.

Mr. Forsyth observes, that much the greater part of the wood of fruit-trees, grows on the north side; and, that therefore, the young trees when set out in the orchard, should be set with the same side to the north as when they stood in the nursery. For this purpose, the north side of the tree may be marked, before it is taken up.

Farmers should attend more to the cultivation of the pear-tree in their orchards. They are, perhaps, as profitable for cultivation as the apple-tree; they suit a stiff soil better; they may be equally improved by grafting; they are less liable to the ravages of insects; and the liquor called *perry*, which is made from them, is, perhaps, in no way inferior to cider, and is capable of the same improvements, by refining, freezing, &c. The cultivation of peach orchards, extensively, where the climate is suitable, is also well worth the attention of the farmer; besides their being fine for eating, and for various family uses, they are excellent for feeding and even fatting hogs, and the liquor made from them, when distilled, has considerable resemblance in taste to brandy. They are at the same time easily cultivated, and require but little ground. The best kinds, however, like the apple, and pear, are only to be obtained by inoculation.

See articles INOCULATION and PEACH-TREE.

The practice of pruning large apple-trees so severely as is done by many farmers, is absurd; as such a profuse mangling of the limbs cannot but lessen the quantity of fruit and injure the tree. The practice is not warranted by any writer on the subject. The suckers, the dead limbs, and those which rub against another, or that cross each other, should be taken away; but not many more. The proper time for doing this is early in the spring, or late in the fall.

I know a farmer who has a beautiful thrifty young orchard, growing on a fertile sandy soil, who every spring whitewashes, with lime, the bodies and some distance up the limbs of his trees; this is believed to be effectual in keeping off all insects and preventing the growth of moss. Mr. Forsyth recommends, for the same purpose, a mixture of fresh cow-dung, old urine and soap-suds.

It sometimes happens, that wood-peckers will fall upon apple-trees and pick the bark full of holes, which very much injures, and sometimes kills the trees. It is said, that cow-dung plaistered round the tree will cause them to desist.

Sheep sometimes get into orchards, in the winter, and eat off the bark from the trees. In such cases, if they have not cut off quite round the tree, Mr. Forsyth's composition might be successfully used in giving it a new coat; minding in the first instance to prepare the tree, agreeably to his directions, for receiving the wash.

See article FRUIT-TREES.

To make the orchard complete, says Mr. Forsyth, there ought to be, in addition to the apples, a due assortment of pears, plumbs, cherries, quinces, &c. &c. He also recommends, planting a row of nut-trees round the whole, as being not only ornamental, but highly useful in breaking off the high winds.

OVERFLOWING OF THE GALL. See article NEAT-CATTLE.

P.

PAINTING of **BUILDINGS,** &c. For painting the roofs of buildings, Mr. Patterson, of New-Jersey, has, some years since, given the following directions, which have been highly approved, as the best composition known for preserving the roofs of houses; as it is found, that it hardens by time, and is an effectual preventative against the roof taking fire from the sparks of the chimney.

" Take three parts of air slacked lime, two of wood-ashes, and one of fine sand; sift these through a fine sieve, and add as much linseed oil as will bring it to a consistence for working with a painter's brush. Great care must be taken to mix it perfectly." I believe grinding it as a paint would be an improvement; two coats are necessary; the first rather thin, the second as thick as can be conveniently worked.

Painting of wooden buildings, of every kind, is not only ornamental, but the owner is well repaid for this extra expense, by the greater durability which the paint gives to them. The wooden fences also, which are intended to be ornamental, round, and near buildings, should never be destitute of a good coat of paint.

A patent wash may be had of Oliver Whipple, of Columbia District, which is very cheap, having no oil in it, and which answers pretty well for coarse outside painting.

The patentee says it will last six years.

PARSNIP; (*Pastinaca.*) The cultivation proper for parsnips, is very similar to that of carrots, and the same kind of soil and manures are suitable for each. They, however, require the soil to be very deeply dug; eighteen inches is not too deep. They are full as good for feeding and fatting cattle as carrots, and are about equally productive. They might be cultivated to advantage for feeding in the spring, when the stock of carrots have become exhausted; as the best way to keep them over winter is to let them remain in the ground during that season. When dug in the fall for family use, the best way to keep them through the winter, is, to bury them in dry sand. In spring, those left in the ground and wanted for that use, should be taken up before they begin to sprout.

Probably the farmer would find the culture of parsnips nearly as profitable as that of carrots, particularly for spring feeding. They are planted in beds and sown or drilled in rows across the beds, having the rows about ten inches apart. The plants in the rows should, at the last hoeing, be thinned to the distance of about four inches. Those which are pulled out in thinning will then be good food for swine.

Freezing does not injure this root; and, therefore, those which are kept in winter for family use, had better be kept in rather a frozen state than otherwise; because, if kept too warm, they will sprout, and this spoils them for eating.

PASTURE. The subdivisions of land that is kept for the sole purpose of pasturing, should depend as well upon its fertility, as upon the number of the different kinds of cattle that are to be fed on it. Fifty acres of land that would only feed three cows during the season would not pay the expense of subdividing. On the contrary, if the farmer has but three cows, and has three acres of the best pasture land, he ought to divide this into at least two parts, so that the one can be growing while the other is feeding. Again, if he keeps twenty cows, and has twenty acres of the best pasture, he will find his account in having it divided into four parts, and pasturing each enclosure three or four days alternately. In this way pasture lands will keep at least one fourth more of cattle, and will keep them much better, than if the whole pasture were in one field.

Not only a change of pasture is beneficial, but a change of different kinds of cattle in the same pastures should be attended to. Thus let the milch-cows take the first cropping of each field, in rotation; then the horses and oxen, and the sheep next; in this way the last feeder will eat much grass that has been rejected by the former.

Wet, miry spots in pastures should be drained off, either by open, or hollow drains; for by this means, the grass in such spots will be doubled in quantity, and much improved in quality. Bushes should be cut out and destroyed; thistles, and other noxious weeds should be mowed down before they go to seed, and every means taken to eradicate them.

It is never advisable to pasture lands too closely, particularly in the fall, as this only tends to diminish the quantity the next year. In this respect it is the same with pastures as with meadows; the closer they are cropped the less will be the next year's supply.

Where the pasture has yielded much feed, there will, of course, be much dung dropped; to beat it to pieces, and scatter it over the field, will tend constantly to recruit it.

Sheep require no water in their pastures; it is also the better opinion, that calves should have none; and, generally speaking, that horses should have little or none, except when they are worked. The effect of this treatment is, that they become habituated to lie by in the heat of the day, and feed at night, when the dew is on the grass, which renders it more nourishing. Cows, however, ought to have water; and where their pastures afford none, the better way is to sink a well at that spot where the pasture lots corner together; and then with a little machinery, which will be but a trifle of expense, sufficient of water may usually be raised every day by the winds, for the purpose of filling the troughs as often as they are emptied. The methods of doing this are so simple and easy, that they are hardly necessary to be described.

See further, article WIND-MACHINERY.

In place of wells, however, artificial ponds are recommended by some.

See article PONDS.

In pastures which are on side hills, water may be easily obtained in another way; that is, by digging horizontally into the hill till you come to it, and then carrying it out in a pipe, or conductor, made for the purpose. Another method is to dig a well on a steep part of the hill, and place a syphon in it, with so small a pipe that it will not let off the water fast enough to exhaust the water in the well.

Another method of making a well, as recommended by M. Cadit de Vaux, is to bore a hole into the earth, with an augur or borer made for the purpose, until sufficient of good water is found. If that which is first found is not good, bore deeper, until you come to better; and bore sufficiently deep to afford a full supply. Let the hole be about eight or nine inches in diameter. As the augur gets filled with earth it is taken up, emptied, and let down again. After the hole is made, a wooden tube is inserted in it, and the water is raised by pumping.

This is a very cheap and safe method of making wells, and might be advantageously performed where the earth is free of stones and rocks.

Lastly, as a matter of ornament and of profit, let your pasture lands be planted with some useful trees, and probably, for this purpose, the locust will be found the best.

See article LOCUST.

The sugar-maple may also be found very advantageous, where the soil is suitable to it, and where a yearly supply of maple sugar is desired, which will be found an article of no small profit.

See article SYCAMORE.

For the best grasses for pastures, *see* article GRASSES.

PASTURE OF PLANTS. Every plant requires a given quantity of earth to nourish it, into which its roots extend for that purpose; and the quantity thus required is called the requisite *pasture* of the plant. Some require more earth and some less. Some require a greater superficial extent with less depth; while others require a greater depth with less superficial extent. For instance, a plant of Indian corn requires a superficial extent, of say, three feet in circumference, and a depth of six inches; while a root of the beet, carrot, or parsnip kind, requires a superficial extent of, perhaps, only twelve inches in circumference, but a depth of, say, fifteen inches. A plant of flax, on the contrary, will not require more than six inches in circumference and five inches in depth.

It will probably be found, that the greater depth is given to all plants, the less circumference they will require; that the roots will, in that case, shoot further downwards; and, therefore, the deeper you plough, the thicker you may sow. This is is a matter of nice calculation, and well worth the attention of the ingenious farmer.

In order to illucidate this, the proper method is to try various plants in beds of the same soil, culture, and dimensions, but dug of different depths, and the plants set at different distances, and then the results will lead to the truth. Thus, for instance, make four beds of carrots, which shall be dug equally well eight inches deep; let the roots in the first bed stand at the distance of four inches from each other; those of the second at the distance of six; those of the third at the distance of eight; and those of the fourth at the distance of twelve inches; and then let it be ascertained which bed has the greatest weight of carrots. In the mean time, have four other beds dug twelve inches deep; and four more dug eighteen inches deep; and plant one of each of them at the respective distances above mentioned, and ascertain what are the results of each. The same experiments can be tried with equal exactness on most other plants, and the results equally well ascertained.

PEACH-TREE; (*Amegdalus.*) Peaches are of two kinds, the clear-stone and the cling-stone; but there are good varieties of each. The same sorts can only be raised by grafting or innoculation; this may be on apricots, or on plum-trees, and will make the grafted trees longer lived.

The trees should have a warm, dry, fertile soil; a sandy loam is best. If the spot where they are planted be sheltered from the northerly winds, it will be the better.

To raise the young trees, take stones that are fully ripe, and plant them in October, they will come up and grow to a good size in the course of the summer. They are to be kept clear of weeds while in the nursery. At a year's growth they may be grafted, or innoculated, and after two summer's growth, they may then be transplanted. This may be done when the leaves have fallen in autumn, or in the spring. Take plants with one strong clean stem, or if they have two, cut one away, however fair. Let the downward root be cut off, in order that the tree derive its nourishment from earth nigh the surface, which will make the fruit less crude and finer tasted. Be careful not to plant the trees too deep, for this is injurious to all fruit. Let the pruning of the new planted trees be omitted till they have taken root.

Mr. Forsyth gives some particular directions for training, pruning, &c. the trees, to make them good bearers; all of which may be well enough for the climate of England, but does not seem necessary to be observed here. Where the climate is suitable for peaches in this country, that is, where the frosts of the winters do not kill them, they generally bear so much that the trees are frequently broken with the fruit, if part of it be not taken off.

Mr. Forsyth also gives a list of the best peaches raised in England, which ripen at the different months of the season for peaches; but no doubt, this country is capable of affording varieties equal, and perhaps superior, if sought after.

In making a proper selection of trees from which to graft, or inoculate, a due regard should be had to three essentials:

1. To obtain the grafts or buds, from trees bearing the finest fruit.

2. That this fruit should ripen at different times, from the earliest to the latest of the season for peaches; and,

3. That the grafts or buds be taken from trees which are plentiful bearers, but not such as bear so plentifully as to be broken by their fruit.

But perhaps the too plentiful bearing of trees is a quality not properly descendible to those which are raised from them by grafting or otherwise. It would be well to ascertain this point by experiment.

See further, articles FRUIT-TREES, NURSERY, TRANSPLANTING, &c. &c.

PEAR-TREE; *(Pyrus.)* This tree will grow better on a stiff clay than most other fruit-trees; but the soils which best suit the apple-tree are also most suitable for it. A scion of this tree may be grafted on an apple-tree; but it does not answer so well as when grafted on a quince, for dwarf-fruit; and a quince answers well to be grafted on a pear-tree. The pear will also grow on the white-thorn. The best way, however, is to graft the pear on its own natural stock, selecting scions from the best trees as in the case of apple-trees.

Let some part of the selection also, as in the case of peach-trees, last mentioned, be made from trees whose fruit ripens at different times, in order to have a full supply for family use. Generally, it may be observed, that the culture which is proper for an apple-tree, is also proper for a pear-tree.

See articles APPLE-TREES, ORCHARD, FRUIT-TREES, NURSERY, TRANSPLANTING, &c.

PEA; *(Pysum.)* There are a variety of peas, some of which are more and others less valuable for cultivation. Those most valuable for garden culture, are the small early peas, and the marrow-fat peas, as they are commonly called. The former do not grow more than three feet high; they ripen early, but are not very productive. The latter ripen later, but are much more productive. They require a double row of bushes to each double row of peas, setting the bushes firmly in the ground on the outside of the rows. The bushes should be of good length, as the stalks will grow five feet high, in a tolerable rich soil. The other kind, also require bushes, which may be shorter.

Peas of every kind for family use, may also be sown in the field, in the broad cast way, and this is the cheaper way of raising them, as the trouble of raising them in gardens is very considerable.

The culture of field-peas is considerably attended to among our German farmers. The product is generally about eighteen bushels to the acre; but in addition to this, there is the haulm, which serves to keep their horned cattle alive until the return of better times; for with such food the winter must to them be a dreary season indeed. In favor of this culture, it should, however, be observed, that the crop, though of trifling value, does little or no injury to the crop of wheat which always succeeds it. A change of seed, would, no doubt, be productive of larger crops.

Peas are subject to a bug which eats into the heart of them. It does not, however, hinder them from growing, but if they be not destroyed, they will infest the next crop. To kill them let the peas be thrown into hot water, and kept in it a few seconds, and then be taken out, dried, and sowed immediately. The same method is to be taken to fit such peas for cooking; as by such treatment the bugs will drop out after they are dead, and may then be easily separated from the peas. In such case, they are, however, to be kept longer in the hot water.

The time for sowing field-peas, or planting garden-peas, is as early as the ground can be well prepared. A dry soil is the best for them. The usual quantity sowed to the acre is two bushels, though some say, that the farmer will be gainer in sowing three; as the thicker they are sowed the less liable they are to fall flat on the ground, which prevents the filling of the pods.

PERRY. To make good perry, manage the pears in the same manner that apples are directed to be managed to make good cider, with this difference, that the pears need not be sweated so long as the apples, by being laid in heaps for that purpose.

See article CIDER.

A drink called *perkin*, is also made from the pressed cheese, of pears in the same manner as *ciderkin* is made from that of apples.

PLOUGH AND PLOUGHING. In constructing a plough, the essential point is to make it run as easy through the ground as possible, and at the same time do its work effectually. In order to run easy it should run flat, not be raising up behind; and the share and mould-board should be so shaped as to assist jointly in turning over the sward. For this purpose the sward should be gradually raised by the share, as soon as it is cut by the coulter, till it comes in contact with the mould-board, and by it as gradually turned over. The share may also be so contrived, and shaped, as to cut the sward itself, and this is probably the better way.

The shorter the beam of the plough, and the higher it is raised from the chip, the more it will raise up behind in ploughing; and the longer the beam and the lower it is placed, the more evenly it will run. In very rough grounds, however, the beam must be placed pretty high, to avoid the stones, &c. that come in its way; but in smooth grounds, as all grounds ought to be made, the beam may run very close to the ground.

For the purpose of gaging the plough, when turning over a sward of smooth surface, instead of the whole plough, one small wheel of cast-iron, properly fixed under the end of the beam, would be found much better.   This can be so contrived as to be raised or lowered, so as to make the plough run deeper, or shallower, at pleasure.

Cast-iron plough-shares have been found to answer well in smooth lands, and are much cheaper than those of wrought iron.   They may be had in New-York.   The chip and the share may also be cast together.   The mould-board may also be of the same material, or the share and it may all be cast together, and the chip cast by itself, and fastened to the share underneath.

Under different articles of this work the necessity of *frequent* and *effectual* ploughings—of ploughing when the dew is on, as being preferable to ploughing at other times—and of ploughing after the first turning under the sward, when the ground is neither too wet nor too dry, particularly in clay lands—have been duly insisted on, and need not here be repeated.

For TRENCH-PLOUGHING, *see* that article.

In breaking up the sward of a side-hill, it should be ploughed horizontally, with the furrows turned downwards, and at the next ploughing the hill should be taken diagonally, having the furrows when ascending to turn downwards, and when descending to turn upwards. In this way pretty good work can be made; but in ploughing diagonally in the opposite direction, nothing can be done with the plough while ascending the hill.

Mr. Livingston describes a "double-firred" plough which he saw in different parts of France, "which has a moveable mould-board fixed on hook at the share, and by a pin at the broad end which passes through the mould-board and into the beam; when they come to the end of the furrow, instead of making a land, they shift the mould-board, which is done very quickly, and has the advantage of throwing the furrows all one way." Such a plough would, no doubt, be useful in ploughing side-hills, where the ground was not too rough and stoney.

A field was summer fallowed, one part of which was ploughed three times, the other part was ploughed eleven times, and a crop of rye was all harrowed in at once. That part of the field which was ploughed but three times did not produce half the crop which the other part yielded.

All sward grounds which are designed for spring crops, should be ploughed up in the fall, in order to be more easily mellowed in the spring; and all ploughed grounds of a wet or stiff soil, which are in like manner designed for spring crops, should be thrown up in high ridges in the fall, in order that the soil be kept drier than it otherwise would be, and of course more easily fitted for a crop in the spring. Where grounds, however, are liable to be washed by heavy rains, care ought to be taken to run the furrows, or the ridges, not up and down the descents, but gradually slanting, or diagonally, so that the waters will not incline much to follow the furrows, but soak away into the soil.

PLUM-TREES; *(Prunus.)* Mr. Forsyth recommends the following selection of plum-trees for a small garden:

The *white prismordian*, small, yellow, mealy; ripens latter end of July.

Early damask, middle sized, flesh good; ripens early in August.

Red Orleans, large, rich juice; ripens latter end of August.

Green-gage, several varieties, fine tasted, distinguished by its size and colour; ripens in August and September.

La royal, equal to the green-gage, but a shy bearer; red colour; ripens late in September.

Drap d'or, a good plum, and plentiful bearer; ripens late in September.

Saint Catharine, one of the best; rich juice and good bearer; fruit hangs very long on the tree.

Imperatrice, has an agreeable flavor; ripens middle of October; should not be gathered till it begins to shrivel, when it tastes like a sweetmeat.

The management proper for raising this tree is the same as that for peaches.

See article PEACH-TREE.

Mr. Forsyth particularly directs the tap roots and the fine hairy roots to be taken off before transplanting; and that the lateral roots should be spread near the surface, in order to make the fruit fine flavored. He directs that the ground should be deeply dug before planting. Where the trees bear too heavily, part of the fruit should be taken off before it is half grown.

A good sandy loam, well manured, is the best for this tree. Stiff clays are very unfit for it. Mr. Livingston mentions a *drap d'or* which stood fifteen years in a stiff clay, and had not grown to the height of nine feet; when, on removing it into his garden, which is a loam on sand, well manured every year, it grew more in two seasons than in the preceding fifteen years.

See further, articles FRUIT-TREES, NURSERY, TRANSPLANTING, &c.

POLL-EVIL. An imposthume on the poll of a horse. At first, says Mr. Gibson, it requires no other method of cure than is proper for boils and inflamed tumors, but it sometimes, from neglect, or mis-management, becomes a sinuous ulcer. He says, the matter is apt to lodge in a small sinus which is under the poll-bone, unless care be taken to keep the part firm with a bandage ; that if the tumor has a large cavity it should be laid open, and if it acquires an ulcerous dis-position, it should be treated as such.

See further, articles TUMOR and ULCER.

PONDS. Those which may have no natural outlet may never-theless, in most cases, be drawn off by sinking a well, or hole, through the stratum of clay, or other close earth which holds the water, until a stratum of gravel shall be found, into which the water of the pond may be carried, where it will sink away. The well, or hole, should be filled up with stones, and the waters of the pond directed by ditches into it. Frequently the bottoms of ponds are found to be fine rich earths, and well worthy of cultivation. The draining of such ponds is also highly requisite for the purpose of avoiding the *miasma* which proceeds from them and which is so productive of fevers.

Artificial ponds are sometimes made at the corners of two or more pasture lots for supplying cattle with water. One of an hundred and twenty feet circumference should be about five feet deep in the cen-ter. To make it retentive of water, it must be lined with a thick lay-er of tough clay and fresh slaked lime, mixed well together, and beat down hard with wooden beetles or sledges ; and on the top of this beat in a good layer of coarse gravel. The edges, and for some distance down the sides of the pond, should then be faced with a solid pave-ment of stones, so large as not to be moved by the treading of the cat-tle. Moist places, and such as where water can be collected together after rains, are best for ponds of this kind.

POPPY ; (*Papaver Somniferum.*) There are two species of this plant, the double poppy and the single.

Doctor Ricketson says, that either of the species yield the same quantity and quality of opium. He directs the seeds to be planted in beds, about the middle of May, in rich moist ground, the plants to stand at the distance of a foot apart. They are to be kept clear of weeds with the hoe.

The plants, he says, yield the most juice during their flowering, and immediately before and after. At this time he directs the stalks to be cut off about an inch below the heads, and as the juice exudes, to take it off with a penknife. The part cut off will at first yield juice as well as the standing stalk. When this ceases to run cut it off a little lower, and so on, till all the juice is extracted.

The juice is to be evaporated in the sun till it is sufficiently dried.

POTATOE; *(Solanum.)* This is a native of America, and was first introduced into Europe by the famous Sir Walter Raleigh.

This root, when boiled, is found to be wholesome and nourishing food for man and beast. Many families of the peasantry of Ireland have little else for subsistence than potatoes and milk, and frequently nothing but potatoes with a little salt; yet these are as healthy, vigorous, and well made, as any people in Great-Britain.

Potatoes are usually propagated by the roots; but they may also be raised from the cuttings of the top branches when set in the ground, and these will even strike root if planted bottom upwards. The sprouts taken from the potatoes in the spring will also grow, and it is said, that a piece of the heart of a potatoe will also do the same.

From the seeds contained in the apples, potatoes may also be raised of various kinds, differing from that which bore the apple; and this is the way in which new kinds of potatoes are to be obtained. For this purpose, let the apples be gathered after the seeds are fully ripe; mash them together in some water till the pulp becomes all washed away and separated from the seeds; then dry the seeds, and the next spring sow them in a bed, which is to be kept clear of weeds, until the young plants shall have acquired their growth. The potatoes raised of this year's growth will be small; but let them be sorted, and the next year planted, each kind by itself, and the products will be full grown, or nearly so. Farmers should frequently attend to this method of acquiring new sorts of potatoes: as those which have been planted for several years are always found to have degenerated, and eventually, will produce little or nothing. Some of the new sorts, thus produced, will be found to excel in size and greatness of product, and others again in dryness and superiority of taste; and thus, the farmer can be accommodated with such as are best for the table, and with such as are best calculated for feeding swine, &c. For this latter use, I have lately seen a new kind which grow to the length of eight inches, and will probably yield double of most other kinds now in cultivation. One potatoe of this kind when cut into as many pieces as there were eyes, and planted in four hills, gave upwards of a bushel. Arthur Young, Esq. makes mention of a thousand bushels having been raised to the acre in Great-Britain; and I think it not improbable, that this amount could be raised here of this kind of potatoe.

The best soil for potatoes is a mellow sandy loam, or gravelly loam, a fertile sandy soil, or a rich black earth : Any soil, indeed, except clay, can be made to produce pretty good crops, with proper manures, if it be not too wet and cold. The kind of dung used, ought to be adapted to the soil ; such as cow-dung and hog-dung for more light and sandy grounds, and horse and sheep-dung for more moist soils. Let the ground be turned over in the fall; in the spring, immediately before planting, plough in a plentiful supply of suitable dung ; run very light furrows about three and a half feet apart ; drop the potatoes, whole, along the furrows, at the distance of about eighteen inches apart, or, if cut in two, at the distance of a foot apart, and cover them with a light furrow run along on one side, or with the hoe. When the plants have grown to the height of six or eight inches, run the plough along on each side of the rows, as close as possible, without injuring the plants, turning the furrows from them, then immediately turn the furrow back to them, and thus the soil becomes sufficiently re-mellowed to keep up a due degree of fermentation about the roots. Let this ploughing be followed with the hoe ; then in due season give them another ploughing, sufficiently deep, turning the furrows to the rows. Follow again with the hoe, destroying all the weeds, and if any afterwards arise, let them again be destroyed by the hoe, so that none shall be suffered to go to seed. From the first to the tenth of May is the best time to plant potatoes in order to obtain the largest crops.

The digging may be performed with the plough, running a furrow first on each side, and then through the middle of the rows ; but perhaps, as good a method as any, is, to take a broad spade, or shovel, and run it under the bunches of potatoes, for when planted, as above directed, they will grow in bunches ; raise up the whole mass, shake it, and the earth will fall first, leaving all the potatoes on the top of the ground.

I have seen it stated in some of our newspapers, that plucking off the blossoms, just before the apple is formed, will tend very considerably to increase the crop. The farmer will do well to ascertain the truth of this.

If dung is to be applied to the rows, it should be placed under the potatoes. The process, however, of dunging in this way is tedious, and by running the loaded cart so often over the ground, as is neces-sary for this purpose, it becomes so much hardened, and of course, in-jured for good cultivation afterwards, that on the whole, it is doubtful, if any thing be gained by this method of manuring the crop. In light sandy grounds, however, it may be best.

Last spring, I planted about twelve square rods of ground in my garden with potatoes in hills. In each hill, of about half this ground, was put one whole potatoe, and dung was put under them. For the four first rows the very largest potatoes, and they were uncommonly large, were selected to plant; and for the four next rows the very smallest were selected, and planted one in a hill. The weight of po-tatoes planted in the latter rows was not a fourth of that of the former. On the rest of the ground the dung was scattered, and two whole po-tatoes, of ordinary size, were planted in each hill. The result of all this was as follows : The four first rows produced nearly double the quantity of stalks which was produced by the four next. The stalks of the remainder of the piece were not so large as those of the first four rows. When the potatoes were dug, no essential difference was observed between the product of the four first rows and the next four planted with the smallest potatoes. They were all fine large ones. The remainder of the piece produced about an equal quantity to the hill, but there were a greater proportion of small ones among them.

I also planted two small beds after the Irish fashion. They were cut in the usual manner and set about ten inches apart. When dug they were sufficiently numerous, but much smaller than those which were planted whole.

On the whole, I am rather of opinion, that cutting potatoes is of no service to the crop, but perhaps an injury ; and I am also further of opinion, that this is the principal, and perhaps the only cause of their degenerating so rapidly as they are found to do. The laws of vege-tation do not indicate a necessity of cutting them to pieces to make them grow better. It would also seem by the above, that there is no necessity of planting the largest potatoes, but that at least those of a moderate size will answer as well as any.

Potatoes will answer very well when fed raw to horses; that is, they will keep them sleeck and in good condition ; but for fatting any animal, particularly swine, they should be boiled.

For the best method of boiling them, *see* article SWINE.

For preserving potatoes for family use, in winter, the best way is to mix them with alternate layers of dry sand ; and when spring arrives let them be taken out of the sand, well dried, and stowed away in a close chest, or box, into which the light cannot penetrate, and put in the garret or some other dry place. It is also said, that for keeping them during summer, a slight scalding with boiling water, and then drying them again, is very serviceable in preventing their sprouting; which always very much injures them for eating. If, however, they be entirely deprived of light and kept entirely dry, they will sprout but very little, if any; but if light be let in at any small hole the sprouts will directly start, when the weather is warm, and point their way to the spot from whence the light issues. This is a very striking case to shew how necessary light is to vegetation.

To raise potatoes with a mere covering of straw, lay them on a clean sward, and cover them over with straw to the depth of about eight inches. In due season they will be found nearly as well grown as if they had been buried in the ground, and will be drier, and better tasted for early eating.

From this root an ardent spirit can be distilled; but this is not properly the business of the farmer. Starch of the best kind can also be made from it in abundance, and it is believed, that the manufacturing of this would be found very profitable.

The method of raising potatoes in beds, as is practised by the peasantry of Ireland, is calculated to produce more to the acre, but is attended with more manual labor; the spade being used instead of the plough. But though there be more labor in getting the seed into the ground, still there is less in attending to them afterwards; as in this way there is no ploughing and hoeing the crop, but merely weeding it a little and keeping the trenches clean. The young plants so soon cover the beds, that but very few weeds have a chance of growing. For raising a crop in this way, a piece of sward ground, or any other, is first well covered with dung, then the ground is marked out for beds about five or six feet wide, leaving a sufficient space between each for digging the trenches. The potatoes are then cut, and set in rows across the beds, about ten inches from each other, and they are then covered to the depth of about two inches or more, by the earth which is dug out of the trenches.

In this way good crops of potatoes can be raised on any wet meadow grounds, that have a sufficient depth of good soil; as by means of the trenches the ground is laid sufficiently dry. It would also seem, that some kinds of noxious weeds might be destroyed in this way; for by covering them over while in their growing state, they would be smothtired and completely killed. Beds, made in this way, round the borders of fields, might often be useful for destroying many growths of weeds, briars, bushes, &c. which frequently encumber such parts of the field.

Great crops of potatoes are sometimes raised in the following manner, and this is probably the best, where the ground is well prepared. Manure the ground well; have it well cleared of the seeds of weeds, and make it sufficiently mellow; then begin on one side of the piece and run a light furrow, and set that with cut potatoes, at the distance of ten or twelve inches apart: The next furrow which is to be run along side of this covers these, and that is again set with potatoes as before, which are covered by the third furrow, and so on till the whole ground is planted: Then run furrows through the whole, eight feet apart, for the purpose of walking in when weeding. When the potatoes are to be gathered, run a furrow through them, beginning on one side as before; pick up what potatoes are thrown out; then run another furrow, and again pick up what are thrown out by it; then a third, and so on till the whole ground is gone over. Then harrow the ground and pick up what potatoes are disclosed by this operation; and again harrow and pick up, by which time the ground will be pretty well cleaned.

The farmer will find the cultivation of potatoes very profitable, if he duly attends to the selection of such kinds for planting as are most productive, and at the same time cultivates them in an effectual manner. They are equally good for feeding and fatting all sorts of cattle when boiled, and the expense of this is but trifling, if a steam-boiler be used for the purpose. It is said that planting in the full of the moon will increase the crop.

POULTRY. Mr. Wakefield, a spirited farmer near Liverpool, say the compilers of "The Complete Grazier," keeps a large stock of poultry in the same enclosure with singular success. He has nearly an acre enclosed with a close slab-fence, about seven feet high: The top of the fence is every where sharp pointed, like pickets, though perhaps this is not necessary. Within this enclosure are put up slight small sheds, well secured from rains, however, for the different kinds of poultry, and it is supplied with a small stream of water. The poultry are regularly fed three times a day with boiled potatoes, which is their only food, except what grass may grow within the enclosure.

The dung of the poultry, which is exceedingly rich, is carefully saved for use; and the turf of the enclosure is occasionally pared off for mixing with composts.

It would seem, that in the vicinity of large towns particularly, this might be made a profitable employment. But it is believed, that the better way would be to keep the different kinds of poultry separate, as they are not apt to agree well together. Something shall now be said of each sort separately.

Of the *dunghill fowls*, as they are usually called, there are various breeds, which it is perhaps unnecessary to designate. When well kept, a good hen will lay from one hundred and fifty to two hundred eggs in a season, which may be at least considered worth a cent each. If her eggs be not taken from her she will bring forth three broods in a year, if well kept, and each brood may be estimated at, say, eight grown chickens.

Guinea fowls, also, lay many eggs in the course of the season; but as they are naturally fond of wandering away and laying them where they are not easily to be found, it is not probable they could be confined to an enclosure like the one in question. Their flesh is of a little value.

The young brood of *turkies*, might probably, be most advantageously brought forth in an enclosure like this, and after they had acquired sufficient strength, let go abroad to shift for themselves.

The *black turkey* is the most hardy. The young of this fowl are tender and apt to die. The Swedish method of making them hardy, is to take them as soon as they are hatched, or as soon thereafter as they are found, and plunge them in cold water, and force each one to swallow a pepper-corn.

After this they are subject to another fatal malady which must be removed. In order to this, when any of them are found drooping, pull out such feathers of the tail as are filled with blood, and the chicken will presently recover.

This fowl is profitable to raise in many situations. They are also of great use in destroying insects, particularly grass-hoppers.

The turkey derives its name from the country from whence it was originally imported. It appears, however, to be the same with that which runs wild in the interior of our country.

Of *geese* there are two sorts, the wild and the tame. In general, they breed but once a year, but frequently twice, if well kept. Three geese should be allotted to one gander; for if the number be increased

the eggs will usually be rendered abortive. About twelve or thirteen eggs are enough for a sitting. While breeding, the goose should
have corn and water placed by her, and the gander should at this
time have free access to guard her. The nest should be sufficiently
high round the sides to prevent the eggs from rolling out, as they are
turned by the goose every day. It is well also to break the egg
slightly near the beak of the young gosling when they are about to
make their way out.

Geese are particularly profitable for their feathers; and although
the plucking of them so often, as is practised by some, appears barbarous, yet it is found that they thrive better by repeated pluckings than
where they are permitted to shed their feathers in the natural way,
which is at the time of moulting.

In Lincoln county, (Great-Britain,) where they are raised in the
greatest numbers, they are plucked five times a year; the first time
at Lady Day, for feathers and quills, and four times afterwards, between that and Michaelmas, for feathers only.

Tame ducks, of which there are varieties, are the same as the wild.
They begin to lay early, and afford a considerable number of eggs,
which are nearly as good as those of dunghill fowls. About twelve
is enough for a duck to sit on. Ducks are greedy feeders, but not
nice as to their food. They are quickly fatted on animal food, of
which they are fond, and their flesh then tastes like that of the wild-
duck. They are useful in turnip fields while the young plants are
liable to be preyed on by insects.

Poultry is most easily fatted when kept in a dark place; and boiled
grain is generally best for the purpose of fatting.

PYRITES. *See* article MANURES.

Q.

QUINCE-TREE; *(Cydonia.)* This tree is easily raised from layers or cuttings. A moist soil suits it best. Let the cuttings be planted early in the spring and be watered in dry warm weather. They require but little pruning, except to keep them clear of suckers, dead, and cross limbs; and where they have too many luxuriant upright shoots in the top these should be taken out.

Mr. Forsyth says, they are apt to have rough bark and to be barkbound. In this case, he directs to shave off the rough bark, scarify them, and then to brush them over with his composition.

He says, they should be planted at some distance from apple and pear-trees, lest their farina should mix, which would cause the apples and pears to degenerate. But perhaps this is mere theory.

R.

RADISH. This root being liable to be eaten by worms, the following method is recommended for raising them: Take equal quantities of buck-wheat bran, and fresh horse-dung, and mix them well and plentifully in the ground, by digging: Suddenly after this a great fermentation will be produced, and numbers of toad-stools will start up in forty-eight hours: Dig the ground over again and sow the seed, and the radishes will grow with great rapidity and be free from the attacks of insects. They will grow uncommonly large. Buck-wheat bran is an excellent manure of itself.

RED-TOP; *(Poa Trivialis.)* This grass is suitable for dry upland, or for moist soils. It makes good pasture and good hay, but is not so productive as herds-grass.

See article GRASSES.

ROLLER AND ROLLING. The roller is useful in smoothing the surface of meadows that have become uneven, and for passing over grounds newly sown with grain, or that are to be laid down to grass. They are further useful in breaking the lumps of baked earth in a clay soil; but for this purpose, a roller filled with iron spikes has been preferred.

See article SPIKY ROLLER.

The use of the roller on grounds sowed with different kinds of grain, particularly barley, which is dry and husky, is to cause the mould to enclose the seeds; much of which, by laying in cavities that soon become dried, would otherwise fail of vegetating. It is also useful in light dry soils for preventing their moisture to evaporate too easily. Perhaps the roller is as useful for this purpose as for any other, in regard to its application to crops of grain. It is also useful in depriving certain insects of their hiding places in the cavities of the soil.

The rolling of land in tillage, should be done when the ground is so dry that it will not stick to the roller; and in grass lands it should be performed in the spring when the ground is soft and wet.

A wooden roller should be about twenty inches or two feet in diameter, and about six feet in length. It should be round and of an uniform surface. Where the roller is made of stone, it should be about fourteen inches in diameter, and of the length above mentioned.

ROOTS. The most essential divisions of these, are those of the *tap*, the *bulbous*, and the *fibrous* kinds. The carrot, parsnip, beet, clover, &c. are tap-rooted; the potatoe, onion, turnip, &c. are bulbous; the plants of wheat, barley, oats, herdsgrass, &c. have fibrous roots. Tap roots have also fibrous roots, which like all others of that kind, extend horizontally, far in every direction, and become so fine that they are imperceptible to the naked eye. The bulbous have also such fibrous roots, and one kind, the turnip, has also a tap root in addition to its fibrous roots. Trees have also tap and fibrous roots.

Some tap roots will extend downward, as far as they can find the soil sufficiently opened to receive them. I have known an instance of a parsnip taken from the ground, three feet in length. This shews the necessity of having the soil deeply mellowed for tap roots; and the fibrous roots extending horizontally so far in every direction, where they can find mellow earth to penetrate, shews the necessity of having the ground well mellowed to a sufficient depth to receive them.

ROTATION. *See* CHANGE OF CROPS.

RUNNET, or RENNET. A good method of making this is as follows: Take the maw of the calf; empty it of its curd; wash it; soak it in strong brine till it is well salted; dry it on boughs made for the purpose; then take two quarts of strong brine that will bear an egg, blood warm, and let the maw steep in this twenty-four hours, when the liquor will be fit for use; bottle it up, and cork it tight, and it will keep for a twelvemonth. About a tea-cup full will be sufficient for ten cows. Some direct spices, and a lemon sliced, to be put into this liquor.

Another method is to take the maw, emptied as before, and fill it with an artificial curd made of new cream; into which put three eggs beat fine; a nutmeg grated fine; and three tea-cup fulls of fine salt; mix the mass well together; tie up the mouth of the bag; lay it under a strong brine for three days, turning it over daily; then hang it up in a dry cool place for six weeks, when it will be fit for use. When used it is first to be dissolved in warm water.

The acid contained in the maw is very apt to become rancid, and to putrify, if a sufficiency of salt be not applied; care must therefore be taken to prevent this by a due supply of this article. No good cheese can be made unless the runnet be good.

The runnet-bag may also be salted and dried, as before directed, and pieces of it occasionally used, by being previously soaked in warm water, and a quantity of this water used in proportion to the quantity of milk to be turned.

In Holland the cheese-makers use no runnet, but instead of this they use a small portion of spirit of sea-salt, (*muriatic acid,*) for forming the curd. This gives the cheese a taste somewhat different from that made with runnet. The acid should probably be diluted. The quantity, which is just sufficient, may be ascertained by a few experiments.

RYE; (*Secale.*) There is but one kind of rye, although it is distinguished by the names of winter rye and spring rye. Take winter rye and sow it later and later, each year, in the fall, and it may at length be sown in the spring, and then it is spring rye: Or take spring rye and sow it at first very late in the fall, and then a little earlier every succeeding fall, and it will become confirmed in the habit of winter rye.

A sandy or gravelly soil will produce as good rye as any other. It will, however, grow pretty well on almost any soil that is not too wet. It will grow year after year on the same soil without exhausting it, provided the stubble be constantly ploughed under, immediately after taking off the crops. It will grow very well on a poor soil, and on the very richest. Mr. L'Hommedieu makes mention of twenty square rods of ground, of gravelly soil, which a neighbour of his manured with four thousand fish, called menhaden, and sowed with rye. In the spring, the piece was twice successively eaten off close to the ground, by sheep breaking in, after it had acquired a height of nine inches the first time and six inches the latter. These croppings, however, only served to make it grow thicker and stronger than before; and when harvested, it produced sixteen bushels, or at the rate of one hundred and twenty-eight bushels to the acre; giving to the proprietor, according to the calculation of Mr. L'Hommedieu, a clear profit of ten dollars sixty-two cents, after deducting the cost of manuring, tillage, &c.; or at the rate of eighty-five dollars to the acre of clear profit.

Mr. L'Hommedieu, however, supposes the crop would have been lost by lodging, had it not been for the two successive croppings of the sheep. Would it not be well to try similar experiments with wheat?

Winter rye may be sowed early in the spring and used as pasture during the season; or it may be sown at the usual time and serve for a sheep pasture a while during the next spring without injury to the crop. It may also be mowed for hay two or three times during the summer, when sown in the spring. For such uses, however, the ground should have more seed than the usual allowance, which for early sowing in the fall, is about a bushel to the acre, or a bushel and a half for later sowing. Spring rye should also have this latter allowance, and be sown as early as the ground can be well prepared.

Rye is subject to rust, but seldom or never to smut. It is also liable to a distemper called the spur.

See article SPUR.

That which is intended for family use ought, if the weather be good, to be harvested even as early as when the rye is yet in the milk, and let lie on the ground for some days to dry and harden. By this means the grain will make a much whiter flour, though the product will not be quite so heavy as when it stands till it is fully ripe.

Rye, as it is usually cultivated, is not an article of much clear profit. Yet, it may be well enough for the farmer to cultivate some of his gravelly or sandy lands in raising this grain, particularly in parts of the country where wheat is not natural to the soil, or where he can make his ground yield him yearly as much as fifteen bushels to the acre. In order to acquire this yearly product, he ought to plough the stubble under as soon as the crop is taken off, which helps the ground, and serves to destroy the seeds of weeds. Let it lie till about the first of September; then plough the ground again, and harrow in the next crop. Some assert, that in this way the crops will increase in quantity. Allowing, however, the average product to be fifteen bushels an acre, and allowing seven bushels of this to pay all the expenses of ploughing, &c.; harvesting and threshing, &c.; then allowing four bushels more to pay for the rent of the land, the clear profit would be four bushels, equal to about three dollars an acre. This, indeed, would not be sufficient to tempt the farmer to go largely into the cultivation of rye; but if by manurings, applied every other year, which should cost him not more than the value of ten bushels of rye to the acre, he could make his lands give a yearly average of thirty bushels an acre; he would have a yearly clear profit, equal to fourteen bushels an acre, which would make the business of raising rye a little more respectable. If the ground, however, becomes too weedy, it must be summer fallowed.

Bread made entirely of rye is laxative and good to prevent costiveness. It is usual to mix some flour of Indian corn with that of rye, in making bread, which serves to prevent its clamminess.

R.

CONTINUED.

[NOTE.—*The following articles were furnished by the Author, after the sheet containing the preceding articles under the letter* R. *had been put to press—which rendered it inconvenient to arrange them in the alphabetical order in which the other parts of this work are done.*]

RABBITS. "In some situations these animals may be kept to advantage, as they multiply exceedingly, and require no trouble in bringing up. They delight in the sides of sandy hills, which are generally unproductive when tilled, but level ground is improper for them. The fur of the rabbit is worth thrice the value of the carcase. Therefore, supposing the rabbit to consume a quantity of food in proportion to its carcase, it is a species of stock nearly three times as valuable as either cattle or sheep. Rabbit warrens ought to be enclosed with a stone or sod wall; and at their first stocking it will be necessary to form burrows for them until they have time to make them for themselves. Boring the ground horizontally with a large augur is perhaps the best method that can be practised. Eagles, kites and other birds of prey, as well as cats, weasels and polecats, are great enemies of rabbits. The Norfolk warreners catch the birds by traps placed on the tops of stumps or trees, or artificial hillocks of conical form, on which they naturally alight." *Encyclop.*

Would not the rearing of rabbits be profitable in this country? We have no eagles or kites to molest them; they breed very rapidly; their food is cheap and easily provided; a fence to enclose a warren can be made of boards, at no great expense, which will keep out cats and polecats; and as for weasels, we have but very few of them in this country.

RATS. These are a very unprofitable stock for the farmer to maintain, and the sooner he disposes of them the better. For this purpose the most effectual method is to give them arsenic. Set some plates where the rats frequent, with a little wheat-flour or other food which they like, put into them; let them bait on this for two or three nights; then add a little arsenic to the flour, mix it well together, and place it as before, and they will eat it very readily, which will soon dispatch them. When this dose is administered, care should be taken to cover the milk-pans and whatever else they can drink at; as the arsenic occasions a burning thirst, which induces them to go in quest of whatever will quench it. Perhaps it would be as well to set some water for them to drink at.

A trap for catching rats is made as follows, and is much recommended:—Take a barrel, or keg, with one head out; put in it water enough to cover the bottom about two inches deep; in the middle of this set a piece of brick or stone; cover the head of the cask with a piece of smooth dried sheep-skin, or perhaps good smooth stiff paper will answer; in the middle of this cut two slits about six inches long, at right angles, so as to form a cross; immediately over this suspend the best kind of bait for the rats, placed sufficiently high;—now when the rat comes to take the bait, in reaching up to it he slips into the hole, by the four corners of the parchment or paper giving way. He now gets upon the brick in the middle of the water, and begins to utter signs of his distress; this brings others to him, who fall in in the same manner. Presently they begin to fight for the possession of the brick, and the noise of this brings others, who fall in in like manner; and thus all within hearing of this scene of confusion follow on and share the same fate.

Another good method is, by suitable baits to draw them into a large box, or cage, by means of an entrance guarded within with sharp-pointed wires, similar to those of the mouse cage.

While the farmer is divesting himself of his rats, let him not neglect his mice, for they, too, are quite expensive in keeping.

REED; (Arundo.) A species of this plant is wonderfully productive in the rich bottom lands of the Missisippi and elsewhere in that direction. Many of the plants are said to grow twenty feet high, and they grow so thick that it is difficult to get through them. Cattle are very fond of them, and subsist almost entirely upon them in the latter part of the season. But where they are fed off year after year they at length disappear.

Would not this plant be valuable for cultivating as an artificial grass, particularly for soiling? *See* article SOILING. If this reed, or cane as it is usually called, would grow after repeated mowings during the summer season, it would probably be found very valuable as an article of food for cattle. By cultivating it, and sowing it thicker than it grows in its natural state, it would be much improved as an article of food. It would be desirable to have some trials made of this plant. If it would start again after every mowing, it would probably yield double of any artificial grass now cultivated.

There are smaller species of this plant which infest low grounds where the soil is good which are not relished by cattle for food. These are easily destroyed by draining the land, or by ploughing it up in ridges. Soot and ashes will also kill them.

RIDGLING: A name given to a half castrated animal. A horse of this description is as troublesome as a stallion, and yet not fit to be relied on as one. "A ridgling hog," says Mr. Deane, "will never be fat, nor grow so large as a barrow, till his castration be completed; as it may be by making an opening in the belly, when the case is most difficult. They should either be killed young or completely castrated. The flesh of a ridgling pig is good, but that of an old one brawny and disagreeable."

S.

SALT. *See* article **MANURES.**

SALTS. Various kinds of salts are found in plants: They are, therefore, essential ingredients in their composition; of course, if any soil contains but little of the requisite salts, the plants which most require any of the different kinds must languish for want of them: In such case, a mere trifle of such as may be wanted, properly distributed in the soil must have a surprising operation as a manure. In short, whatever the soil is deficient of, which is an essential part of the food of plants, a little of that given to the soil will have a tenfold greater effect than any other manure would have, though that manure might produce equally beneficial effects in another soil where it is most wanted.

Probably common sea salt is, in general, more wanted in soils which are out of the reach of the sea atmosphere than any other. A little, therefore, of this, where it is most requisite, may have a great effect; and more might be injurious; for if this article be too plentifully applied to the soil, it destroys all vegetation.

An intelligent farmer once observed to me, that during our revolutionary war, when common salt was so dear that he could not afford to give it to his cattle, his barn dung seemed to do his lands but little service; but that he had found the case much altered since, when by the cheapness of this article he was enabled to deal out sufficient of it to his stock.

I lately saw a small pamphlet, published in Maryland, describing the surprising effects which common salt, mixed with a small quantity of rich mould, and thus sown on the soil, produced; particularly in crops of flax and wheat. The lands on which these experiments had been made, were sufficiently remote from the sea; but few cattle were ever raised on them; of course the soil has had little or no salt since it was cleared. This soil had also been exhausted with the culture of tobacco and Indian corn. All these circumstances may *have* contributed to render a little of this manure of singular use to it.

Mr. Deane says, he has always found common salt much more beneficial to the soil when mixed with composts than when sown in its crude state. He also mentions some trials made of this manure on onions, turnips, and carrots, the latter only of which he found benefitted by it; but, perhaps, the manner of the application to the two former, and the quantity given, were both unsuitable.

Mr. Elliott mentions five bushels of crude salt being sown on an acre of flax, which had a surprising effect; and that he found it very beneficial when sown on wheat. Let the farmer make various trials of this manure, and use it as he finds it best.

See further, article SEA-WATER.

SALTING OF MEAT. In packing down pork, sprinkle in what is equal to four quarts of rock-salt to a barrel; then make a pickle sufficient to cover all the meat, as strong as it can be made with salt, and when cold, pour it on. When the pickle becomes much coloured with the blood of the meat draw it off, boil it, take off the scum, till it becomes clear, and apply it again. Repeat this, if the pickle again becomes coloured too much, and add more fresh brine, if necessary. In this way, pork will keep sweet throughout the ensuing summer, and will be free of rust.

This method is also good for preserving beef, though the following is better.

For a barrel of beef, says Mr. Deane, take four quarts of rock-salt *pounded* fine; eight ounces of saltpetre, and five pounds of brown sugar; mix them well together, and with these ingredients pack the *meat down* very closely, so as that they will of themselves cover the whole with brine. The next spring draw off the brine, clarify it, as *before* directed, adding a little salt to it, and apply it again, and the beef will keep very sweet and fine tasted during the whole summer *following.*

This method of curing meat, it will be seen, is something similar to *the best* method of curing butter, and it is also an excellent method for curing pork and hams. The ham of some of the southern states is allowed to be equal to that of Westphalia; but whether this be owing to this method of curing, to the climate, or to the manner of keeping hogs there, is perhaps uncertain. When hams have been sufficiently cured in this, or any other way, they should be smeared over with molasses—smoked sufficiently and suddenly—the quicker the better;

and let them then be well sprinkled over with slaked lime and put away in casks, filled with bran, to keep during the summer. The lime will serve to keep all insects from them.

SAND. Considerable has been said of this earth. *See* articles EARTHS and MANURES.

Pure sand is entirely barren. What are usually called sandy soils must contain a mixture of other earths, if they possess a greater or less degree of fertility.

The difficulty with sandy soils is, that they do not sufficiently retain moisture, unless they have a close understratum. Where this is not the case, they are only permanently benefitted by carting earths on them which are most retentive of moisture.

SAP. Plants derive their sap principally from the roots. Before it has entered these, it is called the *food of plants.* It is supposed to be absorbed by the capillary roots in the form of vapor, which, being rarified by the heat of the atmosphere, ascends, and extends through all the pores of the plant; and here is imperceptibly carried on that chemical process which eventually serves to bring it to perfection.

SCRATCHES. This is a disease in the legs of horses, occasioned by bad blood, or too hard labor. The skin of the legs becomes cracked open, emitting a reddish coloured humor. To cure the disease, wash the cracks with soap-suds, and then rub them twice a day with an ointment of hog's-lard, mixed with a little sublimate mercury.

SEA-WATER. This fluid is said to contain nitre, sulphur, and oil, besides common salt, and is therefore preferable to that article for manuring, either when put in composts, or otherwise.

Mr. Deane mentions one hundred hills of potatoes which had two quarts of this water applied to each, immediately after planting, and that the quantity of potatoes in these hills was half as much again as the same number of adjoining hills produced. Probably half the quantity of water applied to each hill would have had a better effect. He mentions also a piece of flax, one side of which was short and yellow, but which by being sprinkled with this water, in ten days equalled the other side, and eventually outgrew it.

The above was on clay ground adjoining the sea-shore. The watering of the potatoes cost about an hour's labor of one man. Mr. Deane says, its effects when applied to sandy land appeared to be equally great. He recommends steeping the seeds in the water before sowing or planting, and applying it to the ground immediately after they have been committed to the earth.

It would be easy to carry this water some distance on the land to advantage. For instance, take a one horse cart, and suspend a tight box, rightly shaped, under the axletree, the box having a hole in the upper side: You then drive this cart into the water, so as to cover the box, and it fills through the hole: When it is carted out to where you want it, it may be sprinkled out, evenly over the ground, as the cart moves along, in the following easy manner: You take a tube, say twelve feet long, and, say an inch square within; on one side of it bore small holes, say three inches apart, and close the ends of the tube: You then attach this tube to the under side of the box, crossways, at either end of it; then the water is let out of the box into the tube by an aperture for the purpose; and as the cart moves along, the water runs out of each of the small holes in the tube, and thus sprinkles over a piece of ground of twelve feet wide, till the whole is exhausted: With the next load you begin where the water ceased running before, and thus continue the watered strip across the field. You then take another strip of twelve feet wide adjoining that last watered, and thus you proceed.

With this machine, a man with a horse, could probably draw out, and spread, twenty-five loads per day, to the distance of half a mile: and this quantity would perhaps be sufficient at one time for an acre of ground. At the same rate he could draw out enough for half an acre to the distance of a mile.

Perhaps the better way would be to have a valve in the under side of the box, which would press open to let the water in, and close again when the box had filled. The wheels of the cart which carries it should be pretty high, so as to have the under side of the box as much as a foot from the ground.

It has, I believe, been generally supposed, that salt or sea-water has not much effect as a manure, on soils lying near the sea; but if this be a mistake, and the cases above reported by Mr. Deane be found a standard specimen of the effects to be constantly produced from this manure, it would perhaps be found profitable to adopt means for carrying the water as far into the interior as possible. This, where the country is level, and rises but little above the sea, would be attended with no difficulty, save the expense of the aqueduct for carrying the water. This could be made of wood, and as it would be constantly filled with salt water, this would probably preserve it for a century. The water is to be forced up the tube of the aqueduct by the aid of a plunger and valves, which is to be drove by a little wind machinery, which it is unnecessary here to describe.

Whether the profits to be derived from putting a plan similar to the foregoing into operation would warrant the expense, must depend upon the results of experiments to be properly and faithfully made. Our sea-coast, and the contiguous islands, offer millions of acres to be benefitted by such a method of fertilizing lands, if the plan should be found advantageous.

SEEDS. Many seeds will retain their vegetative faculty for several years; others again cannot be made to germinate after the first year, unless uncommon pains be taken for that purpose.

See article GERMINATION OF PLANTS.

All seeds require fresh air, and if long deprived of this they will lose their vegetative quality. If some kinds be buried deeply under ground, however, they will retain this quality for twenty or thirty years.

Some seeds will lie a year, sometimes two or three years, before they will come up; and for this reason, when seeds are brought from a distant country and sown, the ground should not be disturbed during that length of time.

Seeds of the dry kinds are best preserved in their pods, or natural coverings; but those of all soft fruits, &c. should be taken out, cleansed and dried.

SHEEP. Mr. Livingston has treated this subject with so much research and ability, that the reader need require little or no further information than what his essays contain; but as this work would be imperfect without treating of this important article, and as the writings of Mr. Livingston and others are too voluminous for insertion, it becomes necessary to condense the subject, so as to present it in a small compass.

Animals undergo changes by domestication. Qualities which they possessed in the wild state, but which are no longer useful in the domestic, become less and less visible; and owing perhaps to this circumstance and to others, even their appearance becomes more or less altered. The ears of wild animals are erect, which enables them to hear with more acuteness; but some of the sheep of Sicily and of Italy, says Mr. Livingston, have been so long under the protection of man, where this quality is not so requisite, that their ears have become pendant. Lord Kaims observes, that when sheep run wild they go in droves; that the males are the protectors of the flock, and that the strongest claims precedence of the rest; that when they lie down at night, some stand as sentinels while the rest sleep; but these traits of instinctive sagacity they in a great measure lose when man becomes their protector.

M. Buffon and others have supposed the *mouflou musmou*, or *argali*, which is still found in the wild state, to be the original stock of the present sheep. This animal is swift of foot, and in cold climates has merely a coat of wool under a coat of hair. In warm climates it has nothing but a coat of hair; and such is the case with sheep which have been long accustomed to such climates. It would seem to be the economy of nature that some graminivorous animals when domesticated, but still exposed to the rigors of the seasons, become more inert, of course possess less animal heat, and therefore require a more woolly coat: While others of the carnivorous kind, which are more sheltered by man, but whose habits still require their wonted activity, and of course retain their animal heat, require less clothing, or a mere coat of coarse hair. This perhaps may be the reason why sheep have more wool and less activity than the argali; and why dogs have coarser hair than wolves. If this, however, be thought sufficient to account for the difference between the argali and such sheep as shed their coats yearly, it is still difficult to assign a reason why the merino sheep never sheds its coat; for this, if left on for years, does not fall off, but constantly increases in length and quantity. Probably different climates and soils have done much in producing marked differences among sheep; and probably different kinds, as we now find them, have descended from stock which were of the same genus, but possessing properties different from each other.

Mr. Livingston observes, that "as this quadruped has probably been found throughout all the mountainous parts of Europe and Asia, and perhaps even in Africa; as its young are easily tamed; as its milk, its flesh and its skin, are extremely valuable to man in a savage state, it is highly probable that it was amongst the first quadrupeds that were domesticated; and from this circumstance it has perhaps wrought no less a change in man, than man has in it,"—that it "is highly probable we are indebted to it for the conversion of man from the wild wandering savage to the mild and gentle shepherd."

It may be found equally true that different soils are best suited to different breeds of sheep, and that the soil often serves eventually to

27

produce a difference in sheep. "Fat pastures," says Mortimer, "breed straight, tall sheep, and the barren hills short, square ones." The island called *Smith's Island*, lying off the eastern cape of Virginia, has been found remarkable for producing a breed of sheep of uncommonly fine wool. The large long-wooled sheep of Great-Britain require rich pastures; and a moist soil will suit them better perhaps than it will any other sheep. A wet soil, salt marshes excepted, is, however, unfriendly to sheep of all kinds. The merino sheep require good pastures, and such as is produced on dry soils. Farmers, in stocking their farms with sheep, ought to pay attention to the selection of such as are best suited to their soil. Much of the high moist lands of this and the neighbouring counties, it is believed, would be found tolerably suitable for raising the large long-woolled English sheep.

It is highly desirable that our country should be stocked with sheep of various kinds, in order to supply itself with the various sorts of cloths which are necessary in different uses. In England they have the *Tees-water*, the *Lincolnshire*, and the *Dartmoor* breeds, which yield fleeces of long coarse wool, weighing on an average from eight to eleven pounds; and the average weight of their carcases per quarter is from twenty-five to thirty pounds. The wool of these sheep, and of the *Heath*, *Exmore* and *Berkshire* breeds, which are smaller, and have still coarser wool, is proper for the manufacture of blankets, carpets, &c. The *New-Leicestershire*, or *Bakewell* breed, and the *Cartwold* and *Romney marsh* breeds, have also long wool, but somewhat finer, being better fitted for the manufacture of worsted fabricks; and the average weight of their fleeces is from eight to nine pounds —the average weight of their carcases per quarter is from twenty-two to twenty-four pounds. The *Bakewell* is an improved breed, which was engrafted upon some of those before mentioned, and are highly esteemed for the fatness of their carcases and the fine taste of their mutton. In addition to these the English have various other breeds, besides the merino, yielding fleeces of short wool of various quantities and qualities, the finest of which are the *Dunfaced* and *Shetland* breeds; the next finest is the *Hereford* or *Ryeland* breed, and the next the *South-Down*. Mr. Livingston says the latter very much resemble our common sheep, having wool about equally fine, and that in England they are esteemed next to the Bakewell breed.

Mr. Custis, of Virginia, is rearing a new breed, which he calls the *Arlington* sheep, that yield fleeces of long wool, well fitted for the manufacture of worsted fabricks. They are a mixture of the Bakewell breed with a long-woolled Persian ram, which was imported by General Washington. They promise to be a valuable acquisition to our country. In addition to these are the *Smith's Island* sheep, before mentioned, which are also the property of Mr. Custis, and which on account of the fineness and largeness of their fleeces, promise to be highly valuable, provided the breed do not degenerate in a few years when taken from that island. They are shorn twice a year, and some of the fleeces weigh four pounds at each shearing.

Another breed of sheep ought to be noticed, as being peculiar to this country; these are the *otter* sheep, so called on account of the length of their bodies and the shortness of their legs. They were first found in some of our Atlantic islands, and are indeed a rickety, crippled looking race. Their wool is of a medium fineness, and of a medium length; it is neither of a proper length for combing, nor yet for broadcloths. The advantages of this breed consist chiefly in their inability to be mischievous, in leaping fences, &c. and their disadvantages consist in their proportionate inability to escape from dogs, &c. But the man of taste and feeling will make another objection to them —their form is not pleasing to the eye, and their rickety, hobbling gait, is calculated to excite pity instead of pleasure.

Another breed of sheep, which are found in almost every quarter of the globe, are the *broad-tailed* sheep. These are of different kinds, and yield fleeces of different qualities in different climates. In the Levant their wool is fine, at the Cape of Good-Hope it is coarse, and at Madagascar it is mere hair. They are generally larger than the European sheep, and the tails of one kind weigh in many instances fifty pounds; being "so weighty that the shepherds are compelled to place two little wheels under each to enable the sheep to drag them." "The composition of this excrescence," says Mr. Livingston, "is said to be a mixture of flesh with a great proportion of fat, and to be very delicate food; but the animal has little other fat, the tail being in him the repository of that fat which lays about the loins of other sheep."

As it is hardly probable that this excrescence could have been inherent in the original stock from whence these sheep descended, but has most probably been produced either by accident or by art, it is perhaps one of the most extraordinary instances to be found of an alteration produced in the form of an animal by domestication.

A yearling sheep has at its first shearing two *broad* teeth before, beside its narrow teeth; when sheared the second time, it has four; the third time, six; and the fourth, eight. They are then said to be *full mouthed.* The teeth of ewes begin to decay at the age of five years, those of wethers at seven, and of rams at eight. At this age a ram should be castrated, and turned off to fatten with other old sheep. Ewes will fatten faster during pregnancy than at any other time. If properly kept, and no accident befalls them during pregnancy, they are capable of yeaning till the age of ten or twelve; but they frequently become barren much sooner, by reason of poor keeping, or by injuries received during pregnancy. When this is the case, and they grow weakly, they should be fattened with other old sheep. Those set apart for fatting should be kept separate, on good feed, and have some Indian meal daily. It is said that a sheep is never made very fat but once, and that then is the proper time to kill it; but perhaps this is not founded in truth.

The proper time for shearing is when the weather has set in pretty warm, but sooner where the wool is falling off. The wool of merino sheep must be washed after shearing, as it cannot be washed to any effect while on their backs. The shearing of these may be later, as their wool never falls off. Sheep of the common kinds may have their wool washed while on their backs; but in that case they should be kept some days previous to shearing in a clean pasture, in order that their wool may again imbibe some of the oil which is lost by washing, which will render the shearing more easy, and require less oil to be afterwards added for spinning.

In shearing, care should be taken not to cut them; and this is more particularly necessary with the merino sheep, whose fleece is so close as to render this operation much more slow and difficult, double the time at least being requisite for shearing one of these that is necessary for one of the common kind. Would not shears with blades much *narrower* than those of the common kind be much the best for shearing these sheep? In England it is a common practice after shearing to smear the bodies of the sheep with a mixture of tar and fresh butter, which serves to cure the wounds in the skin, and to fortify their bodies against the cold. This mixture may be improved by the addition of a small quantity of sulphur. The sheep should again be anointed in the month of August, by introducing the ointment from head to tail, and also on the sides and back, by parting the wool for the purpose. This composition should, at all events, be applied to the wounds. It serves effectually to destroy all the ticks, which are very pernicious to sheep. The practice of penning up large flocks of sheep together in a close place during the shearing is very injudicious; they should be penned up in the open air, and but a few brought together at a time. The common practice of tying the legs of the sheep together while shearing, is hurtful to them; as it compresses them into a situation which is unnatural and painful. Rather let each foot be tied by itself, in its natural position, to a small piece of wood, with cross pieces at each end, which may be easily contrived and made for the purpose.

During cold rains and cold nights, after shearing, they should be placed where they can go into their house, or place of shelter, when they please; as they know best when they want shelter, and when they become so warm as to require the open air. They should at all times, but particularly at this, have plenty of salt, as this is a stimulant which enables them the better to withstand the cold. A warm sun is hurtful to the backs of sheep after shearing, and for this reason their pasture should have some shade, to which they can retire during the heat of the day. After shearing, their skins should be carefully examined to see if they have any appearance of the *scab*, and those which have, should be kept apart from the rest till cured, as this disease is contagious. This, too, is the proper time to examine them as to their *age* and *health*, their *bodily defects*, and also as to the *quality* and *quantity* of their fleeces: Those which are found old and broken mouthed—sickly and infirm—ill formed—ewes that are bad nurses, and lose their lambs from want of milk—those whose wool is in small quantities, which is often the effect of age or sickness—and those whose wool is bad, either by being mixed with short hairs, or which are rough on the thighs; these should all be marked, in order to turn them off, and be put in good pasture for fatting.

The wool of yearling sheep should be kept by itself, because not having the same texture or strength which the wool of older sheep has, it will make the cloth shrink unequally if mixed with such wool. The other fleeces may be sorted at shearing time, making separate parcels of the thighs, the belly, and the back and sides. Wool should not be kept long without washing, as in that case it is liable to ferment and spoil in hot weather.

After shearing, the horned sheep should be examined to see that their horns do not press on the scull, or endanger the eyes, either of which may kill the animal. Where this is the case the horns are to be taken off, and for this purpose Mr. Livingston recommends sawing them off with a fine stiff-backed saw, then to apply some tar to the stumps, and tie a double linen cloth over them to keep off the flies.

At this time also the lambs should be docked, castrated and marked. Mr. Livingston recommends the Spanish custom of docking the tail, as conducive to cleanliness. The castration is best performed by taking away the testicles at once. This operation may be performed on lambs when not more than ten days old, and the earlier this is done the finer will be the wool and their flesh. If rain or cold weather succeeds this operation before they are cured, they should be housed, otherwise they will be in danger of dying. Another method of castration, which is probably best for grown sheep, is to tie a cord tightly round the scrotum, and after five or six days, when the part below the cord is dead, cut it off just below the string, and tar the wound. This is, however, a dangerous operation when the weather is warm; cool dry weather should be chosen for it. "In Spain it is usual, instead of either of these operations, to twist the testicles within the scrotum, so as to knot the cord; in which case they decay gradually, without injuring the sheep."

Splaying ewe lambs increases their wool, makes them fatten better, and it is said improves the taste of their flesh. If this operation is to be performed, which perhaps will seldom be found advisable, it should not be attempted before the lambs are six weeks old.

Where ewes are to be turned off for fatting, the lambs must be weaned early; and then let the ewes have the ram again, which will make them fatten better. Lambs thus weaned should be put in a pasture of young tender grass, out of hearing of their dams, and an old wether or ewe should be put with them. Care must also be taken to milk the ewes every day or two for the first week, until their milk dries up. In all other cases the weaning of lambs, before the time when they naturally wean themselves, is believed to be by no means advisable, as the lambs are injured by it at least as much as the ewes are benefitted. This may, however, be found advisable where it is wished to have the ewes impregnated earlier than the usual time, for the purpose of raising very early lambs. These, Mr. Livingston advises, should be shorn the first year; as the divesting them of their fleece may be a matter of some considerable profit, and it renders them more comfortable during the summer. Lambs, however, which do not come until the snows are gone are always most easily reared; and in order to this, the ram must be kept from the ewes in the fall datil about five months previous to that time. Such lambs must be kept from the ram until the second fall.

In Spain twenty-five ewes are allowed to one ram. Mr. Livingston thinks forty by no means too many; and instances are not unfrequent where one ram has served double and even treble that number. If the ram, however, be not well kept, where so many ewes are allowed, he will be in danger of being injured.

The best time for sheep to feed in pastures is while the dew is on; and this they will readily learn if there be no water in the fields where they are kept. Water is not necessary for them during the season of pasture, but in winter they should have free access to it, although they can do many days without it.

When sheep are badly kept they take colds, and discharge a mocus from the nose. Good feeding, together, with some pine boughs given them occasionally, will cure this complaint. If pine boughs cannot be had, spread some tar over a board, and over this spread some salt, which will induce the sheep to lick up all the tar, and this will effect a cure.

According to experiments made by Mr. Daubenton, a celebrated French agriculturalist, it seems that the sheep of France, which are generally of the height of about twenty inches, eat about eight pounds of grass per day, or two pounds of hay per day, which is about the same thing; as eight pounds of grass when dried will make but two pounds of hay. An acre of pasture, then, which in the season would yield of grass what would be equal to two tons of hay, would probably support about eight sheep through the season. It must be remembered, however, that animals consume food in proportion to their size, and that the sheep here described are below the common size of sheep in this country.

Mr. Daubenton also observes, that when his sheep were fed on dry fodder during the winter season many of the younger ones, and those which were weakly, dropped off;—that on opening these, he found the food in the third stomach, or that which receives the food after the second chewing, to be so dry as to be unfit for digestion, and to this cause he ascribes their death. This state of the stomach, he very justly concludes, is produced by the sudden change of food from grass to that of dry fodder; and the remedy pointed out, which is very natural, is merely to feed them with a due proportion of suculent food. For this purpose, carrots, potatoes, turnips and cabbages, are all very good; and though cabbages cannot be conveniently used in this climate for this purpose, yet the roots above mentioned may be kept in cellars, buried in dry sand, and occasionally fed out to sheep to great advantage.

Feeding sheep with a little Indian corn, about half a gill to each per day, is very beneficial; it keeps the flock in good heart; it enables the ewes to rear their young much better; and it serves to prevent the wool from falling off in the spring. Carrots, potatoes, &c. no doubt answer the same valuable purpose.

For early feeding for the ewes which have lambs, a small field of rye, thickly sown, is very good. They may be taken off in time for the crop to come to maturity, and in that case they will do it no essential injury. A small field of cabbage-turnips would probably be the best. (*See* article CABBAGES.) Vetches, clover, tall meadow-oats, and other grasses which start early, are also very good for this purpose.

Sheep should have hay during winter of the best quality, and for this purpose red clover is esteemed the best. If about a peck of salt were applied to every ton of hay when carted into the mow, it would no doubt be found very good for them. The rack in which the hay is put should be upright, so as that, in feeding, the seeds and other matter will not fall into the wool about their necks. Under the rack a trough should be fixed, which will serve for catching the seeds of the hay, as well as for feeding the sheep. They should be kept by themselves, and not suffered to run among other cattle; their yard should be spacious, though in proportion to the number in the flock; and their shelter should be close over head, but the sides not so close as to preclude a due circulation of air among them. Perhaps it is best to have it close on all sides but the south. The shelter ought also to be spacious, so as not to crowd them too closely together; and it ought to have some small apartments in which to keep the ewes a few days previous to yeaning, and for two or three days afterwards. These should be fed during this time with succulent food, and their apartments should be kept well littered. The fence round the sheep-yard should be such as to keep out dogs.

If the flock be large, so that a separation of it during winter would be advisable for promoting the health of the sheep, the better way is to put the full grown wethers by themselves. This is the more advisable because they do not require so good keeping as the ewes and young sheep; and when kept with these they are enabled, from their superior strength, to take the best and most of the food to themselves.

In regard to folding sheep on small or on large pieces of ground, *see* article FOLDING.

Flocks of sheep thrive much better by being changed frequently; but those will be most benefitted which are taken from poor pastures and put into better. Their pastures should be clear of weeds, as the burs produced by some spoil the wool, while others often prove hurtful to them by eating; they should also be clear of all briars and bushes, for these serve to tear off much of their wool in the spring. Clover is the best pasture for them. The shrub called *laurel* is poisonous to them when eaten, and ought therefore to be removed from their walks.

To prevent wolves from killing sheep, says Mr. L'Hommedieu, make an ointment composed of gun-powder and brimstone, powdered fine and mixed with tar and currier's oil, and with this anoint the throats of the sheep. This must be renewed as often as the ointment loses its moisture, which will be four or five times in a season.— Wolves have been seen to seize sheep anointed in this manner, and finding their throats thus fortified, have left them without doing them any injury.

Having said thus much of sheep in general, something shall now be said of the *merino* sheep in particular.

These sheep are certainly much the most profitable to raise, where the soil and climate are suitable to them. Perhaps it may be found that some parts of this state may not be so suitable for them as others; as some farmers of this county (Herkimer) are making complaints of being unsuccessful in rearing them. The climate, and much of the soil, of the Mohawk country is moist, and this circumstance may perhaps not prove so favorable for their propagation here. Let experiments, however, be fairly and fully made upon them before any hasty conclusions are drawn. Most of the sheep of this kind which have been brought into this part of the state were young, and such as were probably rejected from the flocks of those who sent them abroad for sale. The last two winters have also been uncommonly severe on all sheep.

Mr. Livingston has stated the result of his sheep-shearing of the spring of eighteen hundred and eight, and this will perhaps serve to convey as adequate an idea of the importance of the merino sheep as any thing that can be said.

28

From twenty-nine common sheep he had upwards of one hundred and fourteen pounds, which he sold at thirty-seven and an half cents per pound. This, allowing one dollar and fifty cents for the expense of keeping each sheep for a year, fell short three cents on each fleece of paying for their keeping. Eighty-three half-blooded ewes gave upwards of three hundred and ninety-three pounds; and forty-seven half-blooded wethers gave upwards of two hundred and thirty-six pounds. This wool sold for seventy-five cents per pound. Clear profits on the fleece of each ewe two dollars and three cents; on the fleece of each wether two dollars and fifty-five cents. Thirty three-fourth-blooded ewes gave upwards of one hundred and fifty-six pounds, and three wethers of the same blood gave upwards of sixteen pounds. This wool sold for one dollar and twenty-five cents per pound. Clear profits on the fleece of each ewe four dollars and seventy-five cents; on the fleece of each wether two dollars and twenty-five cents. Seven full-bred ewes gave upwards of thirty-six pounds, and one ram, fourteen months old, gave upwards of nine pounds. This wool sold for two dollars per pound. Clear profits on the fleece of each ewe eight dollars and seventy-five cents; on the ram seventeen dollars and twenty-five cents. This wool was all sold at the above prices without being washed.

By the foregoing it will be seen that if the farmer expects to derive large profits from these sheep, he ought not to rest until he has got into the full bloods of this breed, or into the fifteen-sixteenths, which will answer about as well. The profit of the lambs, it will be seen, is not taken into consideration in this statement.

If these sheep are thus profitable for their wool, it is also well ascertained that they are at least as profitable as any others for fatting.

Mr. Young took a merino, weight eighty-four pounds—a half South-down, quarter Bakewell, and quarter Norfolk, weight one hundred and forty-one pounds—and a Southdown, weight one hundred and thirty-six pounds; these were fed abroad together a certain length of time, and then weighed. The first weighed one hundred pounds; the second, one hundred and forty-eight; and the last, one hundred and forty-four pounds. Thus the merino gained more than double the quantity of flesh which the other two gained.

He also made another experiment, which served to shew that a merino only eats in proportion to its size. By this he found that three merinos may be maintained four per cent cheaper than two of the Southdowns. The weight of the merino upon which this trial was made, was ninety-one pounds; that of the Southdown, one hundred and thirty-two pounds.

Mr. Livingston says the size of the ewes, more than that of the ram, governs the size of their lambs; that the ewes of a small race cannot bear large lambs, though the ram be ever so large. For this reason the lambs which are raised from a merino ram on our common ewes, will be larger than those raised from one of our common rams on merino ewes. This is the reason why rams of the large English breeds, when brought here, do not produce a race any way corresponding to their own size. Mr. Livingston therefore recommends engrafting a merino stock upon our common ewes, to increase the size of the breed; though if they only eat in proportion to their size this is not so material. In the selection of the ewes take those that are at least three years old, as large as can be obtained of the sort, with the belly large and well covered with wool, chine and loin broad, breast deep, buttocks full, the eyes lively, the bag large, and the teats long. In addition to these qualifications, they must have fine short thick wool, their bellies well covered, and with the least hair on the hinder parts. In the choice of the ram, which we will suppose to be three-fourth-blooded, and which can be purchased for twenty-five dollars, select one that is of good size, broad in the chine and loins, deep in the carcase, the back straight, the ribs well set out so as to give room for a large belly well covered with wool, the forehead broad, the eyes lively, (a heavy eye being a mark of a diseased sheep,) testicles large and covered with wool; let him also be strong, close-knit and active, of which you may judge by taking hold of his hind legs; and lastly, let his wool be of good quality, and as clear of hair on the hinder parts as possible.

The product of such a ram with common ewes, would be lambs possessing nine twenty-fourth parts of merino blood; and twice repeating the process on the females of the successive products, would give three-fourth-blooded lambs. Two further repetitions from a full-blooded ram, would give lambs possessing fifteen-sixteenths of merino blood, which is probably sufficient. The ram, however, ought to be changed at each time; as it is believed that the rearing of succeeding stocks between which there is the closest consanguinity mus eventually tend to degenerate the breed.

See article CATTLE.

In Spain, where by the extent of the pastures the number of the merinos are limited, it is usual to kill off some of the most indifferent lambs, and thus two ewes can be given to suckle one of those surviving. This is usually effected by putting the skin of the dead lamb over a living one, which commonly induces the dam of the dead one to recognize the living as her own. Where this fails, the ewe is held for the lamb to suck her; and she is confined with it a day or two, by which time she generally adopts it. This custom is only in part advisable here; that is, whenever a lamb dies, to accustom its dam, in this manner, to give its milk to another lamb.

It has been feared by some that these sheep, when no longer migratory, and changed from their accustomed climate, will degenerate, and their wool grow coarser, but experience does by no means warrant these apprehensions. They have been kept stationary for more than eighty years past in Sweden, and nearly as long in France, and yet have suffered no deterioration. Mr. Livingston thinks the wool of his merino sheep which he has raised here finer than those which were imported. It is a general rule with animals which shed their hair, that the farther north, the warmer, and of course the finer, is their coats; but as these sheep never shed their wool, the rule does not necessarily include them. Their wool is in this respect similar to human hair; but this is always found the finest in the colder climates.

Apprehensions have also been entertained that these sheep, having in Spain been long accustomed to situations where winter is scarcely felt, would be found unable to stand the severity of our winters; but the fact just mentioned of their being successfully reared even in the cold climate of Sweden sufficiently obviates this objection. Mr. Livingston says, that "like all other sheep they will be found the better for good keeping, yet they will not suffer more than others from neglect; and that they will, in every mixed flock, be found amongst the most thrifty in the severest weather."

Some, again, may suppose that the country will soon be stocked with merinos, and that the price of their wool will then fall to that of common wool; but such should remember that more than half the civilized world is destitute of these sheep, and that while they continue to remain so, the sheep, the wool, or the fabricks made from it, will be eagerly sought after. In the course of a century, North and South-America will probably contain two hundred millions of people, and the wants of these alone will at that time require three hundred millions of merinos. There is certainly no danger of the price of merino wool falling much for twenty years to come.

The ewes of this breed seldom produce twins; though, if necessary, they may be made, like other sheep, to breed twice a year. Ewes of the English Teeswater breed have been known to bring five lambs in a year. The ram, when put to the ewes, should be better kept than usual; and for this purpose should be fed two or three times a day with a slice or two of bread, made of Indian meal, which may be given to him by hand. When the ewes are not suckling lambs, they may at any time be brought to take the ram, by feeding some Indian corn to them. The first lamb of a young ewe will never be so strong as those succeeding, because she will not have the same strength, nor the same quantity of milk which she will have afterwards.

There are different breeds of merinos in Spain, says Mr. Livingston, and the wool of some is inferior to that of others; some selling there for only sixty cents a pound, while others sell for a dollar. The best flocks are those of the *Escurial*, of *Gaudaloupe*, of *Paular*, of the *Duke D'Infantado*, of *Monturio*, and of the *Nigretti*. The first exceeds for fineness of wool; the second for fineness of form, and fineness and abundance of fleece; the third, with similar fleeces, are larger bodied. "The lambs of this stock and of that of the Duke D'Infantado, are commonly dropped with a thick covering, which changes into very fine wool." The Nigretti are the largest breed.

After merino wool has been sorted as before directed, and is to be manufactured in the family, let it be covered with soft water, mixed one third with urine, and let it stand fifteen hours, or longer if the weather be cold. A cauldron is then to be put on the fire, with some soft water, and let two thirds of that which covers the fleeces be added to it. When so hot as that the hand cannot bear it, take out the wool, put it in a basket, press out the liquor, put the basket in the cauldron, and there wash the wool by pressing, without any wringing of it, and then cleanse it in running water. If the water in the cauldron becomes too dirty, take more water from that in which it was first soaked. Dry the wool in the *shade*, not in the sun; let it then be beat with a rod, which takes out all seeds, &c. and softens it; then pick it, by opening it lengthways carefully, and card it with *cotton*, not with wool, cards. Carding-machines are advised not to be used for this wool, unless particularly fitted for it.

The above is the European method of managing this wool before carding, &c. but Mr. Livingston thinks that if the wool be carefully picked and carded, so as to get out most of the dirt, and wove in this way, that it will answer without washing, in which case less oil, or grease, will be necessary.

Common wool cannot be carded too much—merino wool may. In spinning, the warp must be twisted the opposite way from that of the woof, which should be spun more loose, or slackly twisted, than that of the warp. For spinning the woof, the wool is to have one pound of oil, or grease, to every four pounds; but for the warp, one pound of oil to every eight pounds of wool is the proper allowance. This is for very fine spinning; but for spinning coarser yarn less oil is necessary. Olive oil is the best for greasing the wool; neat's foot oil is also very good; and no doubt the oil which is produced from the sun-flower would be found as good as either. *See* article SUN-FLOWER.

The farmer will find a great addition to his profits from his merino wool by converting it into fine cloth, in his own family, if this can conveniently be done.

Sheep of all kinds are subject to fewer diseases in this country than in most others. This article shall, therefore, be concluded with noticing those most prevalent here, and the remedies for each, together with some slight notice of some which prevail abroad.

Those of grown sheep are as follows:—The *scab*. This appears first by the sheep rubbing the part affected, and pulling out the wool in that part with their teeth, or by loose locks of wool rising on their backs and shoulders. The sheep infected is first to be taken from the flock and put by itself, and then the part affected is to have the wool taken off as far as the skin feels hard to the finger, and washed with soap-suds and rubbed hard with a shoe-brush, so as to cleanse and break the scab. Then anoint it with a decoction of tobacco water, mixed with a third of lye of wood ashes, as much grease as this lye will dissolve, a small quantity of tar, and about an eighth of the whole mass of the spirits of turpentine. This ointment is to be rubbed on the part affected, and for some little distance round it, at three different times, with an interval of three days between each washing. With timely precautions this will always be found sufficient. In very inveterate cases, Sir Joseph Banks says mercurial ointment must be resorted to, with great care, however, keeping the sheep dry; the wool to be opened, and a streak to be made down the back, and from thence down the ribs and thighs. Fine wooled sheep, and rams which have been much exhausted by covering, are most subject to this disorder, and in fine wooled flocks it is most difficult to cure. It is said that it may be communicated even by a sheep lying on the same ground on which a scabby one had shortly before lain, or by rubbing against the same post.

Pelt rot. In this disease the wool falls off, but the skin does not become sore, but is merely covered with a white crust. *Cure*—Full feeding, warm keeping, and anointing the hard part of the skin with tar, oil and butter, mixed together.

Tick. As these occasion a constant scratching they prove injurious to the wool, and they sometimes occasion the death of lean sheep. *Cure*—Blow tobacco smoke into every part of the fleece, by means of a bellows. The smoke is taken into the bellows, the wool is opened, the smoke is blown in, and the wool is then closed—this is repeated over every part of the body at proper distances. It is quickly performed.

Dogs. These often prove more injurious to sheep than all their other maladies put together. *Cure*—A fine, say of a hundred dollars, upon every man that keeps a female of these animals above eight inches high; or a yearly tax, say of twenty dollars, laid upon the owners. Extirpate the *females* of this race, and the whole breed would soon disappear. The legislature may easily enforce a law of this kind without danger of its being *unpopular*, which it is said would be the fate of a law taxing the whole race of dogs.

Staggers. A disease of the brain which renders them unable to stand: Incurable by any means known which would warrant the expense. *See,* however, what Gibson says, article STAGGERS.

Colds. The principal indication of this is the discharge of mucus from the nose. The cure has already been noticed. Whenever this, however, becomes habitual with old sheep they should be killed off.

Purging. If any are severely afflicted in the spring with this, which sometimes happens after being turned out to grass, house them, give them a dose of castor oil, feed them with dry food, and give them some crusts of wheat bread. A slight purging will not hurt them.

Hove. Sheep, like neat cattle, when put into clover pastures, sometimes have their stomachs distended by wind, so that they will die if not relieved. The swelling rises highest on the left side, and in this place let the knife be inserted, or other means used, in the manner directed for neat cattle.

See article NEAT CATTLE.

The diseases of lambs are—

Pinning. When the excrement of the lamb becomes so glutinous as to fasten the tail to the vent, it must be washed clean, and have the buttocks and tail rubbed with dry clay, which will prevent any further adhesion.

Purging. Put the lamb with its dam into a dry place, and give her some oats, old Indian corn, or crusts of wheat bread. If the dam has not milk enough, give the lamb cow's milk, boiled, or let it suck a cow.

Sometimes it may be found necessary to bleed sheep to allay some inflammatory disorder. " Daubenton recommends bleeding in the lower part of the cheek, at the spot where the root of the fourth tooth is placed, which is the thickest part of the cheek, and is marked on the external surface of the bone of the upper jaw by a tubercle sufficiently prominent to be very sensible to the finger when the skin of the cheek is touched. This tubercle is a certain index to the angular vein which is placed below." The method of bleeding, after finding the vein, it is hardly necessary to describe.

Philip De Castro, a Spanish shepherd, has written a short treatise on the diseases of sheep in Spain, and of their management there, and he recommends that bleeding should be performed in a vein in the fore part of the dug. The essay of this shepherd is believed to be worthy of some further notice.

He says the merino sheep of Spain are subject to the following diseases :—The *scab ;* cured by juniper oil when the weather is wet, or by a decoction of tobacco in dry weather : *Basquilla ;* occasioned by too much blood ; cured by bleeding in the dug, as before mentioned : *Moderez ;* (lethargy,) occasioned by pustules formed on the brain ; the sheep keep turning, while feeding, to the side where the pustules are formed ; few recover, and the disease is infectious. Some get well in part by pricking the part affected with an awl ; but those attacked with this disorder should be killed off : *Small-pox ;* being blisters, which first appear on the flanks, and spread over the body ; it is produced by drinking stagnant waters. The diseased sheep are to be kept apart from the rest, as the disease is infectious, and when the blisters break anoint them with sweet oil : Lastly, *lameness ;* this appears to be the same as is described by Mr. Livingston.

He observes that " the legs of sheep are furnished with a duct which terminates in the fissure of the hoof; from which, when the animal is in health, there is secreted a white fluid, but when sickly these ducts are stopped by the hardness of the fluid." He adds, that he had " in some instances found the sheep relieved by pressing out the hardened matter with the finger from the orifice of the duct in each foot; perhaps it may in some cases be proper to place their feet in *warm water*, or to use a *probe*, or *hard brush*, for cleansing this passage." He concludes by observing, that probably the ill health of sheep, in wet or muddy pastures, may in some measure be ascribed to the necessity of keeping these ducts free and open.

The compiler of " The Complete Grazier," however, mentions another kind of lameness in sheep which is called the *foot-halt*. It is caused by an insect resembling a worm, two or three inches long, which is found to have entered between the close of the claws of the sheep, and worked its passage upward between the external membranes and the bone. To extract the worm move the claws backwards and forwards in contrary directions, and it will work its way out. In Great-Britain this disorder is chiefly confined to wet pastures.

De Castro also mentions diseases to which the merino lambs are subject, in Spain, when brought forth in wet weather; such as the *lohannillo*, (gangrene,) which has no cure: The *amarilla*, (jaundice,) which is infectious, the flesh and bones of the lamb turning of the colour of yellow wax; for this a small quantity of the flax leaved daphne guidium is good: The *coviro*, a lameness of the feet, which appears to be the stoppage of the excretory duct before mentioned. Generally, he says the lambs are subject to the diseases of the ewes, and that the same remedies are requisite.

Sheep in Great-Britain are subject to the *rot ;* but it is believed that this disease has never been known in this country. Another disease, however, which the British writers mention, our sheep are sometimes liable to ;—this is, being *maggotty*, occasioned by being fly-blown, and if not timely remedied the maggots will eat into the entrails in twenty-four hours ; cured by corrosive sublimate and turpentine rubbed into the sore. Sheep in Great-Britain are also subject to diseases called the *red-water* and *white-water*, from the colour of their urine; no cure known—supposed to be occasioned by eating poisonous weeds.

Frequently changing flocks of sheep from one farm to another, where the pastures are equally good, is very beneficial to them. I know a flock which for several years past have been pastured on different farms, by being let out to different farmers on shares, which are much the finest looking sheep to be found any where in the neighborhood where they belong.

The farmer who would rejoice to see our country so far independent as to become stocked with woollen fabricks of our own making, must feel himself impelled by his patriotism to endeavor to afford his share of supplies of wool, which are so needful to our infant manufactories; and he who is insensible to a love of country, may still find a powerful incentive to the raising of sheep, in consulting his own interest. The raising of merino sheep, in particular, is undoubtedly very profitable; and the nearer the farmer brings his breed to that of the full blood, the greater will be his profit. Like every thing, however, which innovates upon ancient usages, the merino has its prejudices to encounter; and the savage who first introduced the use of the bow and arrow to his countrymen, no doubt had the same. But let the sensible and spirited farmer persevere; and in the end his merino flock will afford him a rich harvest, the pleasure and profit of which his weaker neighbor must forego as a tax on his prejudices.

SILK WORMS. For raising these worms, (says Mr. De La Bigarre,) the first step is to procure the eggs, which should be from a climate similar to that where they are to be hatched. Good eggs take, successively, the colours of gridelin, purple, and lastly, an ash-coloured hue; they will crack under your nail, while the bad ones will make no noise when pressed in the same manner. Leave them on the cloth where they were laid by the female, and keep them in a dry place where they will not freeze in winter, nor be too much heated in spring. When about to be hatched take them off the cloth; and when the first buds of the mulberry come out, proceed to hatching them. Divide them into ounces, and put each ounce into little flat boxes, lined and made soft in the inside, and let them be kept in a constant degree of warmth equal to ninety-six of Farenheit's thermometer. Some put them into little bags, and carry them under their clothes in the day time, and under their pillow while sleeping; but perhaps the better way is to keep them in a small apartment constantly warmed by a stove or otherwise. The bags must be opened every day to give them fresh air, while hatching. When the eggs turn a whitish colour it is a sign the worms will soon come out; and then, if in bags, they must be stirred up five or six times a day, to give the young embryos sufficient air; but if they be in boxes, they can be thinly spread over the bottom, and then opening the boxes once or twice a day will answer. The time usually required for hatching is about eight or nine days, sometimes longer. If too much heat be applied in hatching, many of the worms will perish in raising. An ounce contains about forty-two thousand eggs, but among these may be many bad ones, which, if they do not hatch in two days after the first hatchings, may be thrown away.

The eggs of the yellow cocoons are to be preferred, as they give the most and best silk.

If you hatch in bags, as soon as you find some of the worms coming out, put them all into such boxes as before described. When a sufficient number have come out, take a piece of parchment fitted to the inside, cut it full of holes like a sieve, lay it over them, and on it spread some tender young mulberry leaves, and the worms will then come up through the holes to feed on them. When a sufficient number have thus come up, take up the parchment, by strings fixed to it for the purpose, and place the leaves and worms in a larger box, or shelf, lined with white paper. Fill only about a third of the bottom of this box, or enclosed shelf, with leaves; because as the worms grow larger they require more room. Here you feed the worms till after their first moulting. In the meantime the parchment is to be laid on with leaves, as before, to take out other supplies of worms; and if these be taken out on another day they are to be put in another box or shelf; as those hatched on different days are to be kept in different boxes. At the end of two or three days all the good eggs will be hatched, and the rest may be thrown away. After they are hatched they must be kept in about the same temperature of heat for ten or twelve days. They are to be fed twice or three times a day with tender leaves till the time of the first moulting; and let those leaves previously fed, be eaten before fresh ones are given.

In about six or seven days they generally arrive to their first moulting, if properly kept in regard to warmth, cleanliness, &c. If they should be as long as a fortnight before moulting they will not do well.

In their moultings they lie in a torpid state, in which they leave their old coats and acquire new ones. They moult four times before they begin to spin. While in this state they should be kept rather warmer than usual, and should not be disturbed. Previous to each of these times they look dull and weak, they lose their appetite, the skin becomes bright, and they seek for a place to lie by themselves.

They lie motionless for about two days. They will not all moult on the same days, but in three or four days the business will be over, which may be discovered by the colour of the skin, and by their activity; and then it is time to change their litter and clean the shelf. In order to get them out, spread over them some fresh leaves, upon which they will crawl, so as to enable you to lift them up. Put one half of these into one shelf of the same size, and the other half into another; and this enlargement of their room must be repeated after every moulting, as they are constantly growing larger.

After the first moulting, some of the worms will be reddish, some ash coloured, and some of a blackish hue. The reddish ones may be thrown away, as they will not come to any thing. More worms perish in the third moulting than in any other.

The mulberry leaves must be picked when perfectly dry; and as this cannot be done every day, a store of them is to be kept on hand, laid in a cool dry room, and stirred up now and then to prevent their heating and wilting. The number of meals, after the first moulting, is to be governed by the appetite of the worms; and if this be not good it is most probable that they want more heat. Don't deal out the leaves faster than they are eaten.

In seven, eight, or nine days, they will moult a second time; and so on for the two following times. The larger they grow the less heat they want. After the third moulting, open the windows each day to give them fresh air. The shelves are to be cleaned after each moulting; and where the intervals between the moultings are unusually long, let them be cleaned twice. When too much crowded, take some out on leaves, as before directed, and place them elsewhere. They cannot bear to be touched by hand unless very gently.

The white mulberry leaves are best for feeding the worms; and the tender young leaves of young trees are to be preferred at first, but in their more advanced stages they want older leaves; and these may be of older, or grafted, trees. Other kinds of mulberry, however, will answer. If the leaves cannot be had dry, let them be dried before they are used, as wet leaves are hurtful.

When they are past the last moulting they eat greedily, and want more food than before. At the end of seven or eight days they begin their cocoons. During all this time let them daily have fresh air, and let their shelves be cleaned.

When you find them creeping about without eating, as if in search of something, with their bodies of a bright straw colour, it is then time to prepare bushes, fixed on tables, for them to climb on and fix their cocoons. The bushes are to be dry and clear of leaves, and set in rows with their tops leaning together. Under these lay some mulberry leaves, for the further feeding of those which may not be quite ready for spinning, and don't let the worms be crowded too much on the tables. To put them on the tables, you apply your finger, to which they readily attach, then put them on a smooth varnished plate, to which they cannot adhere, and empty them carefully on the table. Those that incline to feed longer will do so, and those that do not will ascend the boughs. The spinning is completed in three or four days; but as they do not all commence at the same time, pick off the cocoons in about twelve days after they have begun to spin.,

The chrysalis contained in each cocoon is killed by placing them, in baskets lined with brown paper, in an oven heated nearly warm enough to bake bread; if this be not done the chrysalis eats its way out of the cocoon, and thus spoils the contexture of the silk. They are to be kept in the oven till the ratling noise, which they occasion while dying, has abated. Then take them out, and wrap them close in a blanket to suffocate those which may not yet be dead. Previous to the operation of baking, the outer coat, called tow, is to be taken off; and the same is to be observed with those which are kept for seed.

In reserving these, take equal numbers of males and females of the yellow kind. The male cocoon is sharp pointed; the female round at each end. After being divested of their tow, string them together, male and female alternately, upon a coarse thread, letting the needle go merely through the surface of each, for fear of hurting the chrysalis within; hang these in a dry place till the butterfly comes out. One pound of cocoons will give an ounce of eggs. When the butterfly has come out, the males are known by being sharp pointed, the females being larger and full of eggs. Place them all on a piece of black cloth, and put the males and females together in pairs; let them remain so three or four hours; and then throw the males away, leaving the females to deposit their eggs. These are to be well dried on the cloth on which they are laid, and put in a fresh room during summer, and out of the way of frosts during winter.

Bad management and other causes occasion some disorders among the worms. Some become fat, and do not moult, but continue eating, having a whiter and more oily appearance than the rest. After the third or fourth moulting some become lean, refuse to eat, turn soft, and become smaller than formerly. The yellow worms never appear but a little before spinning, and instead of becoming mature, swell up with nasty yellow spots on their heads, and at last over their bodies. All these, when discovered, are to be thrown away.

The other method recommended by the same writer, is to raise these worms on white mulberry hedges. A hedge of this kind of three years old, he says, begins to be fit for the worms, but those which are four or five years old will be better, as they afford the worm more places of retreat in storms. Two or three days after the first moulting, and in a fine warm day, put the young worms on the hedge, by means of leaves as before mentioned. The feathered end of a goose-quill is very good to raise them, or move them in different places. Put them on the hedge at the rate of about one hundred to every two rods, but thicker where the hedge is older. Worms thus raised in the open air, says the same writer, are free from all disorders; their only fate depends on the season; and our summers are preferable to those in Europe for raising them. In this way, care must, however, be taken to keep certain birds from them.

The same writer also remarks, in a note to his observations on the diseases of this worm, that he was afterwards informed of an experiment made in this state, by which it appears that this climate is more favorable for raising them under cover than that of Spain or France. Out of six thousand worms raised by Mrs. Montgomery, but very few died; and her success in raising them was equal in preceding years. In Europe, he says, four fifths of them perish before spinning.

SLIPS. These are twigs torn from a tree or shrub, to propagate by planting in a moist soil. Let two thirds of their length be buried, and they will strike root more readily than cuttings. This, says Mr. Deane, should be done as soon as the ground is thawed in the spring. They should be set, if possible, as soon as they are taken from the tree; otherwise let their ends be enclosed in wet clay until the time of setting.

They should be set in fine rich pulverized earth, and should be frequently watered, particularly when the ground is dry.

Some twigs will in this way grow very readily; others, again, are more difficult to grow. Mr. Deane advises to place those most difficult to grow, in pots, where they can be more carefully attended to.

It is said that some trees which are not natural to be cultivated in this manner, will not grow so large as when raised from the seed.

Where fruit trees are cultivated in this way, the trees thus raised will bear the same fruit as those from whence the slips were extracted. It is said that the life of a fruit tree raised from a slip or cutting, will end nearly at the same time of that from whence the slip or cutting is extracted; but this seems very doubtful, and in most instances unworthy of belief.

SMUT. The cause of smut in wheat has been productive of much investigation and speculation; but since the means have been discovered of *preventing* it, we may well rest satisfied with this.

In the year seventeen hundred and eighty-seven Mr. Young sowed fourteen beds with the same wheat seed, as black with smut, he says, as he ever saw any. The first bed was sown with this wheat without washing, and this had three hundred and seventy-seven smutty ears: That washed in clean water, had three hundred and twenty-five: That in lime water, had forty-three: That in lye of wood ashes, had thirty-one: That in arsenic, had twenty-eight. Again—That steeped in lime water four hours, had twelve: That in lie four hours, had twelve: That in arsenic four hours, had one. And again—That which was steeped in lie, as before mentioned, twelve hours, had none —and that which was steeped in the same kind of lie twenty-four hours, had none: That also which was steeped twenty-four hours in lime water, had none: That steeped in arsenic twenty-four hours, had five.

Thus it appears as a matter of certainty that steeping the seed wheat twenty-fours in lie will effectually prevent smut. Let the lie be made pretty strong, and if the wheat is steeped longer than this length of time it will not injure it, unless it be kept too warm. Lime water, and salt brine, applied in the same manner, will no doubt answer the same purpose.

If steeping in arsenic a longer time should prove effectual, this would also be an excellent antidote to birds; or to prevent them from picking up the seeds, the lye water and arsenic might be used together.

It has been observed that seed wheat which has been well ripened before harvesting is much less liable to smut than that which has been cut early. Let the wheat for seed be the last harvested, and let it be kept by itself, perfectly dry, until it is threshed out. Perhaps the better way would be, to thresh it out in the field when in a very dry state. The reason assigned for this is, that smut is believed to be somewhat infectious; and that therefore if wheat entirely free of this disorder be put in a mow with smutty wheat, the whole mass will become more or less infected with smut, by reason of the sweating or heating of the mow.

Wheat that is very smutty in the field should not be harvested until the crop is so fully ripe and dry that it will shell out considerably in harvesting; by this means the grains of smut are mostly broken and dissipated by the harvesting and threshing. Threshing in the field would no doubt in this case be preferable; as the drier the crop is when threshed the more readily would the smut grains be broken.

SNOW. In the northern states snow is very useful in protecting winter grain and grass from the severity of the frosts. Winter grain or grasses which have been covered through the frosty season, will grow much more rapidly in the spring than those which have lain bare. Snows may, however, fall too soon, and lie too long for winter grain, as in that case it is apt to be smothered.

Snow is useful in preserving all fresh meat during the cold season. Let the meat be first a little frozen on the outside, then put it, on a cold day, into casks filled with snow, laying the snow between each piece so that they will not touch each other, nor the sides of the cask. The whole is to be constantly kept liable to the action of the frosts; and in this way the meat will neither grow dry, nor lose its colour, during the frosty season.

SOILING OF CATTLE: Feeding cattle in stalls during the growing season, with grass cut and carried in to them. It is particularly recommended for milch cows, working horses and oxen, and for fatting cattle; and Mr. Young also recommends that swine be soiled in a yard for the purpose.

The advantages of this method of husbandry have been experienced in Europe; and it is strongly recommended by Mr. Young, by the compiler of "The Complete Grazier," and by other eminent farmers of Great-Britain. A communication of Dr. Thaer, physician to the Electoral Court of Hanover, to the English Board of Agriculture, as to the result of the experience of the Baron de Bulow and others, lays down the following as facts which are incontrovertible:—

1. A spot of ground which, when pastured, will yield only sufficient food for *one* head, will abundantly maintain *four* when kept in the stable.

2. Soiling affords at least double the quantity of manure from the same number of cattle; for the best summer manure is produced in the stable, and carried to the fields at the most proper period of its fermentation; whereas when spread on the meadow, and exhausted by the air and sun, its power is entirely wasted.

3. Cows which are accustomed to soiling will yield much more milk when kept in this manner; and fatting cattle will increase much faster in weight.

4. They are less subject to accidents and diseases; they are protected from the flies which torment them in the fields during warm weather; and they do not suffer from the heats of summer.

There are other advantages attending this method of husbandry. The trouble of driving the milch cows to and from the pastures, three times a day, is saved; the working horses and oxen are always at hand, so that no time is lost in going after them; and, what is of no small importance, when the cattle are housed the growing crops are in more safety.

For the most profitable cultivation of the earth, it is requisite that it should be in the highest state of fertility. Some manures will enrich a soil to a certain extent, while others will make it still richer. Generally speaking, barn dung is the only manure to which every farmer is accessible, with which grounds may be fertilized in the highest degree. But how is a sufficiency of this to be had?

If all vegetables were buried while green in the soil where they grew, the manure thus afforded by them, together with what additions the soil receives from the air by the requisite ploughings, would be constantly increasing its fertility. The vegetable mass produced on a farm is indeed left on, but with much waste, not only in the drying of the vegetables before they are put into the barn, but in the drying and washing of the dung, and the evaporation of its best parts, when left in the barn-yard, before it is mixed with the soil; and by the still greater waste when dropped in the fields.

The essential point, then, is to make and save the greatest possible quantity of barn-dung manure from a given quantity of ground; and this is only to be accomplished by soiling.

For this purpose, therefore, some of the most intelligent European farmers have barns with cellars under them for the purpose of receiving the dung of the cattle, and into these the dung and litter is constantly thrown, where it is prepared, by a due state of fermentation,

30

for mixing with the soil. Suitable earths are also laid behind the cattle to absorb their stale as it runs backward; and these, when saturated, are also thrown down and mixed with the dung. Others, however, object to cellars as the receptacles of the dung, on the ground of their being too cool for the process of its fermentation during summer, and prefer sheds adjoining the barn, to keep the dung under cover to protect it from the rains. Where cellars are used they should not be too deep, and should be well opened for the admission of warm air during summer.

The quality of the dung of cattle depends much on their food; that therefore which is made from green grass will be found superior to that made from dry hay; that which is made from fatting cattle is the best of any.

Having observed thus much, I will proceed to lay down a system of field husbandry, in connection with the plan of soiling cattle, which I presume will be found far more profitable than the usual method of field culture.

Take a field of proper extent, say for instance forty acres, as nearly square as may be, and of as nearly uniform soil as can be had, of a good gravelly loam, sandy, sandy loam, or other good arable soil, and sufficiently level: Clear it of stones, so as that it can be tilled in the most complete manner: Build a barn in the centre of this field, with a walled cellar under it, with a door to drive in with a cart on one side, and another to drive out at the opposite side. The barn is to be proportioned to the size of the field, and a communication to be made to it on the side most convenient, by a lane. For a more minute description, a plan of the whole is here laid down.

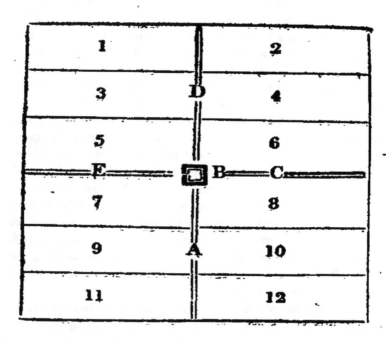

A. The lane to the barn.

B. The barn with a fence round it, communicating with the lane.

C. D. E. Divisions of the field into four equal parts, where strips of land are left unploughed wide enough for a cart to go upon.

1. 2. 3. &c. Subdivisions of the field, on which are cultivated crops of roots, grain and grass, in rotation.

In this barn stables are to be fixed for keeping a number of milch cows, working horses and oxen, or fatting cattle, proportionate to the size and products of the field. They are to be kept on grass, cut and carried in to them during the growing season, and on hay and other food during winter. The cows should be let out each day during the three milking times, and all the cattle should have a constant supply of water from a well made near the barn for the purpose.— During summer the water may be carried to the cattle in troughs in the stable, but in colder weather the cattle must be let out to troughs of water in the yard. As Lucerne starts early in the spring, and grows late in the fall, it will probably be found one of the best grasses for early and late feeding. Perhaps some other grasses may be found best in particular soils, and for particular purposes.

See article GRASSES.

The common trefoil, or red clover, which is mostly cultivated in this country, is very good for soiling. The morning's supply of grass should be brought in the afternoon, and that for the afternoon in the morning; though if it be a fact that dew is nourishing to cattle, it would seem the better way to bring in the whole supply for the day in the morning. A light hand cart is to be used for bringing in the grass from the parts of the field nearest the barn.

After such a field has been brought under complete cultivation, and enriched by this mode of culture, it will probably keep, winter and summer, about twenty-five head of cows, and fatting or working cattle. The Lucerne may be made to yield sufficient for soiling about six head per acre, or six or seven tons of hay per acre, if used for that purpose. Some other grasses will perhaps yield nearly equally well. The common red clover may be made to yield four tons of hay per acre at two mowings, and is excellent as a lay for other crops. About four hundred loads of the best barn-dung would probably be afforded yearly from such a field, which would be at the rate of ten loads per acre each year.

The extra labor required for cutting and carrying in the grass, and cleaning the stalls of the cattle twice a day during summer, would probably employ one hand two thirds of his time. In return for this, the farmer saves the rent of at least twelve acres of the best pasture land, which may be put at five dollars an acre, and his cows give more milk, and his fatting and working cattle keep better and thrive faster. Here, then, the farmer is amply repaid for his extra labor. But the great superiority of the soiling system lies in this—by the great quantity of excellent manure thus afforded the farmer is enabled to carry on a system of field culture that will be found to average one half more of clear profit than can be expected in the usual mode.

It will be seen by the drawing of the field that it is to be divided into twelve parts, and that the divisions are long and narrow; this renders them more convenient for ploughing, as will be presently insisted. We will begin with division number one.

This is to be turned over in the fall to rot the sward, and well mellowed in the spring. All the dung made during winter is to be ploughed in, and the ground planted with potatoes. *See* article Po-TATOES. If properly cultivated, between three and four hundred bushels of this root may be expected from the acre. As no soil can be too rich for Indian corn, give the ground another dunging from the stock of dung made during summer, plough it in, and next season plant it with this. *See* article INDIAN CORN. Nearly one hundred bushels to the acre may be expected of this. The next season it may be sown with hemp, and a large crop expected. *See* article HEMP. After the hemp has come off, let the ground be lightly ploughed, and, after all seeds have come up, harrowed or drilled in with wheat. *See* article WHEAT. Of this crop a hundred bushels may be expected. If it grows too rank in the spring let it be mowed off at a proper time. Let red clover be sown on the wheat in the spring, and lightly brushed in with a brush harrow. Some gypsum may be advantageously applied to the clover every spring. After the second crop is taken off the second year, let the sward be well turned under and harrowed in again with wheat, with clover sowed the next spring, and gypsum applied as before; and after two years more of clover crops let the ground be turned up in the fall to begin again with potatoes.

In the mean time other courses of crops may be occasionally pursued, so as to have a due supply of Lucerne constantly on hand.— Probably it might be found most advisable to cut up the crop of Indian corn as soon as the ears have become sufficiently hardened, carry it off to the sides of the piece, there set it up in shocks to ripen, and in the meantime sow the ground thus cleared; as in this way, the ground being well manured, and, by two hoed crops, well cleared of weeds, would afford the largest crops of this grass. Gypsum, or other good top-dressing, should also be applied to it, as might be found requisite. Other grasses should also be tried, for soiling particularly; as some of these may be found best for some soils, especially for light sandy, or hard dry gravelly ones. Where carrots are to be raised, after the ground has been properly prepared, it would be found most advisable to keep it under this culture for several years. *See* article CARROTS.

The above is merely an outline of the method of managing the divisions of the field; and this management, or something similar, each is in turn to undergo; varying the crops, however, to suit the soil, and so as to have at all times a due supply of those which are necessary for carrying on the business of soiling to its requisite extent.

It has been before mentioned that the divisions of the field are long and narrow, which are unfit for convenient cross-ploughing. No cross-ploughing is intended here; it is only useful in tearing tough swards to pieces. Here there can be no tough sward formed; and as it is only requisite to re-mellow the ground, it can be as effectually done by ploughing one way as by cross-ploughing. In order to keep the vegetable mold of an even depth over the surface, the furrows should be turned first the one way and then the other: beginning to back-furrow where the last parting furrows were made, and then the next parting furrows will be where the last back-furrows were made.

In ploughing the lengthway of each division, and having no short furrows, the work will be much accelerated, as no time is lost by too frequent turnings. The same may be observed in regard to hoeing the rows of hoed crops, and cutting the swarths in reaping and mowing. With long furrows, long rows and long swarths, the work goes on more rapidly than with short ones.

Any calculation is here omitted of stating the probable expense of these crops, and from thence shewing the clear profit of each, as every intelligent farmer can do this for himself; but on an average it may safely be affirmed that the clear profit will average at least twenty dollars an acre. The plan it will be perceived is best calculated for having a dairy combined with it, and this naturally includes the rearing of swine. See article SWINE. It will also be perceived that it is best calculated for particular pieces of land of greater or less extent as they may be found. Small pieces may, however, be advantageously cultivated in this way, even of as small extent as ten acres; and in such case it would be most advisable to set the barn on one side of the field, and run the narrow divisions quite across it. This plan of husbandry appears to be peculiarly calculated for redeeming from barrenness many light sandy, or poor gravelly tracts of land; and generally it seems well adapted to almost all lands that are tolerably level.

See further, article IMPROVEMENT OF LANDS.

It has been observed, however, that those cows which have been always used to be kept by soiling during the growing season, are usually more profitable than those which have but newly been put to this method of keeping.

SOOT. Forty bushels of this to an acre, is a good top-dressing for almost every kind of summer crop, or for winter crops, when sowed on them in the spring. Let it be powdered fine before it is applied. It is also very good for cold grass lands.

It is recommended to be sown over turnips, not only for the purpose of manuring the ground, but for keeping off insects. For this purpose let it be finely pulverized and sown in the morning while the dew is on, and let it be in moderate quantity, lest it should injure the young plants, to which it will adhere and repel the insects.

See article MANURES.

SOWING.   There are three methods of committing seeds to the ground.

1. In hills, which is usually called planting.
2. In drills, or continued rows: And,
3. In the *broad cast* method, or a cast of the hand.

For making seeds vegetate more readily, *see* article GERMINATION OF PLANTS.

By the drill method of sowing, about one half, at least, of the seed requisite for sowing may be saved; which with regard to wheat, particularly, is a matter of some consequence.

See Rutherford's essay on this subject, article DRILL.

For the proper time of committing each kind of seed to the ground and the quantity to be sown of each, *see* the articles of which the seeds are to be sowed.

A general rule which prevails in regard to sowing seeds, is, that the largest and most full grown be sown.   It is said that small seeds produce small stalks and small seeds, and large seeds the contrary. This, it is believed, is a matter well worth attending to, particularly as it respects the different kinds of grain which are not wholly naturalized to our climate or to our soil.

Sowing too early in the spring may be as injurious as sowing too late; for if the ground be not well pulverized, and sufficiently warmed before sowing, the seeds will come up slowly, and be stunted in their growth.

Duhamel found by experiments, that few seeds will come up if buried more than nine inches in the soil; that some will rise very well at the depth of six inches; and, that others again will not rise if buried two inches.   Those seeds which, in vegetating, are thrown out of the ground, such as beans, &c. ought to be buried lightly; and, in general, it may be observed, that very few seeds require to be very deeply buried.   In light soils they should be buried deeper than in stiff and cold ones.   When the ground is rolled after sowing, seeds will come up with a lighter covering of earth than where this is not done.

Much depends on having the seeds sowed as evenly as possible; and for this purpose they ought to be sowed when the weather is not windy, particularly those which are light or easily wafted away.   In sowing some seeds, it is advisable to go over the ground twice ; sow-ing one half of the intended allowance of seed one way, and the other half crosswise.

Previous to sowing, the most seeds should be steeped in some fer-tilizing liquor, and then dried, either with lime, ashes, or gypsum. For the prevention of smut, lye, &c. has already been mentioned.

See article SMUT.

Mr. Johnson recommends, adding about six ounces of saltpetre, to be dissolved in as much lye as will immerse a bushel of grain. This he advises more particularly for Indian corn and wheat ; and he men-tions an instance where it made a part of a field of wheat, the seed of which had been steeped in this way, as much as twenty-five per cent better than the rest of the same field. Let the seed be steeped about twenty-four hours.

Grain that is designed for sowing should always be kept well aired, for if deprived of this for a considerable length of time, it will not ve-getate. Mr. Miller took fresh seeds of different kinds, a part of each he put into phials, and sealed them so as to exclude the air, and the rest he kept exposed to it. After a twelvemonth he sowed each on different parts of the same bed, when all of those came up that were exposed to the air, but none of those which were excluded from it.

Where land is very rich, it ought generally to have more seed than if it be poor ; and if the size of the grains be large, the quantity sown should be greater than where they are small.

SPAVIN. A swelling about the joints of horses, causing lameness. There are two kinds of this disorder—a blood spavin and a bag spavin. The former is a swelling of the vein that runs along the inside of the middle joint of the hind legs, which is frequently attended with a lameness of the joint.

To cure it, says Mr. Gibson, first apply restringents and a bandage tightly drawn round the joint ; for these, if early applied, will general-ly effect a cure ; but if by these means the vein is not reduced to its usual dimensions the skin should be opened, and the vein tied with a crooked needle and wax-thread, passed underneath, above and below the swelling, and the turgid part will then digest away with the liga-tures. Let the wound be daily dressed with a mixture of turpentine, honey, and spirit of wine.

The bag spavin is merely a cyst, or bag, filled with the gelatinous matter of the joint, irrupted from its proper place. To cure this, cut into the bag, and let the matter discharge ; then dress the sore with lint dipped in oil of turpentine, putting into it, once in three or four days, a powder made of calcined vitriol, alum and bole. By this method of dressing, the bag will come away, and a cure will be effected without any visible scar.

Should this fail of a cure, the hot iron is directed to be applied; and in that case, if the joint becomes inflamed, apply a poultice over the dressings till the swelling is reduced.

SPAYING. It is recommended to spay sows, as this prevents conception, and will cause them to have more fat than the barrows. Heifers are also splayed in Great-Britain where they are raised merely for fatting. The method of performing this with effect is best learned by practice.

SPELT. This is a grain much used for bread in Germany. It is said to have been the ancient frumentacious tribute which the Romans formerly exacted from that country. It resembles wheat, but is smaller, and darker coloured, and is bearded, with only two rows on an ear.

It may be sowed in autumn, or in the spring, and delights in a dry soil.

SPIKY ROLLER. This instrument is much recommended by some English writers for mellowing clay ground that is baked in clods. It is also recommended to be passed over fields of wheat in the spring, for the purpose of loosening the ground, and then to be followed by a brush-harrowing. This would no doubt be very useful; and would afford a fine opportunity for sowing clover-seed on the crop. Its further use is to tear and loosen old grass-bound meadows, for the purpose of making the grass grow more thriftily again.

It is merely a wooden roller with iron teeth, or spikes, drove into it. They are to be about seven inches long, and drove three inches into the wood, and set four inches apart, in diagonal rows round the roller. The outer ends are not to be sharp but square.

SPINAGE. See article GREENS.

SPROUTS. Where woods are cut off which are apt to sprout, the best way is to persevere in destroying the sprouts as fast as they appear, because the longer they are suffered to grow, the more difficult it becomes to extirpate them, particularly in wet meadow lands. In these the difficulty is increased on account of their taste being less palatable than those of uplands, and therefore cattle are less inclined to eat them. In such grounds, the best way is to cut off the sprouts

31

four or five times in the first season, and this will pretty much destroy them. If a swamp can be flooded two or three years, it will effectually destroy sprouts and every other growth; or if it can be drained dry, it so alters the nature of the soil, that its growth of wood soon inclines to die for want of its usual moisture.

The best method of destroying sprouts, is to beat them off from the stumps. This can be done with the pole of an axe, and the more the stump is battered, and its bark beat off round the roots, the more effectually will the further growth of sprouts be prevented.

SPUR. A disease in rye. The grains which are affected with it are larger than the rest, mostly crooked, bitter to the taste, projecting beyond their husks, dark coloured, rough, and deeply furrowed from end to end.

This kind of diseased grain sometimes proves very destructive to those who eat it. In some parts of France, where the disease mostly prevails, the peasants who eat it are liable to be attacked with a dry gangrene in the extreme parts of the body, which causes those parts to fall off, almost without pain. " The Hotel Dieu, at Orleans," says Duhamel, " has had many of these miserable objects, who had not any thing more remaining than the bare trunk of the body, and yet lived in that condition several days."

It is not every year that the spur produces these effects ; and if the grain be kept a certain time before it is eaten it will not be hurtful. It is believed, however, that no very bad effects have been known in this country from eating this kind of rye.

STABLE AND STALLS. The stable should be so well inclosed as to defend the beasts from the winds and storms, and at the same time it should not be too warm, lest it make them tender when exposed to the weather.

The stable should have a good floor, descending a little backwards, so that the stale will run off behind. It should be divided into separate apartments, or stalls, for each beast to stand by itself. There should be a good manger for horses, and the rack which holds their hay should be upright and not too high. Some prefer putting the hay into a very large manger, or trough, made for the purpose, and what is left by horses can in this way be given to other cattle, as they will eat it very readily.

Stables should be kept clean and well littered, to keep the beasts comfortable when they lie down. Some advise boring holes through the floor to let off the stale more readily. For horses there should be sufficient room in the stalls to turn their heads to every part of their bodies, and to raise them as high as they please.

STAGGERS. A disease in some kinds of cattle. If the staggering of a horse be owing to hard usage, Gibson directs to take a pint of blood from his neck, and then a quart from some vein in his hinder parts, and that he be then kept on moderate cleansing diet.

When the disease arises from an apoplectic disorder, he must be treated as before, and exercised every day with chewing assafœtida, savin, and all other noisome things, which will keep him in constant action, and forward the circulation of the blood in the small vessels. Afterwards, recourse must be had to clysters, strong purgatives, rubbing and exercise.

When it arises from a swimming of the head, the animal reels, turns round, and falls. For this, take an ounce of senna, boiled in five pints of water, with four ounces of common treacle, and the usual quantity of oils or lard, to throw in as a clyster, and repeat this for two or three days; after this he may have a drench of beer, in which the roots of peony, angelica, rue, rosemary, and flowers of lavender have been steeped. If the disease continues obstinate, balls of cinnibar, and assafœtida, with bay-berries, will be proper here, as in apoplectic cases.

Mr. Gibson condemns the practice of putting ginger and other stimulating things into the ear as dangerous, though it may sometimes prove beneficial.

STALE. It is believed the stale of cattle is almost as valuable as a manure, as their dung, and that pains ought therefore to be taken to prevent its being lost.

For the best method of preserving it in stables, *see* article NEW HUSBANDRY.

The Hollanders, it is said, are as careful in saving the stale of their cattle as their dung. The older it is, the better, as a manure. Old urine is also said to be an excellent application to the roots of trees; but too much ought not to be applied, for in that case it sometimes kills them.

See article MANURES.

See further, article URINE.

STOCK. When an English farmer speaks of *stocking* a farm, he means the requisite number of ploughs, harrows, carts, and other implements of husbandry, beside cattle of different kinds, for carrying on the business of husbandry on that farm to advantage; in the same way that a merchant or manufacturer speaks of the stock, or capital, which is requisite to carry on any branch of trade or manufacture. But farmers in this country, being but little used to renting farms, do but seldom enter into calculations of this kind; and by this means the word *stock* has here acquired a different meaning in regard to farming business; it means merely the number of cattle of different kinds which a farmer keeps on his farm. It would, nevertheless, be well for those who are obliged to rent farms in this country, to examine first whether they can acquire the requisite *stock* for any farm, agreeably to the English meaning, before they attempt to hire; as by not having this they often injure themselves, as well as their landlords. '

Young stock are always more profitable than old; as these, when turned off to fat, do not answer so well as those which are but little past their prime. It costs more to fatten old cattle, and their meat is not so valuable.

Stock should be suitable to the soil on which they are fed. If their pastures be chiefly dry hills, sheep is the best. If they be grounds fit for the cultivation of clover, and various other grasses, the dairy, or fatting of cattle, may be best; and if they be wet grounds, which only produce coarse grasses, the raising of horses will be found most profitable.

The profit of raising horses depends much on the breeding mares, and also on the price which can be obtained for horses. Generally speaking, the farmer will do better in turning his attention to the best breeds of sheep, if his pasture lands be suitable. The dairy is also profitable, where properly managed with regard to the milk; and also with regard to raising a due proportion of swine, with the aid of clover, and the skim-milk, whey, and butter-milk together.

See articles DAIRY and SWINE.

But as stocks of cattle are found to degenerate, unless pains be taken to prevent it, an essential point of husbandry lies in taking the proper steps for improving the breeds. Some cows will give double the quantity of milk which others give, and of better quality. Some bulls beget much finer and larger calves than others. Some sheep bear more wool, and of better quality than others; and some rams beget lambs possessing these qualities in a superior degree to others. Similar observations may be made of some breeds of horses and of swine. The essential point, therefore, is, for the farmer to be diligent in selecting those breeds which are found to be most valuable, as well from those raised in his own stock, as from those which may be obtained elsewhere. Let him persevere in constantly selecting the best breeds for a stock, rejecting all others, and he will presently find his stock very greatly improved.

In Great-Britain much pains are taken to improve the breeds of cattle and the success attending such exertions are very encouraging. In some of their agricultural publications mention is made of prodigious prices being given for certain animals of superior breed : Such as a bull of Mr. Paget, having been sold in the year 1793 for four hundred guineas: Heifers belonging to him for eighty-four guineas a piece; and ewes for sixty-four guineas a piece. In *Monk's Agricultural Dictionary*, there is also mention made of a Mr. Richard Ashley having swine, the boars of which he let to sows at half-a-guinea each; and of a Mr. Bishop who sold his pigs, at weaning time, for two guineas a piece. Such examples might also be produced here, if the requisite pains were taken, and the profits attending them are surely sufficient to gratify even avarice itself.

Above all, let the farmer keep no greater stock than he can support well. The half of any given number of cattle, where they are well kept, will always be found to yield as much clear profit to the owner, as the whole when kept in poor condition. Poor keeping also learns cattle to be unruly ; and when they have learned this effectually, they only prove a bill of expense, instead of an article of profit, to the owner.

STONES. Where arable lands particularly abound with these, no good culture can be carried on. The first step then is to clear such lands of the stones, and let this be done effectually ; carrying off the small ones and digging out the large ones, so that there be no obstructions to the plough.

Some lands may indeed be too stony to be cleared of them to any present advantage. Let such be left to the prowess of future generations ; they will undoubtedly find their account in clearing such, and find use for the stones. If they be not all wanted for fences, buildings, &c. they may be found useful in making hollow drains, &c.

If stones be very badly shapen, so that they will not lie in a wall, perhaps the better way may be to throw them aside, and make hedge fences; but if they be chiefly well shaped, let them be made into walls; for these, if properly made, will last an age, with some trifling repairs. The best method of making these, is to dig a trench where the wall is to be made, to the depth of about eighteen inches ; into this throw all the small and bad shaped stones, until the trench is filled; then on the top of these build the wall, in a mason-like manner, to the height of about five feet, and throw the earth dug out of the trench up against the wall on each side; and in this way it will stand for a length of time beyond the memory of man. If a trench be not dug in this manner, the next best method is to plough deep trenches close on each side of the wall, after it is built, and throw the earth thus ploughed up, against the wall.

Where stones are very large, and cannot be removed without breaking them, the best way is to split them to pieces. For this purpose, drill two holes in opposite sides, according to the grain of the stone; then fill each hole with two half cylindrical pieces of iron, and between these drive a long steel wedge. In this way large stones or rocks may be split out into proper shapes for good building stones, or for other purposes. Building fires on large stones will also render them liable to be broken to pieces while they are thus heated.

By experiments accurately made, it is found, that small stones on the surface of the ground, are beneficial, in a small degree, in increasing its products; but they are too troublesome in good cultivation to be desirable on account of all the benefit to be derived from them.

Where ground is full of small stones, they may be drove down so as to be out of the way of the scythe, by having a roller passed over the ground in the spring, when it is very soft, as the stones are then easily pressed into it.

STOOKING or SHOCKING. Let ten sheaves be disposed in two rows, each leaning against the other; then let two sheaves be laid on the top, so as that the but of one lies under the but of the other, having the heads hanging downwards. In this way, wheat or other grain will keep very well. Another method is to make little stacks of an hundred sheaves or more, in each. They are made with the heads inmost and uppermost, and over the top of the whole, a large sheaf is tied close to the but end, and the other end spread all round the top of the stack, to preserve it from the rains. This is, no doubt, the best method for saving the grain from the effects of long and heavy rains.

STRAIN or SPRAIN. Horses are liable to strains, particularly in their shoulders. Anointing them with spirits of turpentine in the part injured, will help them for a while, but will not afford a permanent relief. Washing the shoulder when that part is affected, with brine, as warm as it can well be borne, will effect a cure in a few days. Let it be done twice a day; and letting the animal rest from labor will generally perform a cure in a few weeks at farthest. If these will not answer, let warm poultices be applied, of bran, boiled in vinegar, with a sufficiency of hog's-lard to prevent its growing hard; let this be repeated, if necessary, until the cure is completed; and then mind to keep that part covered a while, so that it shall not be affected by colds.

STRAWBERRY; *(Fragaria.)* The *Chili;* the *haut-boy;* the *wood;* and the *scarlet strawberry,* are each esteemed; but the latter is mostly cultivated. A light loamy soil is best for raising them; and it should not be dunged much, lest they should run too much, and of course be less fruitful.

They are first to be sown from the seeds, in a bed, which is to be kept clean of weeds. In this they are to be kept three years before transplanting. They are to be transplanted in September or the beginning of October. The ground into which they are to be transplanted, is to be laid out into beds four feet wide, with alleys between each, of the width of two feet. The plants are to be set fifteen inches apart, in rows each way. Mr. Miller says, " the plants should never be taken from old neglected beds, where the plants have been suffered to run into a multitude of suckers;" that those should be avoided which are not fruitful; " and those offsets which stand nearest to the old plants should be preferred to those which are produced from the trailing stalks at a greater distance."

When they become unfruitful, which is generally at the end of three years, they must be again transplanted.

Mr. Miller directs, that the vines be kept clear of weeds during summer, and that all the runners, or suckers, be pulled off as fast as they appear, which will be productive of a plentiful crop the next spring after planting. The old plants produce the fruit; the suckers yield none until after a full year's growth; and they serve to rob the old plants of that nourishment which is so essential to their fruitfulness.

In autumn, let the plants be again divested of their strings and runners, and the beds be again cleared of weeds. Mr. Miller directs, that some tanner's bark be then spread over the ground, and that this when afterwards buried in the soil will serve as a dressing for the vines. He further directs, that some moss, or straw, perhaps, will do as well, be spread round under the vines to keep the fruit from the ground.

An improved method of cultivating the Alpine strawberry, is as follows :—

"Sow the seed on a moderate hot-bed in the beginning of April, and as soon as the plants have acquired sufficient strength, transplant them in open beds. They will begin to blossom after midsummer, and afford an abundant autumnal crop."

Mr. Knight, who reports the foregoing method of treatment, thinks, that this plant should always be cultivated as an annual one.

STUBBLE. Where the stubble is large, as it will be where the grain is large, and is reaped, the ground will be very considerably benefitted by ploughing it under as soon as the grain is taken off; whereas if it be suffered to stand until it is perfectly dried, and all the juices evaporated, it will then do the ground little or no good. In this way too the seeds of many weeds are prevented from ripening.

SUNFLOWER; *(Helianthus.)* It is found, that the seeds of this plant afford an oil equal to that of the olive-tree; and it is said, that seventy bushels of this seed may easily be raised from an acre. The plant will grow in almost any soil that is sufficiently strong; and it is by no means difficult to cultivate. It is believed, that the cultivation of this plant for making oil, might be found very profitable. The seeds are also very good for feeding poultry during the winter season.

From a bushel of this seed, says the Editor of " *The Watchman,*" a gallon of oil, as fine as that which we import from Florence, may be obtained at any time, quite soft, bland, and fresh; and the mass that remains, after pressing out the oil, is of excellent use to feed hogs, poultry, &c. He further observes, that the inhabitants of unwholsome places should be diligent in cultivating this plant, on account of the vast quantity of oxygene gas which it produces; it having been proved, that near twenty times as much of this gas is produced in twenty-four hours by one plant, in light and clear weather, as a man respires, in an impure atmosphere, in that space of time.

The plants should be raised in rows and cultivated in the manner of hoed crops.

SURFEIT. A disease to which cattle, and particularly horses, are liable. In horses it is generally the effect of intense labor, or overheating. The skin becomes dry and full of dander, or of scabs, if the disease be more inveterate. The hair of the animal stands out, and he has a dull sluggish look.

Some have merely this look and appearance of the hair, while they grow lean and hide-bound, without any irruptions of the skin. Some have what is called a wet surfeit, in which case sharp thin humors run from the scabs. This is often attended with great heat, inflammations, and sudden swellings of the neck, which causes great quantities of briny liquor to issue from that part, and if not allayed will collect on the withers, and produce the fistula, or about the head, and produce the poll-evil.

To cure the dry surfeit, the author of " *The Complete Farmer*" directs, first, to take away three or four pounds of blood, and then give the following purge, which will work as an alterative, and should be repeated once a week for some time.

" Take succotrine aloes, six drachms, or one ounce ; gum guaicum, half an ounce ; diaphoretic antimony, and powder of myrrh, of each, two drachms, and make the whole into a ball with syrup of buckthorn."

In the intermediate days, an ounce of the following powder should be given, morning and evening with his feed.

" Take native cinnabar, or cinnabar of antimony, finely powdered, half a pound ; crude antimony in fine powder, four ounces ; gum guaicum in powder, four ounces ; make the whole into sixteen doses for eight days."

The medicine must be repeated till the horse coats well, and the symptoms of the disease disappear. If the scabs do not come off, anoint them with mercurial ointment. This ointment alone well rubbed into the blood, and aided by purges, will also commonly effect a cure.

For the wet surfeit, bleed plentifully, avoiding externally all repellers, and in the morning while fasting, give cooling physic twice a week, composed of four ounces of lenitive electuary, four of cream of tartar, and four of Glauber's salts, quickened with a little jalap.

After three or four of these purgings, give two ounces of nitre, made into a ball with honey, every morning for a fortnight ; and if successful, repeat this a fortnight longer. The above may also be given with the horses food ; or a strong decoction of logwood may be given alone, at the rate of two quarts a day. Where the disease proves obstinate, the medicine must be continued a considerable length of time, to prove effectual.

The horse should be kept dry, and his food should be cool and opening. If he is hide-bound, give him fenugreek seeds for some time.

Where the disorder proceeds from worms, give the mercurial physic, and afterwards the cinnabar powder, as above directed.

The author, from whose work the above directions are taken, observes, however, that as this disease is not always original, but attendant on others, in the cure, regard should be had to the first cause, and thus the removal of the complaint may be variously affected.

SWARD. A stiff green sward is an infallible indication of the ground being in good condition for bearing a good crop; but it is not an equally certain indication of a good soil; as the sward may be the effect of strong manuring. Some soils again which incline to moss, when they have lain untilled for some time, exhibit a greater degree of poverty than they really possess. Earths, however, which, without manuring, bear a stiff green sward, may always be pronounced good, whatever may be their colour; but perhaps only good for certain productions.

A stiff sward, well turned over, will generally bear a pretty good crop, of any growth which is suitable to the soil; as the rotting of the sward keeps up a fermentation in the soil nearly equal to that which is produced by repeated ploughings. This remark, however, more properly applies to rich mellow soils; those that are naturally stiff or hard, generally will not sufficiently ferment to bear a good crop by the mere rotting of the sward.

A clover sward, that has been mowed and well turned over, makes a very fine lay for wheat, where the soil is not too stiff or hard; but where the clover has been fed off, it is not considered quite so good; as in that case the ground becomes harder by the treading of the cattle. Much, however, in that case, depends on the natural mellowness of the soil.

Clover forms but a crumbly sward; Timothy is stiffer; but the English blue-grass, (poa,) forms one of the strongest. This, where it is very strong, and the soil full of vegetable matter, may be cut and used as turf.

Strong swards usually accumulate along the sides of fences, and where cattle much resort, which may be used to advantage in composts. See article MANURES.

When the sward of mowing ground binds too much, it is usually most advisable to break it up and till the ground. If this be not done scarifying, and compost manures are to be resorted to. The binding of the sward in mowing, or in pasture grounds, is principally the effect of close feeding. Let a sufficiency of fog, or after-grass, be left on such lands, and they will not be apt to bind.

Generally speaking, there is no method so easy, and cheap, of covering dry soils, which are poor or exhausted, with a fresh green sward, as with the use of gypsum; and this should always be done before such grounds are broken up; as in that case, double, or perhaps, treble the crop may be expected from them that they will yield if broken up with a light, poor sward on them. Let the gypsum be sown on such lands early in the spring, and by the first of the following July they will be covered with a fine sward of white clover; and when land is well covered with this grass, it is in good condition, with the aid of good tillage, to bear a plentiful crop.

SWARTH-RAKE. This is a rake about two yards long, with iron teeth, and a bearer in the middle; to which a man fixes himself with a belt, and when he has gathered as much as his rake will hold, he raises it and begins again.—*Complete Farmer.*

For another kind of rake, *see* article HAY-MAKING.

SWINE. "*The Cattle Society of Pennsylvania*," recommend crossing the *Guinea breed* of hogs with the best kinds of our common swine, which, they say, forms a breed the most profitable of any.

The *Chinese breed* are very good. The large long bodied hogs with long ears, leaning forward, are most profitable to fatten the second year.

Particular pains should be taken to select and improve the breed of hogs, as some kinds are much more profitable for raising than others. After a proper improvement of the breed, the next point is to select the finest for breeding sows, and for boars.

The marks of a good hog are, a moderate length, in proportion to the size of the body; the head and cheek plum and full; neck thick and short; quarters full; carcase thick and full; hair fine and thin; with a symmetry adapted to the respective breed to which he belongs. Above all, it is essential, that he be of a kindly disposition to fatten early.

The sow will bring forth a stronger and better litter, if she be kept till she is a year old before she goes to the boar; and he should be kept till that age before he is put to sows. He should be kept in good condition for the purpose, and as the author of "*The Complete Grazier*" says, should not serve more than ten sows in a year. The sows should also be kept in good condition, but not too fat; as in that case they will not produce an abundant litter of pigs. As they will usually pig twice a year, they should be put to the boar at such times as will bring forward one litter in April and another early in September. To cause them to go to the boar, if they miss the right season, give them some parched oats in their wash, or the small end of a runnet-bag. If well kept, however, they will seldom require any stimulus to coition at the proper times. Those are reckoned the best breeders which have about ten or twelve paps. They should be kept clean and well littered, but should not have too much litter at the time of pigging, lest they overlay their pigs in it. At the end of a week or ten days, they should be let out of their sties into their yard, for three or four hours each day. Where several sows are farrowing, about the same time, they must be kept in separate apartments in the sty, lest they devour the pigs of each other. Young sows will sometimes eat their own offspring, which may be prevented by washing the backs of the pigs in an infusion of aloes; and, for this purpose, the sows must be watched when bringing forth. It is said, that supplying them with plenty of water at this time will prevent any mischief taking place of this kind.

The sucking pigs intended for market, should be killed at the end of about three weeks. The finest ones should be saved. By this time the rest will be able to follow the sows, when the males may be castrated, and at the end of another week the females may be spayed. This latter operation will greatly promote the growth and fattening of the females. The castration and spaying may as well, however, be deferred till the age of six weeks.

Where the pigs are to be weaned, Mr. Young says, it should be at the age of two months; and they should be kept in the sty by themselves and suffered to run into a yard. They should be kept clean, and well littered, and should have plenty of food, which may be boiled potatoes, or carrots, for a fortnight, when raw ones will prove good food. They should also be baited every day for a month with oats, and after this may have a thin drink of pea, or buck-wheat meal, (Indian-meal will no doubt answer as well,) boiled in water, unless there be a dairy; in which case, a mess of milk or whey may be substituted. Too much should not, however, be given them at once, as Mr. Deane says it is known sometimes so to inflate them with wind as to kill them. Mr. Young says, their being kept very cleanly, so as to have fine clean coats, is as essential to their growth as good feeding, until they are turned out with the larger hogs into the clover field, which, after the age of three months, will keep them very well during the rest of the growing season.

It has been uniformly remarked, that though these animals are naturally filthy, if left to themselves, yet the cleaner they are kept, the better they will grow and fatten.

Boiled or steamed clover hay will serve to keep hogs during winter; but, perhaps, the addition of some potatoes or carrots boiled with the hay, would be a very proper addition. The clover should be cut a little sooner than usual, and should be well cured, and have about a peck of salt to each ton, when laid down in the mow. For boiling in this case, as well as for boiling roots, and for other purposes, a wooden vessel full of holes at the bottom is placed over the boiler, which holds the water, and which is heated underneath; being set in a brick stove or furnace for the purpose. The steam from the boiler rises through the holes in the bottom of the vessel which holds the articles to be boiled, or steamed, and after passing through them, is let off at the top; not faster, however, than is necessary, being partly confined by a lid. If the hay, or other articles, are to be boiled in water, the steam is conducted by a tube into the bottom of a vessel holding the water, into which the articles are put. The steam-boiler is a very essential article in the rearing of swine and for other purposes, and no good farmer should be without it.

The sows may be allowed to breed till they are six years old, and the boar until he is five. After this the former is to be spayed and put up to fatten, and the latter is to be castrated, as being no longer fit for use. His flesh will make good bacon when fatted.

In preference to feeding swine on clover in the field, during summer, Mr. Young prefers soiling them in a yard for the purpose; and in this case he makes use of Lucerne, cichory, clover, tares, and other green food, cut and carried in for feeding them. The water crowfoot (*rununculus aquatilis,*) is also highly recommended for this purpose. This method, however, though it may save some ground in pasture, and may afford the means of making considerable manure, does not seem so apparently beneficial as the practice of soiling some other cattle. Mention is made by Mr. Young, of his having fed sixty-four hogs, great and small, on two acres of clover alone, during one season, and that they all grew very well. The pasture in which they are kept should have a supply of water. Before they are turned into the pasture, and while they are young, let the top of the gristle of the nose be pared off with a sharp knife, which will ever afterwards prevent their rooting up the sward. It answers the same purpose as ringing them.

Perhaps the best method of keeping swine during summer is to have two small enclosures; the one to be kept for feeding them, while the other is under tillage for a fresh supply of clover, or other good grass, when that in the first has failed. And as they are fond of sweet apples, which not only serve for food, but will even help to fatten them, let the enclosures be planted with a few trees of these, of the best yearly bearers, selected for the purpose; some being early ripe and some later; in order that a constant supply may be afforded during the season. The trees should, however, not stand so closely as materially to injure the ground for cultivation. Peach-trees may also be advantageously used for the same purpose till the apple-trees have sufficiently grown.

Boiled clover has been mentioned as affording a good food for hogs during winter. In Great-Britain boiled carrots, potatoes, &c. are mostly used for the purpose by those who go largely into the raising of swine; but here the greater severity of our winters is not so favorable for this practice; the farmer here, must, therefore, consume most of his stock of roots before the frosts set in, and must principally rely on his boiled clover, with some small addition of roots preserved from the frosts, for food during the winter season. No doubt a little Indian meal sprinkled among the hay, and boiled with it, will be an excellent addition.

Hogs for fatting should be in a healthy state; and to increase their appetite let a dose or two of sulphur be given them in their food. Change of food is also good to increase their appetite; but laxative food should be avoided, as they are seldom costive. When found so, a little rye will help them. Probably changes of boiled roots, and of meal and water at intervals, would be found best. Mr. Young says, the best method of feeding all kinds of grain to hogs, is to grind it to meal, and mix it with water, in cisterns made for the purpose, in the proportion of five bushels of meal to a hundred gallons of water; the mass to be well stirred several times each day, until it has fermented and become acid, when it will be ready for use. In this way two or three cisterns must be kept for fermenting in succession; but he says, the profits will amply pay the expense. For the same reason the grains of distilleries, and the refuse of starch factories are excellent for fatting swine. Mention is made of one of the latter at Lambeth, (Great-Britain,) affording sufficient to fatten 10,000 hogs in a year. Pea-soup is also accounted excellent for fatting; but in this case the expense of boiling the peas is incurred. Boiled Indian corn is also very good, or this grain may be soaked so as to answer well, though perhaps it is better ground into meal. Indian corn of a former year's growth is much the best.

In recommendation of peas, together with a mixture of barley meal being used for fatting, the author of " *The Complete Grazier*" asserts, that the pork fatted with this grain will rather swell in boiling and have an improved flavor, while that fatted with beans will shrink much in boiling, will loose much of its fat and be of inferior taste. The cause of meat sometimes shrinking very much, and loosing much of its oils in cooking, seems not to be well understood ; though the knowledge necessary for preventing it would be highly desirable. Generally speaking, it is believed, that the more fully any animal is fatted the less its meat will shrink and part with its oil in cooking.

Whatever method of fattening swine may be adopted, it is essential that they be kept *warm* and *clean*, by having plenty of litter, particularly when the weather becomes colder and by keeping the sty frequently cleaned ; and, that they should have as much solid food and drink as they require. Their meals should also be regular, and as nearly equi-distant in point of time as possible.

It is observed by the author of " *The Complete Grazier*," that where many hogs are put up together to fatten, they will fall away at first, if ever so well fed ; which he attributes to the noise and confusion produced among them by this new state of keeping : He observes too, that in such cases it is not unfrequent for one of the family to become so much the object of hatred to the rest, as eventually to be killed by them; and from all this he infers, that it is much the better way to have them in a number of small companies, detached from each other, so that the noise and bustle will be less, and in order that they may more unmolestedly enjoy that repose which is most suitable to their drowsy faculties. For this purpose the sty should have a number of distinct apartments, separated by close partitions from each other, and where the inmates of each can come forward separately to the general feeding trough, and retire separately again to rest.

Where a hog has surfeited itself by eating too much, the same author recommends giving it half an ounce of flour of sulphur in some wash, once or twice a day, for two or three days; by which time its appetite will be restored. Mr. Deane advises, that posts be set up in the sty for them to rub against, as they are usually much inclined to rub themselves.

The business of fatting hogs should be begun so early in the fall as to be completed before the cold weather sets in ; as after this they will fatten very slowly. Let it be commenced by the middle of September, and then the killing may commence about the middle of November.

Swine are liable to some diseases, which are here noticed, with the best remedies for them.

Measles.—This disorder is mostly in the throat, which is filled with small pustules, and sometimes these appear on the outside of the neck. The animal affected looks languid, with red eyes, and looses flesh. *Cure.*—Give him small quantities of levigated crude antimony in his food.

The mange, like the scab in sheep, is a cutaneous irruption of the skin, occasioned by want of cleanliness in the hogsty. It is known by the violent rubbing of the animal till he tears the pustules, and thus produces scabs. The cure, as directed by Dr. Norford, is first to wash the animal well with strong soap-suds; then anoint him with an ointment formed of an ounce of flour of sulphur ; two drachms of fresh pulverized hellibore ; three ounces of hogslard ; and half an ounce of the water of kali. This is to be rubbed in at one time, and is sufficient for a hog weighing an hundred. If properly applied, no repetition will be necessary, if the hog be afterwards kept clean. Where he has a slight cough, he directs doses of antimony, from half an ounce to an ounce and a half, according to the size of the animal, to be finely pulverized and mixed with his food for ten days or a fortnight. But where from long neglect, the neck, ears, and other parts become ulcerated, they should be anointed every third or fourth day with an ointment made of equal parts of tar and mutton suet, melted together, till the cure is completed.

The murrain, or leprosy in swine, is known by the shortness and heat of the breath, hanging down of the head, staggering, and secretions from the eyes. It is said to be caused by hot seasons, when the blood becomes inflamed.

Remedy.—Boil a handful of nettles in a gallon of small beer ; add half a pound of flour of sulphur, a quarter of a pound of anniseeds, pulverized ; three ounces of liquorice and a quarter of a pound of elecampane, and give this mixture in milk at six doses.

The gargut is an inflammation of the udder, by being filled with coagulated milk. It chiefly happens where sows are too fat at littering; and where they are thus affected the pigs will not suck. In slight cases the udder may be bathed with camphorated wine; but the milk must be squeezed out by hand, if possible. If relief cannot thus be given, it is best to kill the animal.

Dry cough and wasting of the flesh, is best remedied by a dry warm sty, with a regular supply of food that is calculated to keep them cool, and to allay the irritation of the lungs.

Fever, or *rising of the lights,* seems to be caused by over feeding, and may be removed by doses of sulphur and oil

Like many other employments, that of rearing and fatting swine will be found more profitable the more largely and spiritedly it is entered into; and in order to this the farmer must have his hogsty of an adequate construction; his pastures adjoining; his steam-boiler; his clover-hay; together with a due supply of roots and grain for feeding and fatting. The business is most advantageous when connected with a proportionate dairy; but by following the plan above laid down may answer very well without.

SYCAMORE; *(Acer.)* This tree is commonly called maple. There are but three kinds in this country, the white-maple, the red-maple, and the rock or sugar-maple. The latter kind is excellent for fuel, even when green, but it is most valuable for its juice in making sugar, and of this kind only something shall be said.

Where the farmer wishes to save his sugar-maple trees, he ought not to tap them in the common way, but instead of this, bore a hole two or three inches into the tree, out of which the sap can be drawn, and let it be plugged up after the sap has done running. The method of making the sugar is too well known to need any minute description. It would be often well, however, if those who make this sugar, were to observe more cleanliness in regard to the vessels in which the sap is gathered. Old troughs which have lain for years exposed to the weather, are not very proper receptacles for the sap, if regard be had to the cleanliness of the sugar, and of course to its value. Some make use of vessels made in the form of pails, which they keep for the purpose, and this is certainly at least more cleanly. The vessels can be laid up every year, after the time of using them is past, and be preserved many years.

Where farmers are clearing off pasture lands which abound with sugar maple, it would be well to preserve these trees, as they do no injury to the pasture; but the difficulty is, that as soon as they become more exposed to the winds they are blown down. But let the farmer

33

preserve all the small maples which he finds in such grounds, and in a few years these will grow up with sufficient strength of root to withstand the winds, and become an article of profit and ornamental to his farm.   They may also be very easily dug up in the woodlands, and transplanted into such pastures.   This is a piece of economy which the farmer would do well to observe, if he wishes his farm to yield due supplies of sugar when that article shall have become more scarce. Twenty trees to an acre would do little or no injury to the pasture ; and ten acres of such a maple orchard would in a few years yield no inconsiderable quantity of sugar.   By boring the trees as above directed, no essential injury is done to them, so that they might be increasing in growth for half a century, or perhaps double that length of time.

The trees may be propagated by cuttings or by the seeds.

T.

TAIL-SICKNESS. *See* article NEAT CATTLE.

TALL OAT-GRASS. *See* article GRASSES.

TALL MEADOW OATS. The Rev. Mr. Muhlenburg, of Lancaster, Pennsylvania, speaking of this grass, in 1793, says, that he found it the earliest, latest, and best for green fodder and hay, which he had tried. It blossoms in the middle of May and the seed ripens about a month after. It grows best in a clover soil, and the leaves are from two to four feet high before it blossoms. In the blossom the stalk rises from five to seven feet.

He says it should be cut in the blossom, about the beginning of June. The seed may be sown in the spring or fall, and should be lightly harrowed or brushed in. It may be mixed with clover to advantage. He observes, however, that horses do not like it green, but eat it when made into hay.

No doubt this is a very good grass, but it is inferior in quality to Lucerne.

TEAMS. Our teams are of three kinds; teams of horses, of oxen, and of oxen and horses together. In Spain and Italy they have teams of cows, and sometimes of cows and bulls together. In the northern parts of Europe the rein-deer has been subjected to the harness, and Mr. Livingston is of opinion that the elk and the moose might also be brought under the like subjection to advantage in this country.

The advantages of horses in teams are their superior docility and quickness of motion; and their disadvantages are their greater expense in raising and keeping, and their being of no value after their time of service is over. On the contrary, the advantages of oxen are their cheapness in raising and keeping, and their value for beef after their proper time of service has expired; and their disadvantages are their slowness of motion and their greater untractableness. Probably they might be rendered more tractable if some effectual method were devised for driving them with lines; in that case the extra expense of a hand to drive them in ploughing would be saved, and the ploughing better performed.

Say that a good span of farming horses are worth, at four years old, one hundred dollars: At fourteen years from that time they are worth little or nothing; of course, another sum of one hundred dollars, must at the expiration of that time be expended in the purchase of a new span. This sum to be paid at the end of fourteen years is about equal to fifty dollars paid down. In order, therefore, to keep good the span, a capital of one hundred and fifty dollars is necessary; which is equal to an expenditure of ten dollars and fifty cents a year. A yoke of oxen at four years old, are worth, say, sixty dollars; and allowing them not to depreciate in value till turned off for fatting, they require an expenditure of four dollars and twenty cents a year, as the interest of the capital laid out for them. Say that the horses will cost fifteen dollars a year more than the oxen to keep them, and provide harness for them: Say also, that they do an hundred day's work in a year, and that the oxen, working a quarter slower, require one hundred and thirty-three days to perform the same labor: Then if one hand only is employed with the oxen, his wages and board during the extra thirty-three days, at fifty cents per day, would still leave a balance in favor of the oxen of four dollars and eighty cents for the year's work; but if they should require a boy to drive, while another hand holds the plough, then the balance would be very considerably in favor of the horses.

On the whole, it is believed, that oxen may be found the most profitable team in some situations, particularly in new countries, and in rough lands; and in other situations again, such as in smooth lands, and where the best cultivation is required, probably, horses ought, for most uses, to have the preference.

Lord Kaims, however, expresses an opinion very different from this. He says that oxen are preferable for husbandry in many respects. They are cheaper than horses, as it regards their food; the method of keeping them; the superiority of their dung; their being subject to fewer diseases; and their suffering no deterioration by age. He says, that a couple of oxen in a plough require not a driver more than a couple of horses; that the Dutch at the Cape of Good Hope plough with oxen, without a driver, and exercise them early to a quick pace, so as to equal horses both in the plough and in the waggon; that the people of Malabar use no other animal for the plough, nor for burdens; and that about Pondicherry no beasts of burden are to be seen but oxen. He further justly remarks, that if oxen were more generally used, that the articles of beef, candles, and leather, three essential necessaries of life, would become much cheaper.

The compiler of " *The Complete Grazier,*" also says, that Messrs. Culleys, of Northumberland, Great-Britain, employ one hundred and fifty oxen in the draft; that they are used singly in carts, and two in a plough with cords, or lines, without a driver. He however observes, that they do not perform their work with the same dispatch as horses. He further observes, that " in the North of England, it is not an unfrequent occurrence to to see a light ox saddled, and briskly trotting along the road, obedient to his rider's voice ;" and that " Sussex oxen have beaten horses at the plough, in the deepest clay." He recommends the Hertfordshire and Devonshire oxen as being the most speedy.

See the description of the Devonshire breed of oxen in article NEAT CATTLE.

The slowness of oxen is partly natural, and partly acquired by overloading them. This, therefore, should be avoided. When their work is easy they may be quickened without hurting them, and their contracting a habit of moving so slowly, as some do, may be thus prevented. They always become slower as they grow older, and for that reason they never should be kept longer than such age as they will still make the best beef, which is probably about the age of seven or eight years.

In a team of part oxen and part horses, either the gait of the oxen must become quickened, or that of the horses made slower; but, perhaps, a little of each would be the consequence, and in this way the oxen would be the better, though probably at the expense of injuring the horses for almost every kind of work, when they are worked by themselves.

Mr. Livingston makes mention of a contrivance he had seen in Italy, that was attached to the noses of the oxen, which was principally used for governing them ; and by means of it he thinks he had seen them drove with lines. " It consists," says he, " of two flat pieces of iron that turned at the lower ends, and formed a forceps, these bars shut over, and when closed, the ends gently pressed upon the cartilage of the nose of the ox. They were kept close by being tightly bound at the top, and strapped against the forehead of the oxen."

" If we may argue the utility of a practice from its extent," says Mr. Livingston, " we must prefer drawing by the horns to any other mode; nine tenths of Europe make their cattle draw in this way, and from what I have seen of their performance, I am persuaded that it is to be preferred to the yoke. A bull's strength appears to be placed in his neck, and in drawing in this way the whole of it is exerted; his motion is not impeded, or his skin chafed as it is by the yoke."

" In the mountains of Savoy," says Mr. Livingston, " I saw many cattle, chiefly cows, drawing by the horns, not in carts but in waggons. How far the working of cows is advantageous, deserves consideration. It is observable, however, that our cows are in general much smaller than those usually worked in Europe."

" Yokes," he observes, " are used in some parts of Italy, but they differ from ours. Instead of bows, there are four flat pieces of wood, which hang from each side of the yoke, and are about ten inches long, and hollowed so as to fit the sides of the neck: They are so thick as to admit a rope or chain to pass through them, by which they are fixed to the yoke, and each pair of them are united by a chain, or rope, under the oxen's neck. You will see that the draft is in this case by the top of the shoulders only, and I believe it is to be preferred to our bows on that account, because the bow by pressing the shoulder blade impedes the motion of the animal." For holding back, whether they draw by these yokes or by the horns, he says, " the end of the pole projects considerably beyond the heads of the cattle, and turns up very much; to this is fixed a leather strap that goes round the horns of the oxen, so that they keep back the weight by their horns, and with much more ease than ours do by twisting their necks."

In England they are worked in a harness, which, were it not more expensive, and more troublesome, ought to be preferred to the method practised here.

I think it highly probable, that the great pressure of the bows of our yokes against the shoulders of the oxen, and the enormous weight they are often injudiciously made to bear on their necks, when in carts, are the principal causes of our oxen moving slower the longer they are used.

In all teams, where two animals draw against each other, the weaker one should have the longer end of the ox-bow, or whiffle-tree, by which they draw, in order that when drawing they may pull evenly.

If oxen learn to crowd each other, use them to a shorter bow; if they draw apart, use them to a longer one.

THISTLE; *(Carduus.)* The common kind of these are easily kept out of the fields, by plucking them out while young, or mowing them before they go to seed. But there is a species of thistle gaining ground in the northern parts of this state, called *Canada thistle*, being imported from Canada, which threatens to become a serious evil to our soil.

See article WEEDS.

See also, article FULLER'S THISTLE.

THORN. The English Thorn being liable to be killed by the severity of our winters, it becomes advisable to make use of that which is natural to our climate for making hedges.

See article HEDGES.

It has, however, been found difficult to make the seeds of our own thorn to germinate; but it is believed that this may be easily accomplished, if the means be applied which have been recommended in a preceding article.

See GERMINATION OF PLANTS.

After the seeds have been cleaned, and treated as directed in the above article, let them be sown in the fall, in beds of warm rich mould having a southern exposure, at the depth of little more than two inches. When they come up let them be transplanted into other beds, and kept clear of weeds till they are fit to set out in the hedge, which should be at the height of two feet.

Probably it may be found, that immersing the seeds about half a minute in hot water, holding a solution of saltpetre, would be found sufficient to make them germinate. Hot water and saltpetre, have each been found to quicken germination.

THRESHING. This, when performed with flails, is but slow work. Threshing with horses is considerably more expeditious. Some of the German farmers of this county and its vicinity, thresh with a roller, which turns on a centre at one end, which is small and confined to the floor, at that end, by an iron pivot on which it turns, and the other end is large in proportion to the increase of the circle which it makes. It is drawn by a horse, and is usually of the length of about twelve feet. It is set full of little square pieces of wooden teeth, leaning outwards, with the ends cut off slanting, agreeably to the superfice of the roller. With this a man and horse will thresh out about twelve bushels of wheat in a day.

In Virginia, where the greatest crops of wheat are raised, they generally thresh them out in the fields, and for this some use patent threshing machines, and some make smooth circular earthen floors of eighty feet diameter, or more; on this the wheat is set with the heads upwards, and then waggons and horses are drove round on it till that floor is threshed; then more is constantly thrown on, till one hundred bushels, or more, are threshed out, when they separate the wheat from the straw, by forking it up, and proceed to clean the wheat, and then proceed as before, till the business is completed. Threshing machines are, however, the best; and the expense of them is but a trifle for those who raise large crops of wheat and other grain.

TILLAGE. A great part of this work relates to tillage, or the culture of land; the reader must therefore refer to the various articles which treat of this subject in all its branches. Any uncommon mode of culture, however, or any miscellaneous observations relating to the subject, will naturally form the substance of this article.

Under the article, SOILING OF CATTLE, is laid down a method of tilling a small piece of land, wherever such may be found suitable for the purpose, which the writer of this work has ventured to recommend. The mode of culture there recommended is uncommon; the land is divided into narrow strips, and these are to be ploughed but one way. Further, therefore, to assist in convincing the most bigotted, that there is nothing extravagant in the plan of cultivating in narrow strips, and ploughing but one way; the mode of cultivating two fields, which is practised by the inhabitants of *Market Weighton*, in Great-Britain, as published in the "*Rusticum Museum*," shall be here noticed.

These people have five fields, in common, for culture; three of a clayey soil, and two which are more sandy. The latter supply them with rye, hay, and pasture for their sheep, &c.; and are tilled in the following manner:—The fields are raised in ridges, which are four mowing swarths wide; the middle, or higher part of each ridge, of the width of two swarths, is cultivated for rye, and the remainder of each, or the moister parts, alternately for mowing and pasture: When the rye is growing the grass strips are mowed; and the next season, when rye strips are fallowed for another crop of that grain, the grass strips afford pasture for their sheep, &c.; the dung and stale of the the flock serves as a light manuring for the ground every fallowing year; and this serves constantly to produce strips of good rye, and mowing ground the next year. It would seem by the description given of these grounds, that the soil is somewhat wettish though sandy.

Here, then, is ground tilled to advantage, as is said, in very narrow strips, and without any cross-ploughing. It is however believed, that such fields might be cultivated to much more advantage on the soiling plan, heretofore recommended, or something similar.

In tilling lands, it is essential that it be done *in the right season;* that it be done *effectually;* and in order to this, it is of the first importance to have the implements of tillage *well constructed,* and kept in good order.

Again, lands should always be applied to that tillage for which they are best adapted; or, in other words, in which they will constantly yield the greatest *clear profit.* If, therefore, the farmer has lands which are only fitted for grass, let him not work against wind and tide in trying to raise grain on them. If he has broken hills, and declivities, they will generally but poorly repay the unpleasant labor of cultivating them with the plough and the hoe; rather let such be kept for sheep-walks, for orchards, for raising timber, or perhaps for the culture of the vine, as they may be found best adapted. If his lands are rocky and stony, to plough and hoe them is a difficult uneasy employment; and never can be productive of much profit, till the impediments to the plough and the hoe are removed. If they are too light and sandy, they may nevertheless be made to yield good crops of tap-rooted plants, such as carrots and clover; or of such as ripen early, as rye for instance; or that bear drought well, as burnet, sainfoin, Lucerne; or of such trees as flourish in sandy soils, as the locust, Lombardy poplar, olive, &c. If the lands be boggy, when well drained, they will be found very profitable for hemp, which they will bear yearly, with the aid of small yearly additions of manure; but, if the lands be moderately level, smooth, and of a good medium soil, that is, such as is equally adapted for grain and for grasses, there let the farmer pursue the culture of a rotation of crops, in such manner as he finds will afford him the greatest clear profit; and in doing this, it is believed, that he cannot adopt a better plan than that recommended under article SOILING, &c. or something similar to it.

The expense of any kind of tillage never should be regarded where clear profits proportionately great may be safely calculated on, as a general result. Thus, if it costs fifty dollars an acre to till and gather an acre of carrots, and that acre, upon a yearly average, will give five hundred bushels, the crop at eighteen cents a bushel, which is certainly not too high, gives thirty-five dollars per acre as the clear profit, after taking out five dollars an acre for the use of the land; a profit much greater than can be realized by raising any kind of grain. Neither should the expense of tillage be regarded where the clear profits will be great, though not to be realized in some years, if it may be calculated on as a reasonable certainty, that those profits will eventually be realized.

TIMBER. The right time for felling trees for timber is in December and January, when the sap is down, as in this case it is less liable to be eaten with worms.

By experiments of Mr. Buffon, it is found that trees which are stripped of their bark in May or June, while standing, and then cut down the next winter for timber, are found to make the most solid, heavy, and strong timber, even the sap is then good. The bark of oak, and some other trees, may, at that time, be stripped off to advantage for the use of tanning.

Soaking timber in salt water is very good to increase its strength and durability.

In order to preserve timber from cracking while seasoning, let it be blocked out for the purposes wanted, and laid in a hay-mow when the hay is carting in. When the hay is dealt out the next winter, the pieces may be taken out well seasoned, and free from cracks. This is an excellent plan for seasoning all kinds of timber for carriages, &c. When this is to be done, if the trees be felled in winter, let them lie in logs until hay-time arrives.

The right time for cutting down trees for timber, is, when they are in their prime; as the wood will then have arrived to its greatest perfection for hardness and durability.

TIMOTHY-GRASS; (*Phleum Pratense.*) This is a coarse grass, but agreeable to all sorts of cattle, and suitable to low moist grounds. It is said to be a native of America. The name of *Timothy* was given it in the southern states, by its having been carried from Virginia to North-Carolina by one *Timothy Hanse.* It is also called *bulbous cat's-tail grass.*

See article GRASSES.

TOBACCO; (*Nicotiana.*) This plant has its name from *Tobago,* one of the Carribee islands. It was first introduced into England, and from thence into Europe, by the famous Sir Walter Raleigh.

For raising the young plants, burn a piece of ground early in the spring, rake it well, and sow the seeds. When the plants have acquired leaves of the size of a shilling piece transplant them. They require a dry, light soil, and a rich one, well mellowed with ploughiags. Dung of the hottest kinds are suitable to it, though cow-dung in sandy soils will do well for raising it. Transplant the young plants when the ground is wet, as in the case of cabbage plants, and afterwards hoe them and clean them of weeds as you do these, and destroy the large green worms which feed on them. The plants are to be set at the distance of about three and a half feet apart.

Cut off the tops of the plants at the height of about three feet, more or less, as they may be more or less thrifty, except those designed for bearing seed, and let these be the largest. The cutting should be done so early as to let the upper leaves acquire a size equal to the lower ones, and let them all be cut off at the same time, whatever the size, in order that good thick leaves may be afforded. Let the suckers which shoot out from the foot of the stalks be also broken or pinched off as they appear.

The ripeness of tobacco is known by small dusky spots appearing on the leaves, and by their feeling thicker than usual. Then cut them down at the roots, on the morning of a sunny day, and let them lie singly to wither; but be careful not to let them get sun-burnt. When withered, lay them in close heaps, under cover, to sweat, for about forty-eight hours or more. After this, hang them up under cover to dry. The way to do this is by running two stalks on the ends of a sharp stick, and thus suspending them across a pole, at proper distances from each other. As the plants become dry and brown, place them nearer together, when the air is damp, so that the leaves do not crumble. When they have hung till all the greenness has left the leaves, and when they are a little damp, strip them off, pack them in casks, well pressed down, and keep them in a dry place. They will be better for use after the first year.

This climate is too cold for raising tobacco to much advantage, except in a few favored spots in the warmest parts of this state. In the colder parts, the leaves grow too thin to be of much value.

Some practice raising crops of this plant in their cow-yards, without much previous mellowing of the soil; but it is generally ill-tasted stuff, and of but little value in the market.

The above is merely an outline of the method of cultivating this plant. For a minute and more particular description, I would refer the reader to "*Winterbotham's View of the United States*," third volume.

TOP-DRESSINGS. *See* article MANURES.

TRANSPLANTING. In performing this operation, the essential point is to set the roots in the ground in a situation similar to that in which they were placed before they were taken out; not only the same depth, but, as Mr. Forsyth says, with the same side to the south which was the south side before: But as they cannot be got out of the ground, nor set again into it with their full length of roots, these must be cut off to a length proportionate to their size. Where they are very small, let them be cut at the length of six or eight inches, and where they are pretty large, double that length, or more: Let them be carefully taken up without breaking the roots, cutting off those that get broken, and cutting them all off at their proper length; and let the hole into which they are to be set, be sufficiently large to receive the roots without cramping them: Then shake in the earth gently about them, so as that each one shall retain its proper position. As it is difficult to give the fibrous roots their proper place, it is generally best to cut most of these off. In fruit-trees, all the downright roots should also be cut off.

If the roots have been some time out of ground, it is advisable to soak them in water for eight or ten hours before they are set in. In a cold or stiff soil they should be set shallower than in a warm mellow one. After they are properly bedded in the ground, a stake should be drove in near to each one, leaning towards them, and to these they should each be tied, to keep them steady; and some mulch should be laid round the roots of each.

In transplanting the smaller kinds of plants, a wet time is to be chosen, and the evening is better than any other time. As much of the earth should be left round the roots, as possible, in taking them out of the ground; and if they are raised with a little instrument called a gardener's trowel, by which a bunch of earth can be raised with them, they will be the better for it. The holes where they are set should be well watered, and the water should previously be well warmed by the sun.

For the times of transplanting different plants, and the distances they are to be set apart, see the different articles which are the subjects of this operation.

TREFOIL. See article GRASSES.

TRENCH-PLOUGHING. This is performed for two purposes; first, to stir up the earth deeper than it can be well done with one plough; and secondly, to turn under an old exhausted layer of earth, in order to turn up a new one that is fresh and more fertile. It is often useful in clay soils, the top of which has been worn out. In deep rich soils, such as intervales, &c. it may also be found good husbandry, where the upper stratum has been long under the plough without manures.

See article FREEZING, where a case is mentioned, shewing the good effects of this culture.

The method is first to run a furrow with one plough the usual depth, then another follows after in the same furrow, and throws up the fresh earth as deep as possible; then the next light furrow is thrown into the bottom of the deep one, and the deep one again follows, and throws up a new layer on the top of the old, and so the work proceeds.

TUMORS. Mr. Bartlet directs, that when these appear on the poll, withers, under the jaws, or in the groins of horses, they should be forwarded by ripening poultices of oatmeal boiled soft in milk, mixed with oil and lard, and applied twice a day, till the matter is perceived to grow soft and moves under the fingers; and then it should be let out by a sufficiently large opening with the lancet. Let the opening be full as far as the matter extends. After cleansing the sore apply pledgits of tow, spread with a salve, or ointment, made of Venice turpentine, bee's-wax, oil of olives and yellow rosin; and let these be administered twice a day, if the discharge is great, till a proper digestion takes place, when it should be changed for pledgits spread with the red precipitate ointment, applied in the same manner.

Should the sore not digest, but run a thin water, foment it as often as you dress it, and apply over the dressing a strong beer poultice, and continue this till the matter grows thick and the sore florid. Should any proud flesh get into the sore, wash it as often as you dress it with a solution of blue vitriol in water, or sprinkle it with burnt allum and precipitate. If these should not prove sufficiently powerful, apply caustics, by washing it with a solution of half an ounce of corrosive sublimate in a pint of water. Where the sore can be tightly compressed with a bandage, however, these funguses may be generally prevented.

Tumors, caused by bruises, should, if necessary, be bathed with hot vinegar or verjuice; and then a flannel cloth should be wrapped round the part, if it can be done. If this does not abate the swelling, especially if it be in either of the legs, poultice it twice a day, after bathing it with wine lees, or beer grounds and oatmeal, or with vinegar, oil, and oatmeal, till the swelling abates; when, in order to disperse it entirely, let it be bathed twice a day with a mixture of two ounces of crude sal ammoniac in a quart of chamber-lie, having rags dipped in this and laid on.

Where the extravasated blood is not dispersed by these means, let an opening be made in the skin, and let the blood out, and then heal the wound.

TURF AND PEAT. Earth covered with grass is properly a turf; but that which is here intended to be spoken of is a fossil which is generally found in low grounds and boggy places. It is sometimes confounded with peat, but that is a different substance. Where turf has been dug, the hole thus made will grow up again after a number of years; but this is not the case with peat. Turf seems generally to be decayed moss, mixed with rotten or moory earth, and aquatic grass roots. It is much used for fuel in some parts of Europe, particularly Holland, where they take much of it from the bottoms of their canals. It is inferior to peat for fuel, and it yields a much weaker kind of ashes, which are, however, of considerable value as a manure. It is prepared for fuel in a manner similar to that of peat.

Peat.—This fossil abounds much in some countries. It is often found under other layers of earth; sometimes in grounds where ponds have formerly been, and sometimes in the banks of intervales. It is composed of the essence of decayed vegetables, wood, leaves, &c. placed in a situation where there is not heat sufficient to produce an entire decomposition. After it has been dug up and exposed for some time to the common atmosphere, it becomes hard like a cinder, but at length gradually undergoes a further change and turns to dust. It is valuable for fuel; and, when burned, the ashes it affords are much superior to common wood-ashes as a manure. Fifteen bushels are said to afford a good top-dressing for an acre, the effects of which will be perceived for three years. The ashes are to be sown by hand, and immediately before a rain, in order that the plants may not be injured by its heat. They are said to have a better effect on winter than on summer grain. For leguminous plants, they make the haulm too luxuriant.

Mr. Elliot, of Connecticut, says he searched for this fossil and found it in seven different places. The best way to find it is by boring. The stratum above it is most commonly mud, or moory earth. It is known by its being entirely free from grit; by its cutting very easy and smooth ; and by its burning very freely when dried. It may be burned into charcoal; and the red sort, Mr. Elliot says, is better for this purpose than wood. When burned for this purpose, it is to be with a fire similar to that in which charcoal is made.

Peat is sometimes confounded with turf; but these are different substances.

When peat is dug for fuel, it is cut with a spade, made for the purpose, having a wing to it at a right angle, so that every time you sink the spade you cut out a block about four inches square and about fifteen inches long. These are to be laid singly on the ground to dry. When partly dried, they are to be piled, open, across each other, and thus in a few days of dry weather they will be fit to carry home for use.

The method of burning peat to make ashes is similar to that of burning clay.

See article BURNT-CLAY.

After you get the fire going, you may burn a thousand loads if you choose. But as it burns more readily than clay, you must keep the fire sufficiently smothered by throwing on fresh peat, dug from the pit, and particularly on any crack that opens. If the fire deadens too much, which may be known by the heat of the outside, run a pole into the heap and it will give it the fresh air which is in that case requisite.

After the heap has been burned, the ashes should be put under cover till they are wanted for use ; or if no cover can be had let them be piled up as high as possible on some very dry spot, and covered with swards, or with such earth as will keep off the rains as much as possible.

Trees are very often found in a perfectly sound state in beds of peat.

The increasing scarcity of wood in many places in this country, will render it necessary that more diligence be used in search of this valuable article.

TURNIP. In England the raising of this root is a part of field husbandry, and are there fed to sheep, while in the ground, and raised up for other cattle during the winter season. The culture of them there, is, however, in part superceded by that of carrots, which is found to be more profitable. In this country the severity of our winters presents an obstacle to their ever being cultivated on the large scale which they are in Great-Britain. We, therefore, merely raise them for the table, and perhaps a few for sheep and others of our cattle.

There are three species of turnips; the flat or round sort, the long, and the French turnip. The former are about as good as any. Of this kind there are the green-topped, the red purple, the yellow, and the early Dutch turnip. The last are sown early in the spring for a supply of the market during summer. The green-topped is the most profitable, as they grow to a larger size, and are mostly raised for winter use.

Turnips require a rich soil, especially where they grow closely together. Raising them on new cleared lands is generally the most fortunate for escaping the ravages of insects. The most suitable soils for them are mellow sandy loams and gravelly loams.

On old ground, the best method is to enclose and break up a piece of sward ground, that is not very full of the seeds of weeds, and fold it till the time of preparing it for the reception of the seeds; then make it fine and mellow, and sow it thickly, in order that in all probability a sufficient number of the young plants may escape the insects.

For keeping these off, *see* article INSECTS.

If the plants be all destroyed, sow the ground again, and again, until it be too late for a crop. I have known a pretty good crop raised which were sown as late as the twentieth of August.

If a sufficiency of the young plants escape the insects, as soon as they have got five or six leaves, go through them with the garden hoe, and thin them while destroying the weeds, until they stand about six or eight inches apart. If they stand further apart, they will grow larger, but will not be so good for eating.

I have seen good crops raised without any hoeing, or attention to them after sowing, particularly in new lands; but they will produce a much greater crop by treating them as above directed; and even the hoeing ought to be repeated if the weeds again rise amongst them. Forty-seven tons, equal to as much as sixteen hundred bushels, have been raised from an acre in Ireland, as is testified by Mr. Baker, under his culture of hoeing. Those who have made no spirited trials will hardly conceive how much the hoeings will increase the product of these crops.

In England some of the most spirited farmers apply the drill husbandry to turnips, as this is found to yield the greatest crops. " For two years past," says Mr. Deane, of Massachusetts, " I have sown turnips in the drill way, in the poorest part of my garden, where a crop of pease had grown the same summer, and never had better turnips. They were sufficiently large for the table, though they grew so near together in the rows that the roots crowded each other, and were not sown earlier than about the tenth of August. The earth was hoed into ridges three feet apart, and a single channel seeded on each of the ridges." Probably two rows on each ridge would have been found more productive.

The same writer observes, that he cultivated them with the drill, in a similar manner, in the way of field husbandry, and found his crops more abundant than those sown in the broad cast way. The ridges were thrown up with the plough, or cultivator, in May, and were kept clear of weeds till about the last of July, when the seeds were sown as before, and nothing more was afterwards found necessary, except thinning and once hoeing. This crop prepares the ground pretty well for a crop of wheat.

If the farmer here enters into the cultivation of this root for feeding cattle, he must gather those which he does not feed out in the fall, and keep them where they will be protected from the frosts. Covering them over with dry sand will keep them well in a cellar which is not altogether free from freezing. Those kept for the table should also be kept in dry sand during winter.

Turnips are excellent for fatting sheep, and they are good for horned cattle, though milch-cows should not be fed very plentifully on them, lest they give the milk an ill taste.

For raising turnip-seed, take some good sized turnips in the spring, and plant them out in beds, at the distance of eighteen inches apart, and keep them clear of weeds. Surround them with some stakes and lath from one to the other to keep them from falling. One pound of seed is the allowance for an acre; but let two pounds be sowed, in order to make allowance for the ravages of insects. In the drill method less seed is requisite.

The French turnip ought to be cultivated in the same manner as is above directed, allowing them more room in growing. They should be sown only about a month earlier than other fall turnips. The method of sowing them in the spring, and transplanting them, is bad husbandry; as the early sowing occasions them to grow hard and sticky, and the transplanting retards for a while their growth, and therefore leaves them a prey to insects for a much greater length of time.

TURNIP-CABBAGE. This is commonly called cabbage-turnip in this country. The stalk rises from the ground like the cabbage stalk, and then extends into a large bulb, or knob, something similar in shape and appearance to a turnip but longer. It is a perennial plant, and will withstand the severity of the frosts of this country. It is good for table use in the spring and does not grow spongy when old, like turnips. On this account it is recommended by Mr. Baker, for use on sea voyages. It has for some years past been cultivated to no small advantage in England for feeding cattle ; and I can see no reason why it might not be raised here to equal advantage for feeding them in the spring.

It is highly probable that this plant would be found very profitable to cultivate in this country for spring food for cattle, and particularly for sheep, as it may stand in the field till spring, without injury from the frosts.

U.

ULCERS. The following are Mr. Bartlet's directions for treating ulcers, in horses particularly.

The first point is to bring them to discharge a thick matter, which may generally be effected with the green ointment, or that together with precipitate. Should the sore still discharge a thin matter, apply balsam, oil of turpentine, melted down with the common digestive, and the strong beer poultice over them.

See article Tumors.

The part affected should be well warmed with fomenting, to quicken the circulation, &c. If the lips of the sore grow callous, pare them down with a kife, and rub a little caustic over them.

Where proud flesh appears, let it be carefully suppressed. If it has sprouted above the surface, pare it down with a knife, and rub the remainder with caustic. To prevent its rising again, sprinkle the sore part with equal parts of burnt allum and red precipitate; or wash it with sublimate water, and dress it with dry lint, and draw the bandage tightly over the sore; for a tight bandage is the most effectual in dissipating these funguses.

All sinuses, or cavities, should be laid open, as soon as discovered, after bandages have been ineffectually tried; but where the cavity penetrates deep into the muscles, and a counter opening is impracticable, or hazardous; or where the integuments of the muscles are constantly dripping or melting down, these injections should be used. For this purpose, take of Roman vitriol half an ounce, dissolve it in a pint of water, decant it into another bottle, and add a pint of camphorated spirit of wine, the same quantity of the best vinegar, and two ounces of Egyptiacum. This mixture is also good for ulcerated greasy heels, which it will cleanse and dry.

These cavities sometimes become lined within with a callous substance, and in such case they should be laid open, and the hard substance cut away. Where this cannot be done, scarify them, and apply the precipitate, rubbing them now and then with caustic, butter of antimony, or equal parts of quick-silver and aqua-fortis.

When the bone under the ulcer has become carious, which may be ascertained by probing it, it should be laid bare, in order that the rotten part may be removed. In this case all the loose flesh should be removed, the bone scraped smooth to the sound part, and then dressed with dry lint, or with pledgits dipped in the tincture of myrrh, or euphorbium.

Where the cure does not properly succeed, mercurial physic should be given at proper intervals; and to correct the blood and juices, the antimonial and alterative powders, with a decoction of guaiacum and lime water, are good.

URINE. *See article* MANURES.

Human urine ought to be preserved, for it is found to be much stronger than that of beasts. It is advisable to have a *stercorary* near the house where the urine should be thrown. This urine when thrown on earth for sime time, and mixed with it, is found to make an excellent mixture.

V.

VEGETABLE OYSTER. This root is commonly so called, on account of its having much of the taste and smell of an oyster, when boiled soft, and then fried after the manner of oysters. It is easily raised, and requires a culture similar to that of carrots, &c. The roots should be dug in the fall, and protected from the effects of winter frosts.

VENTILATOR. M. Duhamel applied the ventilator to grain, in granaries, with excellent effect in introducing pure air, and expelling the impure, in order to prevent the heating of the grain.

Mr. Deane recommends a common hand-bellows for the purpose by carrying the air from it through a tube to the bottom of the grain, in different parts, and blowing in the pure air, which will of course expel the foul. Grain that is to be sown should be frequently ventilated, if kept long in a confined place, otherwise it will lose most of its vegetative power.

VERJUICE. A juice extracted from crabbed unripe grapes, or apples, too sour for wine or cider. The English crab-apple is much used for this purpose, and ours, though different from that of the English, would, no doubt, answer equally well.

VETCH ; *(Vicia.)* A kind of pulse, the pods being like those of pease, but smaller, and it is cultivated like field pease. Some vetches are sown in the fall, and are called winter vetches, and others in the spring, and are called spring vetches. They do not exhaust the soil ; and, therefore, Mr. Livingston supposed, that the spring vetches might be valuable to be sown on summer fallows to precede a crop of wheat. He accordingly made two trials of them, the seed being brought from England ; but the results of these not being perfectly satisfactory, particularly in the product of seed, there is some reason to believe, that the culture was not such as it ought to be. The produce of his best experiment was at the rate of about twenty-five hundred weight to the acre. "The fodder," he says, " appeared to be remarkably succulent, and extremely well calculated for cows and sheep." He is, however, of opinion, that the cause of his failing in the requisite quantity of seed, which in England is twenty-five or thirty bushels to the acre, was owing to sowing too thick, (three bushels to the acre,) and to manuring with gypsum, which he supposes makes the plant run more to haulm than it otherwise would do.

Probably this plant, when the seeds are imported, requires a naturalization to our soil. At all events, if a ton and a quarter of this fodder could be raised to the acre, as a summer fallowing crop, together with a due proportion of seed, the culture of it would be tolerably advantageous by making this the intermediate crop between the breaking up of sward land and a crop of wheat; as only one ploughing is requisite after taking off this crop, for sowing the ground with wheat.

Vetches which are sown in the fall are used in the spring for feeding sheep and other cattle; they may afterwards be mowed for fodder and it is said they may be mowed twice a year in warm climates. Mr. Livingston mowed the crop of his, which grew best, about the twentieth of August; but these were spring vetches.

There are different kinds of this plant, and probably each kind may not be equally well suited to our climate. Probably if further trials were made of this plant, results of a more favorable nature might be obtained.

VINE and VINEYARD. Wherever any kinds of grapes grow wild, they may be there cultivated to advantage for making wines, and may be habituated to a colder climate. In the more southerly parts of this state there are two species of grapes, of which there are varieties; the black-grape, *vitis labrusca*, and the fox-grape, *vitis vulpina*. In the more southerly climates, particularly on the waters of the Ohio and Mississippi, there are much greater varieties of these grapes.

The little black grape grows in plenty along the Mohawk river, but the higher grounds do not produce them. Much of the western part of this state is also equally well calculated for the large grape as the southern. But as different kinds of grapes are successfully cultivated in our gardens, and yet generally with but indifferent culture, it is but reasonable to believe, that in the greater part of this state spots may be selected in which the vine may be cultivated to advantage.

For garden-grapes, Mr. Forsyth selects the *white muscadine*, or *chasselas*, which is a great bearer; the *white sweet-water*, which is very fine tasted, and ripens in September; the *black sweet-water*, which also ripens early; the *large black cluster*, which is harsh tasted, being that of which the Oporto wine is made; and the *small black cluster*, which is pleasant tasted.

The spots most favorable for vineyards are the sides of hills or mountains, descending southwardly, or to the east, but to the south is best, and let the soil be loose and mellow, so as not to be liable to be much washed by heavy rains. Stiff soils are not good; though by carting on much sand, and other loosening manures, they will answer tolerably well. The ground must be well mellowed by ploughings, and mixed with sand, if it be not already sandy, and such manures as will serve to make it rich and keep it mellow. Where the side hills are steep, (and such produce the best vines,) it is advisable to cart on stones of small and middling size to mix with the soil, which help to keep it moist and warm; and a part of them are to be laid along in ridges on the lower side of each row of vines, to keep the earth from washing away. Round the vineyard let a good substantial fence be made, which will serve to keep out both men and beasts. The northerly sides of the vineyard should be well protected from the northerly winds.

For a selection of vines for planting, Mr. Johnson recommends the following as being hardy and best suited to this climate: The *black Auvernat*; the *black Orleans*; the *blue cluster*; the *miller grape*; (these make the best Burgundy,) the *black Hamburgh*; the *red Hamburgh*; the *white Muscadin*; the *Muscadella*; the *merlie blanc*; the *white Morrillon*; the *white Auvernat*; and the *grey Auvernat*.

The seven following kinds also ripen in September, but are not quite so hardy, and should therefore occupy the warmer parts of the vineyard: The *Chasselas blanc*, or *royal Muscadine*; the *Malvois*, or *Malmsey*; the *grey Frontinac*; the *red Frontinac*; the *black Lisbon*; the *white Lisbon*; and the *Chasselas Noir*.

In addition to these nineteen kinds, let the fox and the black grape, before mentioned, as being indigenous, be also added to the list, the former of which is probably inferior to none of them.

The next point is to select the branches for the cuttings with which to plant the vineyard. These are to be taken from the *bearing* part of the vines; and among these such as are short jointed, from which you may expect vines which will be thrifty and fruitful. They should be sound, of a healthy appearance, thick set with eyes, and the nearer the last year's growth the better. Let them be cut close to the old wood, where they will be more firm; and they are not to be cut to their proper length, which is about five inches, until you are about to plant them in the vineyard. Good branches, of the length of three feet, may afford four or five cuttings, though those which are nearest to the old wood are esteemed the best.

Some cut off the branches to be used for cuttings in October, and others again in March or April. If at the latter times, they are to be planted in April or May, and the next winter they must be secured from the frosts by coarse litter piled up round them, which in the spring following may be strewed over the ground for manure. If the cuttings be planted in the fall, they are to be in the same manner preserved from the winter frosts; one method is also to set them out closely in the fall, in some warm dry spot, in a trench about a foot wide, which should be well prepared by digging, and over them erect a roof made of straw, well secured, to keep off the frosts, and the heads of the branches to be kept in an upright position, by poles or laths surrounding them for that purpose, in order to prevent their lying on the ground, and thus becoming mouldy.

In planting the cuttings in the vineyard, after the ground has been well prepared, as before directed, let the thick ends be cut off square with a sharp knife, and the upper ends obliquely, about half an inch above the eye. Plant them at the distance of about eight or ten feet each way, and let the earth be pressed round them with the foot. They are to be set in an inclined position, leaving the upper bud or eye nearly as low as the surface of the soil, and be careful not to injure the eye in treading the earth about it. In the spring, while the nightly frosts prevail, let this bud, or eye, be slightly covered with earth in the evenings, to save it from the frosts, and again uncovered in the mornings.

Remember to drive in the stake, on which the shoot is to be trained, at the north side, so as to give the shoot all the warmth of the sun. When the shoots begin to put forth, for some will rise from under ground, let them all grow for a certain time, in order that you may have an opportunity of determining which is likely to be the best; and these are the roundest, shortest jointed, and the most thick set with eyes. Those which grow long and spindly, with few eyes, are not good. When you have thus selected the best, pinch off all the rest; for all the nourishment which the roots can afford are requisite for its growth. As it advances in growth, fasten it to the sunny side of the stake, so that it be not beaten about with the winds; and pinch off its tendrils, laterals, nephews, and suckers, not closely, however, but at some little distance from the body of the main shoot.

This shoot may rise to the height of eight or ten feet in a summer, if left to grow its full length; but its growth must be checked at the height of not more than four feet; otherwise its strength becomes exhausted in the production of waste wood, and the head becomes feeble, and incapable of bearing the lateral branches, which it is destined to support.

October, or rather when the leaf begins to fall off, is the time for trimming; and then the branch should be cut down to two good eyes not reckoning the lowermost next the old wood, which is called the dead eye; or you may leave several eyes, which, during the next spring, will furnish a number of sprouts, and from these select the five best.

The vine being thus pruned, some direct to open the ground round the roots, to the depth of three or four inches, and to cut away the roots to that depth, not closely, however; and let this be repeated for the first three years; the use of which is to make the vine take deeper root, which it is said makes them more durable, fruitful, and less liable to be injured by droughts.

No particular notice is here taken of the method spoken of by Mr. Johnson, of bending the vines down to the ground at the approach of each winter, during the first three winters, and covering them slightly with earth, to protect them from the frosts; because it is not believed that this process is requisite. If it be found so, the *head* must not be covered with earth, but with chaff, or some such dry stuff, to keep it cool and dry.

The second year's growth should only exhibit two branches trained. The good eyes will all shoot forth in the spring; and let them all grow to the length of about eight inches before you select the two most proper. These should have the characteristics already described, as necessary for the best branch of the first year's growth. Check the branches of the second year's growth at about five feet, pinching off the laterals, &c. at about four inches, as before directed. In the fall when the leaves begin to drop, trim the vines again, as before. Now you have two main branches to trim, and these should be cut down to within four or five good eyes of last year's wood, dealing with the upper roots as before, and burying the vines during winter, as before mentioned, if this be found necessary.

The third year presents two main branches, each furnished with four or five eyes. Proceed as before in the choice of shoots to be reserved, training only two from each branch: Then you will have four main branches this year. If you find your vines begin to bear this year, pluck off nearly all the clusters while young; for by too early bearing the vines become debilitated, and materially injured for bearing afterwards.

With respect to cropping and pruning the vine, be always careful to check its aspiring nature, and keep it of humble size, by which means it is always easy to be managed by manual labor, and less subject to be injured by the violence of winds.

In the fourth year, training again two branches from each trained branch of the previous year, you will have eight branches to each vine. You, therefore, proceed as before in humbling the vine, and proportioning its quantity of fruit to its ability to bear; and remember not to let the vines bear all the fruit they put forth, until they are fully able to do it, without injury to them afterwards.

All this time the ground of the vineyard is constantly to be kept light and mellow, and perfectly clean of weeds and grass. For this purpose, straw, chaff, flax-shives, and every thing of the kind is to be carried on, and spread over the ground, to keep it mellow and moist, and to prevent its washing. Observing this the first four years greatly forwards the vines, and at the same time prepares them for good crops afterwards; nor should the practice be afterwards wholly discontinued.

In planting a vineyard it is also requisite to have a nursery of the vines at the same time, to supply those which may die when planted out. The ground of the nursery should not be so rich as that of the vineyard; it should be kept clear of weeds and well hoed, and it should be planted pretty thickly, in order that the roots do not extend too much.

A vineyard of an acre should contain but two sorts of grapes; and one of two acres should not generally contain more than four sorts. Every kind of grape should be made into wine by itself, and not mixed with others.

The vine, where the climate and soil is most suitable, will grow to a prodigious size, and live to a surprising length of years. Strabo speaks of a vine which was twelve feet in circumference; and Pliny also mentions one which was six hundred years old! In the western parts of this state, and elsewhere in that direction, I have seen them, where from the size of the trees on which they were supported, and they must have grown up with the trees, they could not be less than a hundred years old.

Mr. Johnson observes, that from the prices which grapes have been sold for in our largest cities, the income of an acre of vineyard would amount to six hundred dollars; but, perhaps, this calculation is rather too large. Be this as it may, it is certain that their cultivation, whether they are to be made into wine, or to be picked, and sent into our cities, or elsewhere, for sale, must undoubtedly be profitable.

The method of preserving grapes to send abroad, is to pack them up in dry saw-dust, or bran; and in that situation they may be exported, if they should not be wanted at home, with the same facility and safety that they are at present sent from other countries into this, for sale. Probably they ought to be put up a little before they are fully ripe. In Albany and New-York they sell for as much upon an average as 25 cents per pound.

The foregoing is mostly an abridgement of Mr. Johnson, on the culture of the vine, and very nearly agrees with Mr. Winterbotham on the same subject. Mr. Forsyth describes a new method of training the vines for wall or garden fruit, but this does not seem applicable to the vineyard. His method is exhibited in his drawings, which are well worthy of examination. Other essays on this culture may also be worthy of examination; such as those of Speechley, Miller, Antill, and that contained in the Encyclopædia; and even the song of the first of Roman poets on the subject, if it should not afford additional instruction, may nevertheless be found possessed of charms which may more strongly incline the man of taste to the industrious culture of the vine.

For the method of making the wine, *see* article WINE.

Mr. Livingston, in describing the beautiful country which lies upon the Loire, between Nantz and Orleans, in France, notices " the farm houses surrounded by gardens filled with fruit-trees, with vines, trained up the trees, and extended from one to the other—Every house, he says, is also covered with a large grape-vine, at least on three sides." This practice he very justly recommends for farmers, as being highly ornamental to small houses, useful as it regards health, convenient for shade, while the fruit, though not intended for wine, might be made a source of family comfort and enjoyment. He observes too, that the earth round dwellings is always rich and warm, and therefore well adapted to the grape.

VIVES.　A swelling, says Mr. Bartlet, of the kernels under the ears of a horse, being the part first affected.　They seldom come to matter, but perspire off, if warm clothing, anointing with marshmallow ointment, and a moderate bleeding or two be applied.　But, should the inflammation continue, notwithstanding these means, a suppuration should be promoted.　For this purpose, make an ointment of an ounce of mercury and half an ounce of Venice turpentine, pounded together till the mercury is no longer visible; then add to it two ounces of hog's-lard, and anoint the swellings with this till a suppuration takes place.

For destroying proud flesh in the sore, *see* article ULCERS.

Mr. Bartlet says, that when these swellings appear in an old horse they are signs of great malignity, and often of an inward decay, as well as forerunners of the glanders.　He also says, that in young horses they are critical and should be managed as above, instead of applying the above ointment at first to disperse the swellings, as in that case there is danger that the disease may be thrown on the lungs, or into the thick flesh of the hinder parts of the horse, where they will form deep imposthumes, and sometimes kill him.

W.

WAGGON. *See* article CARRIAGES.

WALLS. Stone walls, for fences, have already been spoken of. *See* article STONES.

The cellar walls of a house should be laid with stone and lime; not only for standing more firmly and a greater length of time, but also to keep out the frosts. If they be not thus laid, it generally becomes necessary to bank up the outsides with horse-dung, or something that will keep out the frosts which tends to rot the sills, and at the same time has a very mean appearance.

The stone walls of many ancient castles and other buildings in Europe are principally held together, not by binding, as is now practised, but by the force of cement. This cement, it is believed, is nothing more than a due proportion of sand and lime, made very thin with water, and poured into the middle of the wall; not merely plaistered in among the stones, as is done at present. The advantage of this method is, that the lime being so plentifully mixed with water, and for such a length of time before it evaporates, has sufficient time in part to dissolve and be again crystalized; and in crystalizing, it adheres to the stones, and thus forms a solid mass. The wall must be saturated with this cement. Even pebble stones may be thus cemented together in a wall, provided they be kept in their places, and the mortar be kept from running out through them till it has become hardened.

The due proportions of lime and sand for making the strongest cement, must, however, be previously ascertained by experiments made for the purpose; as the proportions of each depend on the qualities of each—that is, if the lime have but little of other earthy matter in it, the less of it will answer; and the more sharp and gritty the sand, the less lime will be requisite.

Mr. Livingston mentions the houses built of earth in the neighborhood of Lyons, in France, which are well worthy of attention in a matter of economy. They are built two and three stories high, and many of them have stood a century. The earth used there for building them is a gravelly loam. A clay or a sand will not answer, but almost every other earth will. The earth is pounded hard with sharp edged beetles, being put in frames made for the purpose, so as to give the masses a square shape proper for being laid up in the wall. These walls are sometimes plaistered on the outside, but will answer well without. The barns, and garden walls there, are built of the same material. Columns are also formed of the earth, in the same manner, in moulds made for the purpose. "The extreme cheapness of these buildings," says Mr. Livingston, "the facility with which they are made, their warmth, their security against fires, recommend them so strongly, that I shall make myself complete master of the art before I come over, and teach it to my countrymen." It is to be hoped that a design so patriotic has not been frustrated, and that its execution may be duly appreciated.

WALNUT-TREES; *(Juglans.)* There are but five kinds of these trees in this country, which are—

1. The *hickory*, with a smooth bark and a firm tough wood, excellent for axe-helves, &c. The nut of this tree is not good.

2. The *shagbark walnut*, which is not so hard and tough, but all the red part of the timber is durable, and excellent for fence rails or building. The nut of this tree is the best tasted of any other of the kind.

3. The *black-walnut*, is natural to a more southerly climate than that of this state. The timber of this is valuable in cabinet work, and is also excellent for rails and other uses. The nut of this is large and well tasted.

4. The *butternut*, which is to be found in the more northerly climates, where it grows very large and high in the forests. It is also excellent for rails and other uses, and the nut is well tasted.

5. The *Paccon*, or *Illinois nut*, which grows on the Misissippi and its branches.

The growth of the three latter indicates a fine, rich, dark colored, loamy, or sandy loamy soil.

The *shagbark walnut* is commonly found on a good soil, inclining more or less to clay; and the *hickory*, most commonly on a warm, fertile, gravelly soil.

Mr. Forsyth makes mention of fifty walnut-trees, in Great-Britain, which were rented out for fifty pounds sterling a year; and he says, that the lessee cleared that amount from them. He states, that they are best raised from the nut, gathered when fully ripe. They will be fit to transplant the first autumn after sowing, if they have thriven well—if not, let them continue another year. They are then to be put into beds and transplanted every second year, until planted out for good. This causes their throwing out fine horizontal shoots and brings them to a bearing state much sooner than when they make deep tap roots.

They are to be trimmed up to the height of seven feet, and by that time they are fit to be set out. When set out, he says the ground should be *trench-ploughed*, and the trees set in rows at the distance of six feet, and as they grow larger, those which are found to be the best bearers are to be preserved and the others are to be cut away. In trimming the trees, the ends of the wood cut off are to be covered over with his composition.

See article FRUIT-TREES.

WARMING ROOMS. As fuel is gradually becoming more scarce, it becomes essential to devise the best means of making a little answer every requisite purpose. I shall, therefore, describe a very cheap and simple method of warming a whole house, leaving every one to vary from this method, by the use of stoves, or otherwise, as much as they may think proper.

Take an old potash kettle which is no longer fit for use in a potashery, and which you can usually purchase for ten dollars or less. Set it bottom upwards, on brick-work, built in a circle, suitable to the size of the kettle, about ten inches high, leaving a place to fix an iron door, like the door of a common stove. Make a round hole in the bottom of the kettle, into which insert a stove-pipe, to carry off the smoke. Build another thin brick wall all round and over this, leaving a space every where of about three inches between this wall and the inner brick wall, and the inverted kettle, and leaving also a place for a door exactly where the inner one is placed. Let holes be made through the top of this outer wall to insert tubes for carrying off the heated air into different rooms. Make a fire within the part covered by the inverted kettle, which will burn as readily as it will in a stove, by having a similar door; and as the kettle becomes heated, the air between it and the outer wall becomes also heated and rarified, and of course ascends through the tubes, and is carried into the rooms, while fresh air is constantly pouring in through the outer door to supply the place of that which has been heated and carried off. This while a constant current of warm air is rushing in below and above; a like current of warm air is constantly rushing into the rooms. When the rooms are sufficiently filled with the warm air, turn a stop-cock, with which each tube should be supplied, and no more warm air will be let in, until it is again wanted.

In a room warmed in the usual way, about two thirds of the whole heat of the fire passes out of the chimney. In the mean time all the air in the room will have also passed out of the chimney in less than an hour; and of course cold air from without must rush in to supply its place. Thus the whole air of such room has to be heated over again once an hour; and this is to be done with only a third of the heat afforded by the fire. Now according to the plan here recommended, the air in a room would require a degree of heat equal to warming the whole over again, about once in six hours; as the heated air is not to be allowed to pass off out of a chimney; and for this purpose of heating, at least two thirds of the heat of a smaller fire can be applied. Thus a room, to be warmed in the common way, requires a fire which gives twelve times the quantity of heat that is required in the method above described.

This heating stove may be set in the kitchen, but a cellar kitchen, or one lower than the dwelling and other rooms, would be best. It may also be set in a small building adjoining the house, but let it be set lower than the rooms of the house.

But in order to render this complete, let the steam-cooking, baking, and roasting apparatus be attached to it. For this purpose let the smoke, and the heat that goes with it, pass out through a hole about four inches square, made at the side of the kettle, opposite the door, and let it be carried in a zigzag manner, back and forward, under the bottom of a boiler, made of sheet iron, and this will sufficiently heat the water in that to afford the requisite degree of steam for the vessels used for cooking by steam, as well as for heating water in adjoining wooden vessels of different sizes, to be used for different purposes. The pipe conducting off the smoke, &c. after having passed under every part of the bottom of the boiler, is then to be carried upwards, and passes round three sides of a small oven, made of sheet iron, which is to be used for baking and roasting. The outside of the smoke-pipe is to be coated with plaister, as high as above the oven, to prevent the heat passing off on the outside. Plans of cooking and boiling apparatus, of which the above is in part an outline, have been patented by two gentlemen of Herkimer county.

If it should be found that the heat contained in the smoke-pipe will not sufficiently heat the oven, after heating the boiler, a part of the externally heated air must be carried into the oven for that purpose; but it must be air heated in an apartment by itself, having no connection with the rest of the heated air; and it must be let off very slowly, by means of a very small pipe, into the oven, by which means it will be sufficiently heated before it is let into it. If too much be thrown in, the door of the oven can be occasionally opened, and let a part of the heated air pass off.

Thus, with one half of the fuel, which is used in a kitchen fire-place, every room in a house of moderate size, may be warmed; all the culinary business may be performed; roots may be boiled for cattle in large vessels made for the purpose; and all this may be performed without half the risk from fires which attends the usual methods.

I prefer an old pot-ash kettle for this purpose, on account of its shape, its thickness, its cheapness, and of its being well tried with fire. A small sized one, however, will be usually found sufficient for this purpose.

For close stoves to be set in rooms, it is believed, that the Russian stoves will be found preferable to those made of iron. They are built of brick, and may be made of different forms. They should be supplied with air from without the room they are intended to warm; as this will be a great saving of the heated air in the room. They are used entirely in Russia, and they require less fuel than our iron stoves, as less than two cords of good wood will supply one of them a whole winter. Cooking may also be done in them, as in our iron stoves, by having an oven fixed in them for the purpose.

WATER. This is found by chemical experiments to be the same substance as air, but in a more condensed form; being composed of about eighty-five parts of oxygene, and fifteen parts of hydrogene gas.

See article AIR.

This substance, however, in its condensed and in its gaseous state, is the essential food of plants; as no vegetation can be produced without air, nor without water; but with these alone, every species of plant can be made to vegetate to a certain degree.

It is, however, unnecessary to dwell minutely on this article; but something should be said of its application to meadow lands; of drawing it off where too abundant; and of applying it to plants.

Where water can be carried over lands without too great an expense it should always be attended to, as great crops of hay may be had from such grounds. The means of watering the ground, or of taking it off, should be completely under control; for if too much be suffered to run on, it may do more hurt than good. Chalybeate waters, and such as are impregnated with mineral acids, should be avoided. That which has a rich sediment is best. The quantity should be proportioned to the nature of the soil; as sandy grounds require more, and stiff soils less. The channels should be so made as to carry the water to every part, except where the ground is naturally wet. The main channel should just have descent enough to cause the water to run; and the lateral branches should be run in such directions as that the descent be very moderate, and at the same time convey the water to every part of the ground. Sometimes it is necessary to carry off the surplus water by other channels, where the ground has little hollows running through it.

When the weather is hot the water should be taken off the ground. The night, and days that are cool and cloudy, are the best times for applying it.

In the spring, it should not be applied till the ground is pretty dry; and after the grass begins to start let the quantity be diminished, and let it also be stopped during rainy weather. When the grass is pretty well grown no water should be applied, except in cases of drought. After taking off the second crop, the water may be thrown on more plentifully, but it must be taken off some time before the winter frosts commence.

The foregoing is believed to be the most suitable directions for watering meadows as practised in this country; but this falls far short of the most approved practice in Great-Britain. There the spots selected for the purpose, are so nearly level, after the ground has received its proper shape, that the water, which is let in at one side, will but barely run off at the other. The ground is shaped exactly for the purpose by raising it where it is too low, and sinking it where it is too high; it is then made into ridges about nine yards wide, and a foot in height, with an uniform descent from the middle of each to the extremes; a shallow channel is then made on the highest part of each ridge for conducting the water on them, and another on the lowest ground between each for carrying it off. A canal is made on the upper side of the piece of ground for supplying the water, and another on the lower side for carrying it off, after it has served the purpose of irrigation. Thus the water is let out of the upper canal into the channels made on the higher parts of the ridges, which channels it fills and overflows, just enough to impart a due proportion of water to each ridge. The water thus gently overflowing soaks away through the soil till it is received in the lower channels, and by them it is carried into the lower canal, and thence carried off.

It will readily be seen, that no water should be suffered to run off into the lower canal from the channels which carry it on the heights of the ridges. These should be stopped at their lower ends. The water in the upper canal should be under perfect control; so that no more than is necessary to be let into the higher channels, and that it be taken off at pleasure. Where the supply of water is small, a part of the meadow may be irrigated at a time, and part at another, in succession, till each part has, in turn, been duly supplied. This is to be done by means of flood-gates, to confine the water in the upper canal, to the parts where it is required.

The upper canal is to be supplied from a durable stream, and the more turbid this is, the better. Clear limpid streams are not near so good for the purpose.

This method of irrigation is a beautiful and ingenious part of husbandry; and seeing that it has been so successfully practised in England, it would be desirable that trials of it should be made here; as in many spots it might be found very profitable. For a more full description of this method of culture the reader is referred to " *The Complete Grazier*," an excellent work lately published in England, to which we have frequently referred.

For raising water to irrigate lands, which are above its level, different kinds of wheels may be used, which are so well known as to render a description of them unnecessary. The method of raising water by the force of wind, in the manner that it is raised out of the dykes in Holland, may also be resorted to, if it be found that the profits will warrant the expense. The reader will find in *Darwin's Phitologia*, a description of a very cheap wind-machine for raising water, which probably might be in some places applied to advantage, but most particularly in raising water from wells for supplying cattle with drink.

Water-furrowing lands which are wet, when sown with summer grain, is of great importance in carrying off the surplus water; and the furrows should be made deep, and cleared out with a shovel, and carried in such a direction as will cause the ground to be the least gullied by heavy showers. The same may be said of grounds sown with winter grain; but wet grounds, particularly if they lie flat, should never be applied to this use; for if the ground be ever so well water-furrowed, the furrows usually become so filled with ice as to render them useless. Grounds, however, of moderate descent may be thrown up into high ridges, so as to answer tolerably well, in most winters, for winter grain; but if they be somewhat steep this management usually proves injurious by the washings of heavy rains. Rather let such grounds be hollow-drained, and then neither ridging nor water-furrowing will be necessary.

With regard to watering plants, all that is necessary to be said, is, that cold water, as drawn from wells, should never be applied to them. The water should always be exposed to the sun for such time as will render it as warm as rain-water; and the quantity applied at once should never be very great; but rather like the application of a gentle rain.

WEATHER. It is of great importance to the farmer to be able to foretel, with some degree of certainty, the future state of the weather; but this depends on signs, many of which differ, more or less, in different places, and at best they are often deceptive. The signs of the approach of bad weather, have always, however, been deemed more certain than those of good; but a new discovery has lately been made, which ought here to be noticed, in regard to the signs of approaching good weather.

It is found that the common field spider is endued with an intuitive sagacity in this particular. When the weather is to continue wet and unsettled his labors are entirely suspended. When he is found employed in repairing his works, which the rains have torn to pieces, it is an indication of the return of good weather; and when he is seen drawing long lines, in various directions, a lengthy spell of dry weather may be expected.

When the air becomes surcharged with moisture, it may be known by the clouds increasing in size; on the contrary, when the air is dry, the clouds may be observed gradually to diminish and the small ones at length disappear. In the former case, therefore, rain may be expected; the latter is an indication of prevailing clear weather. An excess of moisture in the air may also be known in warm weather, by the moisture or wetness of the stones. Contrary currents of air in the atmosphere, which is known by the clouds moving in different or opposite directions, are usually productive of rain.

When stormy weather is approaching, neat cattle and sheep seem more than usually industrious in feeding, and seem to leave their pastures with reluctance; swine are uneasy, grunt loudly, and retire to their sties; geese and ducks wash themselves repeatedly; dogs become drowsy and stupid, and seem to have an aversion to food; and cats loose their vivacity, and remain within doors: Swallows at such times are also observed to fly low, and skim the surface of waters, twittering more loudly than usual; and aquatic birds withdraw to the sea-coast or to marshes, &c. A change from unsettled weather to that which is wetter, is indicated by flies stinging and swarming more than usual.

Circumstances contrary to the foregoing evince the continuance of good weather; to which may be added the bees flying abroad and laboring with great industry; crows croaking early in the morning; the red-breast and other birds singing early on the higher parts of the trees; and gnats flying in columnal form in the rays of the setting sun, are all indications of fine weather.

WEEDS. Generally speaking, most of those which are difficult to extirpate by common culture, will be found to yield to constant yearly crops of such plants as grow very high and very closely. For this purpose, several crops of hemp in succession would no doubt be found sufficient to eradicate almost any weed. The tall oat's-grass, and some other grasses which grow very high and thick, would also be found very useful for this purpose.

See article GRASSES.

Crops of carrots and other roots, which require close weeding, would also be found of excellent use in eradicating some weeds. It is also believed, that planting grounds with potatoes after the Irish method, will be found sufficient to smother almost every kind of weed.

See article POTATOES.

Something shall now be separately said of some of those weeds which are most formidable to the farmer.

The *Canada thistle* flourishes in the close and stiff soils; in those which are dry and gravelly, or sandy, it does not prevail. It is extremely injurious in all tillage. In lands, however, which have been closely pastured for a number of successive years, it will nearly disappear; and in mowing lands, its growth will be constantly retarded, and lessened, where the grasses grow luxuriantly, particularly those before mentioned. It is, however, but little injurious in hay, as cattle eat it freely; and they are particularly fond of it when it has wilted, after being newly mown. In the business of soiling cattle, it would, therefore, be of no essential injury; while it would gradually give place to the tall and luxuriant growth of grasses to be used for that purpose.

See article SOILING.

Pasturing, cultivating tall grasses, and keeping the lands highly manured, will probably, in general, be found the most effectual method of getting rid of this thistle, unless the culture of potatoes, before mentioned, should be found sufficient to destroy it. On dry loams, however, or those laid dry by hollow drains, or on some dry marly soils, the yearly culture of hemp might, in many instances, be profitably used in subduing this troublesome weed.

The *common thistle;* (*carduus,*) is easily destroyed by mowing it when in blossom, or by pulling or digging it up in the spring.

The *yellow weed;* (*ranunculus,*) prevails mostly in wettish meadows, where it roots out most of the grass. It is, however, highly relished by cattle in fodder, though its product will be found small when compared with that of the grasses which before filled its place. When eaten green, it is hot and acrid, and cattle do not much relish it.

Hollow draining the lands where they are wet, and manuring, and cultivating them with tall grasses, or in some of the methods before mentioned, which may be most suitable to the soil, will quickly extirpate this weed.

The *white weed, May-weed,* or *ox-eye;* (*chrysanthemum,*) roots out the grasses in pastures and mowing lands, where the ground is not very strong; but where it is well enriched with suitable manures it gives way to the grasses in turn. It never makes its appearance in a very strong tough sward. Cattle will eat it in hay, if it be cut green, and well made, but they dislike it in pastures; and at best its product is but small.

To extirpate this weed, manure the land strongly, and cultivate it yearly with carrots, hemp, or tall grasses, as may be most suitable to the soil. Common hoed crops, when yearly repeated, will also at length subdue it. But where it grows in moist meadows which are not intended to be hollow drained, the best means of destroying it are frequent top-dressings of composts suitable to the soil, (*see* article MANURES,) or pulling it up by hand, which should be done when it is in blossom.

The *daisy* prevails mostly in upland pastures; and sometimes, where the soil is not strong; it chokes the crops of wheat, flax, &c. It is very readily destroyed by yearly hoed crops, by hemp, tall grasses, &c.

The *wild onion* prevails most in Pennsylvania, where it was brought by the Swedes, and used as an article of pasture. It is very injurious in crops of wheat, and by no means inoffensive in those of rye. It is also bad food for milch cows, as it imparts its taste to their milk, butter, and cheese. Yearly hoed crops, hemp, and tall grasses will gradually subdue it. Frequent ploughings and harrowings, when the ground is dry, is also beneficial. Let the Irish method of planting potatoes be also tried.

The method commonly used in Pennsylvania for thinning this weed, is one or two hoed crops, and then oats sowed thickly. Long pasturing or mowing the ground, will tend gradually to extirpate them, especially if the growth of the grass be luxuriant.

The growth of weeds which are commonly called *cockle* and *steencrite*, are often injurious to crops of wheat and rye. The seeds of these weeds are usually carried into the fields in the barn dung, in its crude state. Dung, therefore, which contains these should not be applied to the summer fallow, but carted out in the spring and used for hoed crops; in this way the seeds will vegetate in the fall, and then the young growth is effectually killed by ploughing for the next spring crops.

Darnel; (*solium,*) says Mr. Deane, "sometimes appears among grain, and is often so fruitful as to spoil a crop. The seeds of it resemble grains of blasted rye. These weeds should be pulled up before they go to seed; but grain for sowing may be mostly cleared of the seeds by swimming it in water."

Johnswort grows on such dry soils as are suitable to the application of gypsum; and this manure, or any other which is suitable to the soil, when pretty plentifully applied, and the land laid down with clover, or other suitable grass, will quickly eradicate every vestige of this weed.

Burdocks, and some similar weeds, should be cut, or dug up while green.

Quitch-grass is considerably injurious to the growth of almost every plant. It prevails in the stiffer soils, and generally in the Mohawk, and some other intervales. It starts afresh wherever its large, strong roots are cut with the plough or hoe, particularly when the soil is rather moist. When it is quite dry, the roots may be dragged to the surface by frequent harrowings, where they will perish; and this, together with long pasturing, or mowing the ground, is perhaps the only practicable method of getting rid of this grass. It should however be observed, that this is a tolerable good grass for either pasturing or mowing, especially when other grasses are sown to mix with it.

Sheep are much better than any other cattle for destroying weeds by pasturing.

As all weeds are propagated by their seeds, none should be suffered to go to seed. This remark is no less applicable to the weeds before enumerated, than to the numerous class of biennials which commonly infest the fields. All weeds, by being suffered to grow, exhaust the soil. The same ground, therefore, which is kept clear of weeds will much easier retain its fertility than that which is suffered to become full of their seeds. Generally speaking, any given quantity of weeds growing with a crop lessens its product in proportion to the weight of the green weeds with that of the growing crop. Farmers should therefore be extremely careful in keeping all weeds out of their grounds, and in destroying the common biennials as fast as they appear, while the ground is bearing crops : And, in regard to those perennials, before enumerated, and all others which may infest the lands, the prevention of their growths is generally infinitely easier than their extermination, after they have got footing in the soil. When, therefore, the farmer sees new weeds start up in his land, let him immediately extirpate them, either by taking them out of the ground, or by smothering them with a sufficient quantity of earth, straw, chip-dung, or other rubbish; and thus he will find that a penny's worth of trouble spent in the prevention of the disease, is worth a pound spent in the cure.

For destroying the common biennial weeds, *see* article SUMMER FALLOWING.

WEEVIL. *See* article INSECTS.

WELL. *See* articles WATER and PASTURE.

WHEAT; *(Triticum.)* Under different articles of this work, to wit :—CHANGE OF CROPS, CHANGE OF SEEDS, DRILL, FALLOWING, GREEN-DRESSING, GYPSUM, HESSIAN-FLY, HARROWING, HARVESTING, MILDEW, SOILING, SOWING, SMUT, THRESHING, and WATER-FURROWING, considerable has been said which regards the culture of wheat, and need not here be repeated.

There are several species of this grain, such as the spring wheat, and of the different kinds of winter wheat ; the *bald*, the *bearded*, the *cone*, the *Polish*, and the *Smyrna wheat*, &c. The latter has a central ear, with several smaller lateral ones, which spring from the lower end of the large one. It requires a rich soil, and it is probable, that in this country, the horse-hoeing husbandry of Mr. Tull, (*See* NEW HORSE-HOEING HUSBANDRY,) would be more suitable for it than for any other kind.

Winter wheat, in this state, and in some more southerly, will grow on almost every dry soil that is sufficiently rich. Very sandy, and very gravelly soils, are, however, the most unsuitable. Dry red loams, with a trifle of clay in them, are perhaps the best. Of the old states, the best wheat, and the greatest crops, are raised in what are called the middle states. Mr. Gregg, of Pennsylvania, lately raised sixteen hundred bushels from forty acres, and crops still larger have been raised in Virginia. In this state, the greatest products are not quite so large, and the eastern states are still less favorable for the growth of this grain.

The time for sowing wheat probably depends much on previous habit. Thus, if it were sown a number of successive years by the the middle of August, and then the time of sowing were changed, at once, to October, the crop would probably be much lighter on that account ; yet where wheat has become habituated to be sown late it will do tolerably well. The later it is sown, however, the more seed is requisite. When early sown, a bushel to the acre is sufficient ; but when sown later, a bushel and an half, or more, may be necessary. In England they sow a much larger quantity than this ; but it is believed to be an useless expenditure of seed. Let the farmer, however, try experiments in this way, by sowing two, three, and four bushels to the acre, and if he finds himself well repaid. by a suitable increase of his crops, let him persevere in sowing that quantity of seed which he finds most advantageous.

Drilling in wheat will save as much as one third of the seed. If wheat is found to grow larger in this way than when sown in the broad-cast, the gain may be much greater. If it be soaked twenty-four hours in lye or brine, with a proper mixture of saltpetre, its smuttiness will be prevented, which in many instances may be a great saving ; and according to Mr. Johnson, the saltpetre will make a very considerable addition to the crop.

See article SOWING.

Thus, by paying attention to these particulars, and some others, the clear profits of a crop of wheat may perhaps be doubled.

Seed wheat should always be run through a screen before it is sown, to take out the seeds of cockle, drips, and other weeds which infest the crop. Care should also be taken not to let the seed get any mixture of rye in it; as the cutting of this out requires considerable labor, and at the same time lessens the crop. The English farmers say, that seed should never be taken of wheat which has grown on sandy land, but from that which has grown on soils most natural to it. The changing of seed should also be attended to, as this grain is found to degenerate if this be not done. The summer wheat which is brought from Canada, is found to produce much larger crops in this county, (*Herkimer*,) than that which has been sown here for some time. Wheat that is carried to a climate much more northerly than that in which it has been long sown, will not answer well, as it will be too late in ripening.

The best preparations for a crop of wheat are summer-fallowing, or a clover sward turned under and the wheat sown on it. The latter is good culture. The former ought never to constitute a part of a good system of farming, on account of its additional expense, unless it be to recruit exhausted lands, or to destroy weeds. But where lands require to be fallowed let the work be done effectually, by repeated ploughings and harrowings, in order that the ground be enriched, and the seeds of weeds destroyed. Beside clover, the summer crops which are found best to precede a crop of wheat, are turnips, peas, vetches, and barley will do tolerably well, but let the ground be ploughed up immediately after the crop is taken off. A potatoe crop is also very good, provided it be got off the ground sufficiently early for sowing the wheat. Indian corn, where the ground is in good heart, will do well, by cutting up the crop while green, and setting it up in shocks to ripen.

Where wheat has lodged so as to fall flat on the ground, the better way is to harvest it immediately; for in that situation it will derive no further benefit from the earth, or from the air; whereas if it be cut, and laid to dry, the seeds will derive nourishment from the stalk; and though they be small they will be as large as they would otherwise have been, perhaps larger, and at the same time will make much better flour. The treatment in this case ought to be the same as in case of mildew.

See article MILDEW.

It is believed, that there is nothing gained by letting wheat stand till it is fully ripe, that is till the heads turn down, before it is harvested. If it stands so long considerable will be shelled out before it is got into the barn; and even if the bulk should in this case be greater, still the weight may not be increased; and as wheat is now sold by weight, not by the bushel; and as it is known that the best flour is made from the earliest harvested wheat; the farmer, from these considerations, may probably be the gainer by commencing his harvest considerably earlier than the usual time. In this way too he will be less in danger of having his wheat grown by long continued rains; for it is found, that wheat which is harvested early, is less liable to grow than that which is cut late. Probably, that which is designed for seed, ought, on this account, to be harvested last, as it will vegetate more readily when late harvested.

As a matter of curiosity, it may be observed, that by frequently splitting the plants of wheat, and setting each part by itself, they may be greatly multiplied. Thus by sowing the wheat in August you may split it, after it has branched out into a number of parts, and this may be again repeated in September, and repeated once or twice again in the spring, until in this way you may make one seed produce more than half a bushel of grain.

Where wheat is likely to grow too large the best way is to feed it down in the spring for such length of time as may be thought requisite, and in this way it will grow up with a stronger stalk, and be less liable to lodge.

See article RYE, for a very extraordinary crop that was raised in this way.

If the wheat cannot be conveniently fed off, let it be mowed off close, as often as may be found necessary, which will answer the same purpose.

In England experiments have been made of transplanting wheat in the spring, by means of which the crops proved very good, and a great deal of seed was saved. This might be found peculiarly useful in wet lands thrown up in ridges in the spring. The expense of such culture would, probably, however, be too great in this country, and therefore, need not be minutely described.

Barberry-bushes or cherry-trees, planted in wheat fields, will make the wheat growing near them blast.

Spring wheat should be sown as early as the ground can be made mellow; and there is little or no danger of its being too rich for this crop. It grows best on rich new lands, or on lands which have been well manured and borne Indian corn, or potatoes, the preceding year. The quality of this wheat is inferior to that of winter wheat, and the crop is usually smaller. It is, however, cultivated with more success than winter wheat in much of the higher lands where the snows fall deep in the northerly parts of this state. The requisite quantity of seed to the acre is about one and a half bushels. Like barley, it is found to degenerate very quickly; and for this reason, new supplies of seed from Canada, or some more northerly climate, are found to be frequently requisite.

A principal difficulty in raising winter wheat on the high lands of the northerly parts of this state, where the snows fall very deep, is, that they lie so long in the spring that the wheat being then, from the warmth of the ground, inclined to vegetate, is prevented from this by reason of the snow which lies upon it, and being thus excluded from the air, it dies of course. The most effectual remedy against this has been found to feed off the wheat closely in the fall, which it would seem, prevents it from starting in the spring until such time as the snows have dissolved.

WHEEZING. A disease of horses commonly called broken wind—caused by surfeits—violent exercise when the belly is full—by being rid into cold water when very warm—or, from obstinate colds not cured.

For the cure, Dr. Bracken advises, that the horse should have good nourishment, much grain, and little hay; and that the water given him to drink daily have a solution of half an ounce of saltpetre, and two drachms of sal ammoniac. It is said that the hay made of white weed will cure this disorder.

WHITE WEED. This weed has various names, such as *bull's-eye*, *May-weed*, &c. &c.

See article WEEDS.

WILLOW; *(Salix.)* There are varieties of this tree, though not many that were found in this country. The weeping-willow and some other kinds are imported.

Some kinds of this tree grow so rapidly as to be valuable to plant for fuel. The twigs of one kind are used for making baskets, &c. Other kinds are good for making hedges in wet lands. Perhaps the shrubby kind that grows along the banks of many of our streams would be very good for this purpose.

For making the hedge, either in the bank of a ditch, or otherwise, stakes of a proper length are cut and set a good depth in the ground, about a foot apart, and they will take root and grow, while new twigs sprouting out from every part soon forms them into a thick bushy hedge. This, when sufficiently grown is to be treated as other hedges.

See article HEDGES.

In Great Britain, some of the larger sorts of this tree are also raised for building timber. In this case, says Mr. Miller, they are planted in rows, and stand six feet apart each way, and are trimmed up the requisite height. When they become too thick, every other tree, in each row, is taken away. They may also be planted along the banks of ditches for this purpose. The sets are seven or eight feet long when planted. The same author observes, that every kind of willow is easily raised from sets or cuttings, which readily take root, either in the spring or fall.

WINDGALLS. These are flatulent swellings on the bodies of horses, but most commonly they are seated on both sides of the back sinew above the fetlocks of this animal : Some times they are in the joints and tendons. They are generally filled with air and thin watery matter. Where they appear in the interstices of the large muscles, which then appear blown up like bladders, they are principally filled with air, and may be safely opened, and treated as a common wound.

When they first appear, they are usually cured with restringents, and bandages drawn very tightly round them ; for which purpose let the swelling be bathed twice a day with vinegar, or verjuice, or fomented with a decoction of oak-bark, pomegranate and allum, boiled in verjuice, and let the bandage which binds the windgall be soaked in the same.

If this should fail, the swelling may be drawn off by blistering, and applying the blistering ointment, repeating it at times, till the humor is all drawn off. Some, however, cut open these swellings, wherever they be situated, and treat them as a wound. But, perhaps, where they are in the joints, the blistering is the safer remedy, as the joints may be stiffened by imprudent management.

WIND-MACHINERY. The saving of labor by the use of the winds, seems to have been but little attended to; and yet it is believed that great advantages might be derived to the farmer from this source.

Suppose, for instance, that an apartment was made under the roof of the barn, at one end, in the middle of which should be properly fixed, an upright shaft, extending up through the highest part of the roof, with four horizontal arms on the upper end, and on these sails fixed for turning the shaft when the winds should blow.—Could there be any doubt, but that this could be made to turn different kinds of machines to be used for different purposes.

In this way a threshing-machine and a corn-shelling machine might be moved with a great saving of manual labor. The cutting of straw and hay for feeding cattle, could thus be almost entirely performed, and the no less important business of grinding different kinds of grain for feeding and fatting of cattle could be performed with equal ease. Perhaps also the breaking and cleaning of flax and hemp could be executed in this way to advantage.

The raising of a constant supply of water from wells, for supplying cattle, is also easily performed in this way; and it is a matter of no difficult invention so to contrive the machinery that it will stop raising water when the trough into which it is emptied, shall be filled to a certain height. Churning may also be thus performed with a very small expense, when the wind will answer.

It is but a trifling objection against all this, that the winds are inconstant, and that they blow unsteadily. The work required to be thus performed requires no great steadiness of operation; and days can always be chosen for performing most of these labors when the winds blow most steadily.

The machinery for some of the purposes before mentioned should be so contrived as to be turned by hand when the winds should not serve. It is immaterial what quarter the winds come from where the sails are fixed on a horizontal wheel, as above intended, as the wheel will still turn the same way. The sails may be of very cheap materials, and the cost of the whole machinery need not be much. Any minute description of the machinery is here omitted, because verbal descriptions of such are necessarily prolix, and at best difficult to be understood; and because, any one wishing to test the efficacy of this method of saving labor, need not be long ignorant of the best means of putting his wishes into execution.

It is believed that Pasmore's machine for cutting straw is the best that is used in Great-Britain. His machine for crushing different kinds of grain between rollers, is also good, as being very expeditious; but probably those machines which grind the grain, in the manner that coffee is ground in small hand-mills, are the best. Descriptions and plates exhibiting his machines, as well as those of Salmon's and

M'Dougal's straw-cutters, may be seen in a new British work, which has been often mentioned in this, called " *The Complete Grazier.*"—Either of these machines might be easily adapted to the purpose of being turned by wind.

WINE. The presses used for making this liquor are similar to our screw-presses for making cider, though they are executed with much neater workmanship.

To make good wine, the grapes of the same vine should be gathered at different times. The first should be of the ripest clusters; and let them be cut close to the fruit to avoid the taste of the stalks. The green and rotten grapes are to be rejected.

In due season the second gathering takes place, when all that are ripe and sound are taken as before. The same may be observed of the last gathering, the grapes of which will be the poorest. To make wine in the greatest perfection, however, the grapes are all stripped from the stems before they are put into the vat.

Wines of different colours are made from the same grape. The French make their white and red wines from the black grape.

To make white wine, grapes sufficient for a pressing are gathered early in a damp, misty morning, while the dew is on. This increases the quantity of wine, but renders it weaker. When the sun comes out warm the gathering is discontinued.

The grapes gathered are carefully carried in panniers on horses, to the press, into which they are immediately put, and the first pressing is given without delay; which should be gentle, for fear of discoloring the liquor. The wine from this pressing is the most delicate, but not the strongest.

After the first pressing, the press is raised, the scattering grapes are laid on the cake, and the second pressing is given, in which more force is used than before. The second running is but little inferior to the first in flavor, or colour, while it is stronger and will keep longer. Sometimes the wine of these two pressings are mixed together.

After these pressings, the sides of the cake are cut down perpendicularly with a steel spade, so far as they exceed the upper part of the press, that is let down on the cake. The cuttings are laid on the top of the cake, and the third pressing, which is called the first cutting, is given. The juice pressed out at this time is excellent. A second and third cutting is in like manner given the cake, with pressings, till the juice ceases to run.

The liquor of the cuttings becomes gradually more red from the liquor contained in the skin of the grapes. The wines of these different cuttings are collected separately, and afterwards mixed, according as they contain the quality that is wanted.

The pressings for the white wine should be performed quickly, that the grapes may not have time to heat, and that the liquor may not remain too long on the *murk*.

In making red wines of the same grapes, they are to be gathered when the sun shines the hottest. They are to be selected and gathered in the manner before directed.

When brought home, as before, they are mashed in a vat, and are then to lie in the liquor for a length of time, which must depend on the heat of the weather, the flavor of the *must*, and the height of colour intended to be given. They are to be stirred frequently, the better to raise a fermentation and redden the liquor.

The authors of the " *Maison Rustique*," say, that for the *Coulange wine*, four hours is sufficient for the grapes to lie in the liquor, and that for the *Burgundy wine* a whole day should be allowed. Others allow a much greater length of time. Perhaps this point will be best ascertained by experience in different climates.

When the *must* or liquor, has lain as long on the husks in the vats as is thought proper, it is poured off, strained and put into casks. Afterwards the *murk*, or remainder of the grapes in the vat, is put into the press, and undergoes the pressings and cuttings before mentioned. The liquor thus obtained, especially if the pressing be so hard as to crack the seeds of the grapes, has a stronger body than the first running; but has not its fine high delicate flavor. Some of it is, however, frequently mixed with the other wines to make them keep better.

Some pour water on the *murk* in the vat, after the liquor is drawn off, which should be done without delay lest the *murk* sour, and leave it in this situation till they find the water pretty well coloured, and judge that it has incorporated most of the remaining strength of the *murk*; they then draw off the water and press out the *murk* as dry as possible, and mix the liquor thus pressed out with the water, and barrel it. It will keep no longer than the following winter, but is brisk and pleasant while it keeps good.

The *murk* is used to mend wines, whether old or new, which want either colour or strength. They are to be turned out of the casks on the murk, after the must has been drawn off, and then well stirred up, and let stand twenty-four hours, if new wine, or twelve hours if old. When a sufficient colour is thus given the wine, and it is no longer too sweet, but agreeable to drink, draw it off, barrel it, and put the murk to the press. New and old wines are, however, not to be mixed in this operation.

The unripened grapes that were rejected at former gatherings, are to hang till they become a little frost-bitten, and may then be made into wine which will answer to mix with other coarse red wines.

When the murk has been fully pressed it will still yield, when diluted with water, fermented and distilled, a spirit for medical and domestic uses.

In some parts of Germany, where the grape does not come to full maturity, the makers of wine have stoves in their wine cellars, by which they are kept warm during the fermentation of their wines, and this, by heightening the fermentation, meliorates them, and renders them more fine. Exposing the casks to the sun will have the same effect in wines that are too acrid to ferment sufficiently.

The people of Champaigne and Burgundy supply the want of fermentation, or of an insufficient one, in their late made wines, by rolling the casks. After drawing the wines off from the first lees, three weeks after being first put up, they roll the casks backward and forward, five or six times a day, for four or five days successively; then two or three times a day for three or four days; then twice a day for four days more; then once a day for a week, and afterwards once in four or five days. This rolling is continued altogether for about six weeks where the grapes were pressed very green, but a less time if they were tolerably ripe.

The finest wines will work the soonest, and the fermentation will take ten or twelve days, according to the kind of wine, and the season of the year. Those that are backward in fermenting may be quickened by putting into them a little of the froth or yeast that works from others. During fermentation, the bung-holes of the casks are to be left open, and should be closed when it abates, which is known by the froth ceasing to rise so fast as before. The cask is also then to be filled to within two inches of the top, and a vent hole is to be left open to carry off all that is thrown up by further fermentation. The filling of the cask should be regularly done every two days for about twelve days, in order that the foulness thrown up by the continued fermentation may be thrown out at the vent hole, or it will fall back into the wine and prevent its becoming clear. After this the cask should be filled to within an inch of the bung every fifth or sixth day for a month, and then once a fortnight for three months longer. When the fermentation is entirely over, the casks are to be filled up, and this is to be repeated once a month as long as they remain in the cellar, in order to prevent the wine growing flat and heavy. They should be filled with wine of the same kind which they contain, which may be kept in bottles for the purpose, and the vent hole should be stopped when the fermentation is over.

The first drawing off from the lees is done about the middle of December, and the casks containing the liquor drawn off should stand without the least disturbance by shaking until the middle of February, when the liquor should be again drawn off into other casks. If there be then still so much lees as to endanger their contracting a putrid taint, let the wine be again drawn off in due season. Sometimes it may be necessary to repeat the racking several times; but let the casks be kept full, and let no wines of dissimilar qualities be mixed.

The lees are to be collected together, and after settling, the thinner part may be distilled.

Brandy is often added to wine when about to be transported, to prevent any further fermentation. Fumigating the casks with burnt brimstone will answer this purpose better; but it is said this will destroy the red colour of wines. The colours of wine, are, however, mostly artificial. A deep yellow may be made by burnt sugar, and a deep red by red-wood, elder-berries, &c.

Turbid wines are fined by isinglass, by putting a pound or two of fresh bloody meat into them, and by other means pointed out under article CIDER.

Where wine has become sour, let some salt of tartar be mixed with it, just before it is used, which will neutralize the acid.

In summer, cool, clear days, with northerly winds, are the best times for drawing off wines to prevent their fretting or frothing.

For making *currant wine*, see article CURRANTS.

Gooseberry wine is made in the same manner as currant wine.

Raisin wine is made as follows: Take thirty gallons of clear rain or river water, and put it into a vessel that will hold a third more; add a hundred weight of Malaga raisins picked from the stalks; mix the whole well together; and cover it over partly, but not entirely, with a linen cloth, and let it stand in a warm place, if the season be not warm. It will soon ferment, and must be well stirred about twice in twenty-four hours, for twelve or fourteen days. By this time, if the liquor has lost its sweetness, and if the fermentation has nearly abated, which will be perceived by the raisins lying quietly at the bottom, the liquor must be strained off, and the juice of the raisins pressed out, first by hand and afterwards by a press, which may easily be contrived, by having two boards and weights laid on the uppermost. All the liquor is then to be put into a good sound wine cask, well dried and warmed, together with eight pounds of sugar, and a little yeast; except that a little of the wine should be reserved in bottles, to be afterwards added during the fermentation, which will take place again. During this second fermentation the cask must be kept nearly full, so that the froth or yeast will run out of the bung-hole. When the fermentation has ceased, which will be at the end of a month, the cask is to be stopped tight and kept a year, or more, and then bottled off.

This wine will be very good at the end of a year and a half, but will improve much by being kept four or five years; as it will then be equal to any of the strong cordial foreign wines, and by proper substances, to give it a color and flavor, it may be made to resemble them.

This is the most perfect of artificial wines, but others may be made cheaper; such, for instance, as supplying the place of every four pounds of raisins by one pound of sugar, so that only a fourth of the quantity of raisins above mentioned may be required; or by adding a proportion of well rectified whiskey to the cask when closed, in which case less raisins and less sugar would be requisite.

Any kind of large raisins will answer as well as Malaga; but the thinner the skin, and the sweeter the pulp, the better the wine will prove to be.

To make *Pomona wine.*—The directions published by Mr. Cooper, of Jersey, for making a wine of cider and other ingredients, which may properly be called *Pomona wine*, are as follows: Take cider of the best running of the cheese, and of the best quality, and add to it as much honey as will make the liquor bear an egg; strain the liquor through a cloth as you pour it into the cask; fill the cask full, with the addition of two gallons of French brandy to a barrel; set it away in a cool place, with the bung-hole open, to ferment; as the fermentation proceeds, it will throw out considerable froth and filth, and to supply the deficiency thus made in the cask, keep filling it frequently with more of the same kind of liquor, kept for the purpose, until the fermentation has nearly subsided; then put in the bung, but not tightly, in order that the liquor may have some further vent, and as soon as the fermentation ceases, close up the vessel. The next spring, rack off the liquor into a new clean cask; and in order to clarify it, Mr. Cooper directs a mixture of sweet milk, the whites of eggs and clean sand to be beat up and well stirred into the cask. (See article CIDER for the particular directions for this.) But it is believed, that about a quart of sweet milk to a barrel, well stirred and mixed with the liquor as it is poured in, will answer equally well and perhaps better. This operation alone will not only clarify liquors, but by repeating it several times, the highest coloured wines may be nearly or quite divested of all their colour. After the liquor has been thus clarified, let it be again drawn off into bottles, or into fresh clean casks, kept in a cool cellar for use. Mr. Cooper says, that his liquors thus prepared, has often been taken by good judges of wine, for the real juice of the grape; and has been pronounced by them superior to most of the wines in use. Age, however, is essential in perfecting this kind of wine, as it is in all others.

Mr. Clark, in his "*Travels in Russia*," makes mention of his having drank mead among the Cossacks of the Don, which was sixteen years old; and this liquor, which is little else than honey and water, he assures us was equal to good Madeira wine. Mr. Cooper adds, that the expense of making Pomona wine does not exceed twenty-five or thirty cents a gallon.

Wine of a tolerable quality may be made of the juice of elder berries, in a manner similar to that of making currant wine.

See article CURRANTS.

Raspberries, and blackberries may also be applied to the same use, and less sugar will be found requisite in making wines of these than of currants.

Under article PERRY, the reader will find some digressive observations, (having been written after most of this work was in the press,) respecting the pear in England called the *Teignton squash*; and that the juice of this pear had been frequently sold in London for *Champaigne*. The circumstance is only mentioned here again for the purpose of observing, in this place, that no doubt many kinds of the pear, as well as of the apple, may be found, by diligent search, and proper experiment, that would form the basis of as fine liquors, and in as great varieties as those which are made of the grape. This fact, however, ought not to discourage the culture of the vine; for, where the climate is suitable to its growth, it is believed, that the products of the grape will afford a wine as cheap to the cultivator as any other, equally good, which can be artificially made.

In making artificial wines, French brandy is used to add more spirit, and to assist in imparting to them the requisite taste. But, as French brandy is somewhat expensive, it may not be amiss here to mention, that a very pleasant spirit resembling that liquor in taste, may be made of the spirit distilled from cider, by putting into it a suitable proportion of dried peaches, baked *brown*, but not burnt; about half a gallon of these, or perhaps less, will impart to a barrel of this distilled spirit a very pleasant taste, smell and colour, after the liquor has had time to ripen by age. Whether this liquor, thus prepared, will precisely supply the place of French brandy in making artificial wines, is not particularly known; certain it is, however, that when it has age it has much of the brandy flavor, and is full as pleasant as that liquor. Common whiskey also, when divested of its essential oil, may in like manner be turned into a pleasant brandy, after it has acquired sufficient age.

WOLVES. For the method of preventing their killing sheep, *see* article SHEEP.

Wolves are easily caught in traps, and as many frontier towns are in the habit of offering considerable premiums for every wolf that may be killed, I will suggest a method of destroying them, which appears to me would be successful.

Build a close board pen out in the wilderness, where the wolves most frequent, so high that they cannot get over it: Let it be about twenty feet square: Leave a hole in each side of it just large enough for a wolf to thrust his head into: Put three or four sheep into the pen and feed them there: Take pieces of tainted meat and drag them along on the ground, off for miles, in different directions from the pen. The wolves coming across the scents made by these trails will follow them to the pen, and when there they will stick their heads through the holes to try and get at the sheep. Let the sheep be prevented from coming too close to these holes.

All then that is further to be done is to contrive traps, which, as they run their heads through the holes, will either kill them, hang them, or otherwise hold them fast till they can be killed or taken; and the different methods of doing this, I should suppose any hunter of common ingenuity could easily contrive for himself.

This plan would be equally useful where the farmer folds his sheep every night to keep off the wolves.

WOOD-HOUSE. Every farmer should provide himself with this building, and into this let him every winter store away wood sufficient for the ensuing year, so that he may have a constant supply of dry fuel. Any kind of wood, or even that which is much decayed, will burn well when dry; and half of any given quantity of dry wood will give more heat than the whole where it is wet and green; so that there is a considerable saving of wood in having it dry, to say nothing of the greater pleasure and convenience which it affords.

A house twenty feet square and ten feet high will hold fifty cords of wood; but if the farmer will be at the pains to have his rooms warmed, and his culinary business performed in the most approved and economical manner, he will find the one half of this yearly quantity of wood sufficient for all his purposes; and thus make a saving in this article alone to the amount of at least thirty dollars a year, and where fuel is dear, to perhaps double that amount.

See article WARMING OF ROOMS.

In cutting wood short, after it is carted home, a saw should be used; as this makes a great saving of the wood, and is at the same time equally expeditious.

WORMS. See articles BOTS and INSECTS.

WOUNDS. Mr. Bartlet directs, that where horses or other cattle receive any large wound, the first step is to sow it up, if it be in such part of the body as will admit of this; for in some parts the wound will be drawn open by the lying down, or rising of the animal. Where the wound is deep let the stitches be proportionately deep, so as to bring the lower parts of it together. The stitches may be half an inch or more apart.

If an artery has been opened, let it be secured by passing a crooked needle underneath and tying it up. If this cannot be done, apply a button of lint or tow, dipped in a strong solution of blue vitriol, close to the mouth of the bleeding vessel, and be careful that it be kept there by a proper compress and bandage till an *eschar* is formed.

The lips of the wound being brought together by the needle or bandage, it needs only to be covered with rags dipped in brandy.

Where the blood of the animal is, however, in a bad state, which may soon be known by the aspect of the wound, and its not healing, the blood should be rectified by internal medicines. The wounded part should be kept as free from motion as possible.

All wounds of the joints, tendons, and membraneous parts, should be dressed with terebinthine medicines, to which may be added honey, and the tincture of myrrh. All greasy applications should be avoided. Fomentations and poultices are also of great use here.

Y.

YEAST. For the best yeast, *see* article BEER.

A method of making what may be called a portable or durable yeast, is as follows:

Take a quantity of hops, suitable to the quantity of yeast you intend to make, boil them well, and strain off the water in which they are boiled; into this water stir in a suitable quantity of flour, and considerable salt, and then add to this a proportionate quantity of good yeast; let this mass rise as much as it will; then stir in fine Indian meal till it is so thick as that it can be made into small cakes of the size of a dollar or larger. When the cakes are thus made, dry them in the sun till they are hard, minding to turn them frequently to prevent their moulding, and then lay them by in a dry place, for future use.

When you wish to have yeast, take one of these cakes, crumble it to pieces, pour warm water on it, and let it stand in a warm place, and it will soon rise sufficiently to make good yeast. A quantity of these cakes may be thus made at once, which will last for six months or more.

YELLOWS. In neat cattle this disease is usually called *the overflowing of the gall*; in horses it is called the *yellows* or *jaundice*. See article NEAT CATTLE.

When horses are troubled with this disorder, it is known by the yellowness of the eyes and of the inside of the mouth. The animal becomes dull and refuses to eat. The fever and the yellowness encrease together. His urine is voided with difficulty and looks red like blood after it has lain some time. The off-side of the belly is sometimes hard and distended. If the disorder be not checked, he becomes frantic.

In old horses, when the liver has been long diseased, the cure is hardly practicable, and ends fatally with a wasting diarrhoea; but, says Mr. Bartlet, when the disease is recent, and the horse young, there is no danger if the following directions are observed:

First, bleed plentifully and give the laxative clyster, as horses having this disorder are usually costive; and the next day give him a purge of an ounce and a half of cream of tartar, half an ounce of castile soap, and ten drachms of succotrine aloes. Repeat this two or three times, giving intermediately the following balls and drink : Take Ethiop's mineral. half an ounce; millepedes, the same quantity; Castile soap, one ounce; make this into a ball, and give one every day, and wash it down with a pint of this decoction: Take madder root, and turmerick, of each four ounces; burdock root, sliced, half a pound; Monk's rhubarb, four ounces; boil the whole in a gallon of forge water down to three quarts; strain it off and sweeten it with honey.

Balls of Castile soap and turmerick, may also be given for this purpose, three or four ounces a day, and will in most cases succeed in effecting a cure.

By these means, the disorder generally abates in a week, which may be seen in the alteration of the horse's eyes and mouth; but the medicines must be continued till the yellowness is removed. Should the disorder prove obstinate you must try more potent medicines, viz: Mercurial physic, repeated two or three times at proper intervals, and then the following balls : Take salt of tartar two ounces; cinnabar of antimony, four ounces; live millepedes and filings of steel, of each, four ounces; Castile soap, half a pound; make these into balls of the size of hen's eggs, and give one of them night and morning with a pint of the above drink. On the recovery of the horse give him two or three mild purges, and if he be full and fat put in a rowel.

CONCLUSION.

To conclude this work, a description is given of a very small farm, suitable for any one who wishes to farm only on a small scale. Such a farm may suit the man of small fortune who wishes to live in an economical manner. The culture of such, or something similar, may also afford amusement to the man of taste.

Take, for instance, a piece of ground of 15 acres, bounded on some highway in front, and let it be, say, 60 rods on the highway, and extending back 40 rods, and cut into divisions as follows:—

The two small divisions which are not numbered, are intended for the house, &c. and for the barn, &c. The two short narrow strips are for lanes, and the long one is merely a cartway across the ends of the strips 8, 9, 10, &c.

1. Orchard;—say, one acre.
2. Ground for raising Lombardy poplars and locust-trees for firewood;—say, two and a half acres.
3. Ground for cultivating grasses for soiling, and for other purposes; say, two and a half acres.

4 and 5. Two hog pastures; the one cultivated with potatoes or carrots, &c. while the other is in clover for feeding the swine; say, one acre. The hogsty is to be set on the corner between the two enclosures. *See* article Hogsty.

6. Currant, and other fruit garden ;—say, half an acre.

7. Kitchen garden ;—say, one fourth of an acre.

8, 9, 10, &c. Divisions of a field, of say, six acres; the five divisions, or strips, are to be cultivated with a rotation of crops; similar to the method described under article SOILING, &c.; beginning with potatoes, then Indian-corn, then wheat, then clover two years, and then potatoes again.

This farm is to keep three or four cows and one good strong horse only. The labor of one such horse, well kept, is sufficient for such a farm, and for other family uses. To keep two horses will create an additional expense of about 40 dollars a year. A one horse cart will be wanted for the farm, and a one horse carriage for the family. The horse and the cows are all to be kept on the *soiling* plan, before described; and about ten or twelve sheep may be kept in the orchard, and in the woodland (marked 2,) adjoining.

The potatoes and other roots which may be raised from this farm, will serve to keep the horse and the cows well, and will also nearly complete the fatting of hogs. The surplus of the Indian-corn, after reserving what is necessary for the family, will complete the fatting. About eight good hogs may be raised and fatted every year. *See* article SWINE.

A plentiful supply of bees may be constantly kept, which will be found very productive. (*See* article BEES.) A small poultry yard for ducks and geese, &c. may also be kept and the fowls fed on boiled potatoes, &c. (*See* article POULTRY.) The orchard, if of the best grafted fruit, will give at least 60 barrels of cider, yearly, after the trees have acquired a good size, and this liquor can also be converted to an excellent account, with the addition of the honey of the bees. (*See* the manner of making *Pomona wine*, under article WINE. The cows will afford milk enough to make three or four firkins of butter, beside what is wanted for the family. (*See* article BUTTER.) The woodland will afford sufficient fuel, if well cultivated with thick growths of Lombardy poplars and locust, provided the house be warmed and the cooking business, &c. be performed in the most economical manner. (*See* article WARMING ROOMS.) In the enclosure marked 3, a sufficiency of Lucerne, cichory, tall oat-grass, or other good grass for soiling may be constantly raised for soiling the cows and horse; while some part of the ground may be in turn, employed in the culture of roots, &c. From the five divisions of the field may be expected, with the *best* cultivation, and highest manuring, about the following amount of different products, viz: 400 bushels potatoes, 80 bushels Indian-corn, 30 bushels wheat, and 8 tons of hay. About one half of the pork fatted every year may be sold. The sheep are to be pastured in the woodland lot and in the orchard. With the growth of the locust, particularly, will always be found a considerable growth of grass. They may occasionally be soiled a little when requisite.

In addition to the ground cultivated for fuel, it would be well to have another wood lot of say, five acres, near the farm, in which, amongst other trees, some that are good for timber should be raised.

Here, then, is a farm of twenty acres altogether, which, if of a good cultivable soil, and cultivated in the most complete manner, and agreeably to the directions contained in the different articles above referred to, will be found amply sufficient to support a common family, living in a prudent economical manner; and at the same time the cultivation of it is calculated to afford *pleasure* as well as profit, while the but too common method of bestowing poor slovenly culture on a large farm is only productive of the reverse.

The foregoing is merely exhibited as a specimen of what may be done on a small scale. The farm, though small, may be still smaller, and tilled with the same advantage; or it may be larger, and the arrangement of it may be different, and yet equally advantageous. At all events, its arrangement and divisions should be suitable to the ground which is selected for the purpose.

THE END.

APPENDIX.

———

THE matter which is arranged under the three following articles was intended as additions to those articles in the body of this work, but were received to late for insertion. The next following article is intended to correct any mistake which might happen by the *tall oat-grass* being called by different names. And the article *weather* was intended as a substitute for that which appears in the body of this work; but as it also came too late for insertion, it is added by way of appendix, omitting those parts which are similar to the two last paragraphs of the same article in the work.

———

CUTTINGS. It has always been said that neither cuttings, slips, or scions should be taken from the sprouts of trees. Forsyth particularly insists on this, alledging that sprouts never become good bearers. Sprouts certainly bear no fruit while they are mere thrifty upright shoots; but it is believed that when they have obtained considerable size, and shoot out their lateral branches, these will become as good bearers as any other branches of the tree. For currants in particular some who have tried cuttings of the sprouts for setting, assure me that they prefer them to the branches; as they grow straight and thrifty, and when they have thrown out their lateral branches, bear exceedingly well.

It has been said, that a cutting, slip, or scion when planted, or grafted, will live no longer than the parent stock, if that dies a natural death. Mention is made in the letters of *Espreilla*, of a very famous pear-tree at Teignton, in Great-Britain, which, on account of the excellence of its fruit for making *perry*, was called the *Teignton squash;* —that all the neighbouring farmers grafted from this tree; and, that when it was found in the last stage of decay, all the grafts which had been taken from it were found in the same condition.

Perhaps it will be found, that cuttings, slips, or scions, will die, when the parent stock dies of natural decay; but that the same rule will not hold in regard to suckers, as these appear to be somewhat of a different kind of growth, and more in the nature of a young tree. They seem to grow with more health and vigor than the lateral branches.

ORCHARD. It has been generally understood, that a peach-orchard of the best selected fruit can only be had by inoculating the young growing trees with the best kinds of fruit; that the stones do not produce the same kinds. Some, however, say, that if the stones be buried immediately, without drying, they will produce the same kind.

It is observed in the letters of *Espreilla*, that in some of the best cider counties of Great-Britain they do not graft their apple-trees at present; but, for rearing young trees they take the *largest* seeds which are found in the *south side* of the *largest apples*, and those of the best selections of fruit; and that from these they raise either apple-trees of the same kind, or others which are found nearly or quite as good. It would be well to make some experiments to test the efficacy of this practice. Probably it will also be found best to plant the seeds as soon as they have been taken from the apple and before they have dried.

PERRY. In the letters of *Espreilla*, which have been before mentioned in this appendix, mention is made that the *perry* made from a famous pear-tree at Teignton, in England, the fruit of which was called the *Teignton squash*, had frequently been sold in London for *Champaigne*. Farmers in this country should pay more attention to the selection and culture of such pear-trees as bear plentifully, and yearly, of the best kind of fruit. *See* articles ORCHARD, PEAR-TREE, and PERRY, in the body of this work.

TALL MEADOW OATS. This is the *avena elatior* mentioned under article GRASSES. It is cultivated considerably in Pennsylvania, and is highly esteemed there for soiling or for hay. It is sometimes called *tall oat-grass*, as in article GRASSES in the body of this work, sometimes *tall meadow oats*, and sometimes *orchard grass*.

WEATHER. It is very essential to the farmer to have a forecast of the weather; not only in regard to summers, whether they will be generally wet or dry, warm or cool; but also what are the every day indications of what the following days are to be. A knowlege of this kind enables the farmer to carry on his business to much more advantage; not only as it regards the products to be raised during a summer, but also as it respects the conducting his labors from day to day. If he can pretty correctly foretell, that a summer is to be uncommonly dry, and of course his crops of grass small, this may indicate the necessity of his lessening his stock of cattle; or if the season is to be uncommonly productive of grass, of increasing his stock. The knowlege of what the coming season is to be, will also enable him better to adapt his culture to it; and the knowlege of the approaching weather, from day to day, will indicate the necessity of driving his business to the utmost at times, and at others again, of desisting from his labors.

The indications of the seasons are scarcely to be learned in the life of man; even the careful observations of centuries are perhaps requisite to attaining a tolerably accurate knowlege of them; nor is it to be expected, that knowlege thus acquired for one country would answer for another; different countries exhibit different signs, and these must be learned on the spot and not gleaned from the observations of others in different parts of the world.

The *Royal Society* in Great-Britain have for more than a century past been making careful daily observations of the state of the atmosphere, and of all signs relating to the weather, by which it is found, that uncommon seasons, whether wet or dry, hot or cold, have always been preceded by certain signs or circumstances; hence a tolerably accurate knowledge is derived of what the coming season is to be, by the recurrence of the signs which are found to precede it. Nothing of the kind has however been attempted in this country, and the experimental knowlege of the British, thus derived, would probably be found no knowledge forus. Indeed, in a territory so widely extended as ours, the seasons may be different in different parts; hence the knowledge we might derive in this way would be very imperfect, unless it were founded on the result of similar observations made in different districts of the country.

In regard to some of the signs of approaching wet or dry weather, they will be found to vary in different places. This may, however, be generally observed, that before the approach of wet weather and during its continuance, the air is loaded with moisture, and until this has been discharged in rain, or carried off by the winds, a return of permanent dry weather is not to be looked for. The presence of a moist, or of a dry air, is easily to be known by the clouds : When the smallest of these increase in size as they are wafted along, then the air is surcharged with moisture, and, generally, rain may be soon expected : On the contrary, when the clouds are seen gradually lessening as they pass along, and the small ones disappearing, this is an indication of a dry air, and the forerunner of a dry spell of weather. The extremes, indeed, of a dry or of a moist atmosphere, are to be known by the extremes of these cases : Where the clouds increase or decrease very rapidly, the former indicates extreme mois'ure, and the latter extreme dryness in the air; and generally speaking, the greater these extremes, the more certainly may the usual results of wet or of dry weather be expected to follow.

But there is nothing certain in these things. The chemical operations of the atmosphere are often extremely sudden ; cool and warm currents of air meeting and mingling together, are often quickly changed into mist or clouds and produce a storm; and sometimes clouds are as suddenly dissipated, and resolved into " thin air again."

Chemists have ascertained that air is merely water in an extreme rarified state, by the operation of *caloric* or *heat*. Heat seems to be the *soul* of Nature—Perhaps something of the essence of DEITY Himself, diffusing his presence through his stupendous works. Certain it is, there could be no life or existence, no visible creation without the presence of heat. This enlivening principle, diffused through the waters of the deep has produced the air or atmosphere in which we breathe ; this air at the same time contains water in solution, which we call moisture ; and this again is susceptible of being changed into

mist or clouds; which, in due season, are either dissipated or converted again into water. Such seems to be the simplicity of these mighty
operations of Nature. We have, however, but faint conceptions how
these wonders are performed; and therein we have nevertheless the
pre-eminence over the lower orders of creation; but they in turn,
seem to enjoy a capacity superior to ours in being able to foresee when
the storms or fair weather are at hand.

Thus, the common field spider seems to possess, intuitively, a
knowledge of what the coming weather is to be; for this knowledge
seems necessary to his existence: and Providence has kindly given
all his creatures to know as much as their condition requires. When,
therefore, this insect is inactive and is not seen engaged in repairing
the damages done by the rains to his works, more rains may shortly
be expected; but when you discover him busy in repairing what the
rains have injured, and in extending his lines in various directions, it
is found an infallible sign that a dry spell of weather is approaching.

Other animals again, are, perhaps, not so fully gifted with this pre-
science, but have still a sufficiency to be enabled to be prepared for
the changes of the weather. (*See* the two last paragraphs of article
WEATHER, in the body of this work, for the signs of fair and foul weather, as indicated by beasts, birds and insects.)

Barometrical observations are useful in ascertaining the coming
weather. "In general it may be expected that when the mercury
rises high, a few days of fair weather will follow; if it falls, rain may
be expected."

The flight of birds of passage to the north pretty certainly indicate
the approach of spring, and their return, that of winter.

In some places certain winds generally terminate in rain or snow.
Such is the case with a north east wind on the Atlantic coast; and,
what seems singular, the progress of the storm is in the opposite direction to the wind. This fact was ascertained some years since, by
noting the time, at different places along the coast, when a northeast
storm commenced; the result of which was, that it was found to have
commenced about twelve hours sooner at Charlestown than at Boston;
and that its progress against the wind was at the rate of about sixty
miles an hour. This is, however, in conformity with a sign of the
weather, which but seldom fails; that is, when the wind is from one
quarter, and you perceive the skies thickening and becoming gradually overcast in the opposite direction, then a storm is at hand, and
the sky in the quarter from whence the wind comes will be overcast
the last.

The weather is generally unsettled about the times of the equinoxes,
and high winds and storms are then to be expected.

"Falling weather oftener happens about the full and change of the
moon than at other times, especially if she be near her perigee at the
time of these changes;" as the attraction of vapors or moisture from
the earth is then the greatest.

When the sky is red before the sun rises, it is generally an indication of rain; but redness after its setting is a sign of fair weather the

next day. The setting of the sun behind a black watery cloud betokens rain at hand; and the same may be observed when the sun wades, as it is called, when going down.

" The falling of heavy dews is a sign of the continuance of fair weather."

When the sun appears very broad and dim, either at rising or setting, this is a sign that the atmosphere contains much moisture, which may soon be expected to condense and fall. On the contrary, when that body appears small, brilliant and dazzling, this is an indication of a dry state of the air. It is also said, that when boiling water evaporates most copiously, this is an indication of approaching rain.

A rainbow in the west, and thunder in the morning, are both pretty certain indications of stormy weather at hand.

A halo or circle round the sun or moon, is also a pretty certain indication of falling weather; and the same may be observed when the stars look dim and appear surrounded with an obtuse light.

Othor signs might be mentioned, but perhaps, most of them would be found local, applying more to certain places than possessing any general characteristics.

INDEX.

A.

B.

C.

ERRATA.

Page 12, 9th line from top, for "*cattle*" read *neat-cattle*.—Page 30, 12th line from top, for "*has already been*," read *shall hereafter be further*.—Page 85, 4th line from top, for "*ground*," read *grass*—and in the same page, 13th line from top, for "*Hedy Sarum*," read *Hedisarum*.—Page 101, 9th line from bottom, for "*new husbandry*," read *milking of cattle*.—Page 157, 3d line from top, for "*saw*," read *raw*.—Page 185, next line to bottom, for "*whole*," read *wheel*.—Page 209, 6th line from top, for "*monflou musmou*," read *monflon musmon*.—Page 219, last line at bottom, for "*cattle*," read *neat cattle*.—Page 241, 8th line from top, for "*cows*," read *sows*.—Page 288, first line on top, for "*warm*," read *cold*, and strike out the words, "*and above*."—Page 291, 11th line from top, strike out the word "*to*."